VANCOUVER
THE WAY IT WAS

VANCOUVER

Pacific Street, in the block just west of Burrard, was a typical street in the West End. The houses were in a quiet corner of the West End, with an attractive southerly view, until the Burrard Bridge opened in 1932. Pacific Street and Burrard were both upgraded to major traffic arteries. The first house–the one on the far left–was built in 1900 for engineer W.H. Patton. The house second from the right was built in 1903, as was the turreted house at 1045 Pacific. There were originally sixteen houses on the block. The two to the west (left) of the painting, built in 1904 for coal merchant A. Blaney and CPR engineer Fred E. Hobbs, were demolished in the Fifties for construction of an apartment. Ironically, the location became so undesirable that the rest missed being replaced by apartments. The two end ones in the painting were demolished in early 1984, while the remaining eight were restored (the one fourth from the right collapsed during the renovation period) and moved onto new foundations at the front of the lots for a housing co-operative.

THE WAY IT WAS

MICHAEL KLUCKNER

with paintings by the author

WHITECAP BOOKS

Whitecap Books
Vancouver/Toronto

First printing: 1984
Second printing (revised): 1985
Third printing (revised): 1986
First paperback edition: 1989
Second hardcover edition: 1993
Canadian Cataloguing in Publication Data

Kluckner, Michael.
  Vancouver the way it was

  Includes bibliographical references and index.
  ISBN 1-55110-102-5

  1. Vancouver (B.C.)—History.
2. Vancouver (B.C.)—Biography.   I. Title.
FC3847.4.K59 1993   971.1′33   C93-091559-3
F1089.5.V22K59 1993

Printed and bound in Canada by D.W. Friesen and Sons Ltd., Altona, Manitoba

To Christine & Sarah Jane,
My Family

Contents

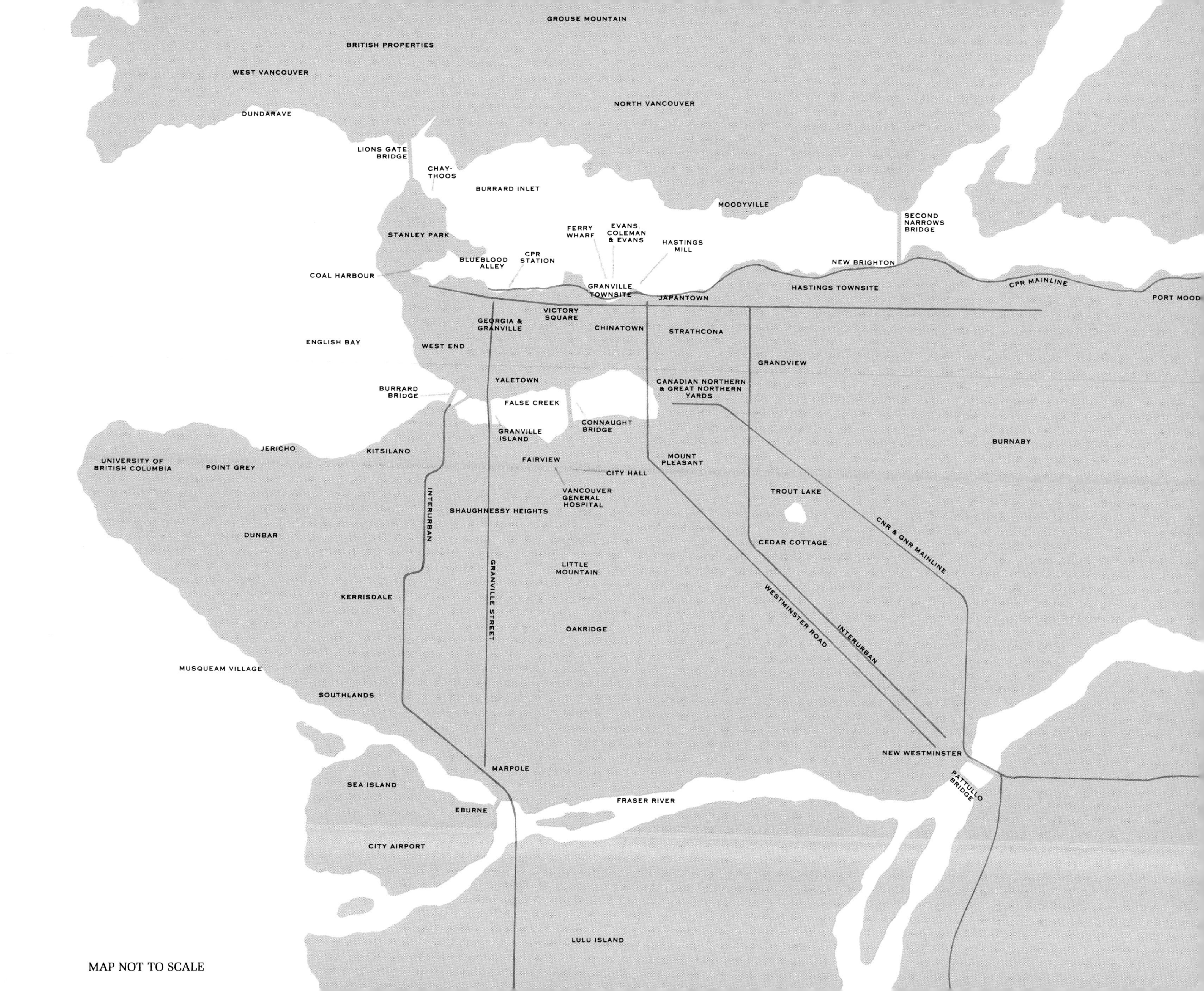

GROUSE MOUNTAIN

BRITISH PROPERTIES

WEST VANCOUVER

DUNDARAVE

NORTH VANCOUVER

LIONS GATE
BRIDGE

CHAY-
THOOS

BURRARD INLET

MOODYVILLE

SECOND
NARROWS
BRIDGE

STANLEY PARK

FERRY
WHARF

EVANS,
COLEMAN
& EVANS

HASTINGS
MILL

BLUEBLOOD
ALLEY

CPR
STATION

NEW BRIGHTON

COAL HARBOUR

GRANVILLE
TOWNSITE

JAPANTOWN

HASTINGS TOWNSITE

CPR MAINLINE

PORT MOOD

VICTORY
SQUARE

GEORGIA &
GRANVILLE

CHINATOWN

STRATHCONA

ENGLISH BAY

WEST END

GRANDVIEW

YALETOWN

BURRARD
BRIDGE

CANADIAN NORTHERN
& GREAT NORTHERN
YARDS

FALSE CREEK

CONNAUGHT
BRIDGE

BURNABY

JERICHO

KITSILANO

GRANVILLE
ISLAND

UNIVERSITY OF
BRITISH COLUMBIA

POINT GREY

FAIRVIEW

CITY HALL

MOUNT
PLEASANT

INTERURBAN

VANCOUVER
GENERAL
HOSPITAL

TROUT LAKE

SHAUGHNESSY HEIGHTS

DUNBAR

CNR & GNR MAINLINE

CEDAR COTTAGE

LITTLE
MOUNTAIN

KERRISDALE

GRANVILLE STREET

OAKRIDGE

WESTMINSTER ROAD

INTERURBAN

MUSQUEAM VILLAGE

SOUTHLANDS

NEW WESTMINSTER

MARPOLE

PATTULLO
BRIDGE

SEA ISLAND

FRASER RIVER

EBURNE

CITY AIRPORT

LULU ISLAND

MAP NOT TO SCALE

Preface and Acknowledgements to the Tenth Anniversary Edition

As a survivor of history as it was once taught in school, and of a large number of chronological history books, I decided in 1983 to write a book that used Vancouver's urban geography and the minutiae that had occurred in various buildings and neighbourhoods as the basis of a detailed city history. I hoped that such a book could not only create more atmosphere than a traditional history, but could also include information—in brief biographies and extended photo captions—that would not fit into a typical book format. The result was *Vancouver the Way it Was*, which explored history through the physical evidence remaining on the streets.

In the study of history some will argue that only chronological is logical, but I believe that human memory is much more anecdotal, and is triggered by recollections of people, places, and events, rather than by dates. A few bars of a popular song will trigger the memory of events that can be pinned to a certain year, whereas the date itself may elicit nothing. As well, chronological histories sometimes suffer from an inability to explore events that occurred over a long span of time; they often propose general themes, then look for specific cases to illustrate them. *Vancouver the Way it Was* in this sense is written backwards, as it starts from the seemingly trivial and looks outward for context.

As I read over what I wrote in the 1980s, I am reminded of another characteristic of this book. In many cases I quoted contemporary newspaper accounts and diaries to reflect the harsh, often bigoted attitudes of the time, and used their colourful but now politically incorrect vocabulary to fit the atmosphere created by old postcards and paintings. Words like "Jap," now repugnant to us, were very much a part of old Vancouver.

The paintings of Vancouver were not copies of photographs, but were done because I could not find historic images of some significant areas of the city. The scenes were reconstructed from a variety of sources, including the buildings themselves if they had survived, written references, contemporary directory information, old pictures of cars and clothing, yellowed newspaper photographs for which neither positives nor negatives appeared to exist, and, occasionally, archival photographs of some portion of the scene. It was "dreaming in colour," I suppose. The 42 paintings from this book were purchased by the City of Vancouver in June, 1984, and form part of the Archives' permanent collection; the painting done on the cover, of the interurban at the Kerrisdale station in the early 1950s, was done late in 1984 and is in a private collection.

In this type of social history, which can draw on few "correct" official documents, much of the information comes from rather uncertain sources, inference, and extrapolation. Although it is impossible to find unimpeachable "social" information through the usual methods of research—in archives and libraries—a researcher can be sure that, as soon as the book is published, someone will phone or write with the "facts." Sometimes, just to make it interesting, two or three people will phone up with different sets of facts about the same event or person! Having received a lot of such information after the first edition came out in 1984, I revised the book for its 1985 and 1986 printings, and have included addenda to this edition.

Individuals who provided material and assistance for the original book were: Ivan Ackery; Christine Allen, who helped prepare and edit the manuscript; Sue Baptie and the rest of the staff of the Vancouver Archives, whose enthusiasm was tireless and knowledge invaluable, and the patient staff of the Vancouver Public Library, Historical Photographs division; the late Raymond J. Bicknell; Bill Cost, who helped copy black and white photographs; Joyce Diggins; Samuel Garvin; Bruce Ledingham; Shirley Mooney; Len Norris; the late Margaret Pawlett; Mrs. J. Ferrier (Barton) Ross, granddaughter of Fitzgerald McCleery; Charlie See; Norma Smith; Willena Stone; Bob Stout; Joe Swan; Gerald Timleck, great-grandson of Hugh Magee; and Alison Wyness, daughter of James Inglis Reid. Bob Herger prepared transparencies of the paintings for reproduction. Kelly Dresser prepared the computer interface for typesetting at Domino-Link Ltd. Michael Burch, Elaine Jones, and the rest of the staff at Whitecap Books were enthusiastic and fearless in the face of huge production costs.

In the years since 1984, I have received useful correspondence and criticism from a number of people, including Gail Darwin, Janey Gudewill, Darrel Harper, Eric V. Jones, Jim King, Stuart Lefeaux, Bea Lineback, G.V. Lloyd, Sheila McLeod, Bob McRae, Jean Milburn, W.V. Owen, Art D.F. Porter, Algernon Strang, Peter Salsbury Vroom, Mildred E. Willis, and Mrs. Frederic G.C. Wood.

Printed sources included: *Vancouver Sun, Vancouver Province, the World,* and the *News-Advertiser* newspapers—the work of hundreds of nameless reporters who chronicled the city's events during the past century; *From Milltown to Metropolis* (Mitchell Press, 1961), by Alan Morley; *Exploring Vancouver* (UBC Press, 1974), by Harold Kalman; *The Shopping Guide of the West* (J.J. Douglas, Vancouver Museum, 1977), a reprint of Woodward's catalogues from 1912 and 1929, *Builders of British Columbia* (Morris, 1982), by G.W. Taylor; *The Story of Vancouver General Hospital* (VGH Public Relations Dept., 1977); *Arches in British Columbia* (Sono Nis, 1982), by Chuen-yan David Lai; *The Pictorial History of Railroading in British Columbia* (Whitecap, 1981), by Barry Sanford; *RCAF Squadrons and Aircraft* (National Museum of Canada, 1977), by S. Kostenuk and J. Griffin; *The Vancouver Book* (J.J. Douglas, 1976), edited by Chuck Davis; *Ten Lost Years* (Doubleday, 1973), by Barry Broadfoot; *British Columbia, a Centennial Anthology* (McClelland and Stewart, 1958); *Flying High* (Transport Canada, 1981), the 50th anniversary publication of the Vancouver International Airport; *Vancouver, The Golden Years* (Vancouver Museum, 1971); *Mart Kenney and His Western Gentlemen* (Western Producer Prairie Books, 1979); *Booze* (Macmillan, 1972), by James Gray; *The Hecklers* (McClelland & Stewart, 1979), by Peter Desbarats and Terry Mosher; *Canada's Diamond Jubilee of Confederation* (Confederation Celebration Committee, 1927); *Canadian Annual Review of Public Affairs* (1907 through 1914 editions), by J. Castell Hopkins; *Who's Who and Why* (1925 edition); *Who's Who in Western Canada* (1911 and 1912 editions); *Who's Who in British Columbia* (1937 edition); *British Columbia* (1912), by Henry J. Boam; *Vancouver Then & Now, 1886-1927*, (Gehrke's Limited, Vancouver, 1927); and, *Vancouver to the Coronation* (Watts & Co., London, 1912), by J.J. Miller.

Introduction

Exploration of the west coast of North America was motivated by the fashion for furs. Russia, Spain, the United States and England competed for control, and voyages of discovery were made by Sir Francis Drake in 1578, Vitus Bering in 1728, Don Juan Perez in 1774, Don Francisco de la Bodega y Quadra in 1775, Captain James Cook in 1778, Captain James Hanna in 1785, Captain John Meares in 1788 and, in 1789, Don Stephen Joseph Martinez, who seized Meares' little fur-trading settlement at Nootka. The next year, Captain George Vancouver was dispatched to explore the west coast and to "take possession of the buildings, districts, or parcels of lands, which were occupied by His Majesty's subjects in the month of April, 1789."

Alexander MacKenzie's overland exploration to Bella Coola in 1793 was followed by the journeys of Lewis and Clarke in 1805, Simon Fraser in 1808 to the mouth of the Fraser River, and David Thompson in 1810. Rivalry among the North-West Company, the Hudson's Bay Company, and John Jacob Astor's Pacific Fur Company in the United States resulted in the establishment of a string of forts through British Columbia and Oregon in the ensuing years. White settlement on the west coast began with the founding of a fur-trading post on the Fraser River at Fort Langley in 1827. The Company never attempted to develop land or attract settlers, although its Fort Victoria outpost on Vancouver Island, established in 1843, had "a great extent of valuable tillage and pasture-land" close by.

In 1849, the Hudson's Bay Company relinquished its exclusive control over Vancouver Island, and agreed to colonize it and manage it on behalf of the Crown, for a rental fee of seven shillings a year. Every purchaser of 100 acres was expected to pay one pound per acre, and to bring three families or six single men. Nanaimo was occupied in 1852, to exploit the rich coal seams which had been discovered there in 1835.

Between 1855 and 1858, gold, rather than furs, attracted whites to British Columbia, and turned the wilderness upside down. Thousands of men flocked to the Cariboo, after the dispatch by Governor James Douglas (a Hudson's Bay Co. employee who had arrived in Victoria in 1843) of 800 ounces of gold to the San Francisco mint. On November 19, 1858, in view of the need for a central governing authority on the lawless mainland, Governor Douglas severed his connection with the Hudson's Bay Company and took over control of both the colony of Vancouver Island and the mainland, under the name chosen for it by Queen Victoria— "British Columbia." The Colonial Office's Sir Edward Bulwer Lytton recommended that the colony receive a corps of Royal Engineers. The 165 men, under the command of Colonel Richard Clement Moody, established the city of Queensborough (later changed by Queen Victoria to New Westminster) on Christmas Day, 1859. By the next year, the population of the interior gold towns was nearly 6,000.

Disillusioned gold-seekers were the first settlers on Burrard Inlet in the early 1860s. They were followed soon after by a few men

Downtown Vancouver in the mid-Thirties. The skyline was dominated by the few landmarks built in the Twenties, including the Hotel Vancouver, the Marine Building, and the Royal Bank skyscraper. The rest of downtown was erected before the outbreak of the First World War. Visible are the English Bay pier, the huge Denman Arena on Coal Harbour, and a CPR Empress ocean liner at Pier B-C. Clearing had commenced on Hollyburn Ridge for the British Properties, but construction had not yet begun on the Lions Gate bridge.

(Preceding page) The Cardero Grocery, on Cardero between Comox and Pendrell, is a typical Vancouver corner store, with apartments upstairs, and rooms in the back for the Chinese proprietors. The store was one of the earliest buildings in that part of the West End, opening shortly after the completion of Lord Roberts School across the street in 1902. Like many of Vancouver's small stores, it was run by a widow, in this case Mrs. Kate Fleming, who presided over it until 1910.

with enough capital to establish sawmills and attract overseas trade. Within a few years, the community of Granville, usually known as Gastown, was a thriving settlement, though very much less significant than New Westminster or Victoria. British Columbians began to lobby for entry into Confederation in May, 1868, for a variety of reasons, including fear of annexation by the United States, a desire for a wagon-road across Canada, and the wish for a more democratic government than that of the Colony. The silk trade with the Far East, and the possibility of more efficient transportation between the Orient and Europe, were further inducements. The colony of British Columbia entered Confederation on July 20, 1871, by which time the proposed wagon road had become a promised railway. On September 16, 1884, when the Canadian Pacific Railway agreed to establish its terminus there, Vancouver was "invented." Almost overnight, New Westminster and upstart Port Moody faded into the background.

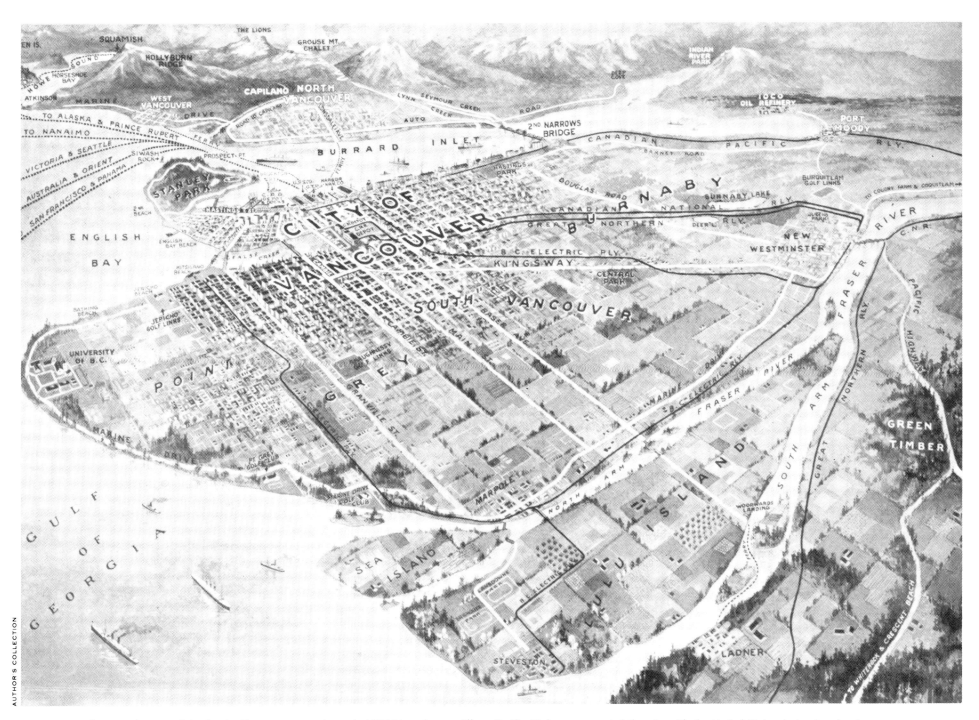

A composite map of the Greater Vancouver area, drawn in 1927. Marpole was still a detached town, separated from the rest of the city by farmland. The East End of the city—much of the old Municipality of South Vancouver—was likewise undeveloped, and didn't begin to fill with housing until after the Second World War. The paved Pacific Highway connected the city with the United States, but only adventurous motorists attempted to drive through the Province to the east. Sea Island, later the location of the City Airport, was still farmland. Vancouver's lifelines to the outside world were the railroad and shipping companies.

11

Vancouver's first boom after the railway's arrival re-created the Gastown area from the devastation of the June, 1886 fire. Following the 1894 Depression, the economy soared on the strength of the Klondike gold rush, and the city expanded southwest along Pender and Hastings Streets west of Victory Square. The boom continued through the first decade of this century, and the Georgia and Granville area—today's downtown—became the city centre. Thousands of families arrived, establishing the suburbs ringing downtown in the years before the outbreak of the Great War. Streetcar lines through the bush aided settlement. As motorcars became popular and reliable, the city spread even further. Dozens of men, who arrived in Vancouver in the years immediately after the Great Fire, left their mark with fine commercial buildings and homes. Their achievements were property development, transportation, lumber and trading, on a grand, pioneering scale of individual initiative that seems Victorian by comparison with the "corporate decision-making" of today. By 1914, Vancouver was a city, but with the outbreak of the War, its development stopped dead. The city remained almost unchanged for the next fifty years.

The Thirties should have been a period of rebuilding and growth with the money from the elusively-prosperous Twenties. Instead, the entire decade was a Depression, followed by the outbreak of the Second World War. The final years of the Forties and the first half of the Fifties were periods of reconciliation—the economic adjustment required to absorb the thousands of returned soldiers caused a serious depression. Industry, which began the difficult adjustment to peacetime, had to retool again for the Korean War. New post-war families bought block after block of small houses in the former farmland and forest of the old Municipality of South Vancouver.

In 1957, the city began to move and change again, with the building of the B.C. Electric building on Burrard, and the demolition of many old West End houses and their replacement by modern high-rise apartments. In the decade that followed, Vancouver changed from a sagging town into a modern, cosmopolitan city.

But the image remains of Vancouver, in the years before the Fifties, as an isolated lumber town far from the world's crises. Much of Vancouver was bush and farmland until the Forties; passable roads ran as far north as Horseshoe Bay, and east to Hope. Only the United States was easily accessible by motorcar. People travelled by ferry across Burrard Inlet, by Union Steamship to the resorts on the islands, and by railway or ocean liner to the outside world. There was a lot of space, but families crowded together at public gatherings and athletic events. The city was smelly and smoky—most homes burned coal or wood and the waterfront was crowded with sawmills and lumber yards. Horses were common on the streets, and chickens in the back yards. Many families in outlying areas still kept cows. Roads were either muddy or dusty. October and November were foggy, and the snow often stayed on the ground in the forest during the winter. It was a very different time.

The view from Grouse Mountain in the Thirties. There were no night-lights at the City Airport on Sea Island, and Lulu Island, now Richmond, showed only a few lights from farms. However, the pattern of the city's main streets, laid out by the B.C. Electric Railway Co. during its aggressive streetcar-track expansion, had been established since 1913. After that, very few pieces of track were laid—only Broadway west of Macdonald and between Commercial and Nanaimo, 41st between Granville and Oak, and a small piece of Clark Drive between Hastings and Venables, were added to the system during the Twenties. One piece of track, on 41st between Oak and Main, was laid in 1911 but ripped up during the War years for its steel and copper. The streetcar system remained intact until the early Fifties, when Brill trolley-buses replaced the "flat-wheelers."

Downtown

The Old City

The Cariboo gold rush of 1858 and the founding of New Westminster the next year precipitated a flurry of interest in the Burrard Inlet area. A British navy survey ship, *HMS Plumper*, discovered coal there in 1859, which caused Morton, Brighouse and Hailstone to pre-empt their celebrated Brickmakers' Claim in Vancouver's West End three years later. In that same year of 1862, the Irish brothers Samuel and Fitzgerald McCleery decided that they would never find gold in the Cariboo, so returned to the coast and began farming along the Fraser River flats. Two New Westminster entrepreneurs, T.W. Graham and George Scrimgeour, decided to log the slopes of North Vancouver, and established the Pioneer Saw Mill at the foot of today's Moody Avenue in North Vancouver, about a mile east of the Lonsdale Esplanade. They promptly went bankrupt, but a savvy Yankee named Sewell Prescott Moody bought the operation and made it a roaring success by 1865. In that year, Burrard Inlet exported its first timber—a shipload to Australia—and the West Coast's reputation for quality lumber was launched.

The activity attracted competition, most notably an itinerant sea captain named Edward Stamp, who had first visited the area in 1858. At that time, Stamp had seen some property on the Nicomekl River in Delta and—attracted by its rich, loamy soil—hired a boat to intercept the steamer *John L. Stevens* at sea. On the steamer was Colonel Richard Clement Moody, the founder of Queensborough (New Westminster) and the Colony's land commissioner; on December 24, 1858, the two met at sea, but Moody refused to give Stamp title to the land. Stamp never pursued it— he left the country and when he returned he had decided to open a lumber mill on Burrard Inlet. (The property on the Nicomekl was eventually occupied by a man named John Hansen, who built a cabin out of split cedar near the corner of Mud Bay Road and Coast Meridian, which burned to the ground on March 5, 1943.)

(Preceding page) Hastings and Columbia was, in 1931, on the dividing line between respectable Hastings Street (the B.C. Electric interurban depot was a block west) and the old City Centre at Main Street, a block east. Unemployed drifters were a common sight on the street. On the southeast corner, Horse Shoe Barbers and the DeLuxe Fruit and Vegetable Company occupied the main floor of the McDonough Hall, built in 1888 on land assessed at $355, the site of the St. Andrews Caledonian Society's first grand ball. The small gabled building at 108 East Hastings, which then housed Mac's Minute "Radio" Lunch, originally housed a carriage repair and cycle shop which became the first automotive garage in Vancouver (page 195). On the left of the picture are the brick sidewall of the first Pantages Theatre and, to its right, the popular White Lunch coffee shop.

Top: the Carnegie Library at the corner of Hastings and Main, built in 1902 with a bequest from American philanthropist and steel tycoon Andrew Carnegie. Its location, on the east side of the city in an area dominated by the Oppenheimer Brothers and the Vancouver Improvement Co., was the last political defeat for the Canadian Pacific Railway. The building to the south was built in 1888 as the city's Market Hall. The theatre which occupied the back half of the upstairs floor was converted into council chambers and offices in 1898. The building was used as a City Hall until 1928, and was thereafter again used as a market hall until its demolition after the Second World War. Bottom: a greatly-retouched view of Hastings Street, looking west

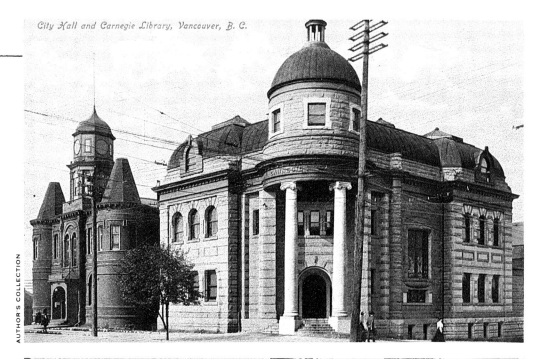

City Hall and Carnegie Library, Vancouver, B. C.

5. Hasting Street, Vancouver, B. C.

from the corner of Carrall Street about 1905. The old Courthouse dome is visible in the left distance. The angled façade of the Palace Hotel, on the right, stood on the edge of the Canadian Pacific Railway's "English Bay line" tracks. The Palace was removed before the First World War and replaced by the Merchant Bank building; the tracks were removed in 1932 when the Dunsmuir Tunnel was drilled. The triangular plot of ground in front of the Merchant Bank is now called Pigeon Park.

The arrival of the first transcontinental passenger train into Vancouver on May 23, 1887. As reported in the Daily News Advertiser: *"The buildings along the principal streets were decorated with evergreens, flags, bunting, etc., while from every flag mast in the city a flag of some nationality was flying out before the breeze. Horses and vehicles were decorated with small flags, brightly coloured ribbons and evergreens. All the ships in the harbour were decked out. At the station, the arch across the track was arranged in a very tasty (sic) manner; on the side facing the roadway was the legend* Labor Omnia Vincit *and over the track 'Orient Greets Occident' and 'Confederation Accomplished'. At 12:45 while all were straining their eyes eastwards, the loud whistle of the engine was heard. 'Here she comes! Here she comes!' was heard on all sides." The station was at the foot of Howe Street. The trestle with the freight cars offshore was in use until the land along Water Street was filled in the 1890s. The arrival of the train spelt the instant demise of New Westminster as a major city, as well as the decline of Victoria. Curiously, it also resulted in the rapid decline of Gastown, as the railway established its operations and facilities on the western side of the new city's downtown.*

William Cornelius Van Horne, general manager and later president of the CPR, visited sleepy Granville on August 6, 1884, and was so enthralled with the hamlet's potential that he decided it needed a grander name. "I name thee Vancouver," he reportedly said. He had no difficulty that September 16, convincing the railway's directors to move the terminus west of tidewater at Port Moody.

In early 1865, with the help of New Brunswick logger Jerry Rogers, Stamp looked over the south shore of Burrard Inlet for a suitable sawmill site. He had decided to set up a steam-powered plant, "much superior" to Sewell Moody's water-powered one, and found the water supply he needed at Beaver Lake in Stanley Park. He and Rogers staked out the lake on June 3, 1865 and Stamp began negotiating with the Indians at the village of Whoi Whoi at the site of Lumbermen's Arch. The Indians were mistrustful of Stamp's plans and feared for the sanctity of their midden and burial ground there, so they told Stamp that the heavy tides through First Narrows would break up his log booms. As an alter-

native water supply, they suggested the Tea Swamp area—the mucky lake bottom between about Main and Fraser south of 14th Avenue which was drained by Brewery Creek. Stamp liked the idea, and found a more protected sawmill site on a point of land at today's foot of Dunlevy, a couple of miles east of Lumbermen's Arch, which offered good anchorage and room for settlement. Negotiations ensued with the Colonial authorities and on November 30, 1865, for the price of $244.04, Stamp's Vancouver Island Spar, Lumber and Sawmill Co.—known to generations of Vancouverites as the Hastings Mill—went into business with an extremely generous timber lease.

Stamp was a rather feisty character, who appeared to have difficulty getting along with even his most trusted colleagues. Jonathan Miller, later the first postmaster of Vancouver and Granville's first Constable, got into a dispute with Stamp over timber cutting on Brockton Point. (Brockton was the engineer on the *Plumper*; the ship's captain was Richards, after whom the street is named.) Eventually, Frederick Seymour, the first resident governor of the mainland Colony, had to intervene on Miller's side. Problems dogged the Hastings Mill from the beginning. Stamp had decided that the best place to dam the Tea Swamp was at about Main and Seventh, where Brewery Creek fell sharply into a deep gully, so he built a flume down the Westminster Road (Main Street) and across False Creek to the mill. The flume leaked and never flowed properly, so it was abandoned in favour of a much longer flume from the only available higher source—Trout Lake at Victoria and Grandview. This new flume was successfully constructed overland from the lake to the foot of Dunlevy, and in June, 1867, Stamp got his mill started. The Trout Lake water was great for steam as it was very acidic—the boilers never had to be cleaned—but the lake was full of beaver that continually dammed the flume's entrance to keep the water level up. Finally, a mill employee named "Silly Billy" Frost—so named because he had sat on the wrong end of a plank he was sawing and deposited himself in Burrard Inlet—was dispatched to live on the site to keep the beavers down.

The peripatetic Stamp ran out of capital within six months and had to abandon the mill in January, 1868. Stamp went back to England, pursued by a legal action for $6,000 in back wages initiated by his former partner Jerry Rogers. The next year, the mill was purchased for $20,000 by Victoria and San Francisco interests under the name of Dickson Dewolf & Co. The difficult days for Hastings Mill were quickly replaced by prosperity as the lumber business grew. On the mill's coattails was the rowdy little town of Gastown, and the beginnings of the city of Vancouver.

Gastown got its start in 1867, when former river pilot John Deighton floated a whiskey barrel ashore at what is now the foot of Carrall Street. He attracted a few mill employees who were inveigled into building him a saloon in exchange for the contents of the barrel. Deighton House—invariably known as Gassy Jack's due to Deighton's reputation as a windbag—was thus established, and on July 20, 1867, he raised the first Canadian flag over his saloon.

15

Jitneys

The enterprising traits of the Vancouver citizenry were rarely more evident than during the three B.C. Electric Railway strikes in 1917, 1919 and 1945. Jitneys had provided some competition for the streetcars since before the First World War, but came out in force when the latter stopped running. Colourful, hand-lettered signs, duplicating the trams', appeared on cars which cruised the tram routes, transporting passengers for five cents or whatever the traffic would bear.

The June 3, 1917, strike lasted eight days and the public, which sympathized with the railway workers, took to the jitneys with alacrity. Although the B.C.E.R. started action against the jitney owners, many of them continued to operate even after the strike was settled. On April 23, 1918, the provincial legislature passed Clause 8 of the Vancouver Bill, putting the jitneys out of business. On August 19, the "jitney amendment" was added to the city's bylaws, over the protests of the Blue Funnel Line of interurban jitneys. On September 12, Magistrate Shaw ruled in Police Court that the jitneys must cease to operate.

The following June 5, the "Vancouver General Strike" was called, in solidarity with the One Big Union's successful Winnipeg Strike. When 1,250 street railwaymen left their jobs in Vancouver,

the jitneys filled the breach again. Big McLaughlins, Maxwell touring cars, and even the occasional Pierce-Arrow packed on the passengers, and tooted their way through the streets, like the one in the painting above, on the Fairview Belt Line. Many charged a dime a ride, and some reportedly made as much as $50 a day, though competition quickly reduced that to $10 or so. On June 30, the street railwaymen voted by a majority of only 45 votes to return, and the jitneys were out of business again.

During the war years, workers who shared expenses and rationed gas getting to work were considered by the City and the cab owners to be operating jitneys. Motorists, who were encouraged by the war department to share all their expenses to save resources, ignored the cabbies. When Wartime Industrial gas ration coupons were cut back, ostensibly due to the "jitney" owners using some of their gas for pleasure, 250 car owners at Westcoast Shipbuilders threatened to leave their "jitneys" at home if the gas coupons weren't restored.

Before the issue could be resolved, the motormen struck in January, 1945. The jitneys came out again, but not in force as on previous occasions. The strike, which lasted for 18 days, proved that people could get around without either trams or jitneys.

Trams & Interurbans

Whereas the Canadian Pacific Railway more or less established the City of Vancouver, and influenced the direction of its downtown and inner-suburban development, the B.C. Electric Railway Co. "laid out" the rest of the city. Its electric tram lines through the suburbs and its Lulu Island and Fraser Valley interurbans had the Midas touch for many real estate promoters, and determined the location of nearly all the main streets outside Vancouver's downtown.

Electricity was introduced to Vancouver on August 8, 1887, when the Vancouver Illuminating Co. opened a 50-volt, 300 street-lamp service with a steam power plant between Hastings and Pender on Abbott Street. Benefits were mainly seen by residents close to the power plant, as the lamps on Granville Street received scarcely enough current to make them visible.

The street railway revolution began with the successful operation of an electrically-powered line in Richmond, Virginia in the early 1880s. The close relationship between property development and good transportation was not lost on David and Isaac Oppenheimer. With partners including real estate developers C.D. Rand, Henry V. Edmonds (Edmonds Street in Burnaby), and John Wulffsohn, they established the Vancouver Street Railway Co. in 1888, and secured (with the cooperation of Mayor David Oppenheimer) a long-term franchise for the construction and operation of a street railway system in the city. The agreement was open-ended, allowing the use of horses, cables, gas or electricity as the promoters saw fit. In 1890, the Oppenheimers were again major backers of the Westminster and Vancouver Tramway Co., which sought to connect the two points of civilization with a regular passenger service. The following year, the C.P.R. incorporated the Vancouver & Lulu Island Railway Co., with an eye to running electric trains to the Steveston canneries (the line, built in 1902, was operated after 1905 for interurban passenger traffic).

The first tram tracks, laid early in April, 1889 from Main and Hastings along Powell Street to Campbell Avenue, serviced the Oppenheimers' large east end real estate holdings. Stables were built at the foot of Carrall along False Creek, and a buyer was sent east to secure the horses which were to pull the trams. However, the company's directors were convinced, primarily by engineer and future mayor James Garden (Garden Drive), to change their order to electric traction street cars (many of the horses did subsequent service with the Gurney Cab Co.). The following June 28, a line opened from Main and Cordova via Cambie, Hastings and Granville to a terminus on Granville between Drake and Pacific. The Fairview Belt Line, which circled through the new Fairview and Mt. Pleasant districts, opened in 1892, but the company foundered in the world-wide depression of the next two years (exacerbated by the severe Fraser River flooding, which closed the CPR line between Whonnock and Ruby Creek for three months in 1894).

The company attempted to sell its railway system to the city for $162,000, but was rebuffed. Later attempts to sell were also unsuccessful, until 1897, when a London-based syndicate headed by Robert Horne-Payne purchased the company. The Vancouver tram company was amalgamated with the foundering Westminster & Vancouver railway and a Victoria streetcar outfit to form, on April 15, the B.C. Electric Railway Co., which came to dominate the province's utilities over the ensuing sixty years.

The New Westminster interurban, incorporated in April, 1890, was the second such railway in Canada (the first was in St. Catherine's, Ontario). The first trip from Vancouver to New Westminster took place on September 11, 1891. The nearly fifteen miles of right-of-way, carved through the forest along the line of Vanness Avenue, was too long for successful power transmission, so a power plant was built in the forest between Edmonds and Highland Park. The plant burned shortly thereafter, and the company's officials were unable to raise the money for a replacement. Subsequently, Henry Edmonds was forced into bankruptcy for debts of $150,000, and Oppenheimer Bros. Ltd. was also foreclosed on. The B.C. Electric Co. took the line over and double-tracked it, beginning in 1906. The line was not abandoned until 1954, and the right-of-way is now again in use for Vancouver's rapid transit system.

The B.C. Electric Railway operated four other interurban lines. The first used the C.P.R.'s line to Steveston, greatly helping the settlement of Kerrisdale and Marpole, and the Lulu Island produce business. In 1908, a connector line was opened from Eburne Station (Marpole) to New Westminster, along the Fraser River. Another line, occupying land now used by Highway 401, was opened from Vancouver along the north side of Burnaby Lake to reach the company's extensive real-estate holdings in that area. The company also built a line which meandered through the Fraser Valley to Chilliwack. The last spike was driven there on October 3, 1910, by Premier Richard McBride, though it was years before the company's English advertising campaign attracted enough settlers to make the line profitable.

The B.C. Electric Co.'s head office was in the building at the southwest corner of Hastings and Carrall (photograph on page 25). It was abandoned by B.C. Electric in 1957 when the company moved to its modern office tower at Nelson and Burrard. Coincidentally, the company abandoned its street railways: the streetcars during the early fifties, with the last ones running on East Hastings street in 1955; the Chilliwack line in September, 1950; the Burnaby Lake line in October, 1953; the Marpole-New Westminster line in 1952; the Marpole-Steveston line in 1958. The streetcars were replaced by the more flexible, rubber-tired buses, which were then considered to be the wave of the future.

The Hastings Mill store, a half mile east, was the only real point of civilization. The store, built in 1865, provided a window onto the outside world with its drygoods and post office. It was located 100 feet west of the foot of Dunlevy, and had a small wharf—the only passenger dock on the south shore of Burrard Inlet. The Hastings Mill area was a good example of probity (though not as strict as teetotalling Moodyville) surrounded by the squalor and shacks of the private community. The area east of the Mill site was called the "Tar Flats"—a collection of shacks and wharves that were "a sort of rancherie," according to pioneer William Henry Gallagher. Gastown was literally a riot, full of Kanakas, squalling children and half-mad dogs. Capt. James A. Raymur—the "polished gentleman" who succeeded Captain Stamp—became resident magistrate for Burrard Inlet when he assumed control of the mill in 1869. His first words upon seeing Gastown were reportedly: "What is the meaning of this aggregation of filth?" Raymur banished the Kanakas and their animals and shacks from the townsite; they settled along Coal Harbour, which became known as the Kanaka Rancherie or the Cherry Orchard, until it was flattened by logging operations in the late 1880s.

Gastown was formally registered as a community on March 1, 1870, and named Granville after the Earl of Granville—the British Colonial Secretary. It was for the next fifteen years a tiny little clearing, bounded by the waterfront, Hastings Street, Carrall and Cambie, containing in 1870 three saloons, one hotel and two stores. As late as 1885 it was just a clearing, extending 350 yards along the shore. The low land just east of the townsite, along today's Columbia Street, flooded regularly during the winter and any high tide, to the point that a canoe could be paddled between False Creek and Burrard Inlet. A wagon trail twisted from Hastings through the trees along a line midway between today's Powell and Alexandra Streets to the Hastings Mill. At the foot of Cambie, there was a rough landing for freight arriving from Port Moody. No proper trail continued west toward today's Granville Street, so the best way to visit John Morton's place "on the bluff" to the west was by boat. The only other wagon trail meandered southeast from Cordova and Carrall, skirting the swamp along False Creek and joining up with the bridge across False Creek and Westminster Avenue, which eventually led the traveller to New Westminster. A small trail ran from today's Victory Square area south over the high ground to about the foot of Granville. Hunters used it. When they arrived at False Creek, they hoisted a stick with a rag for a flag to attract an Indian canoe across from Snauq. Four bits (50 cents) was the typical price of a return trip.

In the early 1880s the residential street was Cordova, while Water Street had all the shops. The south side of Hastings Street was a wall of 250 foot high trees. At the foot of Carrall there was a small float, consisting of two cedar logs lashed together, used for mail delivered by Capt. McFadden's little *Senator* steam tug, which plied the triangle connecting Moodyville, New Brighton and Gastown (McFadden eventually sold out to the Union Steamship Co., which built a proper wharf at the foot of Carrall). Just west of Carrall was the Sunnyside Hotel, a white gabled building with its back verandah built on pilings out over the water, "at least at high tide." Next to the Sunnyside was George ("The Laird of Hastings") Black's butcher shop, also built on piles. There were no buildings on the waterside west to Abbott Street, mainly because the area was usually under water. The land had been surveyed into unsold "wet lots," which were not built upon until filling activity started on the CPR yards after 1886 (the railway tracks ran for years on a trestle off-shore, off Water Street, until the land was reclaimed).

On the southwest corner of Carrall and Water was Gassy Jack's Deighton House. Next to it was the old courthouse and jail, in the area now called Gaoler's Mews, and Constable Jonathan Miller's house faced onto Cordova but backed onto the jail site. The first balloting for the first civic election was held there, as was the first city council meeting in 1886. Next to the Courthouse was Joseph Mannion's Granville Hotel, on the site of today's Grand Hotel at 26 Water Street. Further to the west was Billy Jones' Terminal Saloon, and then the Gold House, owned by "old Mr. Gold." At the corner of Abbott Street, on the site of today's Dominion Hotel, was Pete Clare's restaurant. All of these buildings were built on shorings and piles and planked with board sidewalks right up to the store doors. At the corner of Carrall and Powell was the Ferguson Block, and next to it the town's first Post Office on Carrall Street. There were three small, one-storey stores on the Europe Hotel site. West of Abbott was the unfinished Regina Hotel on the southwest corner of Abbott and Water, Rev. Joseph Hall's Methodist Church on the water side of the street, a block with a few shacks and then the forest.

The custom at the Granville Hotel—and indeed at every hotel throughout the country at the time—was that every guest was entitled to an eye opener before breakfast; that is, they could have a drink before breakfast as part of the price of their room. The practice upon arriving was that a traveller went into the bar before even going to his room, announced to everyone that he was a stranger and asked the "house" (everyone present) if they would have a drink on him. One drink cost a "short bit" (either 10 cents or 12½ cents, depending on who tells the story), but six drinks could be had for a "long bit"—25 cents. Spending was simplified by the fact that there were no nickels in Vancouver for five or ten years after incorporation. Miners still carried scales and a small poke of gold, which they measured out on the bar for their drinks. Drunks were said to be "fond of the flowing bowl," and some became such regulars at Miller's little jail that they were entrusted with the keys and various guard duties. Upon incorporation, the new City treasurer became G.F. Baldwin, a most upright gentleman, who had no source of revenue other than the fines levied on drunks, and was said to consider the money "dirty" and to "finger it very gingerly" when he was counting it.

The Hastings Mill, meanwhile, was exporting millions of board feet of the finest lumber anyone had ever seen: regular shipments of

Richard Henry Alexander came west overland in 1862, descending the Fraser in a canoe. He arrived in Granville in 1870, and worked as bookkeeper and assistant manager at the Hastings Mill until Captain Raymur died in 1882. His son, Henry O. Alexander, born in 1873, was the first white child born in Granville. After a long career in municipal politics and business, he died in Vancouver in April, 1930.

J.W. Horne

J.W. HORNE BLOCK.

James Welton Horne, "a gentleman living on his private capital," speculated wildly in Vancouver real estate. His "office," above, was near the corner of Granville and Georgia (he is in the middle, pointing with the pencil). His most lasting contribution to the city is the Horne Block, on Cordova Street just west of Cambie.

The Horne block at 311 West Cordova was erected in 1889 by J.W. Horne, a Manitoba real-estate developer who was often in the news during the early years of the city. Horne had gone to Winnipeg in 1879, before the railroad arrived there, made a fortune, and moved to Vancouver in 1885. He was a City alderman in 1889 and 1890, and was elected with newspaperman Francis Carter-Cotton as the first city representatives to the Provincial Legislature. Horne donated money during the early 1890s for the beginning of the Stanley Park zoo, and was one of the founders of the B.C. Electric Railway Co. He was known as a staunch Conservative and a prominent resident of the West End, living at 1231 Barclay Street. Horne *owned* the Mission City townsite and, during the debate on the site for a university in 1909, offered twelve acres in Mission City to the provincial government if the university were built there within two years. His Gastown building sits on a triangular lot just west of Cambie Street, the western edge of the original Granville townsite. The streets west of Cambie were aligned with a jog from the older streets when L.A. Hamilton surveyed them for the CPR in 1885 (in order to get the straightest possible streets for the new city).

"Vancouver Toothpicks"—knotless timbers three feet square and 60 feet long. The mill's crews had logged the downtown peninsula, Fairview south to 16th Avenue and much of the Point Grey slope. Early Labour Day parades in the 1890s featured a Hastings Mill float with a "B.C. Dining Table"—a slab of wood four feet by twenty feet long. The value of a typical tree had climbed considerably above the $230 which had coaxed Stamp into his great adventure. Raymur's assistant in the management of the mill was a young Scot named Richard Henry Alexander, whose wife became the social queen and the arbiter of all matters of taste in the little town.

A good example of life in the settlement in the early days is provided by the tribulations of the Dutch barque *Cornelis* of Amsterdam, which arrived in Burrard Inlet on June 26, 1871. She took on a full load of lumber for Valparaiso, Chile and sailed August 1. She was the only ship up to that time to make it through First Narrows under sail without a tug, and reached English Bay safely. However, the wind then dropped, and the ship became stranded at the entrance to Howe Sound. Captain Raymur commandeered an Indian canoe, and was taken to view the wreck on August 9. He discharged part of the cargo and ordered the tug *Grapple* to tow the hulk to Burrard Inlet, where she was beached and had her yards and topmast removed. There, the wreck gradually sank into the beach. One cannon was removed and given to the Indians at the "Mission"—St. Paul's Church near the Esplanade about a mile west of Moodyville. The remains were eventually burned for metal. About that time, a new star was about to rise among Vancouver's lumbering fraternity: John Hendry.

Hendry arrived in B.C. in September 1872 from his native New Brunswick. Finding little opportunity along Burrard Inlet, he worked at sawmills along Puget Sound, ending up at Port Gamble with the Puget Sound Sawmill Co. In December, 1873, Sewell Moody bought the engine from the decommissioned H.M.S. *Sparrowhawk* to replace the engine from his fire-destroyed Moodyville mill. Moody lacked a capable man to rebuild his operation, so sent superintendent George Haynes on a search around the Northwest. He found Hendry in Port Gamble.

Hendry completed the task for Moody and, in 1875, went to Winnipeg and San Francisco looking for lumber markets. He returned to New Westminster, where he built a small lumber mill for W.J. Armstrong. In 1876, Hendry began a partnership with David McNair in a sash and door factory in Nanaimo. Two years later, they moved the operation to New Westminster and called it the Royal City Planing Mills Co., with Hendry as President and General Manager. Over the next few years, he persuaded the Federal Government to improve the passage up the Fraser so that deep-sea ships could unload at the New Westminster docks. He prospered, and by 1890 had absorbed Moodyville sawmill, Hastings Mill and built another Royal City Planing Mill at the south foot of Carrall Street on False Creek, a few steps south of swampy Dupont (Pender) Street.

Other mills that developed around Burrard Inlet in the early years were the Rat Portage Mill at 2nd and Granville, owned later by William Lamont Tait; Robertson and Hackett, formerly known as Fader's Sawmill, at the Yaletown end of Granville Street bridge; and Leamy and Kyle's Commercial Mill at the foot of Ash Street on False Creek. None compared in size with Hendry's operation, which was amalgamated into one giant (for its time) firm called the B.C. Mills, Timber and Trading Co.

The Hastings Mill lease originally included all the land around the mill site, but the owners sold the land from Gore to Carrall to David and Isaac Oppenheimer, who logged it off and eventually built a brick store at the corner of Powell and Columbia (the Pier One Imports Building).

The city's first single-roomed school opened on February 12, 1873 with twenty children in a building on the sawmill site provided by the company. Miss Sweeny, whose father was mechanical foreman, was appointed teacher. The original sawmill, built in 1865, burned on the night of October 28, 1898. The Hastings Mill office, built in 1906 from a prefabricated kit produced by the company, remains as the Flying Angel Seaman's Club at the north foot of Dunlevy Street. The original Hastings Mill store, built in 1865 and the oldest building in the City of Vancouver, was moved in 1929 to its present site at the foot of Alma, where it serves as a museum operated by the Native Daughters of B.C. The mill site was sold in 1929 for port expansion, to the Federal Government for $2.4 million; its famous "flowerpot" burner, which had added a plume of smoke to Vancouver's skyline for over 50 years, was fittingly planted with trees.

The Hastings Mill crew were a rough lot in the 1880s. Employees included the aforementioned "Silly Billy" Frost, "dogfish oil expert and mill oiler" (dogfish oil was the grease for logging skids and machinery; some men made their own and were banished by their compatriots due to the smell, while after 1881 mills purchased their supplies from Spratt's Oilery at the foot of Burrard); and "Dumps" Baker, who worked on the green chain and spent his spare time as a deer hunter—hunting commercially for the butcher shops on Cordova. Baker kept twelve hounds which were said to be so starved they once ate the grease off the sawmill bearings when the mill shut down at noon.

After 1885, when Onderdonk's Yale camp completed its work on the CPR, a number of the ex-railway navvies moved to Vancouver and got jobs at the mill. They worked for $1.25 per 10-hour day and were the toughest lot yet seen. They struck in April, 1886 when mill manager R.H. Alexander refused to reduce the number of working hours.

The old order in Gastown had changed as well. Jack Deighton died in New Westminster in the summer of 1875; his last words were: "Damn that dog! I wish he'd shut up!" Sewell Prescott Moody died the same year in the ramming of the S.S. *Pacific* off Victoria. In 1884, negotiations began between the Hon. Wm. Smithe, provincial Commissioner of Lands, and CPR general manager William Van Horne, with a view towards extending the rail-

Joseph Mannion was known as "The Mayor of Granville" from 1874 to 1886, during the period when there was no civic government. Born in County Mayo, Ireland, in 1839, he intended to enter the Catholic priesthood, but "his studies were interrupted by reports of the gold diggings." He sailed from Southampton and journeyed, via Panama, to Victoria, arriving there on April 10, 1862. Attempting to get to the Cariboo gold fields in a hurry, he spurned the Fraser Canyon trail and became lost in the Bella Coola area for nearly three months. In 1864, he worked for the Overland Telegraph Company's Trans-Siberian Telegraph (which was abandoned after the first trans-atlantic cable was laid in 1866). He bought a half-interest in the Granville Hotel on Water Street in 1874, and ran it as "a respectable first-class hotel." He also owned the Gladstone Inn on the Westminster Road, land in Magee and New Brighton, and much of Bowen Island, where he moved after selling the Granville Hotel in March, 1886. Snug Cove was originally called Mannion's Bay. He left the coast in his later years, seeking a dryer climate to improve his health, and died in Lillooet in September, 1918.

Angelo Calori

Angelo Calori built his Europe Hotel near the Evans, Coleman & Evans and Union Steamships wharves, hoping to catch most of the trade from coastal steamships. By the time he opened it, in 1909, the city's centre had moved far to the southwest.

Vancouver's best "flatiron" building is the Europe Hotel, a relative latecomer to the Gastown area. Erected in 1908-09 by developer Angelo Calori, the building retains its fine stone-work, glass and marble on the main floor. The Europe was described in a 1911 advertisement in the Journal of Progress as being on the "European Plan—We Shall Endeavour to Please You." The building was claimed to be "Absolutely Fireproof and Strictly Modern with All Outside Rooms." It was conveniently located to pick up moderate-budget travellers who arrived at the Evans, Coleman and Evans dock at the foot of Columbia: "Our Autobus Meets All Trains and Boats." The building was designed by Parr and Fee, who built a tremendous variety of Vancouver dwellings, offices and churches, in a staggering variety of styles. Little information remains about Calori himself. He was born c. 1860 in Italy, and went to Victoria from there in 1882. He came to Vancouver in 1886 and was one of the founders (with restaurateur Agostino Ferrera) of the Sons of Italy. In his later years, he bought and lived in the old John Hendry mansion at 1281 Burnaby, where he died on May 7, 1940.

Left: before the Great Fire of June, 1886, all of Vancouver met under the maple tree at the corner of Carrall and Water Streets, still known today as Maple Tree Square. A poster for Vancouver's first election is nailed to the tree. Hartney's Drygoods store occupied the main floor of the Ferguson Block on Carrall Street. Deighton House was on the right. Right: "City Hall in a Tent," possibly the most famous photo of Vancouver, on the city wharf at the foot of Carrall Street after the Great Fire. Back row, left to right, is the first City Council: Joseph Griffiths, R. Balfour, Thos. Dunn, J.J. Blake, Joseph Humphries, G.F. Baldwin, and Dr. McGuigan. Seated: G.E. Coldwell, E.P. Hamilton, J.R. Northcote, Mayor M.A. MacLean, L.A. Hamilton, D. Cordiner, and City Clerk T.F. McGuigan. The man in the background is Mr. Gibson of Gibson's Landing.

way past its proposed Port Moody terminus. A land grant of 6,000 acres was proposed, plus all the unsold lots in the townsite of Granville, and landowners like John Morton were inveigled into giving up as much as one-third of their property in order to entice the railway west. After Van Horne's visit to Granville early in August, 1884, and his obvious delight at the terminus facilities below the bluff on Burrard Inlet, it became evident that the little boomtown was destined for greatness. New settlers, speculators and ne'er-do-wells arrived every day, crowding the hotels and building a shanty-town amongst the stumps around the fledgling city. Flour cost six dollars a barrel and salmon sixty-five cents each. Smelt could be had for fifty cents a bucket.

In January, 1886, over one hundred Granville residents, led by merchant Isaac Oppenheimer, petitioned the Provincial Government for incorporation as the City of Vancouver. Royal assent was received on April 6, 1886, and the city was declared to extend from Heatley Avenue to Trafalgar and 16th Avenue to the water. An election was the first order of business, and qualifications for voting were deemed to be land ownership, or the possession of a cabin, room or lease to the value of five dollars a month. Real estate man Malcolm MacLean ran for mayor against Hastings Mill manager R.H. Alexander. A dispute flared up again between white Vancouverites and "the Victoria crowd" represented by the patrician Alexander; the latter said that he had always run the mill successfully with "Chinamen" and Indians and would do it again, rather than reduce the work day at the mill. In front of a crowd at the Maple Tree he said, probably as much out of frustration as anything: "North Americans are just white Chinamen anyway," a remark which probably cost him the election. At another meeting, when discussing the possibility of a paid Labour Day holiday (first established in 1891) in front of a pro-union crowd, Alexander imprudently punned: "We have enough days of labour without having Knights of Labour." Incensed white workers forged "resi-

dency" permits by cadging room receipts at the hotels along Water Street, and drove away a large contingent of Chinese mill workers who were coming from the Mill to vote. MacLean won the election, 242 to 225. The first council meeting was held in Miller's courthouse on May 10.

The summer of 1886 was hot and dry. The wells were very low, as there had been no rain since May 26. CPR crews were rough-clearing huge areas of the West End south to Davie Street and the False Creek area around today's B.C. Place site. The crews were using a "nine-pin" logging method, whereby the smaller trees would just be sawn through the back and only the big firs and cedars cut through. The crash of one of these forest giants brought down sometimes twenty or thirty smaller evergreens, plus a host of whippy vine maple trapped underneath. The result was a solid wall of tangled wood and brush, some ten feet deep and extending in every direction over most of today's downtown. On June 17, shortly before noon, a clearing fire by some CPR men near the new Roundhouse site (about Drake and Homer) got away. The city didn't burn—"it was consumed." In forty minutes everything was in flames. From 600 to 1,000 buildings were destroyed that afternoon, but no one had any idea how many of the population of 2,000 died. A freak gale carried a wall of flames before it. One stone building survived in the West End; the Regina Hotel, where trapped men, who soaked the walls and saved it from burning, survived. Most of Hastings Mill with the exception of the school survived to be burned 22 years later. Of the 21 sets of human remains which were found and removed to a makeshift candle-lit morgue in the Bridge Hotel at the north end of the Westminster Avenue bridge, only three—found at Hastings and Columbia Street—were identifiable by their features.

Almost immediately, the city began to rise from the ashes. The *Vancouver News*, which had been obliterated, set up and ran a single sheet newspaper the same day in New Westminster. Editori-

ally, it expressed the sentiment that: "The Caldwell Block, wherein the *News* office was situated, was one of the first to be overtaken by the fire, and not even a scrap of paper was saved. Like nearly all others who had started in the new city, however, we perceive that the fire, whatever may be its effect upon individuals, is to the city as a whole not a very serious matter; in fact it can scarcely impede the progress of Vancouver at all." For years afterwards, the "CPR Hotel" (not owned by the railway), just west of Carrall on Hastings, carried a painted banner on its sidewall stating: "Raised From the Ashes in Three Days After the Great Fire." Dozens of other buildings were erected at the same pace. City Council met and—from its temporary headquarters in a tent— passed the city's first building bylaw. It also voted more money for the Fire Department under J.H. Carlisle, who stayed with the Force for over forty years.

On July 4, 1886, the first through train pulled into Port Moody, fulfilling one of the chief conditions of British Columbia's entry into Confederation (although, of course, both New Westminster and Victoria were shattered that they had not been chosen as the terminus). The line between Port Moody and the Vancouver yards took another year to complete and the first train pulled into the new wooden CPR station at the foot of Granville Street on May 23, 1887. The first "ocean to ocean" train consisted of a baggage, a

Funeral at the old First Presbyterian Church at Hastings and Gore, probably before the First World War, as the policeman on the left is wearing a "bobby" helmet. The church became better known as the First United, when firebrand minister Andrew Roddan organized food and aid programs for the destitute in the early years of the Depression.

Jonathan Miller

The Gaoler's Mews near the corner of Water and Carrall Streets dates from the Gastown-era residence of Jonathan Miller, Constable of the Town of Granville from 1871 until incorporation, and afterwards the City's first postmaster. Miller's "police station" was a small, government-built log cottage facing Cordova Street with a "back yard" between Deighton's Hotel on the corner of Carrall and Water and the Granville Hotel at today's 26 Water Street. The cottage had two small log cells in the back yard with doors but no locks. The cottage became known as the "Courthouse" and was the site of Vancouver's first Council meeting in 1886.

Miller was born in 1833 in Ontario and came west in 1862 with wife and daughter via Panama and San Francisco. In the years prior to 1871 he lived at New Westminster but was generally away, operating small logging camps around the Howe Sound area. His dispute with Stamp over logging at Brockton Point soured him somewhat on logging, so when the first Government Agent, Tomkins Brew—who also had responsibility for policing—retired, Miller readily took the proffered job.

In 1873, two of his children started at the Hastings Mill school, and twelve years later were part of the first graduating class. Miller served on the School Board, and, as the city approached incorporation, he operated some small business-sidelines as a teamster and general merchant, in partnership with Thomas Dunn (the building at Cordova and Carrall which houses the Army and Navy store was called the Dunn-Miller block). To occupy his prisoners, he chained them lightly by the ankles and had the one-armed drunkard John Clough supervise them as a chain gang on road-clearing projects like the Cambie Street Grounds and the road to New Brighton (now Wall Street).

After incorporation, he was offered the position of Chief Constable, which he declined in favour of the position of Postmaster—an office he held until 1909. A man named John Stewart, who had worked since 1883 as a "Merchant's Patrolman," prowling the darkened streets looking for suspicious characters, became Chief Constable. Miller died in 1914, on a return visit to Vancouver from his retirement home in Washington.

colonist-sleeper, a first-class, a Pullman and a drawing room car, the engine being profusely decorated with evergreens, streamers and mottoes. As it was the Golden Jubilee year of Queen Victoria, the engine headlight bore her portrait, and the smokestack supported a banner which stated "Montreal greets the Terminal City."

A new school was opened on Cordova Street in January, 1887, with J.W. Robinson as Principal and Miss A. Christie as assistant. Ninety-three pupils registered at the commencement of term; the school finished its first year with an enrolment of 285. Teachers' salaries were reduced by five dollars a month as "they were teaching west of Yale." The new East End School on East Pender— now Strathcona School—was occupied in 1890.

On September 1, 1886, the city's first banking agency opened on Cordova Street under the banner of Bank of British Columbia. The civic delegation, which had gone to Victoria the previous month for a loan for civic improvements, couldn't get it, so they turned to the new bank for the money. During the next few years—the 1888 to 1891 tenure of merchant-turned-Mayor David Oppenheimer— water mains were laid across First Narrows from Capilano, electric light was introduced and the street railway started with new electric trams. Telephone service was extended, the Stanley Park driveway was completed, thirty-six miles of streets were graded, twenty-four miles of sidewalks were laid down and the first attempts were made at a sewerage system to solve the recurring typhoid problem. The old Seymour Street firehall was erected, as was a hospital and a market building near the corner of Main and Hastings, used for years as a City Hall.

Vancouver's first City Hall was the little Courthouse on Water Street attached to Constable Jonathan Miller's house. The second City Hall was a tent, used briefly after the Great Fire. The third was a brick, one-storey building with sheet iron shutters over the windows, at the Powell Street lane directly across from today's Europe Hotel site. It was loaned for civic purposes by the Oppenheimer Brothers, and stood through the Second World War Years. The market building on Westminster Avenue (Main Street) was built by CPR contractor H.F. Keefer, who had built the CPR link from Port Moody into Vancouver and the Capilano-to-Vancouver waterworks. He was one of the original incorporators—in partnership with Henry Abbott—of the Vancouver Illuminating Co. All the bricks were bought from Oppenheimer & Mannion's brickyard on Bowen Island (where the Union Steamships bathing pool was).

A ward system, established in 1888, was finally eliminated in the mid-thirties amidst "pork barrel" allegations. At first, there were four wards: Ward One was the West End, and always sent a "CPR member" to council with the organizing help of R.E. Gosnell; Ward Two was the City Centre, radiating from Westminster and Hastings, which sent a council member who identified with the private landowners; Ward Three was the East End, and Ward Four Mount Pleasant and Fairview. On most issues, the city divided itself right down the middle, with the Oppenheimer camp representing the old City Centre and the News-Advertiser camp, backed

by editor and politician Francis Carter-Cotton, pushing the CPR line. The mayoralty election of 1888 was a trial of strength between the two camps, with the main issue the location of the City Hall. Grocer William Templeton was the News-Advertiser's candidate, running against grocer David Oppenheimer. The two were neck-and-neck until, at a big pre-election rally, Templeton imitated Oppenheimer's German-Polish accent on the platform. The meeting went cold.

The CPR lost that battle, and one more in 1901 which selected the corner of Hastings and Westminster for the new Carnegie Public Library. The library resulted from a $50,000 donation by steel magnate Andrew Carnegie, who had given money all over the world for public libraries, on the single condition that they bear his name in perpetuity. The cornerstone was laid by the Grand Lodge Freemasons on March 29, 1902. The Carnegie Library was the last major civic building in the old eastern Downtown Centre, with the exception of the police stations and court complexes of the ensuing decades. The building served as the City Museum and archives until new facilities were built on Kitsilano Point in the late sixties; the library finally moved to the West Side (Burrard and Robson) in 1957. The original building was renovated, beginning in 1973, and now serves as a community centre for the downtown east-side.

Hastings Street was a secondary throughway until the First World War years. In the early 1800s, streetcars from the Hotel Vancouver vicinity, at Georgia and Granville, travelled east on Hastings only as far as Victory Square; there they turned down the hill and then continued east along Cordova Street, which was the major shopping area for the city. The Lonsdale Block, stretching west from Carrall along Cordova, is one of the survivors from that commercial heyday. Built in 1889, and bought during the Klondike years by North Vancouver property owner A.H. Lonsdale, the building included the store of pioneer drygoods merchant Thomas Dunn, a meeting hall for the Knights of Pythias and offices for the Vancouver Electric Railway and Light Company. It has, since the Thirties, been part of the Army and Navy discount department store chain.

After the wild days of Gassy Jack, Water Street was rebuilt with a number of hotels serving commercial travellers (the carriage trade had moved south and west towards the CPR's Hotel Vancouver).

By the turn of the century, Water Street was the warehousing headquarters for Vancouver's big merchants, a role it continued to fill until the trucking boom of the Forties led firms like Kelly Douglas to the suburbs. "Water Street" fought (and lost to) the Pender Street Chinese wholesalers in the great vegetable wars of the Thirties. The area was slated for razing and redevelopment in the mid-Sixties, through an ambitious scheme entitled Project 200, and some demolition and redevelopment took place, led by the CPR, with investments by firms like Woodward's and Sears. The huge, modern Granville Square tower at the foot of Granville is one result, as is the CP Telecommunications Building at Cordova and Cambie, and the Woodward's Parking garage on Water west of

The B.C. Electric head office and interurban depot stood at the southwest corner of Hastings and Carrall street. In this 1927 photo, a motorbus, possibly from North Burnaby and points east, is parked in front of the station. The little truck behind it is from the Fraser Valley Milk Processors, the forerunner of Dairyland. The interurbans, on the Fraser Valley and Burnaby Lake lines, entered the main floor of the building from Hastings Street. The depot for the Steveston line was at 3rd and Granville, later moved to the southeast corner of Davie and Seymour. The CPR tracks leading to the False Creek roundhouse are visible on the extreme right. B.C. Electric abandoned the Hastings and Carrall building in 1957, moving uptown to Burrard and Nelson (page 113). The main floor of this building was closed in and is now occupied by the Bank of Montreal.

Abbott. During the late Sixties, with the recognition of Gastown as a heritage area, many warehouses were renovated. Art galleries and chic restaurants opened, boutiques flowered and the quaint character of the area proved to be extremely popular with both Vancouverites and tourists. The CPR's last renovation resulted in the Gaslight Square complex at 131 Water, capturing the style and flavour of the surrounding brick warehouses. The city got into the act in the early Seventies, laying the charming street "bricking" along Water, and ensuring the protection of both Gastown and Chinatown from future wanton destruction.

W.H. Malkin

The big warehouse on Water Street, occupied today by the Old Spaghetti Factory and an import business, was, for many years, the headquarters of W.H. Malkin & Co., one of the many enterprises owned by Vancouver grocers who aspired to the mayor's chair. William Harold Malkin, like David Oppenheimer and William Templeton, made his fortune in Gastown, and his reputation as mayor of the city.

Malkin was "every inch an Englishman" and an eternal optimist, fond of saying: "Any young man has a brighter future than we did as young men." He was born in 1868 in Burslem, Staffordshire, and came to Canada in 1884, to be joined later by his two brothers. The three journeyed west and arrived at the "little wooden CPR station" on April 1, 1895. Supposedly they sat down on the benches in the station, and discussed their possiblities for the future. Very soon after, they organized a wholesale grocery business, which prospered from the mining boom in the Kootenays, and later from the frantic rush for the Klondike in 1898. That year they built a warehouse at 139 Water Street, constructed on piles because the water flowed underneath at high tide. Three years later, they incorporated the firm as W.H. Malkin and Co., with W.H. as president and the two brothers as officials. They outgrew the first warehouse, so built another at 353 Water in 1903. In 1907 they commissioned architects Parr and Fee to construct the massive brick and timber warehouse at 57 Water.

W.H. Malkin increasingly left control of the business in the hands of his brothers, while he turned his attention elsewhere. He was president of the Board of Trade in 1902-3, chairman of the B.C. Victory Loan Committee at the end of the First War, and a member of the Royal Commission on Political Campaign Funds which attempted to sniff out some of the funding irregularities of the established political parties. He travelled extensively through Europe and the Far East, and contributed money to the Vancouver Art Gallery fund during the Twenties. He was a great patron of theatre in Vancouver, and after his wife Marion's sudden death in November, 1933, he gave money for the construction of the Marion Malkin Memorial Bowl in Stanley Park.

Malkin's most lasting achievements came about during his term as mayor in 1929-32. He was the first chief magistrate after the city's amalgamation with South Vancouver and Point Grey, having been an advocate of amalgamation during the Twenties. He managed to get money voted for the Sea Island City Airport, and for the construction of the Burrard Bridge.

The Malkins lived in a splendid home called Southlands at the corner of Blenheim and Marine Drive. They owned considerable acreage to the north of the house, six-and-one-half of which were given to the city in 1939 for park purposes. The park never materialized; the last portion of undeveloped land from that period is a clump of forest at 43rd and Balaclava.

Looking west along Water Street from the front of the Europe Hotel in the early Twenties, when the Water Street wholesale grocers were the busiest west of Winnipeg. The Nabob sign in the distance marks the Kelly-Douglas warehouse; the "Malkin's Best" sign adorns the building now occupied by the Spaghetti Factory. The Alhambra Hotel, in the left foreground, was one of the finest in Vancouver, with hot water and a fireplace in each room, and was able to charge one dollar a night to visitors. That lucrative trade helped to prompt Angelo Calori into his Europe Hotel venture.

William Harold Malkin

Malkin was made a Freeman of the city by his successor Gerry McGeer in the Forties. He continued in business as president of Neon Products Ltd. through the Forties. He lived on through the Fifties in excellent health, continuing to support the Art Gallery and local theatre, and died in October, 1959, aged 91.

Robert Kelly

tion Co.'s *Islander* in Skagway for the return to Vancouver, his order book full and his luggage supposedly containing $50,000 in gold. The ship hit an iceberg and sank; Douglas was not among the few survivors. In Vancouver, Kelly continued to prosper, and moved in 1906 to a huge house at 1186 Nicola, across the street from Rogers' Gabriola (page 109).

The firm's trade name—Nabob—was registered in 1905 and became literally a household word in the Lower Mainland. Their coffee was always a big seller—they first sold it in 1896, introduced "Thermatic" roasters in 1927 and "Flav-o-Tainer" packaging in 1940. On May 30, 1940, they achieved another first with a lemon-scented advertisement for Nabob lemon extract in the *Province*.

Kelly Douglas vacated their Gastown premises and relocated on Kingsway in Burnaby near Sears' in 1946. Their Nabob logo—the moustachioed Sultan—has scarcely changed since the turn of the century.

The Kelly Building, at 361-7 Water Street, was begun in 1905 and served the Kelly-Douglas wholesale grocery firm until it moved to Burnaby in the late Forties. Their Nabob brand name was universally known, aided by singers like the "Nabobettes" on the Home Gas Hour of Music on CJOR.

Robert Kelly, the wholesale grocer and influential Liberal, during a visit to Ottawa in 1911.

Robert Kelly, co-founder of the mammoth Kelly Douglas whole-sale grocery firm, came to Vancouver in 1890 from Russell, Ontario, where he was born in 1862. He first worked for Oppenheimer Bros. —the pioneer grocery firm started by David Oppenheimer, Vancouver's second mayor. In 1892, Kelly went into partnership with coffee and tea merchant Thomas Braid. As Braid and Kelly Ltd., they built a warehouse at Dunsmuir and Granville on the site of the Stock Exchange Tower. The enterprise foundered in the depression of 1893-1894, so in 1896, with $14,500 capital, Kelly joined Edward Douglas and formed Kelly Douglas Ltd. Kelly was "short, stocky and aggressive," while Douglas was "tall and easy going"; the two made an effective team and hit paydirt outfitting the goldseekers who swarmed through Vancouver in 1898. Not content just to outfit them and send them on their way, Douglas spent his summers in the Klondike collecting orders from his old customers.

In 1901, Edward Douglas boarded the Canadian Pacific Naviga-

H.O. Bell-Irving

A two-storey brick building at the southwest corner of Cordova and Richards was the scene of the inception of British Columbia's salmon exporting industry, and the business office of one of the province's great families: the Bell-Irvings. The little building, erected in 1889, was demolished in 1932 for the David Spencer Ltd. parking garage (now Sears' Harbour Centre).

The first Bell-Irving to arrive in Vancouver was Duncan, who came in 1883 and was the city's first doctor (unlike his colleague Dr. Israel Powell, Bell-Irving was not heavily involved in property development). However, his brother Henry Ogle Bell-Irving, who arrived here in 1885, was to have the greatest impact on the city. H.O. was born at Lockerbie, Dumfriesshire, Scotland in 1856 and took civil engineer's training at Karlsruhe, Germany. He worked on CPR construction with his friend Henry Cambie, on the mountain sections west of Calgary, and was the man who climbed the ladder to nail up the first "Great Divide" sign when the railway crossed the Rockies. He continued working for the CPR as far west as Salmon Arm, but evidently became fed up with it, and walked the 50 mile gap to the Onderdonk crews who were working their way east from the Fraser Canyon. On the way he was robbed of everything but his survey instruments. When he arrived in Vancouver shortly thereafter, he saw the potential of the little town of 700. Borrowing money from Cambie, he immediately left for England, where he married his long-time betrothed at Torquay. The couple returned to Vancouver and established themselves in Black's Hotel at New Brighton, where the first of their ten children was born. Bell-Irving rowed to work at Gastown every day.

In 1889, he formed an importing business with R.P. Patterson. They chartered the sailing ship *Titania* to bring the first direct cargo of general merchandise to Vancouver from London. For a return cargo, they decided to send tins of sockeye salmon. By this decision, the company "more or less established the westcoast fishing industry." Later that year, Bell-Irving went into partnership with Capt. R.G. Tatlow, later the B.C. Minister of Finance. They moved into the little brick building at Cordova and Richards, and began selling fish. By spring, 1890, he had an option on nine operating canneries—seven on the Fraser near Steveston and two

on the Skeena. On December 22, they formed the Anglo B.C. Packing Co., which was pre-eminent for forty years in the fishing business. By April, 1891, he had raised $330,000 in England to enable him to purchase the canneries. ABC became the largest sockeye company in the world. It sold huge quantities of tinned fish to the U.S. government during the Spanish-American war in 1898, and initiated the shipping of salted, dried fish to Japan in December, 1900. The steamer *Alpha*, which was carrying the first cargo, foundered in a tempest on the rocks off Denman Island while going to Union Bay for coal. (During the early years, fishing was done almost exclusively by whites and Indians operating small sailboats. All of the canning was done under rather dangerous, primitive conditions by Chinese workers using hand-soldering devices. The Japanese domination of the fishing industry didn't become an issue until the 1930s.) ABC provided the 25,000 cases of tinned salmon, which were, on September 4, 1914, "B.C.'s gift to the mother country" at the outbreak of the War. Bell-Irving saw that the superabundance of salmon wouldn't last; after the turn of the century, when Seattle interests entered the business, he lobbied successfully for international fishing treaties.

Bell-Irving moved in the early 1890s to 1151 Seaton Street, where he lived with the elite of the new city—including brother Duncan next door. His house, before its demolition in the Forties, was used as a Seaman's Club. He was Commodore of the Vancouver Yacht Club, twice president of the Vancouver Board of Trade and one of the founders of the Vancouver Club. He served as an alderman in 1888 and was chairman of the civic Board of Works which completed the first road around Stanley Park. He resigned from Council when the City wouldn't grant the money to purchase the twelve remaining waterfront lots on English Bay at the entrance to Stanley Park. He claimed, to much hooting from local pundits, that the city would need them by 1950 for an esplanade along the waterfront.

Henry O. Bell-Irving died in 1931. He left numerous descendants who distinguished themselves, mainly in real-estate and military circles. Henry Bell-Irving was British Columbia's Lieutenant Governor for a term until 1983.

Henry Ogle Bell-Irving, trained as a civil engineer, made a fortune in fish packing.

Isabel del Carmen (Beattie) Bell-Irving (1862-1936), born in Santiago, Chile.

Japantown

The Japanese presence in British Columbia in the past century has been marked by many examples of intolerance and little public recognition of the role played by Japanese settlers on the west coast. Although the old Japanese ghetto, known variously as Japtown, Japantown and Little Tokio (the anglicized spelling changed to Tokyo after the Second World War) was completely eradicated in the first four months of 1942, following the Pearl Harbour air attack, most of the commercial buildings remained in the blocks of Powell Street between Gore and Heatley, and the area has regained its Japanese flavour in the past fifteen years.

The first Issei (Japan-born Japanese, as opposed to Canadian-born Japanese who call themselves Nissei) to arrive on the west coast was apparently a ship-jumper named Manzo Nagamo, who arrived in New Westminster in 1877 and promptly started fishing for salmon in the Fraser River. After travelling around for several years he opened a shop in Victoria. Another well-known early immigrant, and evidently the first Japanese to be employed in the lumber industry (at Hastings Sawmill) was Yasukichi Foshizawa, known as "Indian Yasu" for his knowledge of Indian language and customs. He served as an interpreter for whites working on the coast and was once offered the daughter of an Indian chieftain as a bride (he declined).

By 1890, some 70 Japanese were reportedly working in sawmills in the Vancouver area and, in 1914, builder G. Yoda built a tenement on Fairview Slopes at 7th and Oak to house the single workers in the False Creek mills. A man named Ichitaro Fujii was the first Japanese to marry a white Canadian, at Union, B.C. on January 7, 1887, setting an example of inter-racial harmony that was seldom repeated.

Japanese Canadians wanted to exercise all the rights of Canadian citizenship, although those rights were specifically denied all Orientals by both federal and provincial law. On October 26, 1900, city collector of votes, Thomas Cunningham, said he would "go to jail" rather than buckle under to pressure from Japanese wanting to get onto the civic voters' list. Anti-Japanese feeling was running high throughout the city, but the provincial government said that Canada and Britain's relations with Japan were "too cordial" to permit any further anti-Japanese legislation being passed. Nevertheless, stories repeatedly surfaced in the press about how Japanese were taking over the west coast fishing industry. Dominion Labour Commissioner Brenner said early in 1902 that if the Japanese weren't kept out, "the Indians will be driven off the river" and into a welfare dependency. That summer, Superintendent of Provincial Police Hussey was reported to have chased Japanese fishermen who held up an Indian boat with revolvers and stole the catch. "Net cutting has been commenced at Steveston by the sulky Japs," he claimed, allegedly to enforce their tightly-controlled marketing and price system.

Japanese in Vancouver received a tremendous psychological boost from the outcome of the Russo-Japanese war of 1904-05, when upstart Japan slaughtered tottering colonial Russia. The jingoism of the mother country translated into a tight, proud, self-defensive attitude among the residents of Little Tokio, which stood them in good stead when the city exploded in the race riots of Saturday, September 7, 1907. The hot-headed white mob, having sacked Chinatown, headed for Powell Street looking for more Orientals. The Japanese, who had seen what had happened on Pender, turned out all the lights, armed themselves with sticks, rocks and knives, and set to defending their community. The white mob tried to advance, but were pelted with rocks, pieces of wood and large objects thrown from rooftops. A few windows were broken near Gore and Powell, but the mob had to beat a hasty retreat back to the vicinity of the City Hall at Main and Hastings. The next morning, Powell Street was patrolled by armed Japanese gangs who refused entry to any outsiders. The City Police cordoned off the perimeter of the area to prevent any further trouble. On Monday, no Japanese reported for work (neither did the Chinese). Rumours of armed insurrection so alarmed the populace that gunshops sold out their entire stock on that day.

The riot of 1907 all too accurately reflected the white majority's attitude towards the Japanese. Although the Japanese, as allies of the British Empire, fought loyally during the First World War, and many Japanese Canadians fought and died overseas with the Canadian Expeditionary Force (as witnessed by the Japanese War Memorial in Stanley Park), the public still felt that the "Japs" were "sneaky and untrustworthy," and were trying to take over British Columbia.

By the mid-Thirties 25,000-30,000 Japanese were said to be living in British Columbia, of whom nearly 8,000 lived in Vancouver—most in the Japantown area, but others in Steveston, farming on Lulu Island, on truck gardens along Marine Drive, in a several-block "Japtown" around 5th and Granville and in the valley around Langley. At the foot of Blenheim on the edge of the old Mole farm, there was a community containing a school, several stores, a boat-building plant and a population of up to 600. Of the Japanese population, about 11,000 were Canadian-born. Politicians got good mileage out of a "gentleman's agreement" between Canada and the Mikado, dated 1908, whereby emigration to Canada would be limited to 150 people a year. The hue and cry about illegal immigrants intensified as the Thirties drew to a close. It was matched only by the fears of an "industrial invasion" for the "aggrandizement of Japan."

An editorial in the *Vancouver Province* on April 7, 1937, summed up the popular feeling: "The old Oriental immigrant was objected to because he brought to Canada the low standard of living. . . [of] Asia, and because he worked for low wages and so

Shinkichi Tamura, builder of the New World Hotel at the corner of Powell and Dunlevy, came to Vancouver in 1888 and made a fortune exporting the first wheat and lumber to Japan. He was Japantown's most important banker, through his control of the Japan and Canada Trust Savings Co. He returned to Japan in the mid-Twenties and was elected to its parliament. He died in 1936.

tended to undermine the standards of white labourers." The editorial went on specifically to decry the Japanese, who were an important factor in the fishing industry, "almost a monopoly in truck gardening, gaining a hold on the hothouse industry, driving the white potato grower to despair. He runs woodyards, and is invading the confectionery and dry-cleaning business. . . . In the interior, he has almost a monopoly of the restaurant and hotel business." No distinction was made—then or at any other time—between immigrant Japanese and Canadian-born Nissei.

Another factor which affected the public's attitude was Japan's undeclared, barbarous war against the Chinese since 1931. The Co-operative Commonwealth Federation (CCF), which later was the only federal political organization to oppose the Japanese evacuation from the B.C. Coast, asked for a Japanese boycott in December, 1937 because of that nation's actions in China.

In 1936, a delegation from the Japanese Canadian Citizens' League—led by a young Canadian semanticist working at the University of Wisconsin named S. Ichie Hayakawa—went to Ottawa to appeal for the enfranchisement of Japanese Canadians. It took until March 31 of the next year for the Federal Government to respond: Canadian-born Japanese would not get the vote, they said, until the Province of British Columbia acted to remove *its* discriminatory legislation. Almost concurrently, Japanese financial interests bought up all of the Iron Duke and Granby mines' ore and copper output. The Canadian Legion protested.

In Vancouver in June, Mayor Fred Hume attacked Japanese for "living in scowhouses and paying little or no taxes" but sending their large number of children to school. New Westminster MP Tom Reid got into the act and attacked the Japanese for the same type of thing. Newspapers began to make much of an alleged anti-British feeling noted by travellers in Japan. The Hon. A. Wells Gray, provincial Minister of Lands, threatened to expose Canadians who set up "dummy" corporations to allow Japanese to penetrate B.C. timber reserves. An unofficial boycott of Japanese stores and goods began, due to the bombing of Chinese cities.

On November 17, Archdeacon F.G. Scott, the beloved wartime padré of the Canadian Expeditionary Force, alarmed British Columbians by stating that disguised Japanese naval officers were living in "so-called Japanese fishing villages in B.C." He said that the large vessels in the fishing industry "may belong to the class of mystery ships which England used during the war"—a reference presumably to armed but disguised Q-boats which sank submarines in the Atlantic.

The next day, a completely different group philosophically, the Canadian League for Peace and Democracy (communists "from the relief camps," said the newspapers), clashed with police at Pier B-C to prevent the landing of Japanese Mandarin oranges from the *Empress of Canada*. Twenty-eight people were remanded in Police Court after the incident.

The next month, the Trollers' Association of B.C. demanded that Ottawa deport all Japanese for their "fishing invasion." Alderman Halford Wilson proposed banning all Japanese women to stop the "peaceful penetration of our province." He demanded a new census as a first step towards controlling the Japanese invasion of B.C., industrial and otherwise.

On January 21, 1938, Seattle police discovered a huge time bomb—consisting of 369 sticks of dynamite, 28 fuses and a mechanical device to set it off—underneath the Japanese liner *Hive Maru*. A 27-year old Vancouverite named George Patridge admitted complicity in the scheme, which was "a plot hatched by Oriental agents in San Francisco." The leader—a man named Rolf Forsythe—was described as "an idealist; he believed he could stop the Chinese war by disorganizing Japanese trade." The headlines added impetus to the efforts of Reid, Wilson and MLA Captain MacGregor MacIntosh for a new census and the registration of all Japanese, regardless of citizenship. The newspapers filled with stories about how Japanese were being smuggled into the country; the Japanese population of Richmond, it was said, had increased 300 per cent in 20 years. Whither the 150 a year? An attempt by a few MPs to push a Japanese Exclusion Bill through Parliament was defeated in the House on June 1, 1938, by a vote of 87 to 39; MacKenzie King's government shelved it for a year lest it create discord in the Commonwealth. Japan was still an ally of the British. Japanese spies, said MacIntosh, dominated the west-coast fishing industry. "Nonsense," replied the Japanese community.

The declaration of war on Britain and Canada in late 1939 did little to change the mood on the coast. Japan, which until that time had pursued its expansionist aims in China alone, took advantage of France's helplessness following the 1940 occupation to get France to agree to the "protective" occupation of French Indo-China. In Vancouver that August, Halford Wilson got a City Council resolution passed, demanding the deportation of Japanese illegals. Council urged Ottawa to conduct another census. On August 14, it was decided that Japanese must take a loyalty oath when renewing their fishing licenses (however, it was pointed out that Japanese held only 12 per cent of all licenses on the coast). On October 18, New Westminster dock workers refused to load any more Japan-bound ships.

On January 9, 1941, everyone of Japanese ancestry was banned from Canadian military service; the younger ones expressed public disappointment that they wouldn't be called up. The same day, Prime Minister MacKenzie King announced a new Japanese registration "to protect the Japanese themselves" and to deport any illegals. All Japanese were to be thumb-printed by the RCMP.

On February 8, another spy scare hit the papers when two Japanese tourists were arrested while taking pictures of the waterfront from the CNR dock. They protested their innocence but their film was destroyed. The situation almost exactly paralleled one in May of 1938 when a Vancouver man named J.S. Gilbertson was arrested in Osaka with snapshots of Japanese ships and streets in his possession. An "espionage madness" gripped the city. Halford Wilson continued to make headlines in February and March of

David Oppenheimer

recorded that the brothers skinned CPR General Manager William Van Horne in a poker game during the latter's visit to Gastown. In 1885, they bought the Hastings Mill land from Carrall to Gore (then on the eastern outskirts of Vancouver), cleared it, and opened it for settlement. After the fire, they built a brick warehouse on the southeast corner of Columbia and Powell (the Pier One Imports building) for their grocery business.

David Oppenheimer, a well-known and popular figure around town, unceasingly fought the CPR over the city's development. He was elected alderman in 1887 and became mayor in 1888. During his term of office the city's population rose to 15,000. In addition to his civic duties, he was quite a wheeler-dealer on development schemes like the interurban railway, steamship connections with Australia and the Orient and contracting sidelines like the new City Hall. As such, he represented the only non-CPR financial dynasty in the early city. He established what was then called the Powell Street Grounds as the city's first playing field. Before Oppenheimer's time, all of the ball games were held at the only clearing on Burrard Inlet—a few acres of grass surrounding George Black's Hotel at New Brighton. Charlie Queen drove the stagecoach to New Westminster every day, and in the evenings would drive "the boys" to Brighton for free. The ball ground there was very cramped, and Oppenheimer lobbied furiously for the Powell Street Grounds. Lauchlan Hamilton, the CPR surveyor and alderman, wanted the Cambie Street Grounds location, and paid jailer John Clough's chain gang to rough clear it in 1888. The balance of the work there was done by cricketers and "the baseball boys." The city, of course, ended up getting both parks: Oppenheimer Park was so dedicated in 1902, but was known for years after as the Powell Street Grounds; the Cambie Street Grounds were known as Larwill Park. Oppenheimer Park was the site of many of the Depression-era political rallies and was to have been sold for industrial use in 1957 when the City Planning Department decided the Japantown area should be industrial instead of residential.

Oppenheimer retired from politics in 1891 owing to ill health. A lavish farewell banquet was held for him in the Hotel Vancouver on January 15, 1892. He died on the last day of 1897 in Vancouver, but was buried next to his wife in a Jewish cemetery in Brooklyn (associations with the family's New York home influenced David Oppenheimer in naming Central Park on the Vancouver-Burnaby border).

Oppenheimer had dedicated Stanley Park in 1889 with Lord Stanley; a monument to him was unveiled at the Beach Avenue entrance to the park in 1911. Premier Richard McBride said at the dedication ceremony that Oppenheimer had "played the part of a true man, and lived up to the highest ideals of British citizenship." His brother Isaac died in December 1922 in Spokane; the third brother, Charles, who had stayed in San Francisco, died there in December, 1890.

Oppenheimer Park, bordered by Powell, Dunlevy, Cordova and Jackson, is a tribute to David Oppenheimer, Vancouver's second Mayor and, with his brother, operator of the first "financial establishment" in the city after the Hastings Mill. The Oppenheimer Brothers were pioneer wholesale grocers and great boosters of the east side of downtown during the period when the Canadian Pacific Railway was dragging the population south and west toward Granville Street.

David Oppenheimer was born in 1834 in Bavaria. With his brothers Charles and Isaac, he left Germany in 1848 and went to the United States. They landed in Lafayette, then travelled through New Orleans before heading to Sacramento and San Francisco on the heels of the Forty-Niners. In 1860, David and Isaac went to Victoria and opened a grocery business, with branch offices in Yale and the few other existing interior points, to supply the wagon trains heading for the Cariboo goldfields. In August, 1884, it is

1941, demanding that Orientals be banned from owning property "outside the areas reserved for them," and that all new dressmaking licenses for Japanese be delayed. Japanese reported patiently to the Customs Building at 805 West Hastings to register and be thumb-printed. On May 23, when the first Air Raid Protection blackout was held, Little Tokio was reported to be as black as the inside of a cow.

Although Canada was at war with Germany, the battlefields were on the other side of the world. And, while Canada was about to be at war with Japan, there was little hint of gathering storm clouds in balmy Vancouver during the spring and summer of 1941. Although Wartime Price Controls were in effect, Vancouverites often slipped across the border to Blaine and Point Roberts, where neutral U.S.A. bathed in its post-Depression prosperity. Dancing, drinking, shopping and unlimited tanks of gas were available. The war seemed worlds away. (The first ration books for sugar, coffee and tea came out on August 24, 1942. Butter was rationed that December. By the next February, fats for the making of glycerine for high explosives were in such short supply that a national campaign, under the banner "Out of the Frying Pan, Into the Firing Line" commenced. Local Odeon theatres held movie performances in aid of the Fats Drive. Children with two pounds of fat renderings in a tin were admitted free.)

President Roosevelt responded to the Japanese move on Indo-China on July 24, 1941, by slapping a freeze on all Japanese assets and planting an embargo on her oil supply, a move quickly followed by the British and the refugee Dutch Government in London. It was evident to everyone (as it had been since 1931) that Japan, thus starved, would have to fight in the Pacific. On July 28, the half-loaded lumber carrier *Florida Maru* beat a hasty retreat from Vancouver to Japan.

On Sunday morning, December 7, 1941, the Japanese air force made its attack on Pearl Harbour. In Vancouver, there was a "curious sense of unreality to it all," according to a newspaper report. The Sunday streets in Japantown were quiet. Japanese confectioneries continued with business as usual. On Monday, a spokesman for the Japanese community pledged their "unswerving allegiance" to the Crown. Enemy aliens were swiftly rounded up by the RCMP, Japanese language schools and newspapers were closed, and a roundup of the 1,886 registered Japanese-Canadian fishing boats got underway. That night, there was a small amount of vandalism—an oil-soaked rag was tossed into the woodpile inside the door of the Dunlevy Rooms at 143 Alexander, and a coal-oil lantern was tossed through the window of the Y.Ono confectionery at 2481 West 41st. On Thursday, December 11, Japantown—along with the rest of the city—bustled with preparations for the first real blackout of the war, slated for that night; all suitable fabric was bought up from the stores along Powell. The same day, a patrol from the Royal Vancouver Yacht Club under the name of the "Standing Committee on Oriental Matters" pulled the carburetors from one hundred fishing boats at the foot of Blenheim.

That Friday, amid suggestions of opening new work camps, banning all new Japanese fishing licenses, manning Japanese-owned fishing boats with whites and wild rumours of subversion, the RCMP ordered all Japanese who had been naturalized as Canadian citizens since 1922 to register with them by February 7 at the RCMP Barracks at 33rd and Heather.

On January 3, Mayor Fred Hume warned of a possible Fifth Column and claimed that hundreds of Japanese had fled the city when the registration started. Less than two weeks later, the Federal Government acted: all Japanese males 18 to 45, except those holding police permits, were to be removed from the coast (past a line running along the spine of the Cascades and away from all highways and railways).

On February 4, the first group of Japantown residents—looking surprisingly cheerful—left the city for the east. On the 13th, the paper carried a headline: "All Provinces Refuse Japs. Must Stay in B.C." Plans were then formulated to set up work-camp-style communities in remote, abandoned parts of the Boundary-Similkameen and Kootenays area, at places like Greenwood and New Denver.

On February 14, notices under the banner "To All Male Enemy Aliens" were posted around town, ordering all Japanese to leave the coastal area within 47 days. While German and Italian *nationals* were also affected, *anyone* of Japanese descent, regardless of nationality, was ordered off the coast. Lists of fishboats for sale at bargain prices were published on February 21. The "exodus" from Japantown began a week later.

Starting March 1, a dusk to dawn curfew was slapped on Little Tokio—the "yakan gaishu-tsu kinshi rei" order. The United Church of Canada at 500 Powell held a "last fling" dance in its basement for the young people who were about to be moved out to no-one-knew-where. That week as part of a Victory Loan campaign, "Strang Verboten" occupation orders—detailing what life would be like in a captured Vancouver—were printed in the papers and appeared on billboards and power poles around the city. All stock in Japanese-operated and owned stores was seized and liquidated by the Custodian of Enemy Property. Japanese were ordered to surrender all motor vehicles, cameras and radios at Hastings Park. All such property was seized, and Hastings Park became an impounding and disposal area for all Japanese property. Newspapers were full of advertisements for exceptional bargains on ex-Japanese possessions and the fire-sale stock of retail stores. Little of that money—or the value of the fishboats—was ever returned. Japanese Canadians were lucky to get ten cents on the dollar for their possessions. By April 1, 1942, Japantown was a ghost town.

The landmark from Japantown's heyday is the New World Hotel at the corner of Powell and Dunlevy, built just before the First World War by banker and importer S. Tamura. In the Twenties and Thirties, all of the tenants there, and in the buildings along Powell, were Japanese.

Powell Street between Hastings and Princess–the heart of Little Tokio was evacuated in the months following the Pearl Harbour attack of December 7, 1941. Beginning in March, 1942, all people of Japanese ancestry on the coast, regardless of citizenship, had to surrender cars, trucks, motorcycles, cameras and radios to the RCMP. Most of the goods were surrendered at Hastings Park to the Custodian of Enemy Alien Property. During the latter part of March, Powell Street sidewalks were piled high with baggage of Japanese families who were being moved out to road camps and resettlement communities like New Denver and Greenwood in the B.C. interior. Their moving problem was compounded by the fact that all their vehicles had been confiscated. The streets were deserted. Posters appeared on March 27 under the banner "Notice to All Males of Japanese Racial Origin," ordering all Japanese within the Greater Vancouver area to report to the RCMP Barracks at 33rd and Heather, "unless in possession of a permit to remain in the defense area issued by the British Columbia Security Commission." For the balance of the war, Powell Street east of Main was entirely vacant.

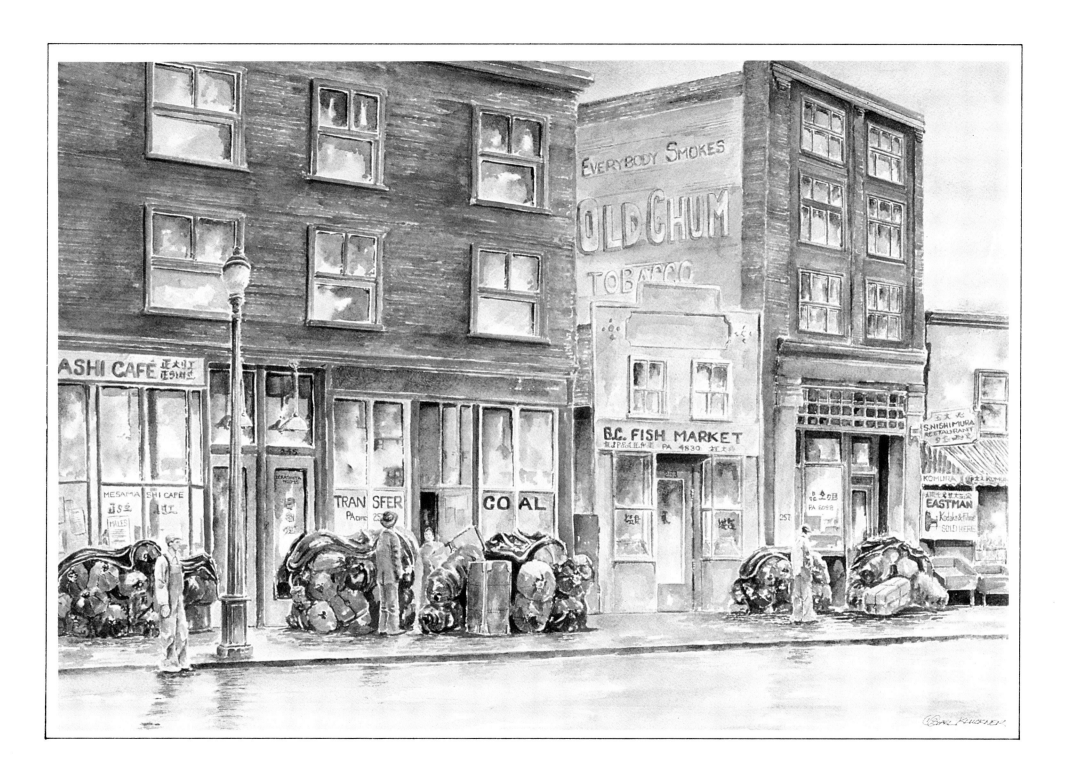

33

The Red Light District

Prostitutes followed the Canadian Pacific Railway workers across the country like a scruffy, pulchritudinous plague. After the driving of the last spike, hookers who liked the west coast settled in the shacks on the "Tar Flats," along the railway line east of the Heatley Street switch. They were thus out of reach of the long arm of the law—Heatley being the city boundary—but the distance caused a shortfall in business. By the turn of the century, the more enterprising Madams had moved to the outskirts of the city along Harris Street (now East Georgia) on the little dent of that road west of Westminster Avenue (Main Street) which deadended on False Creek. This block, which was demolished for the construction of the first Georgia Viaduct in 1913, was popularly known as Shore Street, "The Red Light District," or "The Restricted Area." The brothels were tolerated, although the Board of Police Commissioners in 1910 demanded that they remove the red lights from outside their windows, and ordered the police to continue prosecutions for selling liquor without a license. Public pressure, especially from the Wesleyan Moral Reform league, forced the Police Commission to give the Madams three months notice to vacate as of August 1, 1911. The Madams selected the 500 and 600 blocks of Alexander Street as a suitable new area.

Alexander Street was ideal for the purpose, as it was close to both the Hastings Mill and the docks. By the summer of 1912 the two blocks between Jackson and Heatley were completely occupied by brothels, all registered in the Madams' names. The most famous brothel was the "House of All Nations" at 623 Alexander. According to the November 28, 1912 edition of *The Truth* newspaper, "you can get everything there from a chocolate coloured damsel to a Swedish girl." The same article described Ollie Gilbert's at 510 Alexander as having "a rather sunburnt lady at the piano," while Ollie herself sat at one end of the dance floor, "stowing away the hard-earned money of the young fellows present." There was no pretence of discretion: the front doors stood open and lights blazed out onto the streets. Piano rags tinkled in the summer night air. (The most famous brothel of the period was Edward VII's favourite: the Chabanais in Paris, which had Arabian and Gothic rooms and a fully-outfitted Pullman car.)

In August, 1912, the Police Commission ordered Chief Constable Rufus Chamberlin to clean up the area. Arrests of characters like Elsie Kelly, Alice Bernard, Eunice Longe and dozens of others were made in raids throughout the ensuing months, with the result that, by the end of 1913, the red light district was gone. Arrest statistics for 1912 showed that 19 "Frequenters of Bawdyhouses" were charged, plus 204 "Inmates" and 133 "Keepers of Bawdyhouses." Most of the women were sentenced to six months of hard labour, but given a suspended sentence in order to give them time to get out of town.

The blocks on the waterfront side have now given way to the buildings of the American Can Co., which loom over the remaining houses.

The Alexander Street red light district, called "The Restricted Area" by the newspapers, in 1913. The painting shows the brothels just east of Jackson Avenue. West of Jackson was Japanese, including the Japanese Public School at 439 Alexander. The building at the corner was built, appropriately, as the British Sailors' Home, but was occupied by Dollie Darlington and her associates in 1913. The house at 502 was occupied by one Ruth Richards, and the brick building at 504, built originally as a hospital, had Roma Graham as Madam. Mildred Hill oversaw the activities at the opulent house at 508 Alexander. Some Madams had their names laid in tile in the entranceways–the last remaining one is Fay Packer's (above) in a rooming house at 658 Alexander. The brothels were cleaned up late in 1913. The next year saw the construction of the huge American Can warehouses on the water side, which still dominate the street.

Chinatown

The first Chinese to arrive on the west coast of North America were imported in the late 1840s to aid construction on the Union Pacific Railway in California. A few came north in 1858 to search for Cariboo gold and eventually settled in Victoria, where they were met with unprecedented vilification. Politicians like Premier Amor de Cosmos so abhorred the "Heathen Chinee" that, during the 1870s and beginning years of the Eighties, whites appeared to talk of little else.

Andrew Onderdonk, the CPR-employed contractor who undertook to build the railway through the Fraser Canyon, was met in Victoria upon his first visit to the country in April, 1880 by a group from the Anti-Chinese League. He was to need a minimum of 10,000 railway workers to complete his task (the population of British Columbia was 35,000), but assured the Victoria establishment that he would hire French Canadians if he ran short of local whites, and would only fall back upon Indians and "the beardless children of China" if all else failed. At that time, there were probably about 3,000 Chinese in the province—most in Victoria, and a few in the almost trackless interior and along the worked-out sand bars on the Fraser near Quesnel.

Onderdonk ran into budget problems almost from the beginning and was soon obliged to renege on his promises and hire Chinese. White labourers demanded a minimum $1.50 a day, while Chinese would work for $1 a day and take an incredible amount of abuse. Onderdonk hired his first contingent of Chinese from the Northern Pacific Railroad in Oregon in 1880, and a second one from the Southern Pacific in California in 1881. In the winter of 1881-2, he chartered two sailing ships and brought two thousand more coolies from Hong Kong. (The Chinese were all hired through Canton—where the average wage was 7 cents a day—the only port through which foreign trade was permitted. Thus, when these ex-railway workers began settling in Vancouver, the culture, food and language was primarily Cantonese. In 1911, the great Cantonese revolutionary, Sun Yat-Sen, found safe haven in Vancouver, reportedly in the Chinese Freemasons building at One West Pender.)

By 1886, it became apparent that many of the Chinese who had been inveigled to Canada in the hope of lasting financial independence and an eventual return to China had not been able to save anywhere near the anticipated capital. In Vancouver, they settled into tenements and shacks along swampy Dupont Street (Pender Street) on the edge of False Creek. There were few (if any) women, and the men grew old and died off during the Twenties and Thirties, their hopes of returning to China gradually disintegrating.

The distinctive Chinatown they created, between the Royal City Planing Mills on False Creek and the city's thriving downtown, was a ready target for the Knights of Labour, the Oriental Exclusion League and other white supremacist groups. The area basically kept to itself—at the time, few whites were involved with opium or interested in Chinese-style gambling. However, the importing of Chinese labour, which began in January 1887, tipped the scales. About 20 Chinese arrived from Victoria in the first week of that month, hired by John MacDougall to clear land on the edge of John Morton's property near the north foot of Burrard Street. The group camped by a stream near today's Burrard and Pender corner. On January 10, the Knights of Labour leaders, accompanied by about 250 ruffians, marched to the Chinese camp, escorted the labourers to the CPR dock, passed a hat to collect money for their fares, and sent them back to Victoria. A month later, the Knights' anti-Chinese campaign got into full swing: a boycott was started, businessmen were urged to sign pledges not to deal with any Chinese, and stores which refused to cooperate had black crosses painted on the pavement in front of their doors. Late in the month, when more Chinese had arrived to clear the land, a larger mob listened to Knights of Labour speeches at the Carrall Street city hall and then marched to the camp and sacked it. Chinese were tied together by their pigtails, beaten and had all of their shacks and tents burned. The imbroglio was broken up by Vancouver Police Chief Stewart and Provincial Police Superintendent Roycroft. Nevertheless, that night, many windows were broken in Chinatown and several buildings were set on fire. On March 2, the Vancouver city charter was suspended, and a force of 35 provincial police constables arrived to take over the city. The "Specials" returned to Victoria 17 days later.

By the turn of the century, Chinatown had recovered and erected some substantial buildings—many to house the Benevolent and Freemasonry societies which grew from a need for mutual help and protection. A distinctive Chinatown style of architecture, with deeply recessed balconies, "cheater" stories (inserted between the first and second floors like a mezzanine but not assessed for taxes), and Ming hats and spires, developed along the two blocks of Pender east of Carrall and down bustling Shanghai Alley. Opium was manufactured openly, primarily in the Market Alley between Pender and Hastings, and carried through the streets in baskets. The air had a pungent odour, the streets were full of vegetable peddlers with pigtails and buttonless coats (they used knots), and horse-drawn junk wagons; many buildings housed secret opium dens, baths and hidden gaming rooms. On September 15, 1902, police captured one retreating Chinese by the pigtail during a raid on a club at 38 Dupont. The newspapers carried information on the clubs, their watching women who controlled secret passageways, the back doors and ruined men in the underground opium dens. Harry Stevens, later a Cabinet Minister, made his reputation by exposing the clubs and the degradation of whites in Chinatown in a series of articles in the News-Advertiser. On September 22, fifty

"Sam Kee" was the name of a group of successful importers which lost a valuable piece of property when the city widened Dupont Street in 1912 and filled in the False Creek swamp west of Carrall Street. They were left with a slice of land four feet eleven inches wide and, infuriated, decided to build on it regardless. The resulting Sam Kee building is the narrowest commercial building in the world. Bay windows above give a room width of about six feet, and communal baths used to extend beneath the sidewalk. The building occupies the dividing line between white and Chinese Vancouver. CPR freight trains shunted regularly across Pender and Hastings until 1932. The skyline of prosperous downtown Vancouver was dominated by the World Tower, known from 1924 through 1937 as the Bekins Building. The old Sang Lung Jan building, on the left between Shanghai Alley and the train tracks, was demolished and replaced with a steel fabricating shop. The CPR's first Roundhouse was one hundred yards to the south (left) of Pender on Shanghai Alley, and Dan Sheehan's pioneer Texas Lake Ice & Cold Storage Co. was near the corner.

Chinese who had been charged with gambling appeared in Police Court to plead that they were tired of being raided and paying fines. The judge became interested in their claims that the games were not really gambling, so Police Sergeant Butler demonstrated how chuck-a-luck was played. The lawyer, Crown Counsel and judge then had a game in the courtroom, to the great amusement of all present. Nevertheless, they lost their case.

On March 26, 1903, a bill to increase the poll or head tax on immigrant Chinese from $100 to $500 was introduced in the House of Commons by Prime Minister Wilfrid Laurier. The desired effect—to stop all Chinese immigration into Canada—was not achieved until 1923, when the Chinese Immigration Act was passed. By 1927, the population had actually declined, due to the rapid dying off of the older unmarried coolies; there were then about 20,000 Chinese in the province, mainly in Vancouver's Chinatown.

By 1907, the population of the city of Vancouver stood at about 65,000. The Hundred Thousand Club, formed in August 1906 to increase the population, had done well and had more than doubled the city's size since the turn of the century. However, the prosperity of these "golden years" faltered a little in the spring of 1907 and—although practically no Chinese were employed in "white man's work"—the newly-unemployed white workers turned on them again as a convenient target.

The Asiatic Exclusion League announced a giant parade for Saturday afternoon, September 7, 1907. As many as 30,000—by newspaper estimates—gathered on the Cambie Street Grounds to hear a couple of hours of inflammatory speeches. Led by a brass band and representatives of all the trade unions and military organizations, the crowd then marched up Georgia to Granville, down Granville to Hastings and along to the City Hall at Main near Pender. There, Lieut. Gov. Dunsmuir was burned in effigy (Dunsmuir's Nanaimo coal mines were great employers of Chinese labour). More speeches were made, winding up with a man from Bellingham relating how Bellingham's East Indian community had been sacked recently by white citizens. The mob, suitably inspired, headed down Pender Street, beating everyone in sight and breaking every window. Shops were looted and fires started. At the end of Chinatown, the crowd headed for Powell Street and the Little Tokio area, where they met with a more organized reception. The police and newspapers later blamed the incident on "American agitators," but suggested that it would be much easier for everyone if there were fewer Chinese. The federal government sent its labour minister, Mackenzie King, to scrutinize the damage claims, 250 of which were received. On June 7, 1908, the government paid out a total of $33,000, most of which went to the Chinese merchants. King was revolted to find that opium was manufactured openly in Chinatown—damage claims for lost business had come in from two factories—and with prodding from Moral Reform League spokesmen like Harry Stevens, a Narcotic Control Act was passed in Parliament the following. (The opium factories were

driven underground rather than eradicated; as late as 1938, a fair-sized opium-poppy plantation was discovered in a wooded area just south of the intersection of Marine Drive and Forty First, on the edge of the Musqueam Indian reserve.)

Organized labour remained virulently anti-Chinese until after the Second World War. Typical of this was Article 9 from the Trades and Labour Congress' 1931 "Principles," which stated that an "Asiatic" was "a member of a race which cannot be properly assimilated into the national life of Canada." For the previous ten years the Chinese—who had been effectively barred from work in white industry—had fought against the "Water Street" interests for control of the fruit and vegetable business on the Lower Mainland. Water Street represented the old, white-controlled wholesale firms—the Malkins, Kelly Douglas and the successors to the Oppenheimers. According to contemporary newspapers, there were a "big ten" of Chinese wholesalers on Pender and East Georgia, among whom control of 75 per cent of all the green vegetable trade in B.C. was distributed. "The Celestials locked forces against Water Street," said the papers, and were finally considered victorious in 1933, when both the latter and the Vegetable Marketing Board admitted that they could neither control prices nor keep the Chinese out. The Chinese wholesale dealers had grown from one in 1922 to 21 in 1933. The West End, Kitsilano, Point Grey and Fairview were said to be overrun with Chinese and Japanese corner stores; there were 69 Chinese and 77 Japanese stores in those areas, and there were almost no English Canadians who said they could compete. There were 155 licensed Chinese vegetable peddlers in the city, headquartered at 19th and Main. Newspaper editorialists and politicians like M.L.A. Clive Planta complained about the Chinese's filth, squalor, lack of sanitation, overcrowding and lack of respect for laws.

All of their dealings were considered—in Western eyes—to be under the table. Every morning between two and four-thirty, hundreds of farm trucks made their way to the city from the Fraser Valley, Lulu Island and the truck gardens along Marine Drive. They congregated on the vacant land opposite the CNR station on Main Street before the 6:30 a.m. legal start of business in the city. There they were met by an equally large retail fleet of trucks, which distributed the produce around the city. No money, it was said, ever appeared to change hands.

The anti-Chinese campaign was so insistent throughout the Thirties that in 1938 the Chinese Fruit and Vegetable Merchants' Association started an ad campaign for its 84 stores, stressing their friendliness and good service.

Newspaper items concerning Chinatown in the Thirties mused on the oddness of "blind marriages," or described the "colourful" ceremonies and parades held to mark festive occasions. Some sympathy was directed towards the Chinese for their underdog defensive war against the Japanese, which began in 1931. In February, 1931, the Chinese Benevolent Association raised $16,000 for the Chinese cause. The following March, a shiver went through the

John D. McDougall (1856-1933), the CPR contractor whose employment of Chinese labour on a West End clearing contract in 1887 precipitated the city's first race riot. McDougall claimed to have been the discoverer of "the Klondike" gold fields during an exploration trip in the early 1890s.

(Next page) After five years of Japanese "adventuring," the Tientsin offensive in Northern China in July, 1937 captured headlines all over the world. Vancouver's Chinese community gathered outside the offices of the Chinese New Republic Daily newspaper at 5 East Pender at Carrall to read the war news, written with brush and ink on wrapping paper. Many, it was said, had relatives in the war zone, and even more had contributed to the Chinese national war debt. A "cheerful little laundry man" was asked by a white reporter what he thought of the war. "His round moon face lost its usual grin," the reporter noted. " 'Japanese very bad. Chinese ketchum in the neck too long. By-um-by we put up a good fight.' " He added, prophetically, " 'Now we got too many generals.' " The newspaper, renamed the Chinese Times, has occupied the corner since 1939. The Yukon Uniform Co. moved up the street to 19 East Pender.

city when a car was discovered in the 200-block East Pender, containing six dismantled Lewis guns and 100,000 rounds of ammunition, presumably being prepared for smuggling to the Chinese war zone. Fundraising drives continued throughout the years, including the 1937 "National Salvation" campaign, again sponsored by the Chinese Benevolent Association. After the Tientsin offensive that August, Chinese were often seen in large crowds along Pender and Columbia, reading the hand-printed bulletin boards containing news from the front. Public sympathy was with the Chinese, but few Chinese merchants would state whether there was a boycott, however unofficial, against the stores in Little Tokio. There was no open animosity between the two Vancouver districts, either: "we want to live in peace in this country," a spokesman said. In September, Col. J.E. Leckie was misquoted in Vancouver papers, as willing to raise a foreign legion in Vancouver to fight in China.

The Chinese and Japanese probably felt they were in the same second-class boat in Vancouver, as witnessed by the "white waitress" affair of the last years of the Thirties. In September, 1937, the B.C. Royal Cafe at 61 East Pender, the Hongkong Cafe at 126 and the Gee Kong at 168 were closed by the city for non-compliance with City By-Law 1880, which banned white women from working in Chinese-owned restaurants. The three owners—Toy Chew, Harry Lee and Chinese Benevolent Association President Harry Ting—sued the city but lost. In October, they and other Chinese businessmen were forced to fire all the white girls in their employ in order to get their licenses back. On October 11, thirty of the girls appeared before City Council to demand reinstatement. It was denied. The issue re-surfaced in March, 1939 when other alleged infractions were reported to Mayor George Miller. He passed the decision over to Police Chief W.W. Foster who, on March 20, told Council: "In view of the conditions under which the girls are expected to work, it is almost impossible for them to be so employed, without falling victim to some sort of immoral life." Bylaw 1880 was again enforced. Whites continued to patronize Chinese restaurants, as always.

On December 8, 1941, Chinatown was jubilant when the United States entered the war against Japan. Many Chinese fought and died for the Canadian army over the next four years, and when they returned to Vancouver they settled away from old Chinatown. There was still discrimination—at least one young couple who tried to buy a home in Burnaby in the Forties were rebuffed by hostile neighbours. They moved to Kerrisdale instead. In 1941, Alderman Halford Wilson had attempted to ban Orientals from settling into "better" residential areas, and presented a petition from residents in the newly-developed Highbury area near 41st Avenue. The Chinese consul and the Civil Liberties Union protested vigorously and the issue blew over. During the war, many young Chinese had protested Ottawa's call-up orders with a "No Vote, No Fight" stance. Emancipation was finally granted to Canadians of Chinese ancestry in 1947.

Very little is known (by whites) of the characters who built Chinatown and were important community figures. One "wheel" was named Wong Toy, a "successful businessman, good gambler and philanthropist on the streets of Chinatown." He was active in the three Vancouver Wong groups: the Hon Shing Athletic Club, opened in 1940 to provide recreation mainly for young men; the Wong Hung Kar Tong, the ruling "privy council" of much of Chinatown; and the Wong Wun Sun Society, the most active benevolent association. Wong Toy came to Canada when he was 14 and was "looked after" by the Wong Wun Sun Society. He repaid that debt by service, but oddly enough died penniless after a heart attack in November, 1941, aged a mere 44 years.

Chinatown has changed very little physically since the Twenties. The area is still popular—west of Main Street—with whites seeking Chinese shopping and dining. East of Main is the Chinese market area with its teeming sidewalks, vegetable dealers and poultry shops. The Chinese community is still firmly rooted in the area, but individuals are almost completely assimilated into far-spread white neighbourhoods—quite a feat considering the record of the first four decades of the century.

Chew Woo, also known as Chew Ping Sen (1888-1937), was born in China and came to Vancouver in 1907. He returned to China in 1910 to fight for the overthrow of the Manchu Dynasty, and after his return to Vancouver was an active member of the Nationalist Party. He lived at 815 Princess Street.

Victory Square

The Courthouse, at the corner of Hastings and Cambie, faced onto Hastings Street. Built in 1888, it was the first major public building outside the old Gastown area. It was demolished before the First World War, after the new Courthouse opened in the CPR's bailiwick at Georgia and Hornby. The old Courthouse site was used for recruiting during the Great War years, and a large tent with a marquee occupied the land. After the war, a Cenotaph was erected and the park officially dedicated as Victory Square.

At Cambie, Hastings Street takes a jog northwards, due to the 1885 CPR surveys which aligned Vancouver streets slightly differently from those in the original Granville townsite. On the pie-shaped corner to the southwest is today's Victory Square—the location of the City's original domed Courthouse, built when Vancouver was only two years old. It was the Public Square for the city in the years after the Great Fire. In the spring of 1900, citizens gathered there to celebrate the Relief of Mafeking and lit a tremendous bonfire which burned a hole in the new wood-block pavement. In September, 1901 the city turned out again to welcome the Duke and Duchess of Cornwall and York (later King George V and Mary) during their triumphant parade through the city.

At the turn of the century, the corner of Hastings and Cambie really came into its own. The Klondike rush added new stone and brick buildings to the streets, like the Flack Block at the northeast corner, built with the proceeds of one big gold strike. The Ormidale Block to the east—built with the proceeds of another—the Ralph Block at 126 and the Henderson Block at 122 were all started in 1899. A major draw to the area was "The Arcade" at the northwest corner (today's Dominion Building site) which was opened in December, 1895. Besides being the first office of the Great Northern Railway, it had thirteen shops which ran diagonally from the corner. "Meet you at the Arcade" was a popular phrase of the time. The streets were strung with electric arc carbon lamps, which had

Court House, Vancouver, B.C.

AUTHOR'S COLLECTION

to be lowered daily by the Edwardian equivalent of a lamplighter, to insert a new carbon pencil. Men wore Derby hats or boaters, women, long skirts. The streets were full of bicycles, as no one trusted an automobile for anything other than pleasure. At the numerous bars, like the Strand on Hastings Street, the beer was a nickel a schooner.

Cordova Street began to fade as the city's major shopping thoroughfare by the First World War; it was replaced by the lower end of Granville Street, and Hastings Street from Woodward's Department Store west. The opening of the popular Spencer's at Hastings and Richards added to the area's attractions.

Two major office buildings had risen on the edge of the Courthouse Square shortly before the First World War. The first was the Province Building at 198 West Hastings, erected by *News-Advertiser* publisher and M.L.A. Francis Carter-Cotton— who with real-estate developer J.W. Horne was the city's first representative to Victoria in 1890. After the First World War, the building was occupied by Walter C. Nichol's *Province*, as was the Edgett Building behind it, facing onto Pender Street. The *News-Advertiser* and the *Province* competed furiously with Louis D. Taylor's *World* newspaper, published out of the dramatic World Tower at Beatty and Pender, a stone's throw to the southeast. Although the latter building attracted the most attention and praise, its back-street location was a long way from the hustle and bustle of Hastings and Cambie.

The other office tower to locate at the Courthouse Square was the beautiful Dominion Building, erected through the financial efforts of the von Alvensleben brothers and the Dominion Trust Company. The yellow-roofed, red brick building takes full advantage of the almost triangular lot, providing odd shaped rooms with many windows for its tenants.

Both the Carter-Cotton building and the Dominion Building were erected at the Courthouse Square, even though the Courthouse had moved uptown to Georgia and Howe—a major victory for CPR interests in the City. (The Inns of Court building remained at the southwest corner of Hamilton and Hastings but ceased to be a bastion for the legal profession.) The old Courthouse was torn down shortly before the First World War, and the vacant lot, much of it covered by a large tent with a marquee, was then used for military recruiting. After the war, the Southam family, which had bought the *Province*, donated money for the rehabilitation of the square, and in 1924, when the Cenotaph was erected there, the name was changed to Victory Square.

"The tallest building in the British Empire," circa 1912, stands at the corner of Beatty and Pender in a quiet backwater of brick warehouses. The Tower Building—also known as the World Tower, the Bekins Building and most recently the Sun Tower—was a progressive, attention-grabbing monument to the flamboyant

The painting shows the 300-block West Pender Street, between Homer and Hamilton, in 1914. The real estate boom of 1912 had collapsed, though Dominion Trust—which dissolved in scandal and the suicide of its manager in October—still proudly advertised itself from the roof of the Dominion Building. Vancouver retained its innocence and light-heartedness until after the Battle of Ypres in April, 1915.

Model T's shared the half-empty streets with delivery wagons. Some of the older buildings, like the low one to the right of the Odd Fellows Hall, weren't on the city's water system, and still had water delivered by dray. The Odd Fellows Hall on the corner was built in 1906, as attested by its cornerstone. Its tenant, the National Finance Company, didn't survive the First World War. The building next to it was vacant in 1914 except for a couple of small real estate offices and the London and B.C. Investment Co. All of the small offices on the rest of the block were real estate agents or investment dealers; before the war started, there were more real estate offices than grocery stores in the city. By 1920, nearly all those offices were vacant, victims of the recession (or their proprietors victims of the war). The B.C. Permanent Loan Co., in the neo-classical building at 330 West Pender, which paid four per cent on deposits and had assets of just over $4 million in 1913, had its assets reduced to $2,890,000 by 1922. The firm had a progressive management system, with board members like department store magnate David Spencer and wholesale grocer and future mayor W.H. Malkin. Manager Thomas Talton Langlois was one of the first in the city to advocate a Town Planning Commission, and started the radical, pre-fabricated housing, Talton Place subdivision at 16th and Cypress before the war. The Bank of Canada occupied the building between 1935 and 1966 and installed a machine gun emplacement to guard the expanded vault. Current tenants are wholesale jewellers, who work under the soft light of one of the largest Tiffany-style skylights in the city. The bay-windowed Victoria Block at the corner was built in 1908, the same year as Langlois' little palace. It was home, in 1913, to a variety of tenants including the Rapid Method Music School, the Vancouver Sketch Club and the U.S. Immigration Department. The skyline was still dominated by the spire of the Holy Rosary Cathedral, built in 1898 at Richards and Seymour. By 1914, the bell had already tolled for the old eastern business district; the Dominion Trust sign points west, toward the modern new city centre downtown, where all the money had moved to. When the troops returned to Vancouver, it was to jobs, industry and unemployment, not speculation and huge dreams.

CITY OF VANCOUVER ARCHIVES

Thomas Talton Langlois

Louis D. Taylor, publisher of the *World* newspaper and Mayor of Vancouver. It was a landmark on the east side of downtown until the early Sixties; today, it is dwarfed by the Harbour Centre complex and the B.C. Place stadium three blocks to the south.

The World Tower was never successful financially—even before the First World War the north end of Beatty Street was considered to be off the beaten path. The location puzzled local pundits who suggested that there were many more central building lots available. The World Tower snatched the British Empire height record briefly from the earlier Dominion Building at Hastings and Cambie, but was eclipsed by the Royal Bank's 20-storey Toronto tower in 1914.

The sculptured maidens supporting the cornice on the World Tower are the work of Vancouver's premier sculptor—Charles Marega. He was responsible for much of the ornamental carving and historical portraiture in sculpture-poor Vancouver, including the Joe Fortes memorial at Alexandra Park, the David Oppenheimer bust at the entrance to Stanley Park, the Lions at the south end of Lions Gate bridge, the President Harding memorial in Stanley Park, the Captain Vancouver statue at City Hall, the King Edward VII fountain at the Courthouse and the "Wounded Soldier" being born aloft by an angel at the CPR station.

Marega was born in Genoa, Italy in 1876. He worked and studied in Venice, Zurich and South Africa before arriving in Vancouver in 1910, where he quickly made his reputation. He taught a couple of generations of sculpture students in the Vancouver School of Art at Dunsmuir and Pender. There, while teaching a class in 1939, he collapsed and died.

The *World* fared poorly in its circulation war with the *News-Advertiser* and the *Province*, though Taylor was given to outlandish publicity stunts like the "incredible feat" of the Human Fly on Hallowe'en, 1918. Taylor hired Harry Gardiner, the "Human Fly," to scale the outside of the World Tower: "Up and up he went," noted a reporter, "until, at a great height, he reached the buttress, supporting the overhanging roof, and swung himself over it. The host, watching far below, gasped." The World Building was sold to Bekins in 1924. The tower sported a red neon sign to that effect until 1937, when the *Sun* bought it, after fire destroyed its offices across the street at 125 West Pender, the site of the earlier Imperial Opera House. It became the Sun Tower and the name has stuck, though the newspaper moved uptown to 6th and Granville in the early Sixties.

Directly behind the Province Building, on the south side of Pender Street, was the first properly-established Vancouver hospital. Its predecessor was a quickly-hammered-together wooden shack on the railway's mainline between Hawks and Heatley Avenue on the city's boundary, and was presided over by CPR physician J.M. Lefevre. It was taken over by the city's newly-formed Board of Health in September 1886, by which time it was crowded with the sick and injured of newly-rebuilt Vancouver. The new City Hospital, with breezy front porches and a picket-fenced garden,

The Court House, Vancouver, B.C.

The old Courthouse, looking north along Cambie Street. This scene was used for a postcard, though there was no mention on the card of why the flag flew at half mast. The photograph was taken in 1906, following receipt of the news of the disastrous April 18 earthquake in San Francisco.

opened on Pender in 1888 (page 59). It also rapidly became over-crowded. By 1902, two red-brick additions had been built to accommodate 50 beds. That year, City Hospital became Vancouver General, and an appeal for money was made the following September to finance new hospital facilities in Fairview (page 151).

To connect downtown with the East End, the city (under Mayor Louis Taylor) built the Georgia-Harris Viaduct between Beatty Street and Main Street during the years 1913-15 (Harris Street has since become East Georgia Street). The viaduct, which was opened on Dominion Day, 1915, crossed a small spur of False Creek which used to intrude into the flat land below the Beatty cliff. It was popularly known as the McHarg Viaduct, after Lt. Col. William Hart-McHarg of the Duke of Connaught's Own Rifles, who died at Ypres in April, 1915. McHarg, a much-decorated veteran of the Boer War, was an accomplished marksman. In 1913 he had won the title of World Champion Marksman in the United States and, ironically, Kaiser Wilhelm's Palma Gold Trophy. The old viaduct ran in a north-east direction from Georgia toward the Vanport Hotel and the old B.C. Electric coal-fired thermal plant, now a B.C. Hydro substation at the corner of Main and East Georgia.

A small and quite charming park at the corner of Georgia and Beatty commemorates this early viaduct, which was demolished in 1970; some of the concrete railing with its characteristic star pattern and the (second generation) street lamps have been preserved. The modern six-lane viaduct, built in 1969-70 as the first section of a planned city freeway system, was opened only after intense public protest. The freeway project, which was to include a harbour expressway, the demolition of much of Strathcona and

The Beatty Street ware-houses, looking north from Dunsmuir to the World Tower (by 1928 in its Bekins guise). Most of the buildings are still in use as ware-houses, although the one at 550 Beatty has been con-verted into luxury condo-miniums. The old City Hospital buildings occupied the far end of the block on the left-hand side of the street. The hardtop auto had not yet come into general fashion; nor had the spare tire ready-mounted on a rim. Beatty Street is named after Sir Edward Beatty, a president of the CPR and later founder of the Beatty Steamship Lines. Fires in the warehouses, like the Gutta Percha Rubber Co. fire in 1920 (below right), brought out the Fire Department's long ladders from the fire station at Seymour and Robson.

Robert Cromie (1887-1936) came to Vancouver in 1906 and became J.W. Stewart's private secretary when Foley, Stewart and Welch owned the Vancouver Sun. Stewart made Cromie Sun publisher in 1917, and the latter went on to consolidate it with the News-Advertiser and the Vancouver World.

Chinatown, and a tunnel, called the Third Crossing, under Burrard Inlet, became the Waterloo for the civic Non-Partisan Association administration of Mayor Tom Campbell.

The green building at the southeast corner with the large chimneys is the B.C. Central Heat Distribution plant. Pipes beneath the streets carry steam to heat many of the older office buildings in the city. Vents in the pipes allow steam to escape through grates in the downtown sidewalks—a characteristic Vancouver sight—and power the unique steam clock at the corner of Cambie and Water in Gastown.

The Cambie Street Grounds were, like the City Hospital and the Central High School at Cambie and Pender, slated to be a part of the Civic Centre development of the Thirties, but ended up as the bus depot. The only block which was developed in a manner envisioned by civic planners was the one bounded by Georgia, Hamilton, Dunsmuir and Cambie—today's Queen Elizabeth Theatre complex, erected in the late Fifties. The huge Post Office on the other side of Hamilton was erected a few years before.

Louis Denison Taylor,
publisher of the World
newspaper and owner of
the World Tower at the
corner of Beatty and
Pender. Born in July, 1857,
he was circulation manager
of the News-Advertiser until
June, 1905, when he bought
the World newspaper from
the widow of its founder,
J.C. McLagan. The World,
founded in 1888, was
considered in 1912 to be the
leading Liberal paper in
British Columbia, and had
two fully-leased telegraph
wires. Later, Taylor became
one of Vancouver's most
successful politicians, a
slightly raffish figure
"strictly out of O. Henry."
His symbols were a cigar and
a red tie. Taylor was Mayor
of Vancouver during
1910-11, 1915, 1925-26,
1927-8 and 1932-4. He was
a progressive, a political
opportunist who wooed the
East End and Labour vote.
During the 1923 election, a
complete power failure in
the East End shut down the
trams and caused Taylor to
lose to Charles Tisdall. (The
power failure was allegedly
caused by a woodpecker
which had shorted out the
transformers in the Main
Street substation—senior
B.C. Electric officials produced a badly charred
woodpecker as proof.)
Taylor's greatest political
achievement was spearhead-
ing the civic amalgamation
drive prior to January, 1929.
After his 1934 defeat, he
retired to the Granville
Mansions rooming house,
where he died, destitute and
embittered, in 1946.

Preceding page: looking east along the Georgia-Harris Viaduct in 1918. On the left are bleachers for the Cambie Street Grounds. Horse-drawn wagons still dominated the city's delivery business, and plodded on the left-hand side of the road until 1922.

The Georgia Viaduct, looking west towards downtown in the Twenties. At the bottom left is a small finger of False Creek, jutting into what was to become in a few years one of Vancouver's notorious hobo jungles. The double tracks of the Great Northern main line lead to their Chinatown terminus beyond the right edge of the picture. In the distance, on the left, is the Beatty Street Drill Hall and, to its right, the warehouses and the World Tower during the period when Bekins owned it. In the background distance, left to right, the Grosvenor Hotel (demolished 1983), the Vancouver Block (with the clock tower), the old Hotel Vancouver (demolished 1949), and the newly-completed Hudson's Bay building at Georgia and Granville. The tallest spire is Holy Rosary Cathedral at Richards and Dunsmuir.

47

Beatty Street Drill Hall

The Beatty Street drill hall was established on the high bluff at Beatty and Dunsmuir at the turn of the century. It superseded a small gun shed on the site of the World Tower at Beatty and Pender, where the regimental cannon now flanking the Drill Hall were stored in the years after 1886. This stone castle with its mock-medieval battlements was convenient to the Cambie Street Grounds across the street—a parade ground and marshalling area for the battalions of troops preparing for the Great War.

The Drill Hall was opened on Monday, September 30, 1901 by the Duke and Duchess of Cornwall and York—he the eldest son of King Edward VII, and later King George V; she later Queen Mary. The Duke and Duchess were on a "thank-you" tour pledged to the Colonies by his grandmother, Queen Victoria, in appreciation of the loyalty shown by the Dominions during the South African War of 1899. In September of 1900, Queen Victoria had promised Australia that her son, Bertie, would visit that country and open the new parliament in the spring of 1901. She died in January; her son ascended the throne and announced in February that *his* son, the Duke of Cornwall and York and later the Prince of Wales (so designated November 8), would do the world tour. The royal couple arrived in Montreal on September 16, and travelled across the country by train, accompanied by numerous dignitaries like the Countess of Minto and Prime Minister Wilfrid Laurier. They arrived late in the morning of September 30 at the CPR station and journeyed through the city by carriage under a series of colourful arches erected by the city, the Japanese residents, the Hastings Mill, the Chinese community, and the civic firemen. The Japanese arch, one of the most elaborate, was an imitation stone edifice spanning Hastings Street near Homer, covered with evergreen boughs. It bore on one side the Japanese inscription: "Respectfully We Welcome You," while on the other side it read: "Respectfully We Bid You Farewell."

The procession ended at the Drill Hall, where the Duke presided over the official opening, and presented service medals to the volunteers from the South African campaign. After a tour of Stanley Park, the royal couple left for Victoria.

The Cambie Street Grounds, first cleared in 1887 by the CPR to spur development south and west away from Gastown, became Parks Board property and was officially known as Larwill Park. It ended up as the Vancouver Bus Depot in a "temporary" agreement between Mayor Gerry McGeer and B.C. Electric President Dal Grauer.

Drill Hall, Vancouver, B.C. Love Photo.

Sixth D.C.O.R. on Review Cambie Street Grounds, Vancouver, B.C.

Top: looking east across the Cambie Street Grounds to the Beatty Street Drill hall. The Grounds were also known as Larwill Park, in honour of Albert Larwill, who founded the Vancouver Athletic Club in April, 1906, and are now the site of the "temporary" Vancouver bus depot, built in 1946. In the postcard below, the Duke of Connaught's Own Rifles parade with St. Andrews Presbyterian Church in the background. The first

Vancouver military force was the Vancouver Battery, an outgrowth of the B.C. Provisional Regiment of Garrison Artillery, organized in 1893. It became the Sixth Battalion Rifles, and was named the Sixth Regiment D.C.O.R. on May 1, 1900. By 1912, Vancouver's military garrison consisted of 411 Seaforth Highlanders, 120 members of the 6th Field Co. Canadian Engineers, plus the 411 members of the D.C.O.R.

Dominion Trust

The Dominion Trust building at Hastings and Cambie was the first modern skyscraper in Vancouver. Built in 1909, it was a symbol of Vancouver's modernity and prosperity, and precipitated a reorganization of Vancouver's Fire Department, including the purchase of the first aerial ladder. In this photograph, taken in November in the mid-Thirties, the Cenotaph is bedecked with wreaths. The Bank of Hamilton building west of the Cenotaph was originally called the Inns of Court Building, and provided chambers for many of the lawyers working in the old Courthouse.

The first modern tall building in Vancouver was erected by the Imperial Trust Company at Hastings and Cambie in 1909. The Dominion Trust Company, formed by an Act of the Provincial Legislature in 1908, merged with Imperial and, with the help of German capital organized by Alvo von Alvensleben Ltd., completed the construction. The Dominion building was briefly the tallest in the British Empire, and was the last large steel-framed structure built in the city (later ones used reinforced concrete). In 1912, Dominion Trust had a subscribed capital of $2,250,000, and maintained a secure and solid reputation through the depression of 1913 and 1914. Then, on October 12, 1914, managing director W.R. Arnold stuck a revolver in his mouth and blew his brains out. A quick audit of the company was ordered and an attempt made to unscramble its affairs, but "the mess was found to be hopeless." On October 23, Dominion Trust went into liquidation. It was reported to the provincial legislature on November 6 that the failure was due to "heavy and unauthorized loans made in accounts controlled by Mr. Arnold, and without the knowledge and consent of his directors." Included was a debt of $1,143,000 incurred by Alvo von Alvensleben, who was "temporarily residing in Seattle." Arnold was buried in the Masonic portion of Mountain View Cemetery, with the Mayor and important business figures as pallbearers. Ownership of the building passed to the Dominion Bank, which later amalgamated with the Bank of Toronto. The "crisis in confidence" after Dominion Trust's collapse helped bring down the Bank of Vancouver, which had only opened its doors in July, 1910. It ceased operations on December 14, 1914.

Alvo von Alvensleben

One of the most flamboyant characters in pre-World War I Vancouver was Count Alvo von Alvensleben; he was the chief wheeler-dealer for the German-British Columbia Syndicate responsible for investing (among others') Kaiser Wilhelm's finances, and which was allegedly preparing for German rule in western North America. Some of the investments, like the Wigwam Inn on Indian Arm, faded like butterflies: others, like the Dominion Trust building at 207 West Hastings, have become landmarks in the city. Von Alvensleben was a sport-loving, free-spending, high-living promoter, with interests in real estate, mines, forestry and fishing, who supervised the investment of over $60 million in German capital.

Von Alvensleben was born in 1877, on the family estate in Westphalia, the second son of an old Prussian noble family. He voluntarily resigned his commission as lieutenant in March, 1904, "against the wishes of his father," to do some exploring and pioneering. (Another story was that he was kicked out of the country by his father, after he gambled away his allowance.) He arrived in Vancouver in 1904 with $4 in his pocket and moved into an abandoned shack near the Brunswick Cannery at the mouth of the Fraser River. There he made a living shooting ducks at 35 cents each and catching salmon. During the first two summers he worked at the cannery, but also supplied the Vancouver Club, selling game and fish at the back door. (A few years later, after he had catapulted to prominence and been nominated for membership at the exclusive club, he was dining there with some cronies when he noticed the maitre d' eyeing him suspiciously. "Yes," said von Alvensleben in a loud voice, "I am the man who used to sell you chickens at the back door!")

By 1909, Alvo and his brother Werner were advertising regularly, offering real estate and promotional opportunities for investors. In March, 1909, they were offering land in the Magee area for $1,500 an acre; in February, 1910, they paid $100,000 cash and $200,000 securities for 600 acres on Lulu Island; in August, 1910, they offered for sale the "Portland Canal," 160 acres adjoining the townsite of Stewart in northwestern B.C.; during 1909 and 1910 they built the Dominion Tower at Hastings and Cambie (their involvement with the Dominion Trust Company contributed to its spectacular collapse in 1914).

Alvo von Alvensleben married Edith May Westcott, the daughter of a pioneer Vancouver contractor. They bought the 10-acre estate at 41st and Blenheim in Kerrisdale, built by R.B. Johnson and occupied after the Great War years by *Vancouver Sun* publisher Robert Cromie, who lived there from 1927 to 1939. Thirteen servants were required to maintain the grounds and keep up the

lavish entertainments during the von Alvensleben tenure. He drove a Packard tourer to his office on Hastings Street, and made his chauffeur (James McGrath, later the janitor at Maple Grove School) ride in the back. Like B.T. Rogers, he was a demon driver, and was fined on the average four times a week for speeding. He referred to himself as "the mainstay of the Point Grey Police Department." Miss Ethel Parks, the first teacher at Kerrisdale School at 41st and Carnarvon, cursed Alvo for racing along Wilson Road (41st Avenue), which was "a foot deep in dust."

Alvo ran the British Columbia end of the syndicate from his office at 500 West Hastings, while Werner spent more time in Berlin, cultivating old family contacts for Canadian investment schemes. (Werner made the news for the final time in 1933 when he was arrested and charged with high treason by Hitler following the attempted assassinations of Richard Steidler, leader of the Viennese Tyrolean Heimwehr, and Minister of Security Emil Wehr. Werner was eventually cleared.) Werner placed full-page ads in Berlin newspapers touting the opportunities in British Columbia; Alvo duplicated the ads for Vancouver newspapers,

One project Alvo backed was the $2,000,000 Vancouver Docks proposal of 1909, which would have built 18 wharves and 11,600 feet of breakwater along Kitsilano Point. The brothers' activities attracted some interesting guests to Vancouver: H. von Bergen, a renowned big-game hunter who stayed every summer from 1909 to 1913 in the Hotel Vancouver, and later led an Austrian army corps against Italy during the war; Count von Mackensen, interned in the Vernon army camp during the war, a nephew of the German field marshall who won the Roumanian campaign; Count von Faber Castell, and the propagandists F. Radich and J.J. Weber; Baron Gadenorff, who stormed through the lobby of the Hotel Vancouver, clicking his heels, "hot headed, using his cane like a sword"; Dr. Heinrich Paasche, the vice-president of the Reichstag. These honoured guests were entertained by von Alvensleben, Col. Wilhelm Otto Peters (who had his office at 319 West Pender and ended up spending the war in the Vernon army camp), investment broker Hans von Graevenitz, and the black-moustachioed Imperial German consular agent A.T. von Etlinger (who announced at the outbreak of the war, before being shipped to Vernon: "I am a Prussian and prepared to die for the Fatherland"). The German consulate was at 543 Granville.

Alvo von Alvensleben was in Berlin on a business trip when war was declared; as an enemy alien, he could not return to Canada. His affairs and possessions were seized by the Dominion Government, and on October 21, 1914, it was discovered that he had liabilities of

Constantin Alvo von Alvensleben

Hans von Graevenitz, of the German-British Columbia Syndicate, channelled millions of dollars worth of investment into Vancouver before the First World War. Representing the Imperial German Army, he had an international reputation as an equestrian, and was said to have won more than 500 riding events. He spent the First World War years under detention in the Vernon army camp. His partner G.G. Palmer was a former solicitor in the South African Supreme Court. Their firm, Palmer, Burmester and von Graevenitz, had offices at 411 West Pender.

$3.4 million and assets of only $1 million. Rumours circulated about the Germans' activities in British Columbia: the tennis court at the estate on 41st was supposed to be a concrete gun emplacement ("all nonsense, scandalous falsehoods," Alvensleben said in 1961); Col. Peters owned remote property on the Queen Charlottes where there was supposedly a wireless station and a U-Boat pen. Alvo von Alvensleben went to the United States—neutral until 1917—and took up residence in Seattle.

When he got established there, he wrote to his wife with instructions to pack their belongings and send them down, taking special care with the vintage wines he kept cellared at home. He recommended that they be packed in very large, very heavy cases so they would be disturbed as little as possible in transit. Two weeks later, all the goods arrived in Seattle, except the wine. Von Alvensleben wrote to a friend—a regimental commander in Vancouver with some influence over customs clearances—and protested vigorously. As a resident of the United States, he threatened a diplomatic incident. The friend didn't budge. Finally von Alvensleben offered to give the wine to the friend's regiment on one condition: that every time a bottle was drunk, all would drink a toast to the glory of Kaiser Wilhelm! Apparently, he got his wines within the week.

In 1917, America entered the war and von Alvensleben was interned in a Salt Lake City camp for enemy aliens. After the war, he resumed his business activities in Seattle and, in 1939, revoked his German title for U.S. citizenship. Plain Alvo Alvensleben was involved in British Columbia mining operations during the Forties and Fifties, including the Jingle Pot mine near Nanaimo. He always said that his troubles in Canada were due "to the official policy that people must hate so they could fight." He died in Seattle in 1963, aged 86.

The old von Alvensleben house at 41st and Blenheim, built in 1902, has remained little altered since. Occupied during the Twenties and Thirties by Sun publisher Robert Cromie, it was sold by his widow in the early Forties to Crofton House school, which considered the atmosphere on Jervis Street in the West End to be deteriorating. The school purchased a house surrounded by nearly ten acres of woods, and has since added several buildings and cleared playing fields to the south. The house was built by Richard Byron Johnson, born in London, England in 1868, who helped found the Vancouver Rowing Club when he was twenty years old. He bought the acreage in 1902. At the time, it could only be reached by a sinuous track (dubbed Johnson Road) from Magee Road–now Marine Drive. Johnson died in Vernon in 1958.

David Spencer

In 1948, one of the city's department store chains closed its doors. David Spencer Ltd., with Vancouver headquarters occupying the city block bounded by Richards, Seymour, Hastings and Cordova Streets, reopened as the T. Eaton Co. after reportedly selling for between $14 and $17 million. The sale brought to a close a family "drygoods" history stretching back to 1862, when David Spencer first arrived in Victoria, attracted by wild stories of Cariboo gold.

David Spencer (1837-1920) was born in Wales and was a staunch Methodist. He married Emma Lazenby (1842-1934) shortly after she arrived in Victoria after a meandering, 110-day sea journey from Gravesend around Cape Horn, aboard the bark *Robert E. Lowe*. Rather than strike out for the by-then exhausted goldfields, Spencer made the shrewd decision to invest in little Victoria's future, deciding to open a book shop and lending library for the entertainment-starved town. On January 29, 1864, he placed his first advertisement in the *British Colonist*, stating: "Cheap reading! Three thousand popular novels, also standard works on history, biography and travels. One bit per vol., or one dollar per month. All the English and American periodicals and magazines received by every steamer! Valentines! Sensational and comic, new and beautiful!" (The Valentine craze, a child of the recently devised postal service, had swept the United States at the beginning of the Civil War, to be followed not long afterwards by the Christmas Card craze.)

By 1873, Spencer had prospered to the point where he was importing a wide variety of goods directly from England—a trademark of the company throughout its life. His store, at first called Victoria House, was established at Government and Broad Street in Victoria. During his spare time, he conducted the Pandora Street Methodist Church choir (like all Welshmen, it was said, he loved to sing), and it was there he met Emma. He also found time to sire thirteen children. Their most notable home in Victoria was at Belleville and Government, across from the Legislative Buildings (where the the Provincial Museum now stands) and, at that time, at the south end of the little bridge which crossed the mud flats at the end of James Bay (filled at the turn of the century for the Empress Hotel). One child was delegated to watch for father's approach from downtown. When he started across the north end of the bridge, mother was notified. She quickly set the lunch table and had everything ready when he walked through the door.

Spencer's then-unique business policy—a reflection of his straightforward attitude—was that he sold only for cash. Spencer was able to acquire enough capital to expand his Victoria operation during the 1890s and, in 1906, to buy control of Drysdale and Stevenson Ltd., the drygoods shop on Hastings Street which was famous for the teams of impeccably groomed high-stepping chestnut horses which pulled the company's chestnut-painted delivery wagons. Shortly after, the name was changed to David Spencer Ltd. By 1948, Spencer's had stores in Victoria, Vancouver, New Westminster, Nanaimo, Courtenay, Duncan, Chilliwack and Mission.

David Spencer

The family had a diversity of interests, including 250,000 acres of ranches in the B.C. interior, the *Victoria Times* newspaper and some mining concerns. One small retailing experiment was the Model Market groceteria at 4th and Yew in Kitsilano.

The Hastings Street Spencer's grew in all directions from the original small Drysdale's store. At first, Spencer's expanded north and redeveloped the space on Cordova Street; in 1926 they absorbed and renovated the old Molson's Bank at the western (Seymour Street) end of the block. In 1928, the eastern end of the block was rebuilt with a large, modernistic, nine storey addition which outshone the older Woodward's down the street. In 1932, Bell-Irving's old Anglo-B.C. Packing Co. building was demolished for an extension of the parking garage.

David Spencer Ltd. was the smoking headquarters for many Vancouverites; it imported tobaccos and smoking paraphernalia from all over the world. When Eaton's took over, of course, the tobacco counter was removed. Timothy Eaton never allowed any tobacco sold in any of his stores. Another change, after Eaton's took the store over, was that blinds on the window displays were drawn on Sunday.

Of Spencer's big family, three made their mark. Sara was awarded a C.B.E. for her philanthropic and charitable efforts. Colonel Victor Spencer, a dashing young man in the 1890s, was the most handsome and eligible bachelor in Victoria and was considered very gallant when he went off to fight the Boers in 1899; after his exploits there and in the First World War, he became the vice-president of the family firm. The president was Chris Spencer, known to all his employees as Mr. Chris, who was the true power behind the organization for the last 25 years. Chris Spencer moved during the Great War years to 2150 West 49th (the house that became Athlone School for Boys in 1955 after his death). He considered the Vancouver Symphony to be a "pet," and appeared to have been almost universally beloved at the family store. It was Mr. Chris, 80 years old, who said farewell to the Spencer's employees from the mezzanine in the Vancouver store on December 1, 1948, and introduced them to the Eaton's management team.

After the sale to Eaton's, the Spencer family moved their business operations into the Marine Building penthouse, Vancouver's "most fabulous offices." Eaton's closed its little store at 526 Granville, and announced to the media that the acquisition of Spencer's didn't change its "eventual" plan to demolish the old Hotel Vancouver and erect a new retail outlet there. The old Hotel Vancouver was demolished in 1949, but the land sat vacant until 1970, when the Pacific Centre complex began to rise at the corner of Georgia and Granville.

Hastings Street in the late Twenties, looking west to Richards Street and the Spencer's department store. The department store's building was incorporated into the Sears' Harbour Centre complex in the early Seventies. The revolving restaurant at the top of Harbour Centre is one of the most recognizable features of Vancouver's skyline.

Charles Woodward

The only local retailing firm to survive into Vancouver's second century is the Woodward's Department store chain. In the nine decades since merchant Charles Woodward opened his first little store on the outskirts of the business district, at the northeast corner of Westminster and Harris (Main and East Georgia), Vancouver's roaring expansion has paralleled the store's. Its Hastings and Abbott location has been a landmark to Vancouverites since 1902. The firm has attracted a loyal clientele, distinct from that of its eastern and American competitors, and in the past twenty years it has bucked the trend to move towards Georgia and Granville, and thus been a party to the rejuvenated Gastown.

Charles Woodward was nearly forty when he opened the Westminster Avenue store in 1892 (the building is still there). He was intent on capturing a share of the young province's mail-order business, and, like his main competitors, David Spencer and Timothy Eaton, did not believe in credit. "We keep no books, have no accountants, thereby saving thousands of dollars to those who patronize the store," he wrote in the 1902 catalogue. For the first four years of operation, Woodward was intent on operating an off-the-street drygoods business for the residents of the new city. In 1896 he started a mail-order department and soon after began to publish the catalogues which were, until 1950, a major link with civilization for people in the remote interior and coastal ports of British Columbia. A major stimulus for Woodward was the success of his arch-rival, David Spencer, in Victoria, as was the excitement of boom-town Vancouver in the Klondike years.

Woodward prospered sufficiently to move "uptown" to thriving Hastings Street in 1902. The location has been expanded on several occasions; the six-storey brick and timber section at the corner of Hastings and Abbott is the oldest remaining part, built in 1908. Woodward fought battles with the Pharmaceutical Association to get the right to sell prescription drugs. The store built its reputation on the speed and skill with which orders were filled, the courtesy with which customers were served, and the comprehensive selection of goods available, including bizarre patent medicines and electric belts.

Woodward's, through its catalogues, played a major role in the development of outlying areas. The grocery department, formed at the turn of the century, shipped food all over the province. Shipments to the Fraser Valley went quickly and cheaply on the B.C. Electric's interurban, past stations with names like Milner, Jardine, Harmsworth, Sperling, Warhoop, Coghlan, County Line, and Beaver River. Customers far up the coast, at towns like the vanished Anyox, received their orders by the lifeline of the Union Steamships' coastal boats. Upcountry customers were served after 1917 by the Pacific Great Eastern, which chugged north from Squamish. The firm opened its first store in Alberta in 1926.

WOODWARD'S

Right: Charles Woodward (1852-1937), the founder of the Woodward's Department Store chain. Above: Woodward's second store, replacing his first one at the northeast corner of Main and East Georgia, opened in November, 1903, at the corner of Abbott and Hastings. In the ensuing decades, the store expanded to fill much of the block. (Next page) The typical Vancouver kitchen prior to the Second World War had a woodstove and kindling box occupying space in the centre of the room. Woodward's offered the "Pride of Vancouver" ranges beginning in 1921. The top of the line stove was Woodward's Empire, "made of polished blue steel with duplex grates for coal or wood," with a galvanized reservoir and warming closet. It was "a very good baker," and cost $25.75 in 1912. The mark of a good stove– as far as kids were concerned– was an oven door that was strong enough to sit on. Two blocks of wood on the door made a comfortable seat, which on a winter's day after a play in the rain or wet snow guaranteed chilblains! During the Thirties, many woodstoves were converted to sawdust, using hoppers or worm gears to feed them continuously. If a family owned a kitchen appliance, it was likely a flip-sided electric toaster, which burned out the fuse if it wasn't cleaned regularly. Refrigerators looked like iceboxes with a beehive on top. One woman wasn't convinced that the refrigerator was cheap to operate, because "the light was always on inside." The iceman was a great favourite with kids, who ate the ice chipped off by the picks. Butter was kept in a crock with salt and water in the cellar. Eggs were often kept by coating them in lard and rolling them in sawdust. The cellar was always patrolled by "a good cat."

WOODWARD'S

The Post Office

The square-block sized postal edifice at Georgia and Hamilton proves that, by the mid-Fifties, the postal system had evolved considerably from the balmy pioneer days of Christmas cards, scented missives and longhand love letters. The huge building has been overcrowded practically since the day it opened. Today, the postal service delivers flyers and handbills on a scale never dreamed of thirty years ago.

The south shore of Burrard Inlet got its first post office on May 15, 1869, when innkeeper Maxie Michaud was appointed postmaster at New Brighton. The mail for Moodyville was sent once a week from New Westminster, delivered through the forest by an Indian on horseback, who got $5 for the trip. From New Brighton, the mail went to Moodyville by steam tug.

With the establishment of the Hastings Mill and the community of Gastown, a post office was established in the Hastings Mill store. On February 1, 1886, the storekeeper at the Mill, Calvert Simpson, resigned as postmaster there. The "Granville Post Office" was moved to the east side of Carrall between Powell and Oppenheimer (Cordova). After this building burned in the Great Fire, a post office was established briefly in a shack at the Royal City Planing Mills at the south end of Carrall Street, with Jonathan Miller as postmaster.

On July 2, the post office moved into its own building—a tiny gabled shack with a boom-town front and a small boardwalk for a sidewalk at 325 West Hastings. The next April, Council authorized a coal oil street lamp on a post in front of the building. The little post office had separate wickets for registration, letters and newspapers, plus a few private boxes. It was heated by a wood stove. When it rained, Vancouverites lined up and those at the tail end got wet. The city outgrew that quaint office, and in 1890 a more functional postal building opened at the southwest corner of Granville and Pender.

On August 1, 1910, the grandest of all these post offices opened on the site of Dr. Lefevre's old residence at the corner of Granville and Hastings. The building's "Parisian-influenced" granite upper storey, and the green copper roof and clock tower came to symbolize the Federal Government to Vancouverites. It was occupied by the Unemployed for six weeks in the summer of 1938 (along with the Art Gallery, the Georgia Hotel and the Carnegie Library at various times). The building has been restored by the Federal Government.

The new General Post Office was opened at 349 West Georgia in 1958. With a floor area of almost fifteen acres, the building required the largest welded steel frame in the world to hold it up. There is a heliport on the roof, and a tunnel connects the basement to the CPR station at the foot of Seymour Street. The "people's art"—letter carriers in bas relief on the outside of the building—is unusual for anti-labour Vancouver.

Post Office, Hasting Str. looking East, VANCOUVER, B.C.

AUTHOR'S COLLECTION

The Granville and Hastings post office was the symbol of the Dominion Government in Vancouver. The corner opposite was also significant —for Trorey's Clock, which became Birks Clock when Trorey sold out to Birks. The clock was moved in 1913 to Georgia and Granville, where it remains today, in front of the new Birk's building. Trorey's building was demolished in the late Twenties and replaced with the Royal Bank skyscraper (page 73).

The Strand Bar

The Stanley Hotel bar, at 21 West Cordova, in 1914. It was a typical stand-up saloon, open all night, for a clientele with less "éclat" than the Strand's. All saloons, regardless of their elegance, closed in December, 1916, with the advent of Prohibition (page 220).

The south side of Hastings between Granville and Seymour is today occupied by a solid row of banks. It is all quite prosaic, and few people venture there after closing time. However, the Bank of Commerce at the Seymour corner was once the site of one of the most famous bars in the city. Before Prohibition robbed it of its gaiety, the Strand Hotel was one of the liveliest "genteel" spots in town.

Built in 1889, when Victory Square was the city's centre, the Strand was known as "Vancouver's Lloyd's," after Lloyd's Cafe in London. Most of the port's shipping business was transacted there at noon hour in the dining room and at the bar, much frequented by the ship owners and brokers—the deckhands and other lowly types preferring the Stanley on Cordova Street, where their money went farther.

The Strand was almost like a private club. The head barman, who "had the suave manners of a diplomat," was called Doc; Miller was the head waiter in the dining room. The lunch counter was looked after by a New Zealand Maori named John Bluntish who "treated his shipping gentlemen like children"; he was a trained male nurse and proudly displayed an inscribed gold watch to that effect. Bluntish worked at the Strand until 1918, when he left for the logging camps (producing the lightweight airplane spruce for warplanes) on the Charlottes to nurse victims of the great influenza epidemic; he died there of the disease.

One famous character who was a regular at the bar was a sealer named Captain Alex MacLean, who had supposedly "snatched the largest fur load from the Russians" in the Bering Sea. His large reddish-brown moustache and belligerent manner when tipsy were his trademarks. Jack London, it was said, used MacLean as the model for the villain-cum-hero in *The Sea Wolf*, which didn't please MacLean. London kept out of MacLean's way after the book appeared—at least until 1914, when the latter was found drowned in False Creek.

The Strand bar went out in a blaze of glory on the night of December 19, 1916, hours before "the Drys drove the Demon Rum from the land." In the dying wet hours, there was no way to get close to the bar. The supply of beer ran out, and the bartenders served only straight drinks "and had no time for the usual persiflage." The Strand set an all-time record for bar receipts, even though some of the patrons, as closing time approached, wasted precious moments singing "Sweet Adeline."

The bar never recovered. The hotel was completely remodelled in 1939, but never regained its popularity. In 1946, it was sold to the Bank of Commerce for $215,000. Four years later, it was demolished.

The Great Depression

The breakneck growth and prosperity of the young city was checked by serious economic depressions in 1893-4 (exacerbated by the severe Fraser River floods) and 1913. This last slump was "solved" by the Great War, though British Columbia was on the wrong side of the world to benefit economically. In 1919, the economy slumped again, unable to absorb the returning servicemen. Unemployment remained high for a few years, but Vancouver expanded wildly in the early Twenties. Everyone got a job. Wages rose. Inflation spiralled, but most workers had money left over for the commodities and stock markets.

Grain was the darling crop of the Twenties—the key to future peace and prosperity lay in the abundance of Canadian food and modern transportation methods to feed it to the world. In the heady days of 1928 on the Winnipeg Grain Exchange, commodity speculators pushed the price up to $1.60 a bushel. The 1929 crop was good all over the world, yet the bumper crop from the previous year hadn't been sold. When the crash came, triggered on the New York Stock Exchange, tariff walls were erected so quickly in the United States that trade virtually ceased around the world. Ports like Vancouver became suddenly idle. The Prairies received the coup de grace in 1932 and 1933 with an almost-biblical grasshopper plague and drought. Grain prices collapsed to 38 cents in 1932. Farmers, who had been staggering under debt loads at unheard-of interest rates of eight and nine per cent, simply walked away from their worthless farms, fancy tractors and mortgages. Many who couldn't afford gas took the engines out of their cars, hitched a nag to the front and drove these "Bennett Buggies," named after Prime Minister R.B. "Rotten Bastard" Bennett, to the Okanagan, "where you could reach up and pick the fruit off the trees." Others headed for "the promised land" of Vancouver. The unattached, whether young or old, just drifted. By October, most everyone was arriving in the Terminal City, where things were no better, but at least there was no winter to speak of.

The most enduring images of Depression-era Vancouver—hobo jungles and food line-ups—paint a bleak but incomplete picture of the time. People with jobs had their wages cut back to the point that they were "as poor as church mice," but they clung desperately to security, respectability and pride. Middle-aged men were "retired" on the front stoop of their homes, or evicted onto the street with their family and belongings.

In the summer of 1931, about 200 men built a shacktown on the old Hastings Mill site at the foot of Dunlevy. A camp hierarchy was established, based on the former military rank of the "jungleers," as the newspapers took to calling them. Editorial comment focused on the shame of Great War veterans being reduced to such poverty. The Terminal City Club and the Vancouver Club sent a daily mulligan or soup; Coughlan and Son sent tobacco; Mrs. E.W. Hamber organized packages of boots and socks. The camp was tidy and clean and the jungleers sent a letter to the local newspapers on August 16—appended with all their signatures—thanking the Harbours Board officials for their kindness and cooperation.

Two other camps were established that summer. About 250 men lived under the eastern end of the Georgia Viaduct, near the B.C. Electric Gas Works. They were generally called "the Canned Heaters," for their alleged habit of straining Sterno or Canned Heat through socks for the alcoholic content. About four hundred established themselves in tin and cardboard shacks at the city garbage dump at Prior and Heatley, on the site of the modern Firehall Number One. New arrivals to town—never more than one hundred—camped at the east end of the CNR yards on the grassy banks near Clark Drive. Food line-ups formed behind Andrew Roddan's First United Church at 424 Gore.

Nineteen thirty-one was the year of "direct relief." Eligible men lined up at the old City Hospital Nursery on Pender just south of Victory Square. They received a hunk of meat and a hundred pound sack of potatoes, which they lugged home. Vancouver relief registrants in 1931 included 6,958 single men, 7,136 married men and 601 women. These last really had it hard; they were expected to stay with their parents if they couldn't find anyone to marry them, and any woman with a job was said to be forcing a man onto relief. Of the relief population, 14 per cent were transients and 17 per cent "aliens."

The first of the "red riots" was on August 1, 1931 at the corner of Dunsmuir and Hamilton. Communist organizer Max Herndl was arrested, and unease began to spread throughout the city. The City Health Department, after a typhoid outbreak, got its way and wiped out all three jungles in September, 1931. Transients were moved to the Emergency Refuge at 35 West Pender, or to rooming houses (the city paid landlords 20 cents a day). The City Relief Clothing Store was established at 19 West Pender, just down the hill from the Relief office. City Council discussed, without resolution, a proposal to reduce civic workers to a five-day week in order to create more jobs. In October, the city got some public works projects going and hired labourers at $3.20 for an eight-hour day—a good wage from the perspective of the later labour camps. "Brushing," clearing of undergrowth, was undertaken and roads in the University area were improved. Fraserview Golf Course was built at the end of the year. A military-style relief camp was established on the bluff near the old Stewart dairy on Point Grey. Chancellor Boulevard was cleared through to the university. In all, $2 million was spent in 1931 on relief.

Wages for the working were cut back while the tax and relief payments increased. Everyone's favorite story concerned the shabby guy begging for change at the door, then clinking with a heavy load of coin as he walked down the stairs. Transients talked of "back of the hand" charity, and of eating "Matthew, Mark, Luke

During the summer of 1931, eligible men on relief got an issue of groceries from the Emergency Relief Office at Cambie and Pender, housed in the old City Hospital buildings. Others were shunted to the Emergency Refuge at 35 West Pender, or to private rooming houses around the city. Relief officer W.R. Bone, Esq., supervised the food distribution. In this view, opposite 534 Cambie Street, the former men's surgical ward is visible on the left. The other hospital building visible was the former maternity ward and crèche, which backed onto the lane connecting Cambie with Beatty. The City Hospital was used from 1888 to 1905, when its patients were moved to the new Vancouver General Hospital in Fairview (page 151). It had beautiful flower beds and lawns, "kept in perfect order by the chain gang," steam heat (which sterilized the dressings), a padded cell in the basement, an electrically-lighted operating room facing Pender Street, and a morgue on Beatty. The buildings were subsequently used as McGill University before the latter moved to the Fairview "shacks," then by the Vancouver Social Service Department. In 1946, the old Chronic & Aged Ward on Beatty was used as the "Labour Headquarters." The site is now occupied by a parkade. The block to the west (in the foreground) was occupied by the Central High School, which was demolished in the late Forties and replaced by the Vancouver Vocational Institute. The house at 538 Cambie was raised and a shop inserted underneath it.

and John'' sandwiches at the Sally Ann. In January 1932, the city began refusing bed and meal tickets at the city hostel to single men who wouldn't go to the federal government-run work camps. In order to keep a tighter control of relief payments, the city brought in scrip in February, 1932. Stores and cafes were issued with a list of acceptable goods for which they could accept scrip. The White Lunch, on Hastings near Main, lost its city license after trading scrip for cigarettes. Relief rates were cut back increasingly, to $15 per month plus $2.50 per child for a married couple in 1932. Transients and aliens were considered shirkers and became the city scapegoats, although only 15 per cent of relief payments went to non-Vancouverites. Future Premier W.A.C. Bennett, then a hardware merchant in Kelowna, had his own way of separating the wheat from the chaff: he showed anyone who wanted a meal to the woodpile. If they chopped some wood they would be fed. Rather inflammatory cartoons began to appear, particularly in the *Province*, showing typical ''relief incidents'' of sponging and shirking, with ''taxpayers'' feeding the ''unemployed.'' One ''relief incident'' concerned a family man who had disrupted a City Council meeting and practically assaulted the Mayor because he couldn't afford to heat his house on the $20 relief he got each month. The chief constable was directed to lend the man a crosscut saw and an axe, and show him how to get to the University Endowment Lands. In May, 1933, the city distributed seeds to needy families and invited them to plant gardens on city-owned land.

British Columbia had been ruled by the Conservative party since 1928, when Dr. Simon Fraser Tolmie, the former veterinarian and federal agriculture minister, took over from the Liberals. British Columbians had not yet really gotten used to Party politics (which were introduced by Conservative Richard McBride in 1903) and were prepared to favour or destroy whoever could or couldn't respond to the economic and financial crisis. Two they destroyed were Dr. Tolmie and his finance minister Jimmy Jones, who proposed a tax of one per cent on all income above $25 a week for married men and $15 a week for singles, earning him the moniker ''One Percent Jimmy.'' The proposal, and the government's handling of the economy, were studied by a group of businessmen who lambasted every part of it. Among the recommendations were slashing grants to UBC, shortening the time required to be spent in public school, and discontinuing the publicly-owned PGE Railway. The group recommended that the province's budget be slashed from $25,000,000 to $6,000,000. Tolmie, cut adrift, attempted to form a coalition with Duff Pattullo's Liberals. He was rejected, then demolished in the November, 1933, election after suggesting to the electorate: ''Why change? We are the only group with depression experience.'' The new Cooperative Commonwealth Federation (CCF), fresh from their inaugural convention, and with the ink scarcely dry on the Regina Manifesto, became the official opposition.

The new Premier, Duff Pattullo, attempted some quick action on the plight of the 100,000 jobless (B.C.'s population then was 700,000). He was strongly condemned by Prime Minister Bennett for his radical ideas—a comprehensive medical plan for anyone earning less than $2,400 a year, a new $4,000,000 highway bridge across the Fraser River at New Westminster, new laws for hours of work and minimum pay, and power to call in government bonds and refund them at lower rates.

Meanwhile, drifters continued to ''ride the rods''; they hung onto the frame-stiffening bars underneath freight cars or travelled in comparative style on top or inside. They travelled back and forth across the country in a futile search for work, all the while avoiding the ''railroad bulls.'' Many men walked the old Dewdney Trail from Hope to Princeton on their way to the Okanagan orchards in the spring and walked back again, nearly starved, after the fall harvests. Men who were too slow or clumsy to hop the fast-moving freights went to the ''marble orchard.'' Drifters carried a ''turkey'' —a leather-thong-tied bundle of blankets and effects, which sometimes got in the way when they were running and jumping for a freight, and was responsible for many crushings and decapitations. More wary drifters wore everything they owned: a suit, a couple of pairs of pants, and extra shoes tied around their necks. The most popular song was ''Brother, Can You Spare A Dime.'' The Canadian equivalent of Okies (Oklahoma farmers burnt out by the drought, who chugged into California) were the dust-bowl and grasshopper victims from Saskatchewan and Alberta, who were ''comin' in'' in 1932 and 1933.

In May, 1933, the average rent bill in Vancouver was $5.63 a week. The cost of living was calculated at $15.62 per week for a family of five. The newspapers were full of advertisements for ''mother's helpers'' for the comparatively wealthy families in Shaughnessy, Kerrisdale and Point Grey, and the going rate was $10 per month plus room and board. This seeming pittance was a godsend to country girls who saw no other way of leaving the grinding poverty and claustrophobia of home in the country. Secretaries processing relief requests at the Children's Aid in Alexandra House at 6th and Pine made 40 cents an hour. Once-a-week entertainment was a movie (15 cents at the Roxy) or a milkshake at Peter's on West Broadway, but many could not afford both. If they took the streetcar one way, they had to walk home. Children's streetcar tickets were 12 for a quarter; enterprising youths razored them apart and dropped a half into the farebox, praying that it would land printed side up.

Many a fortune was made by picking up 20 or 50 Kitsilano or Fairview homes with the proceeds from a seemingly small inheritance. The crazes were Shirley Temple dolls, the Dionne Quints, chain letters and miniature golf. People wondered whether ''Bible Bill'' Aberhart's promise of $25 a month to every citizen of Alberta would come true. (Aberhart, the Premier of Alberta, was entranced by the Social Credit theories of Major Clifford Hugh Douglas and his intoxicating ''A plus B'' economic remedy.)

The bitterness of the unemployed was not easily assuaged. On May 4, 1932, many unemployed demonstrated at City Hall. On

Vancouver's squatters survived the Depression with little disruption. From the earliest days, every available piece of shoreline from Second Narrows to New Westminster was crowded with shanties, some built on pilings and floats, with laundry lines and catwalks connecting them to the shore. The painting shows one of the more established communities, at the south end of the Kitsilano trestle, between Granville Island and the Burrard Bridge on the old Kitsilano Indian reservation. Dubbed ''Bennettville'' after the Prime Minister, it was home to families who operated small boats and sold salmon or buckets of smelt door to door. If a horse and wagon or truck was available, firewood was gathered and sold through Kitsilano and Shaughnessy. The squatters were basically self-sufficient, and were left alone by city officials for fear that, if dislocated, they would balloon the city's already-bloated welfare rolls. With wartime came prosperity, however, and on May 26, 1940, the False Creek squatters were given an eviction ultimatum by Mayor Telford, who said: ''It is pitiful to have to throw them out.'' A year later, nothing had been done, but a typhoid scare added urgency when junk dealer George Wilson was found dead in a packing-crate hovel at the south foot of Columbia Street. Four years later, the city removed the shacks under the old Georgia Viaduct by the B.C. Electric gas works. Forty shacks were clustered around the downtown side of the old Great Northern trestle, and in October the GN filed suit against 13 occupants who

CONTINUED ON PAGE 62

September 30, 1932, Prime Minister Bennett ordered a blockade of the "Hobo Specials," as the cross-Canada freights were dubbed. During the year, the Federal Government began establishing work camps "away hell and gone" for the suddenly redundant single men who were plugging up the cities and falling under the thrall of labour organizers and communist agitators. Although a few worthwhile projects were undertaken, including a section of the unfinished Hope-Princeton road west of Foundation Mine and a part of the Big Bend highway, in most cases the camps were like the rock-busting battalions in contemporary prisons. Dig a hole here, fill it back up. Pay was 20 cents a day, the food was awful and camp dormitory conditions were primitive. There was a rash of marriages between single men attempting to avoid going to the camps, and single women attempting to get off the farms and away from their parents. The futility and humiliation of camp life drove more and more of the unemployed back into the city. On July 3, 1933, a large crowd disrupted an eviction on Eton Street in Hastings Townsite. Communist parades became more frequent. A riot in March, 1934 sacked the Men's Institute at 1038 Hamilton. On April 23, 1935, Mayor McGeer "read the Riot Act" to disperse a huge rally at Victory Square. The unemployed, under the leadership of Arthur Evans, went on their famous trek to Ottawa; they were stopped at Regina, where there was a bloody riot on July 1, 1935. Some local men of an idealistic bent volunteered for the "Mac-Paps" (Mac-Kenzie-Papineau Battalion) and fought in the Spanish Civil War.

The climactic event of the Dirty Thirties was the occupation by about 1,600 men of the Post Office and Art Gallery (plus the Carnegie Library and the Hotel Georgia for a brief period) during May and June of 1938. It ended on June 20 in the most brutal riot Vancouver has ever seen, with the forcible eviction of the squatters. There were tear-gassings, beatings and a final window-breaking spree downtown.

By 1938, renewed prosperity was shining through the war clouds. Single men were suddenly worth $1.30 a day. The most apt symbol of the end of the Thirties was the new Lions Gate Bridge, leading to the British Properties, a suburb high on the mountainside, where there was no industry, just a life of residential exclusivity. These new suburbanites could only reach their homes by motorcar. The city never looked back.

CONTINUED FROM PAGE 61
refused to move. Five years later, in 1949, another eviction notice was given to some 700 people whose shacks crowded the Creek. In 1950, Fred Hume's and Jack Price's mayoral campaigns hinged on filling the Creek for industrial land. Most of the squatters were moved out in the late Fifties.

CITY OF VANCOUVER ARCHIVES

Richard B. Bennett, Prime Minister of Canada from 1930-1935, was a rich Calgary solicitor when this photograph was taken in 1911. His patrician, "Tory" attitude during the depths of the Depression made him the namesake for Bennett-villes and Bennett-buggies— symbols of poverty and heartless government throughout Canada.

Georgia & Granville

Even before the railway reached Vancouver, the Canadian Pacific Railway Co. had started work on its Hotel Vancouver, "way out in the woods" a half-mile southwest of the established town of Vancouver. Excavation began early in 1886 at the southwest corner of Georgia and Granville, on the highest point of land in that part of downtown. Skeptics scoffed at the far-away location, but the CPR had the prestige and muscle to move the city south and west towards it (the Great Fire of June of that year helped: no one had a head start). The hotel drew its water from a well, had a breezy front porch (from which, on quiet nights, the creak of ships at anchor could be heard), and attracted guests like Rudyard Kipling, who bought a town lot and wrote sneeringly about the local habit of land speculation during a visit in 1889. The CPR transpacific liners, the trains, and coastal and Alaskan steamers arriving at the Evans, Coleman and Evans wharf at the foot of Columbia, were met by two carriages from the Hotel Vancouver—a fine, covered one with liveried chauffeur for the passengers, and a more functional one for the bags. The Hotel Vancouver carriages were the only ones allowed on the wharves— all others had to wait on the street.

Georgia and Granville is the centre of Vancouver today because of the CPR. The area of downtown west of Granville is the modern, prestigious business district, likewise because of the CPR. And, Vancouver is a major city because of the CPR. In archivist J.S. Matthews' words: "It was all part of a grand plan."

The Hotel attracted some substantial—for the time—buildings to the Georgia and Granville area, including the Elphinstone Block and the Strathcona Block. The Hudson's Bay Co., which already had a store on Cordova Street, built a small store at 622 Granville (the Saba Bros. building; between there and the Georgia Street corner was the New York Block, which housed the CPR telegraph office and Carter's "Temple of Music"). Many attractive churches were springing up in the area: the Homer Street Methodist Church at the northwest corner of Dunsmuir and Homer; the St. Andrews Presbyterian at Richards and Georgia. The Anglican church at Georgia and Burrard, soon to be called Christ Church cathedral, had a granite basement excavated in 1888 but ran out of funds. It was nicknamed "The Root Cellar" for five years until construction was completed. In 1893, the Hudson's Bay Co. built a new store on their now-familiar Georgia and Granville corner; it lasted until 1926, when it was removed and the final section of today's building was completed.

The railway left the block north of their hotel (today's Four Seasons, IBM Tower and Stock Exchange complex) vacant, planted trees, erected an attractive fence around it and established some tennis courts and a gazebo. This "CPR Park" was offered to the city for $17,000; the city declined. During the Great War years, it was used as a military encampment, covered with neat white army tents.

As part of the grand plan, in the spring of 1890 the railway began construction of the Vancouver Opera House, which promised to eclipse the old Imperial at Pender and Beatty and the other vaudeville palaces of the town. Under the direction of lands commissioner J.M. Browning, the theatre was opened on February 8, 1891, with performances of excerpts from *Carmen* and *Lohengrin*. The Opera House was extraordinarily elegant for the time: it had an oil-painted drop screen of "The Three Sisters" (mountains on the Bow River near the railway's Banff Springs Hotel), which had been painted in New York and, because of its length, had to be brought to the city on two flat cars. There were separate box offices for "Gents" and "Ladies." The first passing switch for the Granville streetcar— then a single track line—was directly outside the entrance, so waiting passengers were able to read the marquee and advertisements.

As an attraction, the Opera House duly served its purpose, and by 1910 the Georgia and Granville area was the hub of the city. One year later, on July 9th, the last operatic performance was given at the Opera House. The CPR promptly sold the building to private interests, who painted over the drop screen with garish advertisements, and re-opened it as the New Orpheum, a cheap vaudeville palace. It later became a cinema, first the Vancouver Theatre, and then the Lyric. It ended its days in the late Sixties, when it was

Granville Street looking North, Vancouver, B.C.

102,977

R.V. Winch

The Winch building, erected in 1909 at the corner of Howe and Hastings, was the first modern office building erected west of Granville Street. It cost its builder, Richard V. Winch, nearly $700,000, less than half of the fortune he had amassed in the preceding 20 years.

Winch was born in 1862 in Ontario and managed, as he was fond of saying, "to outlive his insurance policy." He worked at railroad construction in the early days of the CPR until a fellow worker was decapitated in a nitroglycerine explosion, an incident which prompted him to move west. He arrived in Vancouver in 1887, and soon after brought his childhood sweetheart, Isabella, from Cobourg, Ontario to join him. In 1893, he established the Canadian Pacific Canning Co., and shipped the first-ever train load of canned salmon from Vancouver two years later. It sold in Liverpool for $5 a case. At his peak in the early years of the century, he had built and was operating seven canneries and one sawmill, worth a total of $1.5 million. Winch lived in high style during the golden years of the West End. In 1894, he built a mansion at 1255 Comox, which reportedly cost the enormous sum of $75,000 to build and furnish. It contained adjoining billiard and ball rooms, each over 40 feet long, solid oak billiard tables, a grand mahogany staircase and a 600 pound marble bathtub. In 1910, he imported the first two Rolls Royces into Vancouver. The cars cost him $10,000 each, at a time when the road was ruled by $10 horses and $400 Tin Lizzies. The family had regular outings in the Rolls in Stanley Park, and was a common sight around the town. (In 1919, Winch sold the cars—one went to Japan and the other was dismantled. The latter's power plant was bought by logging operator Rod Williams to run a small sawmill at Alert Bay on northern Vancouver Island; it was rediscovered there, still running the sawmill, by a MacMillan Bloedel log buyer in 1960.)

The family had five children. One daughter married Col. Victor Spencer of Aberthau. Isabella died in 1939 at age 79. Winch lived on until 1952—a crusty, eccentric character who truly had outlived his generation. Three years later his mansion was pulled down and an apartment building erected on the site. The Winch building lives on, its future protected by a Heritage designation.

The Winch building, built in what was, until then, a fashionable residential area, was across Howe Street from the Henry Abbott mansion and less than a block from the Vancouver Club (page 102). The Post Office building, completed the previous year, occupies the rest of the block. Henry Braithwaite Abbott, the first general superintendent of the CPR in B.C., was born in Abbotsford, Quebec in 1829. He trained under expatriate Polish railway engineer Casimir Gzowski and, after handling the transportation of troops to the Montreal garrison during the American Civil War, became construction manager of the Sault Ste. Marie division of the CPR. In January, 1886, he took over railway operations as General Superintendent of the Pacific Division. He retired from active service in 1897, but later served as president of the Vancouver & Lulu Island Railway, which became the "Sockeye Limited" interurban to Steveston. His son, lawyer J.L.G. Abbott, was William Hart-McHarg's law partner, and married R.H. Alexander's daughter Elizabeth. Henry Abbott died in September, 1915.

Richard V. Winch

Above left: the MacKinnon building, on the left in the foreground, was built in 1897 with the Klondike earnings of miner J.M. MacKinnon. It housed a Masonic Temple in the penthouse, the Liberal Headquarters on the floor below, and a United Cigar store on the corner. It was superseded in design by the Winch Building, around the corner on Hastings, the Post Office building at the corner, and the Bank of Commerce's temple on the right, and was eventually demolished in 1959 for the United Kingdom building. Above right: the CPR's second station at the foot of Granville street was Vancouver's best example of the "railroad chateau" style. Built in 1899, it was demolished during the First World War years following the completion of the present station, a block to the east. The latter, while no longer used for train passengers, serves as the terminus for the North Vancouver Seabus.

demolished for the new Eaton's department store.

The CPR fought hard to "win" the new Courthouse for its part of town, against East End interests, which had triumphed in the battle for the Carnegie Library at the turn of the century. The $500,000 Courthouse, designed by famous Victoria architect Francis Mawson Rattenbury (who designed the Legislative Buildings) was completed in 1911 and opened on September 18, 1912, during the Duke of Connaught's visit. The elegant, neo-classical building served the city until the opening of Arthur Erickson's eye-catching Courthouse and Robson Square complex during the Seventies. Rattenbury's edifice is now the stately home of the Vancouver Art Gallery.

Splendid offices were built at Georgia and Granville in the boom years before the First World War. The first to be erected was the Vancouver Block, a squarish but modern highrise with a clock tower directly across from the Hotel Vancouver. Henry Birks and Sons, the Montreal jewellers, built a graceful Edwardian office building at the corner, which survived until the Vancouver Centre complex was built in 1974.

Although the CPR had expanded the Hotel Vancouver at the turn of the century, it had burst its seams by 1910, and covered a site of nearly 60,000 square feet, five storeys high. A new Hotel Vancouver was built and opened just before the First World War. The quality of the exterior stone carving and interior finishing has not been equalled in the city since. Its oval Oak Room, ornate ballroom, Peacock Gallery, Spanish Grill and airy roof garden were the pride of the city, although few could afford as much as a cup of coffee there. *That* Hotel Vancouver, which so dominated the skyline until

the late Thirties, was abandoned in 1939 when the new Canadian National Hotel opened down the street at Georgia and Burrard. This third (and current) Hotel Vancouver was negotiated between Sir Henry Thornton and Mayor Louis Taylor during the Great War years, as one of the conditions of the railway's entry into Vancouver. The "old" Hotel Vancouver at Georgia and Granville was quietly closed, and functioned during the war years as a regimental headquarters. It was boarded up at the end of the war, but "liberated" by homeless returned soldiers in 1946. Eaton's purchased the property from the railway and—despite buying the Spencer's Department store building on Hastings in 1948—announced plans to eventually locate a department store on the Georgia and Granville site. After the hotel's demolition in 1949, the site was used as a parking lot until the Sixties, when the entire block was "assembled" by the city of Vancouver for the Pacific Centre mega-project. The Toronto Dominion's imposing black tower now covers the hotel site; Eaton's covers the rest of the block, including the site of the Opera House. The block to the north—the old CPR Park, which had become a motley collection of small stores, was razed in the early Seventies for phase two of the Pacific Centre.

Other hotels in the downtown area in the early years included the Badminton, at the southwest corner of Dunsmuir and Howe. Built in 1890, it was beloved by Vancouverites for its airy porches and covered roof garden. Like the Glencoe Lodge, it fell victim to the Depression and was demolished in 1936. The most prestigious hotel was the Hotel Georgia, opened by the Prince of Wales in 1927 and still one of the finer old downtown hotels. The Devonshire, which until 1981 stood next door to the Georgia, at Hornby and

Georgia, started life as an apartment hotel. It was granted one of the first cocktail lounge licenses in the city in 1954 (along with the Vancouver, Georgia, Sylvia and St. Regis). Its builder and owner, Walter Fred Evans (1874-1949) was one of the important impresarios of early Vancouver, bringing performers like Fritz Kreisler and Dame Clara Butt to town, and was an active supporter of the Symphony Society, as well as being the long-time organist at Christ Church Cathedral.

The foot of Granville Street, in 1886 when the first Hotel Vancouver was built, was the "Blueblood Alley" residential area for the business and railroad elite of Vancouver. The business "anchor" was the CPR's railroad station at the foot of Granville Street. The first little wooden station and platform, built just in time for the arrival of the first train in May, 1887, was demolished in 1898 to make way for a much grander structure. This second station, built in the CPR's famous "railroad baronial" style, had two bulging turrets, and an arch connecting Granville Street with the platforms and trains. It was demolished after the completion of the third railroad station—the neo-classical structure which extends along Cordova Street east to the foot of Seymour. For a brief period during the First World War, the two very different stations stood uncomfortably side by side.

Commercial development crept westward along Hastings Street as early as 1888, when CPR physician John Matthew Lefevre tried his hand at property development no more than 200 yards from his home. His Empire Building, demolished in the early Eighties, was a feature for years on the Seymour and Hastings corner with its British Boot Shop and newsstand. At the Granville Street corner was the Haddon building, occupied by Trorey's jewellers.

Trorey's, Frith's next door, the Semi-Ready suit shop on Granville at Dunsmuir, and the McDowell's Drug store at Granville and Hastings were typical shops in that area in the years before 1910, when the Granville and Hastings area rivalled Cordova Street as a shopping centre. McDowell's Drug Store was in the MacKinnon Building at the southwest corner, kitty-corner from Trorey's. It was built during the Klondike Rush by J.M. MacKinnon, a timber cruiser and miner who was also an honorary Colonel of the 231st Seaforth Batallion. MacKinnon was linked with the "Golden Cache" mining swindle in Lillooet; his fortunes changed and he sold the building to Frederick de la Fontaine Williams of England. McDowell's claim to fame was the seven Sutherland Sisters, who combed their long hair in the window of his drugstore to advertise their miracle hair tonic.

Financial and business interests—as opposed to retailing concerns—had already moved into the Granville and Hastings area in the years before 1910. One of the first was lawyer E.P. Davis, who built a handsome office building next to Lefevre's Empire Building in 1906. The Canadian Bank of Commerce built a magnificent "temple bank" on the southeast corner of Granville and Hastings in 1908; that same year, R.V. Winch started construction on the Winch Building—the first modern office building west of Gran-

The civic welcome on Wednesday, September 18, 1912 for the Duke of Connaught. The Duke, who was Canada's Governor General, paraded through the city under nine arches, erected by the Canadian Pacific, Canadian Northern, and Great Northern Railways, the Italian, Japanese, Chinese, and German communities, the Progress Club, and the B.C. Lumber and Shingle Manufacturers Association (Lumbermen's Arch, re-erected in Stanley Park). Mayor Findlay delivered the civic address of welcome at the Courthouse, after which five thousand school children staged a welcome at little Aberdeen School on Burrard Street. The Courthouse, designed by famed Victoria architect Francis Rattenbury, is now the Vancouver Art Gallery. On the left of the picture is the first Hotel Vancouver and, beyond it, the clock tower of the Vancouver Block on Granville street.

James Inglis Reid

Above: James Inglis Reid. Right: the interior of the shop on Granville Street during the Twenties. The hams on the left are graded Tasty, Choice, Best, and Excellent.

"We hae meat that ye can eat" has been a familiar phrase to Vancouverites for the past seventy years, almost as familiar as the "Dollar forty-nine day, Woodward's" jingle. Whereas the latter day was known rather unkindly as the "Scotchman's picnic," the former is the slogan for James Inglis Reid, the Scottish butcher to the carriage trade, at 559 Granville.

James Inglis Reid was born in 1874 in Scotland and came to Vancouver in 1906. He started the business with the famous slogan in 1913, but at first operated as a general provisioner. In 1917, however, he hired a newly-immigrated Scot named "Horatio" Nelson Menzies, who began to make sausages on the premises. They were such a hit that the matrons of Shaughnessy and the West End—who bought sausages for their servants as part of their regular meat order—began to request them for their own tables. In 1920, the store showed its true colours by turning out 25 pounds of haggis for Robbie Burns' Day (now they make and sell thousands of pounds of it every year). The store quickly developed a reputation for hams and bacon, cured and smoked on the premises, and for years operated on a strict schedule: Monday was sausages, Tuesday jellied tongue, Wednesdays white pudding (made with oatmeal and sausage), Thursdays black (also known as bloody) pudding, and Fridays head cheese.

James Inglis Reid died in November, 1952, leaving an estate of $343,000. In memory of his son Knox, who drowned off Bowen Island in his early teens, a hospital fund was left to pay the expenses of needy boys.

ville Street. In 1910, builder Jonathan Rogers took over the site of the Maison de la Ville restaurant and an old bicycle riding academy, and built his handsome Rogers Building. Concurrently, the Federal Government erected the Main Post Office on the site of Lefevre's house. In 1910, the Bauer Building (now the Pemberton) was built next to the MacKinnon Building on Hastings. In 1912, CPR treasurer W.F. Salsbury sold his old home on the southeast corner of Hastings and Howe Street—across the street from the Vancouver Club—to Credit Foncier for $100,000 cash. They built an office tower there on the eve of the War.

Nearly twenty years later, the old Trorey's store was knocked down by the Royal Bank, which built Vancouver's first really modern skyscraper on the northeast corner of Granville and Hastings. The old MacKinnon building survived until 1959, when it was demolished and replaced by the modern United Kingdom Building. Parts of the MacKinnon building live on, though: a group of sculptors led by Jack Harmon managed to save 40 large sandstone blocks from the demolition crew. The north blocks of Granville, Howe and Hornby streets have become the city's financial district, bustling during office hours but deserted after dark.

A feature of the Granville and Hastings corner in the Twenties was Constable Duncan McKinnon, who, "using his own judgement," directed traffic in his "bobby" uniform, wearing white gloves and waving a white baton—which everyone called his "wand." McKinnon was one of the first constables hired for the new Traffic Department, formed in December, 1921, two weeks before the rule of the road changed over to the right hand side. After a few years, McKinnon got a "Stop/Go" set of iron hands, operated by a lever. The iron stand was inserted into a socket in the pavement in the middle of the intersection. Finally came automatic signals, the first at McKinnon's corner, the second at Robson and Granville in the late Twenties.

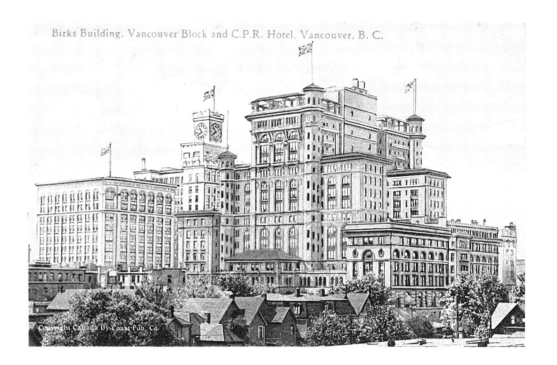

Birks Building, Vancouver Block and C.P.R. Hotel, Vancouver, B. C.

Copyright Canada By Coast Pub. Co.

Hotel Vancouver, Giant Flag-Pole (210 ft.) and Court House, Vancouver, B. C.

AUTHOR'S COLLECTION

Top: looking southeast to the corner of Georgia and Granville, during the Twenties. The "second" Hotel Vancouver dominated the corner until its demolition in 1949. The Birks Building on the left was demolished in 1974 for the construction of the Vancouver Centre complex. Only the Vancouver Block with its distinctive clock tower remains (an earthquake on December 7, 1918 stopped the clock). Below: looking southeast from the corner of Georgia and Hornby. The flagpole on the Courthouse lawn was cut at Stillwater, B.C., and raised on August 29, 1913, by an elaborate steam-donkey arrangement. It weighed nine tons, and was removed on November 4, 1936, "as doubt existed that its condition was still safe." In front of the flagpole, on Georgia Street, stood the King Edward VII fountain, sculpted in 1912 by Charles Marega, and now moved to the west side of the Courthouse. The plaza in front of the Courthouse is now the site of the Centennial Fountain, sculpted in 1967.

*Right: the Royal Bank
tower, at the northeast corner
of Granville and Hastings,
was started in 1929 and
became the city's first
modern skyscraper, in a style
practically created by the
city's "height and tower"
bylaw (page 74). It replaced
the Haddon building, which
had housed Trorey's Jewellers. Harvey Haddon, who
died in London in February,
1931, bequeathed the
money to buy the land at the
end of Kitsilano Point,
adjoining the Planetarium
and Vancouver Museum,
for a park which bears his
name.*

Henry Cambie

The steely-gray office building occupied by the Continental Bank at the southeast corner of Georgia and Thurlow now occupies the site of the first Vancouver home of Henry Cambie. Cambie's estate comprised the area to the west of a ravine which crossed Georgia Street in a northwesterly direction mid-way down the block. On the other side of the ravine—in the pre-Christ Church cathedral days of 1889—was one of the few homes west of the Hotel Vancouver, the residence of land commissioner J.M. Browning.

Cambie's name is remembered not for his house on Georgia, but for Cambie Street—the second street named in Vancouver (the first was Abbott; the third Hamilton, by the surveyor and alderman Lauchlan Hamilton). Cambie lived at 1030 West Georgia from 1889 until 1909, when he sold the site for $35,000 to an apartment builder. Cambie then moved to 1918 Haro, where he lived for the rest of his life.

"The last great railroad builder of the Dominion" was born at Castleton, County Tipperary in 1837, to a family which had settled there in Cromwellian times. He nearly died of poison when a mere baby and was actually taken to the undertaker for burial, but recovered on the table. At 16, the family moved to Canada and settled in Nova Scotia.

His family apprenticed him to an engineering firm and, at age 30, he was put in charge of construction of a section of the Windsor-Annapolis railway in Evangeline, Nova Scotia. There he married Miss Helen Fay. He was put in charge of part of the Intercolonial

Railway, where he worked with his new brothers-in-law. One frosty morning the three were thawing frozen dynamite in preparation for a day's work, when some sticks exploded. The two brothers-in-law were blown to pieces, but Cambie survived.

In 1874 he was sent to B.C. to explore the feasibility of a railroad through the mountains. The Hastings Mill's Captain Raymur told him: "No one but a damned fool would consider it." The next year, he explored the Chilcotin and tested the feasibility of alternate routes to the coast via Bute Inlet, and the Skeena River via Pine Pass. In 1881, when his surveys had proved the benefits of the Fraser Canyon-Burrard Inlet route, he was put in charge of engineering for Onderdonk's tortuous Fraser Canyon section. The worst part, Cambie recalled, was the Cherry Creek bluffs section on Kamloops Lake, where he worked for weeks, in bare feet, suspended by ropes over the cliff high above the water.

With the completion of the railway, Cambie was appointed engineer in charge of the Western Division of the CPR. He resigned from that in 1902, and became a consulting engineer to the company. Although he retired from active service in 1920, he maintained an office in the station and walked to it regularly from his home—a familiar figure in his topcoat, regardless of the weather.

Cambie died on April 22, 1928, aged 91. He had been very healthy, until he caught a cold in his final week. He lived in the last years with his eldest daughter, Mrs. R.G. Tatlow, the widow of the late Minister of Finance.

Glencoe Lodge

CPR Land Commissioner J.M. Browning erected a house at the northwest corner of Georgia and Burrard in the winter of 1886-87. Later, it was extended several times and operated as the Glencoe Lodge, a very respectable residential hotel. For a brief period, before its demolition in July, 1932, it was known as the Hotel Belfred. The site was used for a Standard gas station and parking lot until the early Seventies, when the enormous Royal Centre was constructed. Note the "silent policeman" lane-marker in the middle of the intersection.

CITY OF VANCOUVER ARCHIVES

The Royal Centre at Burrard and Georgia replaced a drab parking lot and Standard Oil gas station which had been there since the Depression years. The gas station's predecessor was the Glencoe Lodge, a famous residential hotel "where fashionable life centred for many years."

Burrard and Georgia was "way out in the woods" in 1886 when CPR land commissioner J.M. Browning built his home on the northwest corner with a view to attracting settlement to the area (in fact, the only settlers he attracted were CPR engineering director Henry Cambie and CPR lands employee Newton J. Ker). Browning's home was called Cottage B, and had a beautiful garden with climbing roses and wonderful flower beds. On his death, the "cottage" was divided into a duplex—one half occupied by Superintendent H.E. Beasley, the other by passenger agent E.J. Coyle.

In April, 1906, it was bought by sugar magnate B.T. Rogers. He leased it in 1907 to Miss Jean Mollison, who had been managing Chateau Lake Louise for the CPR. She renamed it Glencoe Lodge, after the region of Scotland where she was born. It became the city's "most récherche hostelry," in the words of newspaper writer Bob Bouchette, who described it as a victim of the "wolf of Depression [which should have been] chased from the threshhold."

Glencoe Lodge was home away from home to the crème de la crème: the Van Bruyssels of the Belgian consular service; Prime Ministers William Lyon MacKenzie King and Sir Wilfrid Laurier; Lieutenant Governor Henri Joly de Lotbinière; Governor General Lord Aberdeen and Lady Aberdeen; Shakespearean actors Ellen Terry and Sir Johnstone Forbes-Robertson. Guests were entertained by recitals and dramatic presentations (from such long lost celebrities as Patricia Salmon, "now on the New York stage"), sipped cherry wine from Venetian decanters and ate off Sèvres plates while sitting on Chippendale chairs. Both the Canadian and the American Women's Clubs held their meetings there, as did the Philharmonic Society.

In 1912, Miss Mollison expanded Glencoe Lodge by building two large wings running north and west. Although she always felt that she "had founded an institution" rather than a hotel, the Depression hit her hard and, despite her sentimental attachment to the place, she couldn't continue managing it.

Jonathan Rogers

Jonathan Rogers had a vision of Vancouver as a great, growing city and, with his wife Elisabeth, worked for most of his life to improve the recreational, social and cultural opportunities of its citizens.

Jonathan Rogers was born on July 30, 1865 at Plason, Denbighshire, Wales—reputedly a grubby coal town with a decidedly narrow outlook. Although a relative of Thomas Gray (of "Gray's Elegy"), at age 16 he was unable to read or speak English. However, when he was 20, he went to Liverpool and thence to Canada with the idea that cattle could be driven from the freezing prairies to the temperate coast for the winters. He arranged passage on the first transcontinental passenger train through the Rockies in May, 1887—his trip through that mountainous wilderness "undeceived" him, he later confessed. When the train pulled into Vancouver on May 23, Rogers was supposedly the first man off it (although, according to a letter to the *Vancouver Sun* in 1941, this distinction belonged to one W.E. Grant, who lived in later years at 2505 Scott, and was one of the last survivors of the construction crew present at the driving of the last spike). Rogers set up a painting business, and secured as one of his first contracts the painting of part of the new Hotel Vancouver. In the first CPR land sale that year, he bought four lots, then—wearing his Wellington boots—went out looking for them.

In the early 1890s, he became well established as a Vancouver real estate agent and was president of the local YMCA. In 1898, he tried his hand at building, and erected the modest Rogers building on Hastings near Homer Street. In 1911, he built a more impressive namesake, the Rogers building at 470 Granville Street. The exterior of this skyscraper, with its pink marble columns and fine carving, makes it one of the more impressive pre-war commercial buildings left in Vancouver.

Later, Rogers constructed some major projects—the power house at Lake Beautiful (now Lake Buntzen) for B.C. Electric, the Royal Bank skyscraper at Main and Hastings, and much of the St. Andrew's Wesley Church. He also acquired the last remaining undeveloped piece of Shannon farm (north of the Shannon estate at 57th and Granville between Granville and the interurban tracks), where he laid sewers, roads and sidewalks and subdivided the land for an eager group of buyers in what was coyly referred to as "South Kerrisdale." Increasingly, his attention turned to public service. He was president of the Vancouver Board of Trade and, in 1907, ran successfully for the Parks Board, where he exerted a considerable influence for the next 25 years. He might have had even more influence, had he won the 1913 mayoralty race; both he and his major opponent Louis Taylor were disqualified on technicalities, leaving Alderman T.S. Baxter the winner in a cakewalk. Rogers was clearly the candidate for the *Vancouver Morning Sun*, who called him "John the Baptist" for his "moral community"

The corner of Granville and Hastings, looking south, before the First World War. The Bank of Commerce's "temple bank" at the corner, built between 1906 and 1908, dwarfs cars and passersby. The tall building behind it is the Rogers' Building, erected in 1911 on the site of Ferrera's prestigious "Maison de la Ville" restaurant. To the left of the bank, in the three-storey building with the marquee, is the Strand Hotel. The Bank of Commerce extended into British Columbia in 1898 and three years later amalgamated with the Bank of British Columbia, which had been formed by Royal Charter on May 31, 1862, and had opened the first Vancouver bank branch in 1886.

stand and his campaign cry: "Prepare for a Greater City!" Louis Taylor was, of course, backed to the hilt by his own newspaper, the *World*.

During his 25 years with the Parks Board, Rogers guided the development of Stanley Park, and leased the foreshore from Musqueam Indian Reserve at the mouth of the Fraser all the way around to Spanish Banks for parkland. He was convinced that Vancouver needed splendid parks in order to become a splendid city—his public-spirited attitude, concern for recreational amenities, and sensitive public planning, places him in sharp contrast with most of his rich, socially prominent contemporaries.

Elisabeth Rogers was likewise a pillar of the community. She exemplified the progressive woman of the pre-suffragette days. She was founder and president of the local Women's Canadian Club, a delegate to the Red Cross Peace Conference at the Hague before the war, a founder of the Art Gallery (with 10 other citizens she pledged $100,000 in 1925 to start construction of the gallery at 1145 West Georgia) and the Symphony Society. Her daughter Rosemary married Robert Malkin, grandson of grocer and mayor

Jonathan Rogers

William Harold Malkin, in 1940.

The Rogers lived in a grand mansion, Argoed, at 2050 Nelson in the West End. Jonathan Rogers was rendered an invalid by a stroke in 1935 but lived on in reasonable spirits until 1945. Throughout the last years of his life, the achievements of his career in private and public service were recognized and a clamour began to name a city park after him. When he died, he willed $100,000 for a park site, stipulating that it should be in the vicinity of Cambie and Broadway (because, he said, the old Strathcona Park was no longer available to citizens due to the 1936 erection of City Hall). Thus, Jonathan Rogers Park was created in the block bounded by Columbia, Manitoba, 7th and 8th; in the 30 years since the park was dedicated, most of the families have moved away and the area has gradually changed into a light industry and factory location.

The bequest for the park was only a part of Rogers' legacy. He left a total of $258,000 to public causes, the largest single amount so willed up to that time.

Excavation for the Hudson's Bay Co. building at Seymour and Georgia Streets, looking southwest, in 1911. The old "corner unit" building of the Bay is visible on the extreme right. It was finally knocked down on March 27, 1926. The Birks' Building is half-completed in the background. The recently-opened Vancouver Block is visible behind it. The V flagpole in the right background is on the original Hotel Vancouver, which was to be knocked down in 1913 to make way for the elegant "second" hotel. Across the street was the Raeburn rooming house, later the site of the Strand Theatre and now the Scotia Tower. Contractor George W. Ledingham of Ledingham and Cooper is standing beside the shovel boom with his back to the photographer. The Marion steam shovel, with a one cubic yard capacity, transferred earth to the horse-pulled wagon, which probably dumped its load along Water Street to fill in the land at the CPR yards. A powder man is in the left foreground in silhouette with a powder rodding stick over his shoulder. Note the early electric arc lights strung across the excavation, probably for night work. There is no shoring in the excavation–the walls are a sandstone formation.

BRUCE LEDINGHAM

The Roof Garden

View from C. P. R. Hotel Roof Garden, Vancouver, B. C.

AUTHOR'S COLLECTION

The tea garden atop the Hotel Vancouver, at Georgia and Granville, was the most elegant place in Vancouver for afternoon tea dances. Its structural features were highlighted in the "Engineering Record" of April 25, 1914 (after a story on the new Panama Canal). The tea garden was an ellipse, 52 feet by 76 feet, with a roof of glass panels in 5-foot sections. The new (second) Hotel Vancouver was also noteworthy for its interior fire escapes. Its design, like that of the Royal Bank tower fifteen years later, was influenced by a city ordinance, limiting buildings to a height of 120 feet, with a tower eight storeys higher covering no more than one-third of the ground area. Thus, the hotel was designed in a multiple-wing arrangement, using graded levels which relieved the sheer wall-drop to the streets. So effective was the arrangement that, of 500 guest rooms, only 44 had windows facing onto the inner courtyard. The Spanish Grill, during the Twenties and Thirties, featured three dinner combinations, at $.75, $1.00, and $1.50. The most expensive plate offered a choice of Scalloped Chicken à la King, French Steak Sauté, Roast Haunch of Spring Lamb with Mint Sauce, or Cold Young Turkey with Ham. Vegetables were string beans in butter, and potatoes Alma. Chateau Cheese & Crackers accompanied tea on the roof garden.

The Orillia Apartments, at the northwest corner of Robson and Seymour, in 1935. Built in 1903 by William Lamont Tait, it was originally a rooming house in a residential area, but was raised in 1907 to allow the construction of the main floor shops. Later renamed the Capitol Rooms, the building was best known for Sid Beech's Vancouver Tamale Parlour, which served Mexican food just west (to the left) of the rooming house doors, behind the tram. The building was an anomaly for over 70 years, ever since the construction of modern office towers like the 1910 Vancouver Block in the background. It was demolished in 1985, following an extended controversy over its heritage status. W.L. Tait is probably best known for Glen Brae, the twin-turreted mansion also known as the "Mae West house" at 1690 Matthews in Shaughnessy Heights. Born in Scotland in March, 1850, he came to British Columbia in 1891 and in 1902 started the Rat Portage sawmill at the foot of Fir Street. He was one of the first mill owners to hire Indians and East Indians. He had five sons and three daughters, and lived first at 752 Thurlow Street, near Robson, later the site of the Women's Building. He disposed of Rat Portage in 1910, and retired to Glen Brae, where he lived until 1920. He then moved downtown to his Manhattan Apartments at Robson and Thurlow, where he died the following year. Glen Brae achieved great notoriety in 1925, when the Ku Klux Klan bought it as their B.C. headquarters.

A postcard photograph of downtown Vancouver in the early Thirties, looking northwest. It differs little from the view on page 10, other than that, on close inspection, it can be seen that the wall and window detailing on the new, chateau-style Hotel Vancouver on the left has been merely pencilled in. The hotel, a concession agreed to by the Canadian Northern Railway in return for terminal rights in the city, was commenced in 1929. Work stopped as the Depression deepened, and its frame stood abandoned on the skyline for several years. The hotel was rushed to completion in 1939 for the visit of King George VI and Queen Elizabeth. A "farewell" to the 25-year-old "old" Hotel Vancouver was held on May 24, and the new one was royally opened the next day. The "old" hotel, visible immediately to the left of the Vancouver Block, was demolished in 1949.

The Waterfront

Waterfront and Shipping Vancouver, B. C.

From Coal Harbour east to the Second Narrows Bridge is an inaccessible stretch of waterfront—the most industrial of industrial Vancouver. Some of it is very old: the CPR mainline came through in 1887; the B.C. Sugar Refinery warehouses date from before the turn of the century; the Ballantyne Pier was built in 1922, in the great post-war shipping boom. Other parts are modern, like the Vanterm container terminal at the foot of Clark Drive.

Vancouver was put on the world map on June 14, 1887, when the ex-Cunarder *Abyssinia* (chartered by the CPR along with the *Parthia* and *Batavia*) docked at the CPR pier with the first silk and passenger cargo from Yokahama. These ships and the later Empress liners (including the *Empress of Japan*, which first arrived here in 1891 and whose figurehead is preserved in Stanley Park), made the CPR an international success story. The CPR's Pier D, near the foot of Granville, burned in an enormous conflagration in the summer of 1938. "The magnificent Pier B-C," as it was described when it opened during Canada's Diamond Jubilee in 1927, slipped into a decline after the air travel revolution of the Fifties. Only Pier A, the first CPR pier built, and the furthest to the west, survived. The Great Northern Railway built a pier at the foot of Main Street, later the point of departure for CNR coastal boats like the *Prince George*.

The CPR controlled much of the Burrard Inlet waterfront. Its enthusiasm for the dramatic and tricky entry through First Narrows was not shared by competing industrialists, who continually put forth schemes for a new harbour. The Vancouver Dock and Harbour Extension Co. was one which held a good chance of success, and would have completely altered the future development of the Lower Mainland. The harbour was to occupy the entire western shore of Lulu Island, an area of 8.4 square miles. Six long piers, a log pond, and a 1,000 foot dry dock were planned. Railway lines were surveyed to New Westminster and Vancouver, the latter entering a tunnel one thousand feet north of the Fraser River at Eburne Station and connecting to the Great Northern yards on False Creek. A branch tunnel was planned, diverging at about King Edward Avenue northwards, to a point near the Cambie bridge, for passenger access to downtown Vancouver. The firm had intentions of spending $21,000,000 by 1914, but the pre-war Depression killed it.

Top: the CPR's Pier B-C, opened Monday, July 4, 1927 near the foot of Burrard Street, served the CPR's world-famous Empress liners until the collapse of the ocean liner business in the Fifties. The pier was revitalized in the early 1980s, when the old Spanish Colonial façade was demolished and a new cruise ship facility and convention centre built. Its companion, Pier D at the foot of Granville (built 1920), burned in an enormous $1 million fire on the afternoon of July 27, 1938. Bottom: Vancouver's cluttered waterfront, looking southwest near the Union Steamships wharf at the foot of Carrall Street. The large turreted building in the right distance is the old CPR station (page 65) at the foot of Granville.

interior walls and floors are held up by huge beams—"Vancouver toothpicks," turned out by the Hastings Sawmill Co. Nearby, the pioneer Ross and Howard Iron Works located at the foot of Woodland Drive.

In 1914, MP H.H. Stevens bucked the eastern-dominated logic of his colleagues and got Lapointe Pier and Dominion 1—Vancouver's first grain elevator—built at the foot of Woodland Drive. Stevens reasoned that Vancouver was the grain port of the future, and that grain could be stored and shipped cheaply from the west coast via the newly-opened Panama Canal to Europe. The grain elevator cost $1.75 million; shortly after it opened, a landslide blocked the Panama Canal. The elevator stood bleakly empty on the skyline for two years, by which time it had inevitably been dubbed "Stevens' Folly." He was ridiculed by the CPR, the Board of Trade, and Evans, Coleman & Evans. Liberal logic said that wharfage for 79 ships at once—the largest number before the First War—would be adequate for years to come. These groups were convinced that grain would never make it through the Panama Canal, due to the heat. Stevens arranged six highly publicized bulk shipments to England during the last three years of the war, the first aboard a ship called *War Victory*. His contention that grain shipments to England could also be profitable was confirmed on January 17, 1921, when the U.S. ship *Effingham* was loaded with 2,000 tons of wheat, at a carrying rate of $30 a ton (the rate dropped to $10 a ton by the Sixties).

Vancouver's grain transportation trade prospered during the Twenties, largely due to the efforts of future mayor Gerald Grattan McGeer, K.C., who had become special counsel for B.C. in 1916. Through his persistent lobbying, a second grain elevator was begun in 1923, and he got westbound grain rates increased by 10 per cent. Grain shipments grew to 24 million bushels in 1924, and McGeer helped to get Burrard Drydock—the city's first large shipbuilding facility—some government contracts despite Eastern skepticism. The huge Alberta Wheat Pool, near the site of the New Brighton resort, was built in 1927-9.

Another grain pioneer in Vancouver was Ernest Woodward, born in 1884 in Minneapolis (d. 1954). He moved to Vancouver in 1922 and built the first two private grain elevators in Vancouver at the foot of Salisbury near the sugar refinery. They are now the United Grain Growers terminal. In 1924 he built the Columbia Grain Elevator at 2700 Wall Street, east of the main industrial area of the port. Woodward invented equipment to unload boxcars and load ships simultaneously, which became standard in the industry. A crony of Stevens who played a major role in the development of the port was Sam McClay (1875-1958), a member of the first Harbour Commission from 1913-22 and its Chairman from 1930-34, while the R.B. Bennett Conservatives were back in the saddle. McClay's term of office saw the development of Granville Island, and the Second Narrows bridge debacle (page 182). After the latter experience, he seriously proposed that the Second Narrows be dammed and the bridge become a causeway.

(Preceding page) The Evans, Coleman and Evans wharf, at the foot of Columbia in Gastown, was built in 1890, and served a variety of passenger and freight companies, including John Irving's Canadian Pacific Navigation Co. Sailing ships were in use regularly until the First World War years, particularly in the transport of lumber from Hastings Mill at the foot of Dunlevy, and were moved around the harbour by the "mosquito fleet" of steam tugs, with names like Stormer and Etta White, which docked at the Gore Avenue wharf. The H.M.S. Hood (above) was, in 1924, the biggest warship ever to visit the city. The Hood was later sunk by the German pocket battleship Bismarck in the North Atlantic during World War II.

(Left) Captain John Irving (1853-1936), whose Canadian Pacific Navigation Co. was, from 1883 until the CPR bought it in 1901, the largest steamboat operator on the coast. He came to B.C. in 1859. He worked as a steamboat captain on the Fraser and, later, in the Yukon. He was a part-owner of the Moodyville Sawmill and the Vancouver Waterworks. (Left below) 'Whistling Texas,' whose real name was George Booth, was a regular sight on the Evans, Coleman and Evans Wharf. He did odd jobs, beachcombed a little, and carried baggage for steamship passengers. He slept for 35 years in an empty room at Firehall Number Two on Seymour Street, and died in 1936 when he fell from a ladder there.

On the Burrard Inlet waterfront, the most famous of the early docks was the Evans, Coleman and Evans wharf at the foot of Columbia, at which many of Vancouver's distinguished early visitors arrived. The Union Steamships wharf, a block west at the foot of Carrall, was the departure point for coastal steamship service and the North and West Vancouver ferries.

Development of the immense B.C. Sugar Refinery began in 1892. Aided by the prestige and financial support of some CPR directors, Benjamin T. Rogers was able to strike a good deal with City Council when he proposed the refinery: fifteen years without tax and ten years worth of free water. In return, Rogers promised to employ only white labour. The huge, arcaded warehouses stretching along Powell Street were built in 1902; the exteriors are brick, but the

The Greenhill Park

VANCOUVER PUBLIC LIBRARY

The worst disaster since the fire of 1886 occurred on March 6, 1945, on Pier B of the Canadian Pacific dock near the foot of Burrard Street. It had nothing to do with a wartime cargo. The 10,754-ton Dominion government-chartered freighter, the S.S. *Greenhill Park*, was taking on a diverse load of lifeboat flares, aeroplane parts, sodium chlorate, whiskey, lumber, and some odds and ends including pickles, paper and sunglasses.

At a quarter to twelve, just as a crew of fifteen painters knocked off for lunch and started their climb from the double bottom of the freighter, a fire broke out in number three hold amidships. Long-shoremen poured water on it, but the smoke kept getting thicker. At three minutes to twelve, a small explosion blew out the hatch. Longshoremen and painters scrambled for the deck, while men in the loading scows dived for safety in the water. Suddenly, a second explosion ripped through the *Greenhill Park*, heaving her out of the water. A sheet of flame blew out of the number two and three hatches, hurling lumber, pickles, drums and flares high into the air, some as far as Lumbermen's Arch two miles away. Both sides of the ship blew out, leaving ragged holes twenty by fifty feet across, and breaking $30,000 worth of windows downtown. Amazingly, only eight men died, none in the number three hold where the fire started.

The tug *RFM*, skippered by Captain Harry Jones, was pulling a barge to the B.C. Sugar Refinery when the explosion occurred. Jones cut the barge adrift off Brockton and headed directly for the *Greenhill Park*. In a memorable act of bravery, captain and crew managed to get a line onto the ship and tow it away from the wharf. An hour later, after three-and-one-half miles bucking the tide, the *Greenhill Park* was beached at Siwash Rock. The fireboat *Carlisle* pumped nine million gallons of water into the wreck over the next three days.

At high tide three days later, at four o'clock in the morning, the burned-out hull was pulled clear of the beach and towed to Ballantyne Pier. During the tow, the ship nearly split in two. She was patched, then towed to North Vancouver and beached again. On August 20, the *Greenhill Park* was refloated and taken to the North Burrard shipyards, where she was refitted and sold to Greek interests for $165,000.

An inquest, held by Justice Sydney Smith, concluded that "the peculiar combination of articles stowed contrary to the regulations of the British and American governments made the explosion possible," and that "the crux of the whole disaster was the broaching of whiskey barrels in the hold of the ship, and a space giving access to the whiskey existed in the hold after stowage."

The North Shore Ferries

West Vancouver Ferry Number Six passes Pier B-C on its way to Ambleside during the Thirties. The Dundarave pier, built in 1914 for the ferry service, was used only sporadically, partly because it was difficult to approach in rough weather.

AUTHOR'S COLLECTION

Vancouver's smart Seabus, connecting the Lonsdale pier with the former Canadian Pacific Railway station at the foot of Seymour, succeeded a Burrard Inlet ferry service dating from the turn of the century. Double-ended ferries ran from the Carrall Street wharf to the Lonsdale pier in North Vancouver. Another service connected to the Dundarave Pier in West Vancouver.

The North Vancouver service commenced on May 12, 1900. North Vancouver Number One cost $14,201.37 to build, and on its first day had receipts of $42.20. The service was so popular that a second ferry, dubbed the *St. George* after North Vancouver property owner A. St. George Hamersley, was built in 1904 at False Creek. (It was sold in 1932 to a logging company and used as a floating bunkhouse until fire destroyed it in 1960.) The *St. George* was big enough to take both horse and carriage aboard together. A third ferry was launched in 1911 (sold in 1952 to Gulf of Georgia Towing Co., which used the hull as a scow). That same year a new wharf was built to accommodate the huge increase in traffic caused by

North Vancouver's property boom.

The first Lonsdale pier was the terminus for the Lonsdale streetcar, which started service on Labour Day, 1906. The streetcar's turntable was on the edge of the wharf at the bottom of the Lonsdale hill. In August, 1909, the inevitable happened when a streetcar lost its brakes and dived into the water. Motorman John Kelly jumped and broke his leg, but Conductor Jones rode the tram into the water and emerged unhurt. Fortunately, no passengers were aboard.

The North Vancouver service remained popular until the early 1950s, when the automobile and post-war prosperity doomed it. Automobiles were carried by the ferries, one of which is now the Seven Seas restaurant at the foot of Lonsdale. The service was discontinued in 1958. The West Vancouver service, started in 1909 by real-estate promoter John Lawson, was operated by West Vancouver municipality after 1912. The opening of Lions' Gate bridge in 1938 sealed its fate, although the service continued through the war years until February 10, 1946.

H.H. Stevens

The "grand old man of Canadian politics," the "Conservative-Labour Member from Vancouver," and "that old war horse of Vancouver Centre" were three of the more printable nicknames applied to the Hon. Harry H. Stevens, one of the most controversial and successful politicians Vancouver ever produced. More than anyone else, Stevens is responsible for the development of the Port of Vancouver. His public career spanned 60 years.

Stevens was born in Bristol, England on December 8, 1878. His father, in 1890, bought boat tickets to Australia, but changed his mind and his tickets a few days before sailing. The father got work in the boom-town (now ghost-town) of Phoenix in the Boundary-Similkameen, when the mines in that part of the province were the richest in North America. The son's appetite for political harangue was whetted by rallies of the Marxist-oriented Western Federation of Miners. He also heard Prime Minister John A. MacDonald speak during the 1891 election campaign and was so impressed he became a life-long Conservative.

In 1894, the family moved to Vernon. The railway line was washed out at Sicamous, so Harry walked the last 48 miles while the rest of the family followed on an ox-cart. Two years later he left school and did a stint as fireman on CPR locomotive 374—the "Kits Beach train" which is now restored in the Roundhouse museum at B.C. Place. He satisfied his wanderlust by working for the Red Cross during the American Army campaign against the Spanish in the Philippines in 1897.

In 1901, he arrived in Vancouver and got a job as a clerk in the City Grocery at Main and Pender, on the edge of Chinatown. He lay-preached at the Mt. Pleasant Methodist Church and assisted the Rev. Ebenezer Robson (after whom Robson Street is named), including rowing the old man across Burrard Inlet for services to his Indian flock at St. Paul's Church on the Mission Reserve. By 1903, Stevens had become morally outraged at the graft and corruption in Chinatown. Raw opium, which was transported through the streets in baskets, was, he said, claiming more and more white men. Two clerks at the City Grocery were caught stealing from the till to cover their Chuckaluck debts. Stevens went to the police demanding action about the gambling and drug addiction, but got none. Every week he visited Chinatown gambling clubs, opium dens and brothels with his friend Reverend Chown (Chown Memorial Church on Cambie), and published all the details of his visits in the *News-Advertiser*. Through his efforts, and his lobbying of Labour Minister Mackenzie King, who had visited Vancouver in the aftermath of the 1907 riots and been shocked by the opium industry, the Narcotics Control Squad was founded.

In 1904, Stevens became the chief accountant and secretary for a trust company, but remained in the public eye as a backer of temperance and as the main spokesman for the Wesleyan Moral Reform League. He took the day off on July 5, 1905 to marry Gertrude Glover (1880-1966), in a double-ring ceremony with her sister.

H.H. Stevens

Stevens opened a public accountant's office in 1908, but his interests were clearly in the political arena. In 1910, he was elected Alderman. During his term, he helped originate the scheme for the joint sewerage system for Greater Vancouver—a system sufficient for a population of one million and for many years one of the best on the continent; he also proposed the annexation of the municipalities of South Vancouver and Point Grey, which was finally accomplished in 1929.

In 1911, he managed to squeeze MP George Cowan out of the Conservative nomination for Vancouver Centre and was elected to the House of Commons by a huge 3,256 majority. He was re-elected in 1917 as a Unionist by a record majority. In 1921, he was re-elected again as a Conservative, and served as Minister of Trade and Commerce in the Meighen administration. Stevens said later that when he first became an MP "not a dollar had been spent on the Port by Ottawa."

Stevens got the waterfront rights east of Gore and west of Cardero from the Canadian Pacific Railway, which had considered that it had a monopoly on all wharfage and shipping there. During the war, he got False Creek dredged out and Granville Island "built,"

Dr. Samuel D. Chown (1853-1932), the crusading minister who accompanied H.H. Stevens on his tours of Chinatown opium dens and gambling clubs.

and helped Burrard Dry Dock and J. Couglan and Sons by pressuring Munitions Minister Sir Joseph Flavelle into giving shipbuilding contracts to the west coast. When access into the inlet for modern ships was debated, he responded by getting First Narrows dredged from a 400-foot wide channel to 1,600 feet.

Harry Stevens' accomplishments during the Twenties were legion: he was considered to be "The Father of Technical Education" in Canada for his proposals on revamping the school system; he promoted mining exploration and development in British Columbia, reasoning that it would be the province's chief industry in the future; he exposed customs scandals which helped topple MacKenzie King's Liberal Government in 1926.

The 1930 election was a rout for the Conservatives of R.B. Bennett. The Tories won 137 seats, compared with 88 for the Liberals and 20 for an assortment of others. One of the Liberal seats was Vancouver Centre, where upstart Ian MacKenzie knocked off Stevens. Bennett wanted Stevens in the Cabinet, so a byelection was arranged in the East Kootenays in a bit of politicking that Bennett was later to rue. The next few years saw the entire country sink into a Depression from which no one could reason a way out. On the Prairies, political extremism took forms as divergent as the neo-fascist Social Credit and the neo-socialist CCF. A tremendous amount of public disenchantment was directed against companies which were supposedly paying starvation wages to employees. The Prime Minister established a Price Spreads Commission in 1934 to examine the wage and price question, and put Stevens in charge. In September, a row became public between Stevens and Bennett—Stevens published a pamphlet which became known as his "sweat-shop booklet," alleging that mass buying and sweat-shop conditions enforced by the major department stores forced prices down, destroyed the small retailers and crushed manufacturers who wouldn't accept price dictation. Stevens followed the pamphlet with a speech in Toronto, in which he accused R.B. Bennett of being influenced by R.Y. Eaton and Simpson's C.B. Burton. The debate split Bennett's cabinet and threatened the entire government as the country took sides over the affair. Stevens resigned from the Cabinet on October 27, 1934. He became a "national hero" for his efforts on behalf of the downtrodden consumer. He expanded his price-fixing charges in an attempt to get higher rates for Maritime fishermen. On November 5 he told the national press that he was being followed by two Detroit private detectives who were reporting his moves to the Canadian financial establishment. He stated: "Wealth must be used in the interests of the people."

On July 7, 1935, in preparation for the forthcoming federal election, Stevens called a press conference. "I am amazed and appalled at the forbearance of the Canadian people," he said. He announced that he was forming a new reform party "to defend the forgotten man against concentrated capital." One of his platform planks was that the Bennett government's legislation— proposed from the tattered remains of Stevens' Price Spreads Inquiry—was "anaemic, inadequate and ineffective." Stevens stumped the country attracting votes; a meeting on August 5 in the Denman Arena—chaired by First United Church minister Andrew Roddan—was filled to capacity. During the election campaign, R.B. Bennett called Stevens "a traitor to Canada." Although the Reconstruction Party— as Stevens and his followers came to be called—garnered 400,000 votes in the election, they won only one seat: Stevens'. The final tally showed it to be a rout for MacKenzie King's Liberals, who gained 171; the Tories were reduced to a rump of 39, while others took 24 seats.

Stevens continued to preach his radical philosophy, but by the time the war came the electorate was looking for the tried and the true. Stevens was defeated in 1940.

In his last years, he continued the tradition, which he had started in 1908, of walking around Stanley Park on his birthday. On his 85th birthday, the walk took him two hours. On his 91st, he was accompanied by a photographer and reporter. He missed the 92nd, and wanted to walk on his 93rd but an unusual December snow stopped him. He died on June 14, 1973, aged 94.

False Creek

The Canadian Pacific Railway exacted a heavy price from the town of Vancouver for agreeing, in 1884, to move its yards 14 miles west from Port Moody. In exchange for this guarantee of prosperity, called "the miracle wrought by transportation" in a Diamond Jubilee booklet, the railway was given enough prime land to ensure its dominance of civic development for much of the ensuing century.

William Van Horne's delight in the potential of the Burrard Inlet railyards and harbour did not stop the railway from looking elsewhere for land for other facilities. Land was needed for maintenance shops, a roundhouse, workers' quarters, and the acres of track necessary for marshalling the products of the Pacific Rim (for years after the railway arrived in Vancouver, there was so little land along Burrard Inlet that the trains ran on a trestle offshore from Water Street). The Burrard Inlet site was ideal for a passenger terminus, but deepwater navigation through First Narrows was difficult. Van Horne ordered a fixed wooden trestle to be built across False Creek to connect the main line to Kitsilano Point. The trestle was such an obstacle to marine traffic that further industrial development on False Creek was threatened. The City, alarmed, bribed the CPR with an offer of thirty tax-free years for the company's land on the north shore of the Creek if it would locate its yards and roundhouse there.

In addition to its interest in building its main railyards on Kitsilano Point, the CPR announced in 1886 the impending creation of a deepsea terminus, station and hotel. The company made moves to oust the existing occupant, Sam Greer, and started to negotiate title to the Kitsilano Indian Reserve. A suggestion was briefly made for a tunnel all the way to Point Grey, with railyards and a port on filled land at what is now Wreck Beach. The railroad track crossed False Creek on the Kitsilano trestle, continued past the Indian village of Snauq, and deadended at the foot of Trafalgar Street. Thus, the English Bay branch of the CPR was established.

The English Bay line branched off the main line between Westminster Avenue (Main Street) and Columbia and headed in a southwesterly direction through Gastown and Chinatown before it reached the open flats along False Creek. The odd-shaped buildings, particularly the front of the Anchor Hotel on Powell, the diagonal gap through the buildings in the unit block Powell and the angled frontage of the Merchant Bank building at the corner of Carrall and Hastings, show how development adapted itself to the rail line. The Carrall Street crossing was the most important to Vancouverites during the period before 1932, as Hastings was the main downtown throughway and the shunting and chuffing freight trains strung across the intersection created memorable traffic jams. One CPR employee spent his working life in a roofed shed at the corner, in front of the Palace Hotel and the Bijou Theatre, operating the crossing gates and chains which tied up horses, wagons, pedestrians, trucks and the operations of the B.C. Electric interurbans.

The Dunsmuir Tunnel, executed by the cut-and-cover method in

the worst year of the Depression, won the railway a lot of good favour from Vancouverites, both for the employment it created and the elimination of the city's worst traffic jams. Trains henceforth travelling from the main line to English Bay entered the tunnel at a portal drilled in the bluff below Hastings near Thurlow. The track then looped around and travelled directly east along Dunsmuir, veered southeast under the Beatty Street Drill Hall and emerged onto the False Creek flats. For forty years the tracks connected with the railway's marshalling yards and Roundhouse. Since 1983, the tunnel has seen new life as part of Vancouver's rapid-transit system.

For the first few years of operation, while its Yaletown shops were being built, the railway used a roundhouse with a hand-operated turntable on Shanghai Alley, about 100 yards south of Pender Street. The area was quite swampy, although a lot of filling of False Creek had been done for the Royal City Planing Mills and the B.C. Transfer Co. stables at the foot of Carrall Street. A block east, at Columbia Street, extreme high tides turned the area into a slough, and a shallow canoe route separated the western part of downtown from the rest of Vancouver. J.S. Matthews, the future city archivist, described the situation in the late 1880s: ". . . a walk from Water Street to Pender Street at high tide usually meant wet feet; skunk cabbage grew in the muskeg, and the rotting debris sometimes gave off a queer effluvia. At the False Creek end of Carrall Street, an indent brought those waters—and floating logs—almost to Pender Street."

The track, continuing southwest along the shore of False Creek, passed Cassady's Sash and Door Factory and Frank W. Hart's Furniture Factory, side by side at the site of the B.C. Place stadium. The watertower, roundhouse and Yaletown shops were erected at the foot of Drake Street. The only other development on the north shore of the Creek in 1890 was the Fader Brothers Sawmill (later Robertson and Hackett) on the east side of the "Granville Street traffic bridge."

City Council, which was never pleased with the Royal Navy name False Creek, unsuccessfully petitioned the Dominion Government on September 16, 1891, to rename it Pleasant Inlet. It was a much larger body of water than it is today, continuing east past its current limit of Quebec Street all the way to Clark Drive—a total length of about three and one half miles. Since then, it has been filled very extensively to provide more industrial land, primarily for railway and lumber company operations. The big filling sprees were for the Canadian Northern yards during the First World War, Granville Island and much of the south shore during the years after 1915, and the area between Main and Quebec Street from 1972-75 as part of the proposed (and later abandoned) city freeway system. Much of the silt for landfill came from simultaneous dredging of the waterway, which at low tide could practically ground a canoe.

Although the Kitsilano facilities never materialized, the railway used the trestle, and built a spur line to reach the Steveston canneries. In 1905, the line was taken over by the B.C. Electric and used

A late-Thirties view of the north side of False Creek, between Granville and Burrard bridges, with City Hall visible through the smoke in the background. The rigging and wharves of the Vancouver Granite Company are visible in the foreground, immediately in front of the 1886 Kitsilano Trestle. Also in the foreground are the wharves for the MacDonald Marpole coalyard. The firm acted as mainland agents for Nanaimo's Canadian Collieries (Dunsmuir) Ltd., and supplied all the coal required by the CPR. Beach Avenue shipyard, which was sold to Gulf of Georgia Towing Co., was between Hornby and Burrard Streets. Champion & White maintained a sandyard at the foot of Burrard Street, which was removed for the construction of the Burrard Bridge in the early Thirties.

for its Lulu Island interurban service. The old trestle was finally removed in 1982, after it had stranded thousands of vessels on the sandbars around the swingspan (installed in 1898 to expedite traffic) and disrupted the movements of generations of log and sawdust barges.

Lauchlan A.Hamilton, the CPR surveyor who laid out most of the city of Vancouver, had his operations camp during the summers of 1885 and 1886 in a tent on the south shore of False Creek, just east of North Arm Road, at about Third Avenue. The quiet and idyllic camp scene belied the later fate of False Creek— industrial, smelly and smoky for the next 90 years. James Matthews, later the city archivist, took his wife and two small children out in their canoe onto False Creek in 1900; a fuzzy photograph was taken, showing the children at the mouth of a little creek at the foot of Ash Street, amidst bullrushes and slough grass. In the background there is already a pall of smoke—from Leamy & Kyle's mill.

False Creek, by the First World War, was a thriving industrial and lumbering area, with good rail facilities, water transportation, booming grounds for logs and nearby accommodation in increasingly grimy neighbourhoods for its labour force. The north side of the Creek around the Roundhouse was almost completely occupied with railyards, spur lines of which penetrated into the Yaletown warehouse district along Mainland and Hamilton streets. Bachelors lived in sheds on skids and floats around the foot of Helmcken. In the lee of the Cambie Bridge sat the Sweeney Cooperage, a family-operated barrel-making concern, which survived there until the early 1980s.

By the beginning of the First World War, most of the good industrial sites along the Creek had been taken. The City deeded the eastern end of the Creek, from Main Street to Clark Drive, to the Great Northern Railway for its terminal facilities. In an attempt to make better use of the remaining area, the Harbour Commission in 1915 decided to fill the sandbar in front of the Rat Portage Sawmill. For hundreds of years, Indians had used the sandbar as a fish corral. Its extent, when False Creek was in a natural state, was about 20 acres. The Indians encircled it with converging fences of twisted brush sunk into the sand. Rope nets were made from cedar and spruce roots, and fine netting from stinging nettle fibre. The flounders and smelt which blundered in were cut into strips and smoked over hemlock fires. The Indians also caught ducks in English Bay at the mouth of False Creek; small fires were built at dusk on platforms suspended over canoes, attracting curious ducks within a spear toss.

In 1915, dredges that were opening out the shipping channel in False Creek began to pump sand onto the sandbar, instead of filling industrial sites around the edge (or creating Kitsilano Beach, as had been done in 1913). A 35 acre "island" was created, joined to Vancouver by a narrow bridge at 3rd Avenue. About fifty industrial plants went up, including the Britannia Wire Rope Co. build-

ings (now the Emily Carr College of Art), the National Machinery Co. (part of which is now the Public Market), the Arrow Transfer building (now Bridges' Pub) and the Spear and Jackson Saw buildings (now converted into the Granville Island community centre). Railway lines crisscrossed the island and threaded between the sheet iron and timber buildings, to the south shore yards of the B.C. Electric Railway on the old Indian reserve. Granville Island was refurbished in the early Seventies into a market and cultural area.

The first shipyard on the Creek was started in 1892 by Alfred Wallace, who built "Columbia River" salmon fishing boats, with moulded hulls, in floating sheds on the west side of the Granville bridge. His boats became so popular that they virtually replaced the flat-bottomed skiffs on the Fraser River. When completed, the boats were tied nose-to-tail in strings to the Granville Bridge. Wallace got the first Dominion government contract in Vancouver, in December, 1900, to build the steamer *Kestrel*. George Cates established the Beach Avenue shipyard (partly uprooted by the north piers of the Burrard Bridge in 1931), and the McKeens and Walkems built firms like West Coast Shipbuilding Ltd., Vancouver Iron Works, Vancouver Machinery Depot Ltd. and West Coast Salvage and Contracting Co., on both sides of the Creek. The George Cates Co. was bought out by R.J. Bicknell's Gulf of Georgia Towing Co., which operated three tugs and fourteen gravel and lumber barges, serving logging camps and small communities on the coast.

The largest firm was West Coast Shipbuilding at 205 West First Avenue, just east of the Cambie bridge. West Coast built several Liberty-class merchant ships during the war. Their first "Victory" ship was launched at the end of May, 1943. Newspaper ads invited the Vancouver mother with the most sons in the service to come forward and officiate at the ceremony. The Victory ships were able to make it past the swingspans on both the Cambie and Granville bridges, but were stymied by the low Kitsilano trestle. Gulf of Georgia Towing solved the problem by stacking timbers on a barge and positioning the latter under the trestle's steel span at low tide. When the tide came in, the steel span was lifted right off its moorings, and the barge towed out of the way, allowing the Victory ship to pass.

The south side of False Creek between Granville and Cambie bridges was dominated by the sprawling factories of the Vancouver Iron and Engineering Works, which manufactured many of the elevators in the early downtown office towers, did industrial casting and, during the early Thirties, assembled Kenworth trucks. V.I.E.W. finally went bankrupt, unable to pour large enough castings to compete with foreign foundries, and plagued by pollution-related complaints from the surrounding neighbourhoods. Other operations in the area included the Vivian Gas Engine Works at 1090 West 6th, in the building now converted into The Sixth Estate condominiums; Cedar Cove Sash and Door at 1101 West 6th; Sigurdson Millwork, in the building now converted into New Look

Interiors at 6th and Birch; and, a string of B.C. Forest Products sawmills and booming grounds, the last remnant being the Alberta Lumber Co. at 790 West 6th, boarded up in 1981. The B.C. Forest Products mills burned in an enormous conflagration on July 3, 1960, and were never rebuilt.

Until the late Forties, the Vancouver Athletic Park was located at Hemlock Street between False Creek and Sixth avenue. In its last decade, it was home to the Vancouver Capilanos of the old Western International Baseball League. The stadium was torn down to provide the land for the eastern cloverleaf of the new Granville bridge.

The 95 acres of the north shore of the Creek owned by the CPR were to be developed in the early Seventies with a mixture of high-density housing and commercial enterprises. The CPR had intended to flatten its redundant roundhouse and the Yaletown shops and start afresh. No agreement could be reached between the company and the city government over zoning, schools and low-income housing so the project was abandoned in 1977. The Provincial Government stepped into the breach soon after, with the B.C. Place and Transpo (Expo '86) project.

In keeping with the transportation theme of Expo '86, the roundhouse has been completely refurbished, even to detailing eliminated from the original plans, due to the famous CPR cost-cutting practices. Old engine No. 374, the CPR relic which pulled the first train into Vancouver, and had sat at Kitsilano beach since 1947, is now installed in the roundhouse. The immense B.C. Place stadium occupies the former railyard and sawmill land east of Cambie bridge.

During the Fifties, False Creek was considered to be such a liability that serious plans were advanced to fill it in, partly to add industrial land to the growing city, and partly to eliminate the traffic bottlenecks and expense caused by the necessary bridges.

After the 1960 fire, plans were developed and work began to change the south shore of the Creek into a residential area. On the old V.I.E.W. site, pathways and roadways, bearing names like Ironworker Passage, Foundry Quay and Forge Walk, recall the area's lumbering and foundry past. Near the foot of Ash Street, Stamp's Landing commemorates Capt. Edward Stamp, who founded the Hastings Mill. Millbank commemorates Leamy and Kyle's Commercial Mill, which went into receivership in December, 1889. It had a bad reputation, as it was the site of several murders. Leg-in-Boot Square, at the foot of Heather Street, commemorates the finding in July 1887, of a leg in a boot at "that very terrible neighbourhood"; nobody came to claim it although it was hung from a pole at the Police Station for two weeks.

(Top) A "Vancouver toothpick," manufactured by one of the mills on the south shore of False Creek in the early Twenties. "One of our specialties," the beam is 30" x 30" x 45 feet and weighs over five tons. The houses in the background were on Fifth Avenue at Hemlock, across the street from the old Athletic Park. (Below) Members of the Inglis family, and their neighbours from the blocks around Fifth and Pine, walked through

the Indian reserve, picnicked at the beach and swam from a small raft near the foot of Cedar (Burrard Street). Fishermen regularly staked nets in the Creek, as far east as Oak Street, through the Thirties.

(Left) Fire at the Hanbury Mill on the south shore of False Creek in 1915. The old 1909 Granville Bridge with its swingspan (identical to the 1912 Cambie Bridge) is visible at the left of the picture. A dredge can be seen in the middle of False Creek working on the job of filling the new Granville Island. Granville Island was created by some nifty patronage and contract padding, according to Mayor Louis Taylor. Two dredging contracts were let: one to dredge a shipping channel 300 feet wide and dispose of the soil in deep water; the other to fill the island. The two contracts were combined, effecting a neat profit. Granville Island, popularly known as Mud Island, paid no taxes to the city and made a regular $35,000 a year profit for the Federal Government, which had invested $300,000 in the scheme. The first industrial plant was that of the B.C. Equipment Co., which built on the island in 1917. The second was for Vulcan Ironworks. The 1914 Hotel Vancouver and the 1912 Vancouver Block dominated the skyline. The steeples of the Holy Rosary Cathedral rise to the right. Note the two coach-wheeled motorized firetrucks at the mill, the sheds for the greenchain and the ubiquitous beehive burner for sawdust. The mill was built on pilings. The edge of False Creek was a tidal swamp, stagnant with wood chips and rotting shavings. The last operating mill on the Creek was Bay Forest Products on Taylor Street in the shadow of the B.C. Place stadium.

(Right) The south side of Granville Island in 1934, at about the point where the modern footbridge crosses from Foundry Quay. The rather patchy, corrugated iron building to the right of the Spear and Jackson Saws Building is now the recreation building for the Granville Island community centre. Most of the buildings on Granville Island have retained their characteristic corrugated-iron facing and timber construction. Just above the rooflines on the left was the 1909 Granville bridge, built considerably closer to the ground than the modern 1954 structure. In the middle distance, directly above the SAWS sign, is the unfinished, unopened "new" Hotel Vancouver.

90

On July 4, 1960, a $2 million dollar blaze destroyed B.C. Forest Products' False Creek spruce division, and did extensive damage to Alberta Lumber Co. and Bingham Equipment. The fire was started by a short-circuit in a planer shed, and literally took off through the tinder-dry buildings and piles of lumber, jumping 50 feet at a time from building to building. Windows shattered from the heat, and the railroad tracks along Sixth Avenue were bent and twisted. Police fought sightseers in an enormous holiday traffic jam, while police and airforce boats on the Creek fought with pleasure craft which were hampering the city fireboat's efforts. B.C. Hydro crews cut power for the Fairview area. The entire fire department—450 men—fought the blaze for four hours before getting it under control. It was the first five-alarm fire in the city, comparable with the huge Pier D conflagration of 1938, and the million-dollar blaze on election night in June 1949, which destroyed the Excelsior Paper Stock Co. on False Creek. Two hundred and fifty men were put out of work by the blaze. The mills were never rebuilt, as the city saw an opportunity to clean up the Creek and develop a residential community along its shores. The large buildings on the skyline are, left to right: the City Hall, Fairmont Medical, the Vancouver General Hospital, and the domed King Edward High School at 12th and Oak, destroyed by fire in 1973.

Canadian Northern Railway

Attracted by the phenomenal success of the Canadian Pacific, other railways gained access to Vancouver in the early years of the century. Their legacy remains in the False Creek flats east of Main Street, which were filled during the Great War years to provide trackage and terminal land.

Interpersonal rivalry between CPR president Thomas Shaughnessy and the American Great Northern Railway president James Jerome Hill led the latter to seek a Vancouver terminus. The two railways had fought bitterly during the late 1880s and 1890s for the profitable metals trade in southeastern British Columbia. On November 27, 1891, the Great Northern reached the south shore of the Fraser at the little town of Brownsville, across the river from New Westminster, but was stymied there by the width and depth of the river, and the lack of political influence to gain an entry into Vancouver. In 1899, Hill hatched a scheme for a rail line to the booming Yukon, and instructed his Vancouver associate, John Hendry, to secure a charter to connect Vancouver with Dawson City. In 1901, the Vancouver, Westminster and Yukon Railway was established, with rights to build from Vancouver to New Westminster, where it was to connect with Hill's New Westminster Southern railway, a direct link with the Great Northern's continental system. The VW&YR's intention was to cross Burrard Inlet and establish terminal facilities on the north shore, then strike north via Squamish and the Chilcotin for the Yukon. As an alternative to the hated CPR, the railway received wide public support.

The most significant obstacle to Hill's entry into Vancouver— the Fraser River—was overcome in 1904 by a combined road and rail bridge, paid for by the provincial government. The Great Northern (in the guise of the VW&YR) trains entered Vancouver on a line north of the B.C. Electric's New Westminster interurban (later paralleled by the Burnaby Lake interurban), crossed False Creek on a trestle just west of Main Street, and terminated at a station at the corner of Columbia and East Pender. The rail yards stretched south from the station to the shore of False Creek.

Meanwhile, the City had gained from the Province, on November 23, 1900, title to the upper False Creek flats east of Main Street, with an eye on industrial development. In 1908, aldermen prepared a $2 million bylaw for filling the mud flats, then began negotiations with the Great Northern to use the land for a railway terminus. That agreement was signed on August 5, 1910. The Great Northern improved its line, between 1910 and 1913, by digging the Grandview Cut east of False Creek to Nanaimo Street to reduce the grade. In later years, when the Grandview Cut was used by the Canadian National, the climb out of False Creek was the steepest grade west of Winnipeg. The excavation spoil was dumped in the eastern end of the Creek.

Concurrently, the Canadian Northern Pacific Railway was snaking southward from the Yellowhead Pass to Vancouver. The Canadian Northern was the brainchild of promoters Alexander MacKenzie and Donald Mann (Port Mann), who had parlayed the 1896 purchase of a small Manitoba railroad into a national dream. The CN was the object of such public enthusiasm that it became the major plank in Premier Richard McBride's October, 1909 election campaign. The government agreed to guarantee the principal and four percent interest on the construction bonds of all CN lines in the province. (Three years later, McBride ran a similar, even more successful railway-based campaign, which resulted in the formation of the Pacific Great Eastern Railway—now B.C. Rail—and his complete monopoly of provincial politics. Only two socialist opposition members were elected.) The CN reached an agreement with the city to share the flats with the Great Northern, and announced plans to dig a $20 million tunnel from near the south foot of Boundary Road to False Creek.

The Canadian Northern first got into trouble in 1913, when the world economy staggered, and the railway had to request an enlargement of the provincial bond guarantee. Terminal facilities were simplified and, as the world financial crisis deepened, an agreement was hastily worked out with the Great Northern to use the latter's tracks into the city. The CN's last spike was driven in April, 1915, south of Ashcroft, and the first through train pulled into Vancouver on August 28. Wartime shortages and curtailment of Pacific traffic due to the European war zone stifled its hopes of success. It cashed in so many securities with the federal government (which had guaranteed much of the work east of British Columbia) that by 1917 it was effectively publicly-owned. The floundering Grand Trunk Pacific, which had built a transcontinental railway to a terminus in Prince Rupert (completed in 1914), was likewise taken over by the government and amalgamated with the CNPR into the Canadian National Railway.

The Great Northern, cramped in its Chinatown terminus, opened a station on Main Street in 1917. Twenty-five hundred piles to support the CN station were driven in March, 1917. The old Chinatown station became a restaurant, and was finally demolished after years as the "Marco Polo." The GN's False Creek trestle was pulled out after the Second World War.

The Canadian National's promises to the City of Vancouver, in return for which it was allowed entry into the city, were postponed for over ten years. The CN had originally pleged to build, in addition to the tunnel, a large downtown hotel. "Fighting Joe" Martin, during his January, 1915 mayoral campaign, scored political points on Mayor Baxter for handing over the False Creek flats deed to "Bill & Dan" for a "worthless" bond of $1½ million. Later, Mayor Louis Taylor agreed to a compromise put forward by CN President Sir Henry Thornton (the namesake of Thornton Park in front of the CN station), whereby the tunnel was abandoned in return for a 600 rather than a 500 room hotel. Work began on the new Canadian

James Jerome Hill, president of the Great Northern Railway, and the CPR's chief rival for control of trade through British Columbia.

Sir Donald Mann (1853-1934), with partner Alexander MacKenzie, created the Canadian Northern Railway in the decade before the First World War.

Sir Richard McBride (1870-1917), Conservative Premier, dominated British Columbia politics until 1915, when his policies were repudiated. He retired to London as the Province's agent general.

The eastern end of False Creek in the Twenties, looking east. False Creek east of Main Street was filled before the First War years for terminal space for the Great Northern and Canadian Northern (now Canadian National) Railways. The latter's terminal, built in 1917-19, is in the centre, flanked on its right by the GN terminal, built in 1915-17 and demolished in the Sixties. Thornton Park, with saplings, is visible in front of the CN station. The filling of False Creek eliminated the Main Street bascule bridge–first opened as a trestle on October 2, 1872. The trestle with the swingspan in the foreground led to the old Great Northern terminal, later the Marco Polo restaurant (demolished 1983), on Pender at Columbia. A sign on the Marco Polo building (left below) directed passengers on the Vancouver, Westminster & Yukon Railway (which connected with the Great Northern) from Pender Street to the trains.

National hotel at Georgia and Burrard on December 28, 1928.

Over the ensuing decades, passenger traffic declined to the point that, in 1962, the Great Northern abandoned its False Creek station. That station was demolished in 1965 to save taxes, after the City declined to accept it as a replacement for the Carnegie Library, which was then serving as the City Museum. The Great Northern continued to run a Vancouver-Seattle train service for nearly fifteen years. The Canadian National station became the only point of arrival and departure for train passengers in Vancouver, when all Canadian passenger trains were amalgamated under the VIA Rail banner in the mid-Seventies.

Connaught Bridge

The longest-surviving bridge across False Creek was opened in 1912 as the Connaught Bridge, though it was commonly known as the Cambie bridge. The Connaught bridge was identical to the 1909 Granville Street bridge, which predeceased it over thirty years ago.

The Connaught bridge was not the first one to cross False Creek at Cambie Street. Leamy's sawmill built a small skid bridge, not more than ten feet above high water, as wide as a horse crossways, and built entirely of wooden piles driven into the creek bottom, to connect its sawmill with the city. It opened in July, 1891, and cost the mill the princely sum of $12,000. It had a hand-cranked draw-span, which was opened about once a year to test the mechanism. There was little traffic more substantial than skiffs on the Creek at that time.

The City went on a bridge-building spree before the First World War, and approved a new Cambie Street bridge on July 8, 1908 (the contractor who won the tender, Armstrong and Morrison, was concurrently building a bascule span into the Main Street tram bridge). The new bridge opened on September 20, 1912, during the visit of Prince Arthur, who was Queen Victoria's third son and the Duke of Connaught, together with the Duchess and their daughter, Princess Patricia. The Duke had been appointed Canada's Governor General on October 13, 1911. The royal tour of the city passed under many arches, including the Lumbermen's Arch on Pender, and culminated in a civic welcome at the new Courthouse on Georgia Street. (The regiment at the Beatty Street Drill Hall, the Duke of Connaught's Own Rifles, was also named for the Duke. The "Princess Pat's Light Infantry" was named for the daughter.)

At 4:30 on the morning of April 29, 1915, a fire broke out on the centre span of the bridge, causing its collapse into False Creek and $70,000 damage. One man died fighting the fire. Another, fireman William Plumsteel, plunged seventy feet into the water when the span collapsed, but survived to become an assistant Chief. Simultaneously, a small fire broke out on the Granville Bridge. Sabotage was suspected, as the first battle of Ypres took place the week before, and anti-German feeling was rampant. The next day, there was a raid on a Point Grey home, and two German nationals were arrested. Nothing was ever proved. Fire officials concluded that the Granville bridge fire had been caused by a cigar butt, while the Connaught Bridge's oil-soaked timbers (from the increasing number of automobiles) had been touched off by sparks from a mill's beehive burner. On May 3, two more fires started on the Granville Bridge. One was definitely caused by a lighted cigarette, but the other remained a mystery, though a Kitsilano woman said she saw three men fleeing from beneath the bridge. Again, no sabotage charges were ever brought.

The new Cambie Street bridge opened in 1985.

The opening of the Connaught Bridge (commonly known as the Cambie bridge), in 1912, brought out a crowd of Vancouverites for a walk to Fairview from downtown. Straw boaters, cloth caps, bowlers and parasols protected both men and women from the possibility of an unfashionable suntan. After many mishaps, including collisions and alleged sabotage, the bridge was finally removed in 1984 and replaced by a modern structure. Right: the Duke of Connaught.

Granville Bridge

The steel crew on the Granville bridge drawspan worked for contractors Armstrong & Morrison. The balance of the bridge was wooden pilings driven into the silt. The bridge, built in 1909 and opened by Governor General Earl Grey, improved navigation on False Creek. The old wooden bridge which it replaced was so low that kids fished and swam from it during the summer. Six years after it opened, the southern side of the Creek under the bridge was filled to create Granville Island.

Alexander Morrison (left) of Armstrong & Morrison Co. Ltd., builders of False Creek bridges and the first Georgia Viaduct. He ran unsuccessfully for mayor against Louis Taylor in January, 1911. The firm, in 1899, built the first and only automobile in B.C., for use on the Cariboo Road as a stage. It was found to be unsuitable, so the engines were taken out and put into a launch. Morrison bought a steam-powered Locomobile in 1900, the first horseless carriage in Vancouver. His partner Robert Armstrong (1870-1946) owned a stone mansion at the southeast corner of Comox and Jervis. The 132-foot square property, with mansion, sold in 1940 for $8,750.

The Granville bridge was built, and the "mile-long peep-hole" called Granville Street opened, to provide a shorter route to the Fraser River than the old North Arm Road, Fraser Street. Granville Street south of False Creek was called Centre Street until the first Granville Street Traffic Bridge opened on January 4, 1889 (simultaneously, a bridge was built to Eburne across the Fraser River, page 184). At the time, the only clearing on the south side was around the Indian village of Snauq. The bridge was 2,400 feet long, wide enough for two wagons, and cost $16,000. There was a four-foot wide, separated pathway on the west side for pedestrians.

In 1891, the CPR cleared Fairview Slopes, subdivided it and attempted to sell the then remote lots. To spur development, a separate single-track trestle was built in September on the east side of the Granville bridge, and tracks were laid from the Davie Street terminus along Granville to 9th (Broadway), along 9th to Westminster (Main), and back to downtown—the "Fairview Belt Line." The Fairview subdivision collapsed, taking with it the Belt Line, in the depression of 1893-4, but when traffic built up again in the Klondike boom, the Granville bridge quickly became overloaded.

The bridge was barely above the water at high tide, and extended from Beach Avenue to Third Avenue. In 1908, the "high level" bridge was built from Fourth Avenue to Pacific Streets. It had a steel draw-span, and was built to withstand the weight of the heavy interurban cars which had been put on the Vancouver-to-Steveston line. An interurban terminus was built at the Third Avenue end of the bridge. The "high-level bridge" was opened on September 6, 1909, by His Excellency Earl Grey, the Governor-General who sponsored a football trophy for the best amateur team in the country. The bridge greatly aided the settlement of Kitsilano, and made commuting from Shaughnessy a feasible proposition. Its use was discontinued in February, 1954.

The modern Granville Bridge was a recommendation of the Town Planning Commission throughout the late Forties. A rush-hour traffic jam in November, 1945, caused by three small scows keeping both the Granville and Connaught bridges open, was the last straw for many commuters. The new Granville bridge is a fixed span, but high enough to permit all traffic to pass beneath it. Its cloverleafs demolished some of the last Yaletown housing, and the Athletic Park at 5th and Hemlock.

Yaletown

The Canadian Pacific Railway moved its western maintenance centre, complete with hard-drinking workers, houses and the odd family member, from the wild and woolly Fraser Canyon town of Yale to Vancouver in 1886. Yale had been described by Henry Cambie as "... a curiosity in the manner of vice flaunting itself ... along the main streets." The *Yale Sentinel* had boasted in 1884 that the town had more saloons per acre than any place in the world. Many of the Fraser Canyon construction workers followed the railway to Vancouver, some intent on perpetuating the excitement of their leisure time in Yale. The Chinese navvies came at the same time, but settled along Dupont Street (East Pender). The CPR's shops and maintenance yards were established, along with the new Roundhouse, on the north shore of False Creek at the foot of Drake Street. A few blocks west, at the south foot of Granville Street, the community of Yaletown sprung up. It was reputedly too far through the forest for Vancouver's regular police force, so quickly developed a reputation for rowdyness and lawlessness. The Yale Hotel, built in 1890 and originally called the Colonial, is the last remnant of the community's night life. It was a popular spot for travellers arriving, after a day's carriage ride, from Lulu Island and Steveston.

In addition to the railroad workers, Yaletown had a respectable, god-fearing enclave in the blocks of Hornby, Howe and Burrard around Pacific Avenue. This group looked westward to the infant West End, and many of them moved there in the late 1890s, taking the Yaletown Church with them. Most of the old Yaletown houses have vanished and been replaced with small factories and warehouses. Many of those that have survived around the corner of Hornby and Pacific have been converted into restaurants: for example, the 1888 home of paperhanger George Leslie, now Umberto's restaurant at 1380 Hornby, with an identical house on the back lane-end of the same lot, built ten years later for Leslie's married daughter. Other houses, like the Sheehan's on Seymour Street, were demolished during the construction of the exit ramps and cloverleafs for the 1954 Granville Bridge.

Yaletown, in modern terms, comprises the warehouse area along Homer, Hamilton and Mainland streets, abutting the old CPR False Creek yards, now B.C. Place and the Expo site. Mainland and Hamilton represent a unique warehousing area from the age before 18-wheel semi-trailers. The brick buildings have large iron awnings and railroad loading docks on the streets. Railroad sidings used to connect with the CPR yards, and freight cars shared the streets with automobiles until the early Eighties. The warehouses, since converted into lofts and studios, are popular with architects and designers. The streetscape has changed very little since the more mundane occupants—Sherwin Williams at 1128 Homer, Piggly Wiggly Foods at 1000 Hamilton, Empire Brass at 1038 Homer—clogged the streets with loading Ford and Dodge trucks,

and milk and coal went through the streets on drays. The old Blair-Behnsen printers' building on Cambie is now occupied by the retracting-roofed L'Orangerie restaurant. The Liquor Board warehouse at 871 Beatty, directly across the street from the B.C. Place plaza, probably awaits a similar fate.

Mainland Street, in the Yaletown warehouse district, looking north to Nelson Street in the late Twenties. The distinctive iron awnings and loading docks are still in use, although the rail sidings which, until recently, brought freight cars into the streets, have been abandoned. The land in the background on the extreme right was the CPR's Drake Street shops, roundhouse, and railyards, occupying most of the land on the north side of False Creek. The warehouses and streets in Yaletown have recently been converted into chic offices and studios.

The last true Yaletown house stood at 1371 Seymour Street, and was demolished in 1949 for the Seymour Street exit ramp from the Granville Bridge. When the CPR shops left Yale in 1886, and divisional headquarters moved to the foot of Drake Street, a number of workmen's houses were brought to Vancouver in sections on flatcars. The home of Dan Sheehan (on the left) at 1371 Seymour, was one of these. His first city tax assessment for the re-erected house on its 25-foot lot was $5.40. His daughter, Lottie, continued to live in the house until its demolition. Sheehan had built an ice house on Texas Lake, at Choate about seven miles south of Yale, to supply the CPR's passenger trains. When he moved to Vancouver, he established the Texas Lake Ice and Cold Storage Co. at 44 West Pender Street on the edge of Shanghai Alley. It was the first ice distribution firm in Vancouver, and had 174 customers–including the Hotel Vancouver–in 1892. Sheehan also had a plant on Front Street in New Westminster, which became the Cleeve Canning and Cold Storage Co. The Heckington House, next door at 1367 Seymour, was built for Daniel Macdougall, the operator of the Valley Dairy. The dairy was at 856 Howe Street, and its cows roamed quite freely through the vacant lots of the West End at the turn of the century. MacDougall's house was demolished and replaced with an auto parts plant when the area turned industrial.

Burrard Bridge

Snauq, the village at the foot of Burrard Street on the Kitsilano reservation, was the second-last inhabited Indian village in Vancouver. Another Indian community existed near Lumbermen's Arch in Stanley Park, but it was demolished after a smallpox epidemic in the late 1880s. The Musqueam band continues to live along the Fraser River at the south end of Camosun Street.

Snauq was well established before the HMS *Plumper* surveyed the English Bay area in 1859. In 1870, the year before Confederation, Governor Douglas established a 37.45-acre reserve around the village, bounded approximately by First Avenue, Chestnut and the Burrard Bridge right-of-way. Seven years later, the Joint Reserves Committee expanded it to include the Kitsilano Point area occupied today by the Vancouver Museum and Planetarium. In 1886, the CPR negotiated a right-of-way through the Reserve, and bandied about plans for a deep-sea terminal on Kitsilano Point, but nothing ever came of these.

Many Vancouverites, however, considered that the Reserve land was too valuable to be left alone. Their feelings were shared by the Provincial Government, which in May, 1901, formally asked the Indians to abandon the Reserve for another location. The Indians refused. But, as the government agent noted, "the government was determined to get the Reserve, by fair means or foul." The tribe, seeing the writing on the wall, exhumed their dead from the graveyard at First and Fir, and began moving to Squamish and the Capilano Reserve in North Vancouver.

In 1913, with the Reserve vacant, Sir Richard McBride's Provincial government began negotiating directly with 20 Indian heads of families, rather than with the band's legal representatives. A deal was struck for about $300,000. The Indians were assessed "costs" of over $80,000! A commission of $40,000 was given to one man. The balance of the money, some $219,750, was paid to representatives of the families who happened to still be on the site. These ne'er-do-wells lost their money, in the words of the Indian agent, "by violence and trickery." As the negotiated agreement was not endorsed by the majority of the band members, the Federal Government refused to recognize it, and the Provincial Government was severely criticized in the House of Commons on April 24, 1913.

Attempts to establish industry on the land continued. Mayor Louis Taylor sought to interest the Ford Motor Co. in a car assembly plant there. Alvo von Alvensleben promoted a scheme for wharves and a breakwater on the Point. T.D. Pattullo, then Provincial Minister of Lands, lobbied in favour of the 1916 A.D. Swan report, which called for a two million-bushel capacity grain elevator, four main shipping berths, and a lighthouse at the foot of Chestnut Street. H.H. Stevens suggested that it be "disposed to any bona fide concern, as a great terminal point for ocean steamship service, rail

CITY OF VANCOUVER ARCHIVES

WILLENA STONE

Burrard Street Bridge, Vancouver, B. C., Canada

AUTHOR'S COLLECTION

Left top: August Jack Khahtsalano and his wife Swanamia in their canoe near the foot of Chestnut Street on Kitsilano Point, about 1910. The land in the background was part of the Kitsilano Indian reservation, abandoned by the Squamish Indians before the First World War. Left below: during the Twenties, before the Burrard Bridge was built, families used the Indian Reservation beach as an alternative to the crowded West End and Kitsilano beaches. The photograph here, looking north-east, is taken near the modern Vancouver City Archives on Kitsilano Point. Above: Burrard Bridge, approved in the prosperous Twenties but opened in the grim Thirties, was a major link in the city's Town Plan, approved for the amalgamation of Vancouver with the Municipalities of Point Grey and South Vancouver. Old Cedar Street became Burrard Street south of False Creek.

service, warehousing, elevators and such like." During the early Twenties, unemployed returned soldiers were given $4 a day to clear its standing forest.

One of the recommendations of the Harland Bartholomew Town Plan of 1927, which was formulated in preparation for the city's amalgamation with Point Grey and South Vancouver, was the building of a Burrard Street bridge, and the upgrading of Cedar Street (Burrard) and Cornwall to funnel traffic through Kitsilano to Kerrisdale and the University. In January, 1929, plans were put forward by engineer Major J.R. Grant for a double-decked bridge costing $3,180,000, the lower deck of which was to replace the aging Kitsilano Trestle (demolished 1983), and carry trains and

trams. A financing formula involving governments and the CPR was mooted.

Construction began in 1930 on the piers and supports, though no agreement had been reached with the federal government and the railway. The city required eight acres of the Reserve for the south approach, so arbitration was arranged with the Squamish Indians, and three white commissioners were hired, at $50 a day, to negotiate a deal. Over the ensuing 28 days, the commissioners listened to a number of bogus delegations, prolonging the time to make a decision. The final award was for $44,966, out of which $28,854 was charged for costs of the arbitration. Future archivist J.S. Matthews, a friend of Chief Khahtsalano's, who sat in the gallery for much of the proceedings, wrote: "A more scandalous proceeding I have never seen."

The City had more difficulty securing rights to the property at the north end. Twenty-five parcels of land were disputed, and among the major settlements were $125,000 paid to Robertson & Hackett for the Canadian Wood and Coal Co. property, and $37,500 to the Brighouse Estate for the parcel at the northwest corner of Burrard and Beach. On October 31, 1931, W.J. Heaslip was compensated $23,000 for his expropriated property at the southeast corner of Pacific and Burrard.

By late 1931, work on the steel bridge span was well underway, when suddenly "a big financial problem" was discovered—the need to widen streets and buy buildings at the south end of Burrard Bridge. Cedar Street was a narrow two-lane road with tenements and houses built nearly to the road-line. Cornwall Street was, similarly, a mere back street. Cornwall Street owners asked for double the assessed value of their land as compensation. Council recommended 20 per cent over assessed value, and eventually the two sides compromised.

The bridge opened on Dominion Day, July 1, 1932, in the midst of protests by Ratepayers Associations about the cost of the planned "tea party" and celebration ($6,000 had been spent on airport opening ceremonies the previous year). The *Sun* commented that "its appearance will not please everybody, but there is a massiveness about it that is attractive," and suggested that "it gets its beauty from its rugged strength." On July 5, Woodward's displayed a 12-foot long Burrard Bridge cake, with sugar-coated light standards and a small, pastry Mayor Malkin. The first suicide from Vancouver's first tall bridge, was the manager of the foundering Vancouver Import Distributors, J.M. Bean, who dived to his death in October, 1933.

The Provincial Government had released all its interests in the Indian Reservation to the Federal government on February 27, 1928, for the sum of $350,000, although this wasn't paid out until 1947. On April 7, 1946, when the reserve was in use as an RCAF storage depot, the Squamish surrendered the rest of the Reserve to the Federal Government. The Indians eventually received $672,319 for this land.

G.A. Walkem

George Alexander Walkem

Looking southeast from the Cambie bridge on March 21, 1944, at the operations of West Coast Shipbuilders Ltd. The shipyard is in normal operation, with seven Liberty-type merchant vessels under construction. The yards were at First and Manitoba.

(Next page) The Eureka Grocery, now called the Arbutus Grocery, at the corner of 6th and Arbutus in Kitsilano. The store's square "boomtown front" faces onto 6th Avenue, which was the more important of the two streets at the time, as drays and Tin Lizzies had problems climbing the steep Arbutus hill. The garbage truck picked up its load on Arbutus Street, as there are no back lanes in the area, which is traversed by the Lulu Island interurban line a block east. The prosperity of the Twenties allowed even family men to own "flivvers" like the Chevy in front of the store. Soda pop and anything iced were all the rage. Few homes had refrigerators, and iceboxes were standard in most kitchens. The store was built in 1908 for Thomas F. Frazer, then run by a Mrs. Annie Stevenson until 1924, when Mrs. May Worrel took it over.

Many of the early industrial and shipbuilding firms on False Creek, including West Coast Shipbuilders and the Vancouver Iron Works, were founded and headed by George Alexander Walkem, a nephew of George Anthony Walkem, K.C. The latter Walkem was both the third and fifth Premier of British Columbia (the only Premier to have two separated terms), in 1874-6 and 1882-4.

George Alexander Walkem was born in Kingston, Ontario in 1872 and came to Vancouver in 1898. After service in Palestine and Egypt with the Royal Engineers during the Great War, he became a Point Grey Councillor in 1921-22, Point Grey Reeve in 1923-4, and MLA for Richmond-Point Grey in 1924-8 and Vancouver City in 1928-33. He died in December, 1946.

His younger brother, Richard Knox Walkem, Q.C. (1880-1962) was an expert corporate lawyer who was better-known as a sportsman. He came to Vancouver in 1902 with a record from Queen's university as a good track, rugby and hockey athlete. His business activities included the management of West Coast Shipbuilding and a directorship of the *Vancouver Sun*. He was a charter and life member of Shaughnessy Golf club, and a respected amateur golfer.

George Alexander Walkem's stepson, James Charles Byrn (1901-1966), became the chief engineer for the Port of Vancouver after a distinguished wartime career. He served with the Royal Canadian Engineers as Lieutenant Colonel and earned a C.B.E. for rescuing survivors of the Arnhem parachute jump. He was second in command of the 1941 Spitzbergen commando raid.

Walkem's stepdaughter Margaret married Ray Bicknell (1899-1985), whose father had come to Vancouver in 1887 and farmed on Lulu Island west of Brighouse's property. Bicknell started in the shipyard and towing business with his father-in-law in 1928, eventually selling Gulf of Georgia Towing Co. to his nephew Jimmy Byrn in 1970. The False Creek Industries buildings at 860 Beach Avenue were demolished in 1985.

Residential Areas

Blueblood Alley

The 1980s label for the downtown part of East Hastings Street might well be "sleazy" and that for West Hastings Street "commercially prestigious." Yet in the 1880s East Hastings was a major business street for Vancouver, and West Hastings was where all the Canadian Pacific railway executives and business elite lived.

In by-passing Port Moody for the railway's terminus and thus avoiding competition with the established landholders there, General Manager William Van Horne still had to contend with the fact that the community of Granville was largely in private hands. So the CPR established its operations west of the old townsite at the foot of Granville, installed its executives in homes on the bluff above Burrard Inlet, and built the Hotel Vancouver "way out in the bush" at the corner of Georgia and Granville. The rest of the city was dragged west with the railway.

The first inhabitants of the West Hastings area were less posh. The Three Greenhorns built their cabin in early 1863 near the coal seam at the foot of Bute Street, on the site of the plaza of the Guinness Tower at 1055 West Hastings. Eighteen years later, Victoria-resident Joseph Spratt built Spratt's Oilery, the source for dogfish-oil for log skids and the biggest herring saltery on the Lower Mainland, on the bluff just west of Burrard Street. During the latter years of the 19th century, Hastings Street west of Burrard was known officially as Seaton Street, and popularly as Blueblood Alley. Mansions lined the street. One of the first was built at the corner of Hornby and Hastings in 1887 for Henry Abbott, the General Manager of the railway's Pacific Division. J. M Lefevre, the CPR's resident physician, had a turreted home on the large property at the northwest corner of Hastings and Granville (the site of the "old" Post Office). A. St. George Hamersley, the city's first solicitor, lived on Seaton Street just west of Burrard. F.C. Wade, later the province's first Agent General in London, occupied a rambling English country home at 1125 Seaton. John P. Nicolls, Esq., of the pioneer real estate firm MacAuley and Nicolls, was at 1158 Seaton Street. Although there was no basement and they drew their water from a well, he had an unobstructed view of the mountains. A.G. Ferguson, the CPR civil engineer and contractor who was the first chairman of the Parks Board (1888), built a residence

Vancouver Club, Vancouver, B. C.

at 837 West Hastings—the site of today's Terminal City Club. The stable for his fine horses, which he used when inspecting the city's park system (then Stanley Park), was a separate building closer to the street. Col. T.O. Townley, the mayor of Vancouver in 1901, owned a large home at the southeast corner of Hastings and Burrard, with a glazed conservatory leading onto a side garden. Other neighbours included Henry, Duncan and Richard Bell-Irving, and the famed barrister E.P. Davis.

Life in "Blueblood Alley" was very gracious. Eligible girls—as was later the case in the West End and Shaughnessy—held regular "at homes." Carriages brought gowned and hatted ladies along Seaton Street for afternoon teas. Young men, when not taking exercise at the first Vancouver Rowing Club at the foot of Bute

Above left: The original Vancouver Club, at Hastings and Hornby, was located within walking distance of the homes of its members. Established in 1891, this clubhouse had a ballroom (the building on the left), which was demolished in 1913 for the new, Edwardian club building which survives today. The old building operated as a war veteran's club for several years, and was demolished during the Twenties. Next door, on the east side, between the Club and Henry Abbott's home, was the home of Charles Trott Dunbar, a prominent real-estate associate of Ceperley, Rand, Calland and the other big operators of the 1890s. From his office in the Empire Building, at Seymour and Hastings, he managed a Liberal-backed (with F.C. Wade) real-estate and railroad business, including the aborted Port Moody, Indian River & Northern Railway, which cleared a few miles of right-of-way north of Port Moody in May, 1910, with the intention of completing an electric line to Pemberton Meadows. Dunbar made a fortune selling Dunbar Heights lots, which he reported were "selling like hotcakes" in October, 1906. Above: the residence of Thomas O. Townley (1862-1935) at the southeast corner of Burrard and Hastings, in the mid-1890s. Townley was born in Newmarket, Ontario, called to the bar in Manitoba at age 24, and came to Vancouver in 1889. He was soon thereafter appointed Registrar of Land Titles for the District of New Westminster, a position he also held for Vancouver from 1901-1910. In 1901, he was elected Mayor of Vancouver, and was the Lieutenant Colonel of Vancouver's first military unit. Note the wooden sidewalk. The boulevard trees are mountain ash, one of the few native deciduous trees available to early Vancouverites (the other common one, equally unsuitable because of the huge size it attained, was the vine maple). The posts and chains were intended to keep horses from trampling the boulevard grass and munching the foliage.

Street, played tennis or rode about in the mud on the new safety bicycles, dressed in striped blazers, white flannels and straw boaters.

As all of its prospective members of suitable wealth and prestige lived within a few blocks, the Vancouver Club was strategically established in 1891 at the corner of Hastings and Hornby. The original building was in use as a club until the current, Georgian-style edifice a half block to the west superseded it in 1914. The area still retains its strong associations with Blueblood Alley times: apart from the Vancouver Club at 915 West Hastings, there is the Terminal City Club at 837, and the University Club in a Renaissance-style 1929 building (formerly the Quadra Club's) slightly to the west of the Marine Building at 1021 West Hastings.

Until 1908, Granville Street was a firm dividing line between commercial-retail Vancouver and Blueblood Alley. Cannery owner R.V. Winch led the move west of Granville with the first-class Winch building at 739 West Hastings. It was quickly followed by a forest of office buildings, including the Metropolitan Building two years later, on the site of A.G. Ferguson's old home. The exodus of the well-to-do to the south slope of the West End had started at the turn of the century, when B.T. Rogers moved to his stately Gabriola on Davie Street. By 1910, Seaton Street was no longer a fashionable address. Most of the homes were converted into rooming houses and survived in a rather shabby backwater of the city's business district until after the Second World War. The opening of the Marine Building just before the Depression lent prestige to the businesses in the area, but it took the catalyst of both the Great Depression and the Second World War to effect any real change. Some of Vancouver's first apartment buildings were built in the area before the First World War, a good example being the Banff Apartments at Georgia and Bute, which was very elegant in its time, but symbolized, nevertheless, the changing residential nature of the area.

The former Seaton Street is today a canyon of high-rise office towers which have almost obliterated any view of the harbour and North Shore mountains from street level. The Guinness Co. (which partly owned the Marine Building, and financed the Lions Gate Bridge project), built the first of them in 1967, a green glass and enamel slab at 1055 West Hastings. It has been superseded in scale by huge developments like the Oceanic Plaza (also Guinness money, at a British-sounding 1066 West Hastings). From the plaza of the Guinness Tower, it is possible to see the north portal of the 1932 Dunsmuir Tunnel, which connects the Burrard Inlet railway yards with False Creek—now the route of the Vancouver rapid transit system.

The last remaining Blueblood Alley house is the second Henry Abbott home at the corner of Jervis and Georgia. Abbott moved there in 1898, having sold his former mansion to Richard Marpole.

The Three Greenhorns

The Three Greenhorns are normally associated with the West End (Morton Street at English Bay is named for John Morton, and the namesake restaurant is in the Denman Hotel), rather than with the Blueblood Alley area on Burrard Inlet. Nevertheless, their cabin was built on the bluff above Coal Harbour—at about the modern site of the Guinness Tower at the foot of Bute Street—because of the discovery there in 1859 of coal and clay by the naval survey ship HMS *Plumper*.

John Morton was a Yorkshire potter, born in Huddersfield in April, 1834. With his brother-in-law Samuel Brighouse and a friend William Hailstone, he sailed on the maiden voyage of the *Great Eastern* (later the ship which laid the first transatlantic telegraph cable) to New York in early 1862. The trio then travelled to Victoria via Panama and a burro ride across the Isthmus. They visited the Cariboo, but found the promising creeks all staked, so returned to New Westminster. One day, so the story goes, Morton was walking past a shoemaker's shop on Columbia Avenue and spied a lump of coal in the window (the other story is that he saw it in an Indian's basket). He found the "Siwash" who had brought the coal into the shop, and paid the man to take him to the spot on Burrard Inlet. Intrigued by the possibilities of making bricks, Morton convinced his two companions to settle on the spot. The three, on November 3, 1862, pre-empted the 550 acre parcel of land which was to become the West End, between Burrard Street, Stanley Park, English Bay and Burrard Inlet. They paid four shillings tuppence an acre, a total of $555.75. The pre-emption became known as the Brickmakers' Claim; it attracted attention due to its remoteness, and the "Three Greenhorns" were, according to New Westminster and Victoria pundits, doomed to failure. True to these predictions, the three made no money and fought over the value of the land. David Oppenheimer, Israel Powell, and C.P. Rand, under the banner of the Vancouver Improvement Company, bought an interest in the property, renamed it the City of Liverpool and, on March 15, 1882, registered a plan for subdividing the northeast part. It was a failure. In 1884, they were persuaded by the CPR and the provincial land commissioner to give up one-third of their holdings to the railway, as part of the inducement to extend the railway past Port Moody. Morton, who thought the CPR would have to extend to Granville anyway and resisted the land giveaway, quit the area that year and built a ranch at Mission Junction. Brighouse soon left too, and bought land on Lulu Island, near the Richmond end of today's Dinsmore Bridge (a row of poplars marks his front lawn; the home burned down in a Richmond fire department "fire drill" several years ago). Hailstone considered himself cheated by his two friends, and left the city. It took the power and

William Hailstone, Samuel Brighouse and John Morton

prestige of the Canadian Pacific Railway to develop the City of Liverpool area in the late 1880s. Morton returned to the city in his declining years, and died in 1912 in his little cottage at 1947 Pendrell.

F.C. Wade

Frederick Coates Wade, the president of the Liberal-backed Burrard Publishing Co., which published "the official organ of the Liberal Party," the Vancouver Sun.

The F.C. Wade home at 1125 Seaton was a social centre for the Blueblood Alley district during the first decade of the century. It was one of the last of the old mansions west of the Marine Building to survive the march of progress, being demolished in September 1953, to make way for a parking lot.

The house was built at the end of the century for Col. and Mrs. T.O. Townley. It was purchased in 1904 by Frederick Coates Wade, a prominent Liberal with good connections in the United States. Wade, born in Ontario in 1860, had handled the Legare claim against the U.S. Department of Justice for compensation following Sitting Bull's surrender in 1887. In the late 1890s, he acted as legal advisor to the Yukon Council, and in 1903 prepared the Canadian case for the Alaska Boundary "panhandle" tribunal. He enjoyed his time in Vancouver, completed the upstairs of the home, and was particularly proud of his large library, decorated with William Morris art-nouveau wallpaper. The garden had privet hedges and

flowering lilac, laburnum and may. At the side of the house was a croquet lawn, frequented by local girls in white tennis frocks with leg-o'-mutton sleeves. Young men descended a small path down the steep bluff and across the CPR track, to a rocky beach to swim.

Regular guests included poet Rupert Brooke, who died so gallantly in the Great War; surveyor, explorer and incendiary pamphleteer Walter Moberly; the famed Canadian baritone Charles G.P. Roberts; and, American jurist Ben Lindsay, who advised on the founding of Wade's favorite service interest—the Juvenile Court. Mary Capilano, wife of the Indian chief, made the Wade home a port of call when she paddled across the inlet in her canoe. In the spirit of the times, the Wades kept a special chair for her in the garden.

The Wade's home ended its days as a rooming house, divided into many small suites. Its site is now occupied by the Holiday Inn.

The Marine Building

The most prominent legacy of Vancouver's prosperity during the Twenties is the Marine Building at the northwest corner of Burrard and Hastings. It was the first really "modern" skyscraper in Vancouver, and is probably the best example of Art Deco—*Les Arts Décoratifs* from the Paris design show of 1925—left in Canada. The building's shape, with white-crested peaks high on the sides, was described as "some great crag rising from the sea, clinging with sea flora and fauna, tinted in sea-green, touched with gold;" the carved decoration, depicting everything from amoebae and gargoyles to dirigibles and locomotives, is a mini-history in terracotta of human evolution; the entrance portal with its dramatic "deco" sunburst and brass doors is the most imposing of any building in Vancouver.

On March 14, 1929, Mayor W.H. Malkin blew a golden whistle to start construction, four days after the G.A. Stimson Co. had formally presented the plans to the public. Those were heady days: the Marine Building was "to pull the business district to it" and clean up the remains of shabby Seaton Street. The building rose 349 feet high—nearly 25 storeys—and ended up costing nearly $2,500,000. Two huge boilers in the basement consumed up to 400 gallons of fuel oil each day. During the war, due to rationing, they were converted to coal, and then reconverted to oil in 1946. City water pressure only reached to the tenth floor, so a battery of pumps hoisted the water to a tank above the penthouse, which then gravity-fed the rest of the building.

G.A. Stimson went bankrupt shortly after the Marine Building opened. Attempts were made to sell the building to the City for $1 million—the city administration had been holed up in the Holden Building at 16 East Hastings since 1929, while squabbles continued on a location for a new City Hall. The City balked. In January, 1932, a lien by Winnipegger James A. Richardson for $248,820 was discharged, opening the way for a sale. English liquor money was rumoured to be interested. Late that year an option to purchase the building was taken by British Pacific Properties Ltd., the firm headed by Vancouverite A.J.T. Taylor and Londoner John Anderson. The next July, the option was exercised, for a reported $900,000, in "another substantial demonstration of [BPP's] faith in the future of Vancouver."

A.J.T. Taylor moved into the unfinished loft of the Marine Building while his estate at Kew Beach was being built. As the elevators only ran to the 18th floor, he had to climb a staircase the rest of the way to his newly-decorated offices, a bedroom and kitchen. Mrs. Taylor disliked sleeping so far off the ground, as did the subsequent purchaser—a woman named Mrs. Smith who moved out after the shelling of Point Estevan lighthouse in 1942,

A.J.T. Taylor

A.J.T. Taylor was the President of British Pacific Properties Co., the firm that brought millions of pounds of British capital to Vancouver, changed the face of West Hastings Street, built the Lions Gate Bridge, developed exclusive West Vancouver and once and for all changed the way the city worked, slept and moved around.

Born in Victoria in 1887, A.J.T. Taylor started work at age 14 as an apprentice in a Nanaimo machine shop. He earned $5 a month, and supplemented his income by running a boarding house. When he moved to Vancouver, he ran another boarding house across the street from the Marine Building site while he studied for his Professional Engineering Degree. (Years later, when he lived in the penthouse of the Marine Building, he told a BBC radio audience that he could "truly claim to have risen 400 feet in the world.") In 1912, he founded Taylor Engineering Co., and spent the war years and the early Twenties building projects which included an Imperial Oil Co. townsite and the picturesque Dolly Varden Railway at Kitsault in northern B.C.

In 1926, Taylor went to England, where he became managing director of Underfeed Stoker Co. Ltd.—a large engineering manufacturer. While there, he got the idea of interesting British capital in the potential of Vancouver. He developed plans for a bridge across First Narrows and an exclusive residential suburb high on the North Shore mountains. Having interested British financiers, he formed British Pacific Properties Ltd. He was considered quite daft by Vancouverites, who sneered at every aspect of the project—the road through Stanley Park, the fact that the bridge went "from nowhere to nowhere," the cost of British Properties land and the restrictions placed on purchasers. Taylor replied that London, "the lighthouse and watchtower of the world . . . looks to British Columbia as the last great empire for adventure."

Taylor moved back to Vancouver in 1937, when the first 600-acre development (of the 4,000 the company owned) and the Lions Gate Bridge were underway. He lived in the penthouse of the Marine Building (another purchase by British Pacific Properties Ltd.) while his Kew House at Kew Beach was being built. The mansion, on a 27-acre estate west of Caulfeild (now 5324 Marine Drive), is situated on a rock bluff in total seclusion, with a panoramic view over the straits and islands to the west. The home was later bought by Garfield Weston. The size of the estate has since been substantially reduced; the house was severely damaged by fire in 1964 but was restored.

Taylor left Vancouver in 1939 to return to England for a position with the British Ministry of Aircraft Production. He had intended to return to Kew House after the war, but died on July 20, 1945 while in the United States on a business trip.

A.J.T. Taylor

The Marine Building, framed at the western end of Hastings Street, in the Thirties. Its strategic site at the eastern end of old Seaton Street resulted from a difference in the surveys by the CPR and the Vancouver Improvement Co.'s City of Liverpool. Joseph Spratt, of Spratt's Oilery, bought one of the City of Liverpool lots on the edge of John Morton's old homestead, so Hastings (formerly Seaton Street) was jogged to the south to fit around it. In the picture, on the right, Spencer's Department store is visible, as is the Royal Bank skyscraper at Hastings and Granville. The large building on the left is the Standard Building, a fine pre-World War I office tower at 510 West Hastings.

because she was afraid that the Marine Building would be the first target of a Japanese bombing raid. Taylor bought it back and used it as an entertainment studio for his young daughters and their friends. Taylor sold it to British "Biscuit King" Garfield Weston, from whom the Spencer family acquired it after they sold out to Eaton's.

Vancouverites got their first "towering inferno" in November, 1954, when a $50,000 fire took out the elevators and wrecked the offices on four floors. Firemen were initially stymied by the height and constricted stairways, but hauled the firehoses up the outside of the building and eventually doused the blaze. The next day, only one secretary—21 year old Shirley Stanley—climbed all the way to the Penthouse to go to work. "538 Steps and 10,000 Puffs," said the newspapers.

Albert Cadman, the Londoner who was the building's superintendent when it opened, and who spent the rest of his life there, once fell down an elevator shaft after a hasty step through opened doors. A draughting clerk from one of the offices was sent down the side of the shaft with a glass of brandy, while everyone awaited the arrival of a proper rescue crew. The clerk took one look at the battered and bloody Cadman, drank the brandy himself and fainted. In another incident in 1945, Cadman saw a fire starting on a ship in the harbour. He went to tell the elevator operator and, while he was away from his window, the ship, the *Greenhill Park*, blew up, knocking out his windows and scattering shards of glass through his office.

The building has been as lucky as its superintendent. The initial investment proved sound, and many of the original tenants, including the firm of architects who designed it, stayed with it through the decades. It has retained its prestige, though surrounded by many newer, fancier buildings.

A. St. George Hamersley

One Seaton Street resident who distinguished himself in more than one respect was A. St. George Hamersley, "a tall and austere gentleman, prone to wear the English tweed cap with fore and aft peak and a handlebar moustache."

Hamersley was born in 1850 to a prominent Oxfordshire family. Educated at Marlborough, he was captain of the English rugby football team in 1874. As a young man, he moved to the south island of New Zealand, and is credited with introducing rugby there. He was called to the bar, and later made a Lieutenant Colonel for his activities against the natives in the islands' Maori wars of the 1870s and 1880s. While there he met and married Miss Isabella Maud Snow of Wellington. (They had three sons and two daughters; she died on the family estate in Oxfordshire in 1955, at the extraordinary age of 102.)

The Hamersleys came to Vancouver in 1888, where St. George became a legal advisor to the CPR and the city's first solicitor. He was appointed first president of the B.C. Rugby union at its founding in 1889. He kept Rudyard Kipling waiting outside his office for a couple of hours when the English writer was attempting to purchase a town lot.

His reserve hid a very sharp tongue, as Mayor Fred Buscombe discovered. The Mayor owned Skinner's, a store which sold household furnishing and plumbing contraptions in the days before modern toilets were installed inside the house. During a Council meeting in 1904, he unwisely chose to berate the City Solicitor. Hamersley drew himself up, announced that he would not be criticized by "a mere purveyor of chamber pots" and strode out of the Council chambers.

Shortly thereafter, Hamersley lost interest in Vancouver municipal affairs. He briefly tried hop farming in an area around Agassiz long known as Hamersley Prairie. In 1905, he bought District Lot 274 in North Vancouver, the lower Lonsdale area owned by London financier Arthur Heywood Lonsdale, who had held the mortgage, and foreclosed on, Moodyville in the 1880s. Hamersley subdivided the land and managed to attract some settlers to open the district up (the second North Vancouver municipal ferry was named St. George in his memory). He built a house on Second Street between St. Patrick and St. David, but had scarcely moved in when he decided to return to England.

In 1906, Hamersley left Vancouver and, according to his obituary, "will be remembered by County folk principally for the way in which he managed to restore the old mid-Oxfordshire District to Conservatism in the general election of 1910." He served as an MP until 1918, when he retired due to ill-health. He died in February, 1929.

His son, known to everyone as "Tommy" during his boyhood in Vancouver (b. 1892), went to Sandhurst and served in the King's Shropshire Light Infantry in campaigns in Macedonia, France,

Colonel Alfred St. George Hamersley, K.C. The sign on his office door said: "Out on Business." Business was the name of his horse.

India and against the Bolsheviks in southern Russia in 1919. He then joined the Egyptian camel corps and rose through the colonial administration to become governor of Sinai, Egypt in 1936. As El Miralai Major A.H. St. George Hamersley Bey, he was the last British Pasha in Egypt.

Daughter Constance Hamersley was a well-known English academy painter, and during her youth painted many attractive scenes of the Vancouver waterfront.

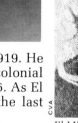

El Miralai St. George Hamersley Bey, known to his Vancouver boyhood friends as "Tommy."

The West End

St. Paul's Hospital, Vancouver, B.C.

A RESIDENTIAL SECTION OF VANCOUVER, B.C.

Vancouver's skyline owes as much to the solid phalanx of apartment buildings in the West End as to the cluster of office towers downtown. The profile of the West End, particularly the English Bay side, bears a distinct resemblance to Waikiki, Miami or Rio: a sweep of sand, a strip of green park and a wall of highrises. Its eastern boundary, Burrard Street, now forms the western boundary of Vancouver's business district. Until the Fifties, much of the Vancouver "downtown" southeast of Georgia and Burrard was also residential, with houses and families and little stores indistinguishable from the West End. The West End is the original Brickmakers' Claim, the 550 acres pre-empted by the "Three Greenhorns"—Morton, Brighouse and Hailstone—in 1862.

By 1890, civilization had extended west of Burrard Street along Haro and Barclay into the West End. Families moved into the area, against the advice of those who insisted that Haro Street was too far from the centre of town. William Shannon, the pioneer dairy farmer of the area around 57th and Granville, built a house at 1108 Haro. Fred Cope, Vancouver's third mayor, built an attractive turreted residence next door, where he lived until bitten by the gold bug (he drowned in a creek on the Skagway Trail in 1897). A public school was established at the corner of Burrard and Barclay in 1892, known as the West End school to distinguish it from the East End school (Strathcona) and the Central School downtown. It was later called the Aberdeen School, and survived as part of the Dawson complex (between Helmcken and Nelson on Burrard) until its demolition in the 1970s to allow for expansion of the B.C. Hydro head office building. Established families sent their daughters to the private Granville School at 1175 Haro, which was conducted by the Demoiselles Kern and later had as its patron the B.C. Lieutenant-Governor, Henri Joly de Lotbinière. The school's motto was "Rien sans Peine" and, like Crofton House School, established two years later in 1898 on Jervis Street, cultivated the virtues of hard work and devotion to duty in the young ladies.

John Moore Bowell, the son of Prime Minister Mackenzie Bowell and the father of prominent local car dealer Mack Bowell of Bowell MacLean, paid $500 in 1890 for the 66' x 132' lot at 1207 Haro; the next year, he paid $750 for the corner lot and built a large, airy residence with an encircling porch, straddling the properties.

Top: St. Paul's Hospital was erected in 1894 by the Catholic Church, "way out in the bush" at the end of the Burrard Street trail. At the time, Burrard Street ended there, but a pathway extended southwest to English Bay, and a rutted wagon trail connected with Yaletown. Below: the extremely fashionable corner of Davie and Nicola in the West End in 1907, coyly described as "a residential section," looking northeast at wholesale grocer Robert Kelly's mansion on the corner. The lawn on the left belongs to B.T. Rogers' Gabriola estate, now restored as the Mansion restaurant.

John Hendry

Left: the John Hendry house, at 1201 Burnaby Street.

John Hendry

Mrs. Adaline Hendry

The Hendry House apartment at Burnaby and Jervis commemorates the site of a Vancouver home of John Hendry—"a man of tremendous vision" who created the B.C. Mills, Timber and Trading Co., the first large lumber conglomerate in British Columbia. (Although the home at 3802 Angus Drive in Shaughnessy is normally called the John Hendry house, Hendry only lived there for a year before his death. It was built for J.E. Tucker, a Texan who came to Vancouver in 1904 and bought the Vancouver Lumber Co.) Hendry's residence on fashionable Burnaby Street was built in 1903 (demolished 1968). It featured a grand curving staircase, mahogany and oak panelling, inlaid floors and a glass-roofed conservatory.

Hendry was born on January 20, 1843 in New Brunswick. He arrived in B.C. in September, 1872, worked at sawmills in the Puget Sound area, and rebuilt Sewell Moody's Moodyville sawmill after it was destroyed by fire. In 1876, he became partners with David McNair in a sash and door factory in Nanaimo. They moved to New Westminster in 1878 and opened the Royal City Planing Mills, with Hendry as President and General Manager. Within a dozen years, he had absorbed the Hastings Mill and Moodyville and built another Royal City Planing Mill at the south foot of Carrall on False Creek. In total, he was employing about 2,000 men by 1890. To supply power for the expanding industrial base of the city, Hendry promoted the Stave Lake Power Co., one of the first modern generating plants in the Vancouver area. He was the Vancouver representative of the Great Northern Railway, and in 1899 secured a charter for the Vancouver, Westminster and Yukon Railway, which was to have connected Vancouver with Dawson, but only got as far as New Westminster.

Hendry married Adaline McMillan, a Pictou girl born in 1862 who came to Victoria at age 10. After Hendry's death in July, 1916, she moved to the house at 3851 Pine Crescent, later occupied by her daughter—the widow of Eric Hamber. The home was notable for its large aviary. Mrs. Hendry died in May, 1946.

W.F. Salsbury

Harwood Street, Vancouver, B.C.

Harwood and Burnaby Streets, on the south slope of the West End facing English Bay, attracted Vancouver's elite in the first decade of the century. Men like John Hendry, W.F. Salsbury, and George Coleman built large houses on huge, manicured estates. The handwritten note on the back of this postcard, evidently sent to a friend in England by a prosperous new Vancouverite, read: "You may think the people here are all heathens and live in log huts. There are a lot of both here, but also a few thousand houses. This shows a few in the west end where I live amongst the upper crust. You may think 'how's it done' well 'wait and see.' I have got most of the flies knocked off since I left Bristol."

William Ferriman Salsbury

One neighbour of John Hendry's on Burnaby Street at the turn of the century was William Ferriman Salsbury, the Treasurer of the Pacific Division of the CPR. His home at 1340 Burnaby commanded an unobstructed view of English Bay. He, along with Hendry and neighbour George Coleman (of Evans, Coleman and Evans), made the Sunset Beach slope the place to live in the first decade of the century; all of them moved to Shaughnessy around the time of the First World War, Salsbury to the house at 1790 Angus, which cost him $25,000 to build.

Salsbury was born on February 16, 1847 in Surrey, England and began his railroading career as a boy working in the Brighton ticket office. He came to Canada in 1870 and became the assistant treasurer to the Grand Trunk railway, then joined the CPR in 1881 as an accountant. As the railway neared completion, he was promoted to Treasurer of the Pacific Division, and arrived in Vancouver on the first through train in July, 1886. Until his retirement in 1921, he was secretary of the Esquimalt and Nanaimo railway and a vice-president of the Columbia and Kootenay railway.

Salsbury's conduct reflected the civic-mindedness and largesse of the CPR in the early Vancouver years. The treasurer and his chequebook could always be counted on to promote the city, its recreational facilities and institutions. He helped to finance the Brockton Point Athletic Grounds and used his influence to secure the Stanley Park lease. He was a charter member of the Vancouver General Hospital Corporation in 1901, helped establish Christ Church, and was one of the founders of the Vancouver Club. His business activities included the New Westminster and Burrard Inlet Telephone Co. (The B.C. Telephone Co. had secured a provincial charter in February, 1884, for a line connecting Port Moody to New Westminster; the New Westminster & Burrard Inlet Co. obtained a charter to run a line from New Westminster to Vancouver. In 1904, the directors amalgamated the five telephone companies in the province, and by 1912 there were 35 exchanges and 30,000 subscribers in B.C.)

After his retirement, he became well-known as a gardener, producing record onions and squash on his 10-acre estate at Gordon Head in Victoria. His retirement and removal to Victoria were perhaps precipitated by the brutal murder on April 12, 1921 of his son Bill (page 214). Salsbury died in January, 1938, in his ninety-first year.

Dal Grauer & The B.C. Electric

Dr. Dal Grauer, and his bride Shirley (Woodward), leaving on their honeymoon world cruise during the Thirties. (Preceding page) The most dramatic change in Vancouver since the Depression occurred in 1957, when the B.C. Electric Railway Co. abandoned its decaying Hastings and Carrall head office (page 28) for a gleaming glass and porcelain tower on the edge of the West End. Its tower was built several blocks to the southwest of the established downtown, in an area of crumbling rooming houses, across the street from the West End's two biggest churches. The painting shows the view from the lane between Howe and Hornby street, now the site of the Law Courts building. No single event during that decade showed better the determination of the B.C. Electric, and the progressive industrialists of Vancouver, to modernize the city. Like the Marine Building nearly thirty years before, the B.C. Electric building pulled the city's business district toward it.

"One of tomorrow's tall buildings," said the promotional brochure on March 28, 1957, "is the new B.C. Electric Head Office structure. During its construction, many people have been intrigued by its unique shape. This is no architectural whim. The unusual appearance is functional. The handsome exterior is a happy product of efficient use of space and the latest techniques in skyscraper construction using modern materials."

Not only was the design of the building revolutionary, its location, far to the southwest of the established Vancouver business district in an area of crumbling rooming houses, was a dramatic statement of the power and position of the B.C. Electric Company and its dynamic President, A.E. "Dal" Grauer. The building, soaring 285 feet above the corner of Burrard and Nelson, featured pre-fabricated porcelain-enamelled steel panels and 50,000 square feet of double-paned glass. The first ground had been cleared in October, 1955 and construction was completed in a record eighteen months. The opening ceremony main program was held in the ballroom of the Hotel Vancouver, with a menu of "Fresh Shrimp Cocktail Ravigote, Consommé au Sherry, Filet Mignon Bearnaise, and Baked Alaska (B.C.E.)." Newspapers editorialized that "few companies were lower in the public's esteem (than the B.C. Electric was) when Grauer took over in 1946." The president had the best office view in the city from "Grauer's Power Tower," a far cry from the slummy surroundings of the company's old head office at Carrall and Hastings.

Dal Grauer was one of Vancouver's golden boys during the Thirties, Forties and Fifties, a "most brilliant young executive" who had a profound effect on the industrial and social development of the province. He was the last president of the B.C. Electric Railway Co.

He was born in 1906 to Jacob and Marie Grauer, farmers on Sea Island who grew potatoes, raised beef and dairy cattle and ran Grauer's Store. Their son Albert Edward got his nickname from "le livre d'Albert" when he was a schoolboy. He was a bright student who graduated early from King Edward High, attended UBC, became Rhodes Scholar for B.C. in 1927, got a Ph.D. in economics at the University of California, and studied law at Oxford. He became, while still in his twenties, the director of the Department of Social Sciences at the University of Toronto. As well, he was an excellent athlete and a member of the Canadian Olympic lacrosse team in Amsterdam in 1928. In 1933, he married Shirley Woodward, the daughter of grain elevator owner Ernest Woodward. He tired quickly of the academic life and in 1939 accepted an offer from the Montreal-based Power Corporation to become general secretary of the B.C. Electric Railway Co. In 1946, after a meteoric

rise, he was appointed president. In his spare time, he continued to manage the Sea Island farm, and became well-known as a breeder of purebred Jerseys and Holsteins. He was also president of the Symphony Society, a member of the UBC Board of Governors, and a member of the Vancouver General Hospital Board.

Throughout his career, Grauer never wavered in his conviction that B.C. had a dynamic and prosperous future made possible by its abundance of energy, and—increasingly as the leftist CCF Party gained ground—that socialism was the major threat to that prosperity. His first battle on assuming the presidency of B.C. Electric was with the historically militant motormen over profits, wages and his desire to implement a 10-cent streetcar fare. The fight continued through October, 1947, by which time a new bus terminal (a "temporary measure," still there) opened on the Cambie Street Grounds and Grauer dedicated $6,000,000 to start the switchover to trolley buses (which required just a driver compared with the motorman and conductor on the streetcars). The last of the flat-wheelers or rattlers ended their days on April 25, 1955, by which time the fare was 13 cents, and Vancouverites were said to be in love with the quiet new trolleys which picked them up at the curbside.

During the Fifties, Grauer masterminded a $650,000,000 program of investment which changed the face of Vancouver and the province. Bridge River and Ruskin power came on stream, and many small communities in the interior were able to phase out their thumping diesel generators. Meanwhile, the Grauers entertained tirelessly at the old Aivazoff home on the Crescent. He was a good after-dinner speaker, and was quoted as saying: "If you're not a socialist before you're 25, you have no heart; if you're one after you're 25, you have no head!"

B.C. Electric had been walking a tightrope since the mid-1940s, when Premier John Hart had hinted that a takeover would save British Columbia millions of tax dollars then being paid to Ottawa. Tax inequities dominated the thinking of the volatile W.A.C. Bennett governments during the early Fifties; by the last years of that decade, the Premier had bigger fish to fry and was feuding openly with the Diefenbaker government over proposals to develop both the Columbia and the Peace Rivers. B.C. Electric refused to commit itself to the purchase of blocks of power from these new mega-dams. The CCF opposition, long proponents of public ownership of utilities, trumpeted the advantages to the taxpayers of a takeover. Bennett held back publicly, but gave B.C. Electric a private ultimatum—buy the power or be nationalized. The company refused to budge.

On July 17, 1961, Dal Grauer was hospitalized, gravely ill with

leukemia. He died two weeks later.

On August 1, 1961, just as Dal Grauer's funeral cortège was entering Christ Church cathedral, W.A.C. Bennett rose in the provincial Legislature to announce that the government was taking over B.C. Electric. The battle over the legality of the move and compensation for the company's shareholders raged for years.

The Sixties were the years of massive power projects in B.C., with the construction of the Columbia River dams and the Peace River project (the W.A.C. Bennett dam). The new B.C. Hydro and Power Authority, formed from the B.C.E.R. and the B.C. Power Commission, has since become firmly established. The familiar red B.C. Electric thunderbird disappeared from the front of buses, as did "Reddy Kilowatt," who promoted better living through electricity.

Grauer had the last laugh on the B.C. government. His $2.8 million estate was legally manipulated to exclude the provincial government from estate taxes. One investment source was quoted as saying that the use of the legal loophole was "almost poetic."

Looking northeast from the bell tower of the First Baptist Church at Nelson and Burrard in the Thirties. The residential West End extended all the way to Robson Street. The major buildings are, left to right, the "new" Hotel Vancouver, the Hotel Georgia behind the Courthouse, the "old" Hotel Vancouver, the Vancouver Block, and, on the right edge of the picture, the Grosvenor Hotel (demolished 1983).

The last remaining homes in that part of the West End occupy the block bounded by Broughton, Nicola, Haro and Barclay, which has been declared a Heritage Park. The 1890 Barclay Manor (formerly the West End hospital), the turreted 1893 Roedde house (built by the proprietor of the city's first bookbinding firm) and three small homes built by the firm of Parr and Fee remain on the block.

Southlands farmer Henry Mole, who had homesteaded the Point Grey Golf Course area in 1863, retired to a home at 1025 Comox when his son took over the farm. In 1894, St. Paul's Hospital was opened "at the end of the trail" at Comox and Burrard. Past the hospital, a trail wound in a southerly direction to Beach Avenue, cleared in the 1880s by a logger named Oben. Another trail wound westwards to the summer camp area at English Bay. Early photographs show the occasional house jutting up above the stumps; none of the swampy ground is planted or drained. A few homes had been built in 1893 "way out in the forest," in archivist J.S. Matthews' phrase, at the southwest corner of Pacific and Burrard. One of these was occupied by the twenty-year-old Matthews and his even younger bride in 1898. He recounted—in his usual dramatic fashion—a walk on the trail to St. Paul's shortly after they moved in: " . . . (they) linger too long in the clearing, now our "West End"; too quickly dusk turns to black night; they are lost in the wilderness. A bright light in an upper window, shining in the gloom as a heavenly star, is their guide; they stumble towards it, and reach home."

Matthews' neighbour down the block, in the first house on the beach at 1172 Pacific, was Major Lacey Johnson, a CPR official who "took the throttle" on the first CPR train entering Vancouver in 1887. Johnson's first house was on the site of the Hudson's Bay Co. building at Georgia and Granville. He was very active throughout his life with the B.C. military and pre-Baden Powell organizations like the Christ Church Boys Brigade, who were entertained, complete with their uniforms and rifles, on Lacey's lawn in 1896.

The southern part of the West End along Beach Avenue was an adjunct to the older community of Yaletown, the residential community for the CPR yards on False Creek in the 1880s. The Yaletown Church, at 1246 Hornby, was built in 1889 to serve that community, but as the parishioners abandoned raucous Yaletown for the West End, attendance at the church declined. In 1898, it was hauled on skids by a horse along Davie Street to the southeast corner of Jervis and Pendrell. There, it was rechristened St. Paul's church and, after a major rebuild in 1905, became the Anglican headquarters for the western part of the city.

Blueblood Alley on Seaton Street began to be abandoned by the "bloods" at the turn of the century. Many moved to the slope above English Bay, particularly on Harwood, Burnaby and Davie Streets. One of the earliest was William Ferriman Salsbury, the treasurer of the CPR land division, who occupied a fine home at 1340 Burnaby with an unobstructed panorama of the sea. B.C. Mills, Timber and Trading Co. owner John Hendry, shipping magnate George Coleman, prominent barrister George H. Cowan, and architect

Thomas Fee owned homes there briefly, before the mad rush for Shaughnessy Heights robbed English Bay of its fashionable status. West End society conducted itself in the most formal British manner: afternoons were reserved by hostesses for receiving at home, picture calling cards were presented, and gentlemen when courting were expected to endure long afternoons of croquet, badminton and lemonade under the watchful eye of the family's bejewelled dowager aunt. Chinese houseboys, clipped hedges, monkey-puzzle trees and stone walls completed the street scene, though, off the manicured properties, the roads were dusty or muddy and the sidewalks were often still planked. The two most splendid houses in the West End were B.T. Rogers' Gabriola, now restored as The Mansion restaurant, and wholesale grocer Robert Kelly's turreted, rambling home, demolished in 1946. They occupied opposite sides of Nicola Street at Davie. Rogers' home had a concrete basement and was built completely of stone quarried from Gabriola Island.

The 1920s and early 1930s were the period of the elegant apartment. Social values which had placed a premium on family life in an ostentatious residence broke down under pressure from jazz, motor cars, travel, and a higher standard of education. The Twenties roared in Vancouver, too; in Chicago and Winnipeg people won and lost fortunes on the grain and commodities exchanges, Vancouverites made fortunes in metals, lumber and shipping. The expensive new apartment buildings in the West End maintained the old standards of design and workmanship—such as high ceilings, wainscotting, leaded glass, and large entertaining rooms—but were built for ease of maintenance. The latest conveniences, including vacuum cleaners, refrigerators, and central heating systems, were provided. The half-timbered Tudor style, so popular a generation earlier in large houses by Maclure and Fox, became popular again for apartments. The Beaufort, at 1160 Nicola, built in 1932, is one example. Another, advertised to Vancouverites in 1928 as "The Ultimate Apartment Building," is Tudor Manor on Beach at Jervis.

The Great Depression put the West End into a tailspin from which it didn't recover until the wholesale redevelopment of the Sixties. Little changed physically until 1956, when the City amended its 1927 zoning bylaw, which had limited buildings in the area to six storeys. The thin edge of the wedge was the B.C. Electric building (page 113) at Nelson and Burrard, a modern office tower in what was then still a residential area, and the luxurious Ocean Towers on Morton Street at English Bay.

The change in the West End during the late Fifties and early Sixties was staggering and lightning quick. Almost overnight, entire blocks of turreted and bay-windowed houses were knocked down and replaced by highrises. The new, compact style of apartment was well-suited to the single office-workers who crowded into the city during the great office building boom of the Sixties.

*J.H. Carlisle (1857-1941)
fought the Great Fire and was
the City's Fire Chief from
1886 until his retirement in
1929.*

Fire Hall Number 6, at Nelson and Nicola, was built in 1907 for the rapidly-populating West End. It was the first fire hall on the continent to be designed specifically for motorized vehicles, and was built at a time of great technical innovation in the Vancouver Fire Department. The Hastings Mill's volunteer fire department bought its first steam pumper, with a copper-riveted hose, from San Francisco in 1867. After the catastrophe of June, 1886, the new city purchased two pumper wagons, with shiny black "Russian iron" boilers, which (until the city's Capilano water system was established) drew their water from cisterns, including one at the southeast corner of Granville and Dunsmuir, filled with groundwater seepage and rainwater. In 1908, when Firehall Number 6 was opened, the city was discarding its teams of horses, and purchasing Seagrave "chemical-engined" fire trucks, with solid tyres and Pres-to-Lite pressure gas tanks on the running boards for the lights. A year later, the building of the Dominion Trust skyscraper at Victory Square prompted the department to buy a Seagrave Aerial ladder, 75 feet tall, tractor-drawn with solid tyres, which was kept in old Firehall Number 1 (now the Actors' Workshop building) at Gore and Cordova. Shortly thereafter, the Department purchased a Webb Aerial ladder, which it kept at old Firehall Number 2 (demolished 1957), on the east side of Seymour between Robson and Georgia. By 1912, the city had eleven firehalls, and a committee of London insurance experts declared that the three best fire brigades in the world were in London, Leipzig and Vancouver. In the group portrait, taken in the early Twenties at the corner of Georgia and Beatty, the Webb and Seagrave ladders are second and third from the right, respectively.

Thomas Fee

The architect Thomas A. Fee, in his chauffeured Packard outside his home at 1025 Gilford (Comox dead-ends at Stanley Park in the background of the picture), about 1918. Fee formed a partnership with J.E. Parr, and built many of the finest buildings in early Vancouver, including the Europe Hotel, the Vancouver Block, the Evangelical Tabernacle in Mt. Pleasant, the Manhattan Apartments on Thurlow, and Rat Portage sawmill owner W.L. Tait's "Glen Brae" in Shaughnessy. Fee (c. 1860-1929) lived first at 747 Hamilton, where he became a common sight in his Detroit Electric automobile, the first one in the city. He later lived briefly at 1119 Broughton before moving, in 1907, to the Gilford Street house. He was expelled from the Vancouver Board of Trade on September 30, 1914, for advocating British Columbia's annexation by the United States, and suggesting that it was unfair not to allow Alvo von Alvensleben's return from Seattle. The Fee Block, at 570 Granville, was the office for their very active property development business. J.E. Parr (inset) developed a reputation for devastating any client or municipal official standing in the firm's way.

117

B.T. Rogers

Very few large houses from Vancouver's grand, elegant age remain outside Shaughnessy Heights. Two of the grandest—Gabriola in the West End and Shannon on South Granville—were owned by Benjamin Tingley Rogers, the founder of B.C. Sugar and one of the wealthiest men in Vancouver.

Rogers was born in Pennsylvania on October 21, 1865, to a family with interests in the sugar business. In his youth, he worked for Havermeyer and Elder, "the sugar kings of New York." After the death of his father in 1889, he moved with his mother Clara to Vancouver. With the backing of some CPR directors —especially R.B. Angus—and the whole-hearted support of City Council, he opened the B.C. Sugar Refinery in 1892. Year by year, "he lengthened his ropes and strengthened his stakes." He married Mary Isabella Angus, the daughter of Victoria merchant James Angus—and R.B. Angus' niece. The Rogers lived in a rambling frame house at 1508 West Georgia (which became well-known forty years later as a boarding house run by an eccentric woman named Edith Fowler). In 1900, B.T. hired Samuel Maclure, who had done renovations to his father-in-law's Rockland Avenue house, to design him a mansion "which will cost $25,000, which is probably twice as much as the next best residence in the city," according to a contemporary newspaper report. The house had the first concrete basement in Vancouver; there were wood-panelled interiors imported from England, eighteen fireplaces and the best stained glass in the city.

Rogers loved motoring and was something of a speed demon. He went the wrong way around the Stanley Park drive one day and was ordered by the constable to "reverse his path, else there will be a summons." On another day, Rogers was accused of "driving his toot-toot wagon on the bicycle path on Powell Street, and was fined $5, or 10 days." One day, about 1900, young Bill Roedde (the son of the Roedde bookbinding family whose 1893 home is now preserved as part of the West End's heritage park) was playing in a sandpile at the corner of Nicola and Barclay, when he became the first person in Vancouver to be hit by a car. Evidently, "the one-cylinder puddle-jumper with a handlebar instead of a steering wheel" skidded out of control, ran over the lad's leg and stalled. B.T. jumped out, cranked the car furiously into life, shoved the boy onto the seat and drove him home. On arrival the boy rushed in to tell his brothers that he had had *a ride* in a motorcar!

On February 15, 1907, Rogers was arrested "for driving 1,046 feet in 44 seconds" (a speed of almost of 27 mph) on the upgrade between Robson and Nelson on Burrard. He was defended by his solicitor, J.W. deB. Farris, who told the court that Rogers asked: " . . . didn't they have to go a little faster to overcome [the hill]?" He was fined $10. Another day, he was evidently racing John

Benjamin Tingley Rogers

George Cowan

The only Vancouverite ever to receive both a Q.C. (Queen's Counsel) and a K.C. (King's Counsel) for distinguished service to the legal profession is George H. Cowan. Cowan, after whom Cowan Point on Bowen Island was named, was the patriarch of a distinguished Vancouver family. The family owned the better part of the south end of Bowen Island, and maintained a sort of family compound there under the stern eye of Cowan's wife, who never permitted a female relative to venture in the direction of the Union Steamship's pleasure palace.

George Cowan was born on June 17, 1858 in Watford, Ontario into a staunch Conservative and Anglican family. In 1894, shortly after his arrival in Vancouver, he founded the first Conservative Association in Vancouver. His residence at 1225 Davie Street was a natural gathering spot for prominent Orangemen like Prime Minister Mackenzie Bowell, who visited in August, 1894. Cowan was created a Q.C. by the Tupper administration, but this was cancelled by the Liberal Laurier administration. He was finally appointed a K.C. in 1905, which stuck. He listed his pursuits in the 1923 *Who's Who in Canada* as "horses, hunting and billiards."

Cowan was City Solicitor from 1907 to 1908, when he resigned to run for Parliament. He was a good lawyer and "a true craftsman of reasoned argument," but had a stutter which detracted from his ability as a speaker. Nevertheless, he was elected as representative for the Vancouver Centre riding, and sat in Opposition. In 1911, he was edged out of the Conservative nomination by the upstart Harry Stevens, who went on to win an overwhelming victory in the anti-reciprocity election of that year. Cowan authored an influential report, "The Chinese Question in Canada," which was generally negative on further immigration or any emancipation for the Chinese.

His son, Major George P. Cowan, was killed in action in Italy in 1944. Mrs. Cowan, like her in-law Mary Rogers, lived on as a grand dowager to the ripe old age of 92, dying in October, 1960.

George H. Cowan, K.C.

Mary Isabella Rogers

Hendry's chauffeur. The newspaper reported: "Mr. B.T. Rogers and two other automobilists fined for exceeding speed on Nelson Street. Harry Hooper, Mr. John Hendry's chauffeur, with visions of himself in jail, gathered in his smiles and stood in his black leather automobile coat in sphinx-like silence. He and Mr. Rogers were fined $16 each." (Harry Hooper had, in 1903, operated the city's first taxi service.) The speed limit at the time was 10 m.p.h on city and town roads and 15 m.p.h. on country roads.

Rogers owned the steam yacht *Aquila* and was Commodore of the Royal Vancouver Yacht Club in 1912. One of his contributions to the war effort was donating the yacht as the mother ship for Premier Richard McBride's navy (the Premier, unimpressed with the Royal Canadian Navy's determination to defend the British Columbia coast, and mindful of German cruisers operating in the Pacific, had purchased two used submarines in Seattle for $1 million shortly before the war). Life in Vancouver during the war was tranquil until 1917, when the city was rocked by its first serious labour trouble. Among those who struck that summer were the employees at the B.C. Sugar Refinery.

On the night of June 17, 1918, Rogers went up early to bed. By 11 p.m. he was dead of a cerebral hemorrhage, aged 53.

The Rogers family continued to make news for a couple more generations. Widow Mary Isabella Rogers lived on to the extraordinary age of 96, dying in October 1965 as the undisputed *grande dame* of Vancouver society. In the Twenties, she moved her four daughters and three sons into the huge new Shannon mansion, and held court there until she sold it to the Austin Taylors in the Thirties. After that, she lived at 3637 Angus Drive. Mrs. Rogers was a founder of the Vancouver Symphony Society, and entertained some interesting guests, including the King and Queen of Siam who stayed at Shannon in 1931. (During that visit, King Prajadhipok noticed two paintings in his room which he declared had been stolen from his palace in Bangkok many years before. Mrs. Rogers's son-in-law bought them in an antique shop during his nuptial grand world tour in the Twenties. The paintings were later donated to the Red Cross Superfluities Shop at 731 Burrard, where they hung for years and "attracted much interest.")

Mrs. Rogers' love of music and interest in the symphony led to her meeting "the dynamic Russian pianist" Jan Cherniavsky, who married one of her daughters (his brother Mischel married another). Son Blythe Dupuy Rogers ran B.C. Sugar until his sudden death in 1920; it was then managed by future Lieutenant-Governor J.W. Fordham-Johnson. Second son Ernest T. Rogers then took it over—he died on July 24, 1939 in Malaspina Strait near Pender Harbour. The family was yachting when a sudden squall knocked his daughter overboard. Rogers dived in, but apparently suffered a heart attack and sank—his body was never recovered. His wife, the daughter of George H. Cowan, saved the child.

Julia Henshaw

Julia Willmothe Henshaw was the only Vancouver woman to appear in "Who's Who" before the First World War. She and her husband were among the first to live on Robson as far west as Denman Street, and received a free pass from the Vancouver Street Railway Co. as an inducement to settle there.

Many of the women in early Vancouver lived comfortably in their husbands' long shadows, content to be distinguished as "superb hostesses" or "patronesses of the arts." Julia Henshaw was both of these, but also achieved international recognition in her own right as a writer, lecturer and botanist. Born in Durham, England in 1869 and educated in England, France and Germany, she moved to Montreal, where she married Charles Grant Henshaw, an investment broker who distinguished himself as a recruiter in the early years of the Great War, and ran the Recruiting Depot at Victory Square. He so enjoyed society entertaining that he earned the nickname "Afternoon Tea Charlie." He was also something of a rogue: according to a story told by newspaperman Alan Morley, Henshaw imported Parisian bathing costumes for an impromptu swimming party; the costumes dissolved after ten minutes in the water!

In 1914, Julia, with her husband Charles in tow, drove the first motor car across the two divides of the Rockies. In 1896, she hiked to the sources of the Columbia and Kootenay Rivers. She was one of the first photographers of the Rockies; achieved international recognition for her mapping of the centre of Vancouver Island in 1910 and 1911; was a pioneer newspaperwoman in Vancouver, with a regular column in the *Province*; wrote the "book of the year," *Hypnotized*, in 1898; wrote the definitive botanical study on the province's flora; was made an honorary captain in the Canadian Army for her war-time lectures and recruiting work, and received the Croix de Guerre for her ambulance driving on the Western Front.

Charles died in Rome in 1927 of a sudden stroke. Before that, they had moved to Caulfeild; a stained-glass window in the St. Francis In The Woods church there commemorates them. Julia Henshaw died, after several years of near-blindness, in November, 1937.

Cedar Cottage

The district south of Trout Lake, the only Vancouver lake outside of Stanley Park, has been known as Cedar Cottage since the early 1890s, when Arthur Wilson built a small cedar cabin east of Knight Road south of the Westminster Road (now Kingsway). In 1893, an Irishman named Moses Gibson started a 19-acre ranch on the land bounded by Knight, Bella Vista, 18th and 20th on the slope above Trout Lake. Gibson had arrived in Vancouver in 1886, and ran the Queen's Hotel on Water Street until starting his farm.

Ranching and dairying were the main activities along the Westminster Road—the Garvin and Jones dairies were established slightly closer to town at Windsor Street—and transportation was relatively easy between New Westminster and the fledgling city of Vancouver. Since the 1870s, carriages and stagecoaches had stopped at the Gladstone Inn at Gladstone and Kingsway to feed passengers and change teams.

In 1900, George Raywood built the Cedar Cottage brewery at the southeast corner of Kingsway and Knight Road, the site now occupied by a Safeway store. The brewery was built on the Gibson Creek which ran through the property, so thick with salmon that they were pitchforked onto the bank rather than hooked. The brewery was set far back from the road in a flower garden. John Bensen, one of the original proprietors, lived in a cottage on the site through the Forties. The brewery found a ready market during the early years; beer was sold, delivered to the home, for 75 cents per dozen pints or $1.50 per dozen quarts. It was bought in January, 1902, by the Royal Brewing Co., and used for brewing heavy English ale. After the brewery discontinued operations, the equipment was moved to the Stanley Park brewery at the foot of Alberni on Lost Lagoon.

The major recreational attraction in the area was Trout Lake, Vancouver's only freshwater beach. Trout Lake was first tapped as the source of water for the Hastings Sawmill boiler, after the dam on Brewery Creek didn't produce enough of a head. The lake was very popular with boys, who swam there in their birthday suits in the summer and shot ducks in the fall, but never caught any trout. During the winter, skaters converged on the lake, which sometimes froze (more often than Beaver Lake, as it was deeper in the forest) and was an easy walk from the interurban stop. Around the turn of the century, a man named Williams set up a tent along the shore, lit a fire and erected a sign stating: "Clothes Checked and Skates to Rent." He was succeeded by a group of local boys led by future mayor Gerry McGeer, who put up a barricade at the end of the Gibson trail and charged 10 cents to pass through to the lake. One winter, about 1905, the lake froze solid and it snowed. McGeer hired dairyman William Hamilton to clear the ice. Hamilton had his horse sharp shod at Lobb & Muir's blacksmith shop on the Westminster Road and was prepared to plough the ice, but that night it rained. McGeer went broke and never paid.

Development of the Cedar Cottage area began in earnest after 1892 when the interurban line was pushed through the forest to New Westminster, following a path parallel to the Westminster Road (what is now called the Vanness Cut, the rapid transit right-of-way). By comparison with the horse-drawn stages and muddy, rutted roads, the interurban's hourly service was a miracle. The electric trains stopped on the hill just above Trout Lake, at the end of a trail from the lake through the Gibson property, at 1627 Vanness. A small commercial community sprang up there, the remains of which can be seen in a few odd-angled, bay-windowed buildings near the tram stop, and in the 3300 and 3400 blocks Commercial Drive. The area became briefly fashionable around the beginning of the First World War, and prosperous families settled on the hill near Clark Park at 14th and Commercial.

Of the buildings left from that period, the St. Mark's Lutheran Church at 1553 East 18th, dating from 1911, is one of the most attractive. Many of the old homes have been demolished and replaced by the stucco, boxy "Vancouver Special" type houses so popular in the East End.

Clark Park was then known as Buffalo Park. In the civic election of 1913, the interurban route down Commercial Drive was the subject of considerable controversy. Critics wanted the interurban route changed so that it ran northwest down China Creek instead. Nothing ever came of it, as no one wanted to spend the money to ease the grade from Cedar Cottage to the False Creek flats.

Fraser Street was then called North Arm Road and had been opened through to the river. The area was best known for its cemetery—now the Mountain View cemetery—and the road was popularly called Cemetery Road. The first 20 acres of the site had been deeded to the city as a cemetery in September, 1887, after Johnny Baker's clearing and Deadman's Island in Stanley Park became overcrowded. The first burial, of a man named Joe Butterfield, was a controversial one, as he was both "a coloured" and a suicide. The first live resident was a man named James Hutson, who had a cottage at 23rd and Fraser. On the southeast corner, a man named Thomas, who was the caretaker of the cemetery for a number of years, built a store (Thomas Road is now called Inverness Street). Other characters in the area were Roxy the Italian, Lump-Jawed Harrison and Pig-Swill Jack. A very early settler was named "Black" Jones. He was a bachelor from Wales, and got his nickname from his swarthy complexion. He cleared the land between Victoria and Commercial, and 37th and 38th Avenue himself with an axe and a handsaw. He then went to Wales and returned to his land with a wife, but died soon after.

Trout Lake was plain Trout Lake until controversy erupted over its fate during the Thirties. Some wanted it filled in because of the acidic water and the clouds of mosquitoes which rose from it

Looking north on Commercial Drive from 20th Avenue to Vanness Avenue in 1915, at the Cedar Cottage shopping district, south of Trout Lake and the modern rapid transit line. The interurban in the distance is about to turn southeast at the rail crossing sign and proceed over the Vanness Cut to New Westminster. Due to the vagaries of the War, many of the shops were vacant by 1916.

during the summer; others thought it would be a good replacement for the rapidly-filling China Creek dump. Into the breach came Mr. and Mrs. Eric Hamber, who bought the land, including the lake, and donated it to the city on the condition that it be named John Hendry park, after Mrs. Hamber's father, who owned the Hastings Sawmill.

South Vancouver

The White Spot at Gladstone and Kingsway is a modern commuter facility. A predecessor on the site at 2219 Kingsway was the old roadhouse known as the Gladstone Inn, a "commuter facility" dating from the stagecoach days. The Gladstone was one of four roadhouses which predated the paving and naming of Kingsway in 1913. Stagecoaches travelling from Gastown to New Westminster could stop at the Junction Inn at Fraser, the Gladstone, the Pig and Whistle at 3399 Kingsway, and the Royal Oak (demolished only in 1968). All were outdated as roadhouses by the opening of the interurban line in 1892.

The Gladstone Inn, which had hitching posts with white china doorknobs on them, was demolished in the spring of 1909, and replaced with the larger Gladstone Hotel, which burned about 1930. It rose again as the Gladstone Club and became the Hi-Hat Cabaret in 1937. For the 30 years prior to 1914, it had the only liquor license in South Vancouver. In July 1916, when it was called the Kingsway Hotel, it lost its operating license because, according to Municipal Council, "it is in a residential area."

The roadhouse was the scene, on April 29, 1891, of the first meeting of the incorporators of the Municipality of South Vancouver—and the place where the name South Vancouver was chosen. On April 13 of the next year, just six years after Vancouver was created, the Municipality was incorporated. It included the entire area from Point Grey to Boundary Road, south of the 16th Avenue City boundary and the Hastings Townsite.

Early settlers who arrived in South Vancouver included the pioneer farmers of Southlands—McCleery, Mole, Shannon, Magee—and a host of lesser-knowns who settled along the Fraser and began logging timber on the south slope in the late 1860s. William Henry Rowling, Obadiah Betts, James Rae, Robert McBride and Sam Taylor staked pre-emptions in the years after the Cariboo gold rush. After incorporation in 1892, William John Brewer of Cedar Cottage was elected the first reeve. A man named George Martin was appointed clerk and general factotum for the municipality, and was paid $50 a month, which the Provincial Government provided as a grant.

Newspaperman S.T. Frost, writing in the late Twenties, described the South Vancouver old-timers as a group of individuals "who feared debt as children are taught to fear the devil." To avoid the necessity of borrowing, much of the work on roads and bridges was done by the settlers in payment of taxes. For the first dozen years, property owners refused to sanction municipal bonds, preferring swampy roads and no sidewalks to any further debt. The residents and property owners in the western section—the CPR lands west of Ontario Street—complained repeatedly about the lack of services and improvements. In 1906 the westerners managed to get Councillor E. Foreman, from the Point Grey section, elected reeve. Foreman attempted to get action on civic improvements and, when he failed, led the secessionist movement which resulted in the formation of the separate municipality of Point Grey in 1908. Point Grey's Municipal Hall was in Kerrisdale—then the major established community south of downtown. South Vancouver finally built its own hall at 43rd and Fraser Street.

The South Vancouverites were a strange, fiscally-tight lot: they refused to tax "improvements" on property until 1919 and had borrowed by 1908, a total of only $185,000 for roads. Their total expenditure on schools to the time of secession was $24,000.

In 1913, borrowing for roads again became the issue which catapulted South Vancouver to notoriety. A paving contract was let for Kingsway, Bodwell and Main streets. Reeve Kerr, in the face of strenuous opposition from council, defended the decision to pave Main Street; he was defeated by Thomas Dickie and resigned. Dickie became mayor and presided over a very stormy few months, with one faction demanding the cancellation of the "unnecessary" paving contract. The argument was so strenuous that Reeve Dickie, too, resigned; other resignations followed, until finally Kerr was elected reeve again. Kerr found that he could float no more municipal bonds and that no bank would lend South Vancouver any money. Tax collections dropped to less than half of the total levy. Municipal work ceased, and most of the civic employees were laid off. In 1915, Edward Gold, who had been most vehement about cancelling the Main Street paving contract, was elected reeve. He attempted to sell local improvement debentures, but couldn't raise enough money, so he in effect mortgaged the Muncipality to the firm of Spitzer, Rorick of Toledo for $790,000 worth of treasury certificates. The tax collection rate dropped to 43 per cent. Gold was defeated the next year; his successor was defeated in 1917. In the spring of 1918, the treasury certificate loan came due; the Municipality had no money, so under the terms of the agreement the Toledo company was entitled to take over bonds valued at $989,902, a considerable increase since 1915. Reeve Russell attempted to sell new bonds in eastern Canada while his councillors appealed to the Provincial Government for a financial bailout. The Municipality hoped that the councillors would be allowed to continue to administer their affairs, while the Province maintained a check on disbursements.

To everyone's surprise, in May,1918 the Province appointed F.J. Gillespie as commissioner in charge of the municipality and summarily dismissed the reeve, councillors, school trustees and police commissioners, without any official warning. Gillespie maintained control until A. Wells Gray was appointed in 1921. The full municipal franchise was restored in April, 1923.

Under the no-nonsense control of the Provincial appointees, a tax sale was inaugurated and improvements were taxed—both of which went a long way towards restoring some fiscal health. During the Twenties, South Vancouver prospered, and the residents voted—along with the residents of the Muncipality of Point Grey—to amalgamate with Vancouver on January 1, 1929.

Mount Pleasant

Charles Doering built one of the first houses in Mount Pleasant, at 262 East 6th, a half-block west of the old Red Cross Brewery at 6th and Scotia on Brewery Creek. Doering, with partner Otto Marstrand, bought out owners William & Barker in 1891 and re-opened it as the Doering & Marstrand brewery. The latter controlled most of the Vancouver bars (the Europe Hotel was the most prominent exception) until Doering arranged its amalgamation with Henry Reifel's Vancouver Breweries in 1907. Doering was an alderman in 1890 and 1891, and died in 1927. Partner Otto Marstrand (1848-1911) lived at 310 East 5th, and was the Danish vice-consul for Vancouver for the five years before his death.

Mount Pleasant was the first suburb of Vancouver to be developed and settled. The first bridge across False Creek on Westminster Avenue (Main Street) was opened on October 2, 1872, and early in the 1880s the land to the south of False Creek on the Westminster Road (first cleared in 1861 as a trail, now Kingsway) to New Westminster was divided and homesteaded. "The people across the Creek," as Mount Pleasant residents were known, settled around the spot where the Westminster Road headed southeast at Seventh Avenue.

Plain Westminster Avenue and 9th Avenue became grand Main and Broadway in 1911, during the pre-World War I real estate boom. Fine structures like the Lee Building at the corner of Broadway and Main, the Mt. Stephen Apartments (now Quebec Manor) at 7th and Quebec and the two huge churches at the corner of 10th and Quebec remain from that burst of speculation and optimism. The old Federal Agriculture building at 15th and Main is another example of how grand Mount Pleasant was 70 years ago; the building has been restored and is converted into offices for social service agencies.

Early activity on the south side of the Creek included the towered Mount Pleasant School, opened in 1892 at Broadway and Kingsway; the Vancouver Street Railway car house at Front Street (1st Avenue) on the tide line; the Doering and Marstrand brewery at 6th and Scotia on Brewery Creek; the cottage of eccentric Julius Caesar, who had a vegetable garden near the False Creek bridge and rolled boulders into the water as stepping stones for his trips downtown; the Sherdahl nursery at 12th and Guelph, now the block containing the Florence Nightingale School; Sam Garvin's False Creek dairy (Dairy License 1 in Vancouver) at Westminster and Front Street; the Jones Milk Ranch, which had 58 cows and produced an average of 110 gallons of milk a day, had its farmhouse at the northeast corner of Kingsway and Windsor; the William Hamilton house, built near Westminster Road on what is now the southwest corner of 18th and St. Catherine's Street (his daughter, Ella Hamilton, born there in 1892, became Mrs. John Murchie of the Tea and Coffee importing firm); the Junction Inn at Fraser and Kingsway, a stagecoach stop in the 1880s like the more famous Gladstone Inn; M.J. Henry's nursery at 14th and Kingsway (now Robson Park); and, Jim McGeer's dairy at 16th and Kingsway.

Samuel Garvin arrived in Vancouver before 1890 and established his operation at the south end of the False Creek bridge. He later worked as a teamster, and lived at 950 East 19th. His son Sammy (1884-1973), who had apprenticed as a boy by driving a milk wagon through the gloomy forests, started a dairy in the 500 block East 10th Avenue. It went broke in 1916. Sammy then worked for Chapman's Motor Freight, and in 1922 started the Independent Ice and Fuel Company at 325 East 5th Avenue. The firm started with one truck which held four blocks of ice. The family changed the firm's name to Garvin Ice and Fuel, and hauled ice, coal, wood and sawdust with a fleet which had grown to 110 trucks by the Fifties. They lived above the 3600-ton ice plant on East 5th, which is now the Malkin and Pinton warehouse. Samuel William, Sammy's son, sold the business to Standard Oil in 1956.

William Sherdahl established his nursery at 510 Westminster Road in March, 1890. In 1896, he advertised four-year-old apple trees for sale, and prospered enough to expand his operations northward to the block at 12th and Guelph.

During the mid-1890s, many of the vacant lots around the central part of Mount Pleasant were filled with handsome frame houses, few of which survived the apartment boom of the Sixties and Seventies. Those around the enormous churches at 10th and Quebec are the grandest, while the cottages northwest of Main and Broadway have a minimum of fretwork and decoration. The prestige of the area was greatly enhanced by the opening of the Fairview Belt tramline in 1892. Eighth Avenue between Kingsway and Brunswick still has some relics from the old Mount Pleasant neighbourhood. The Knights of Pythias Lodge, a boom-town fronted hall at the corner of 8th and Scotia, was built after the club abandoned its original quarters upstairs in the Lonsdale block on Cordova (now the Army and Navy store). The old lodge building is now the residence of the Western Front artists' group, an avant garde centre for Vancouver theatre, music and artistic events. Most memorable was the dadaist Mr. Peanut for Mayor campaign in 1974. (He lost.) Further east on that block are the old Ledingham and McWhinney homes.

The paving of Westminster Road in 1913 (when it was named Kingsway) and the increasing mobility of Vancouver's population dealt a blow to the grand dreams of Mount Pleasant's landowners and developers. The area's old houses have gradually converted into rooming houses or been demolished for apartments, particularly on the steep slope overlooking the Canadian National yards.

Creeks of Mount Pleasant

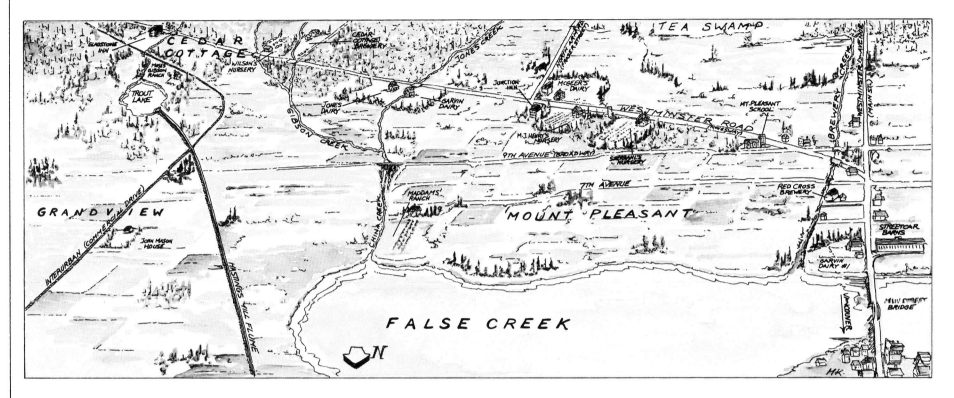

Several creeks flowed through the Mount Pleasant and Cedar Cottage areas in the early years.

The one furthest west was called Brewery Creek. It flowed north from what was called the Tea Swamp, also known as "No Man's Land," also known as District Lot 301. The swamp was a bog like Camosun Bog on the University Endowment Lands, with hemlock trees, scrubby pine, blueberries and Labrador Tea bushes—hence the name. It crossed Broadway under a little bridge a few yards east of Main Street, and headed straight down the hill before draining into False Creek. Small boys discovered that it was the only creek in the area that had eels. Captain Edward Stamp, when establishing a water supply for Hastings Mill, attempted to run a flume from a dam built on Brewery Creek at about 14th or 15th Avenue between Prince Edward and Sophia. The flume didn't have either adequate flow or adequate drop and so was abandoned in favour of one from Trout Lake. At Seventh Avenue, a waterwheel was built to produce power for the Red Cross brewery; all of the broken bottles were tossed into the creek's ravine. The last of the brewery buildings still exists at the southwest corner of 6th and Scotia, and occasionally, during the late summer, hops can be seen growing in the lane there. A block to the north, Brewery Creek passed by the house of Otto Marstrand—310 East 5th. There was a little bridge on 5th Avenue, crossing the creek.

Creek number two ran east of Main through Garvin's milk ranch, and past the small cottage he had built in 1889 at 950 East 19th. The wooden bridge on Westminster Road (Kingsway) which crossed this creek separated Garvin's property from Jones' milk ranch to the southeast. The creek at that point was called Jones Creek; it continued north and passed through the Chinese pig ranches and vegetable gardens at what is now Glen Park. Thereafter it was called China Creek, and ran through Maddams' ranch to drain into the extreme eastern end of False Creek near Clark Drive.

The third creek was called Gibson Creek. It had its source at about 33rd and Knight Road. It flowed through Arthur Wilson's Cedar Cottage nursery near Knight and Kingsway and provided the water for Raywood's Cedar Cottage brewery.

The fourth was a branch of the Gibson Creek, and crossed Kingsway at Commercial Drive.

The fifth, Gladstone Creek, flowed north from the forest past the Gladstone Inn stagecoach stop at Gladstone and Kingsway, finally feeding into Trout Lake.

Maddams' Ranch

Charles Cleaver Maddams' house at the mouth of China Creek, built in 1888. It was the first house in the district, built on the shore of False Creek, and could at first be reached only by skiff. In later years, it had a street address of 941 East 7th Avenue, near the corner of St. Catherine's, and was the last operating farm in Mount Pleasant. The home site and part of the old farm are now parkland along Great Northern Way.

The park on Great Northern Way, below the King Edward campus of Vancouver Community College, was the site of the last farm in the Mount Pleasant area. Charles Cleaver Maddams (1855-1928), who arrived with his family in Vancouver just before the May, 1887 "first train," bought five acres on the south shore of False Creek three years later, built a house, and called the result the Maddams' Ranch.

Charles' father, George Maddams, was a dispatch messenger in Queen Victoria's household, then transferred into the household of Victoria's daughter, Princess Louise. The Princess married the Marquis of Lorne, who became the Governor-General of Canada. Charles Maddams was part of the Marquis' entourage which toured the Canadian Northwest in 1882. Maddams liked Victoria, and obtained a position with B.C. Lieutenant-Governor Cornwall's household, then worked for the "swells" in Victoria's Union Club before coming to Vancouver. He got work as a personal assistant to Henry Abbott, and stayed with the CPR until 1901.

The family initially lived on Cordova Street between Richards and Homer, behind Jonathan Miller's Hastings Street post office. Charles bought the waterfront acreage bounded by St. Catherine's, 7th Avenue and Glen Drive for $400. The Maddams reached their land by means of a skiff from the Royal City Planing Mills wharf at the foot of Carrall on False Creek, rowing along False Creek to their

beach landing at the mouth of a little creek (which became known as China Creek, due to the Chinese pig ranches upstream near 12th and Clark). There were no roads into the area, and the land was heavily treed.

Maddams gave the land rent-free to some Chinese, who cleared it. Two years later, after the streetcar line opened to Seventh Avenue, and Seventh was cleared as a slash road so people could skid lumber over it for house building, the Maddams built a nine-room house at 941 East 7th Avenue. A natural spring was beside the house, and the beach was littered with black lignite coal. The family planted cherry trees in the front yard, and pillar roses and crimson rambler on the side of the house. Fruit trees and berry bushes were planted as cash crops, but rhubarb was their main source of income. They sold it by the ton to W.H. Malkin & Co. With the surplus crop they made apple cider and, one year, some memorable amber-coloured rhubarb wine, which Malkin attempted to sell, but the alcoholic content was too high and he couldn't get permission from the government. One of the Maddams' early neighbours was H.H. Stevens, who built on the east side of the China Creek ravine, at 1451 East 12th Avenue.

Financial survival was a struggle, and the Maddams tried raising, at various times, pure-bred chickens, geese and pigeons for market. The sons shot ducks by the hundreds from their canvas canoe in False Creek (son Clarence, aged 16, was shot dead on the beach in front of the house in a hunting accident). Salmon were readily pitchforked from the creek. Maddams, who had bought other property in the heady years before the Great War, "got into trouble with the compound interest" and lost his "ranch" for taxes in 1923. The Great Northern railway, which had filled the Creek during the War years, ended up buying part of the acreage; a proposal by Rainier Breweries to buy the rest of the land fell through when the city, under pressure from more established breweries, wouldn't grant a charter.

During the late Twenties and Thirties, the city used the China Creek ravine below the Broadway trestle as a dump (two bridges, one at 12th Avenue and the other at Broadway, spanned the Creek). Neighbourhood residents organized in 1941 against the stench from the dump, and five years later the city abandoned the East Broadway site and created a new dump at 63rd and Kerr, far from any houses. The garbage was covered over in the early Fifties, and a high-sided wooden cycle track built in time for the 1954 British Empire Games. The cycle track decayed through the Sixties, was restored in the Seventies, and finally demolished in the Eighties for a new location for the King Edward campus of Vancouver Community College (formerly at the old King Edward High school site at 12th and Oak). That "small odoriforous waterway" called China Creek, which wound across Mt. Pleasant's False Creek flats, was put into a conduit in 1951.

(Left) The Sullivan-Taylor Motor Co. in the unit block Kingsway, about 1918. Sullivan-Taylor was later replaced on that block by the Johnston Motor Co (below left). Sullivan-Taylor retailed Fords (at that time Model T's, in, as Henry Ford said, "any colour you want, as long as it's black") out of a desanctified church dating from the 19th century Westminster Road days. Gas was available at 25 cents a gallon and the firm sold Dunlop tyres. A Christie Biscuits sign had been painted on the south roof of the church. (Below right) The Mount Pleasant Baptist Church was erected at the southeast corner of 10th and Quebec during 1909 and 1910. In 1912, it was realigned to allow for addition and new construction. G.W. Ledingham and Co. poured a new foundation and basement after the building had been jacked up, moved and finally placed on large beams. The Baptist Church is one of three churches on that corner, while the fourth corner is occupied by a government building named for H.H. Stevens (page 84). The finest house remaining in that part of Mount Pleasant— dating from a generation earlier than the church–is the Davis Home at 166 West 10th Avenue, built in 1891 and restored in the Seventies to its original condition by the descendants of the original family.

(Above) The corner of 8th and Main, looking southwest, in the Thirties. The F.W. Woolworth Co. still operates in that location, with that sign. The large Lee Building at the corner of Broadway and Main no longer has the neon-advertised Aristocratic restaurant on its ground floor. It is a good example of pre-World War I commercial architecture, with two deep light wells at the back to give some natural illumination to all the tenants' offices. The expensive stone facing on the Main side of the building is repeated on the Broadway side, indicating that Broadway and Main were equally important in the developer's scheme of things. The Main street tram tracks with their granite-set ballast brought prosperity to the area immediately before World War I. One of the finest buildings (right) was built for G.L. Pop Furriers at the northeast corner of 6th and Main.

G.W. Ledingham

From 1903 until the early 1950s, the house at 348 East 8th Avenue, at the corner of 8th and Brunswick, was occupied by the Ledingham family. The house was built at the turn of the century for contractor Peter G. Fenton, who lived there until he sold the house to James McWhinney, a lumberman who lived next door at 342. The latter sold the house to Ledingham. George Ledingham, born in January, 1875, in Ontario, came to Vancouver in 1897 and worked as a labourer on projects around the False Creek area. He boarded on Davie Street for $4 a week and worked six ten-hour days for 15 cents an hour. A couple of years after his arrival, he imported his childhood sweetheart, Helen, from Ontario and delivered her in his buggy to friend Fitzgerald McCleery's farmhouse for her first few days of chaperoned stay before their marriage. Shortly after they moved into the house on East 8th, Eula, the first of three children, was born. Their middle child Bruce—who ran the family contracting business until his retirement—attended Mount Pleasant school and had two paper routes, but still had a lot of time left over to enjoy a rambunctious life. He, his younger brother and young Samuel Garvin played in the Brewery Creek ravine, rode freight cars around the Canadian Northern yards on False Creek, where they got chased by the "brakies," and threw potatoes at the Chinese ironers in the Sing Kee laundry behind the 6th Avenue brewery. On their bicycles, they made trips to the China Creek trestle, where they swam in a little pool they called the "Bananahole" (they had to stay upstream of the acid and garbage dump which is now the King Edward campus of Vancouver Community College), or rode all the way to the Jericho Golf Links to pick up golf balls.

In 1927, Ledingham built a large garage behind the house, which has "G.W. LEDINGHAM CONTRACTOR" lettered in plaster above its doors. South of them, on 9th Avenue, on the site now occupied by Kingsgate Mall, stood Mt. Pleasant school, the earliest permanent school building outside of the downtown area. The community opened its first school for 42 pupils on November 12, 1888, in a one-room building at the corner of Westminster and 9th (Broadway and Main). The electorate authorized an eight-room brick building with a slate roof and a tower in June, 1892. Later, an additional eight rooms were added to the west (Dawson School at Burrard and Nelson, now demolished and the site of a B.C. Hydro parking lot, was built at the same time to identical plans). The school was demolished in 1972.

BRUCE LEDINGHAM

(Next page) The Ledingham house, at the corner of 8th Avenue and Brunswick in Mount Pleasant. Lumberman James McWhinney lived next door. In the background is the Mount Pleasant School, built in 1890 on the triangle of land now occupied by the Kingsgate Mall shopping centre. George Ledingham's first car was an EMF 30, built by Studebaker.

Strathcona

Ninety years ago, the city had an eastern boundary at Heatley Street, several blocks east of Main. Beyond that was forest and swamp. The "East End"—the area now called Strathcona, just east of Chinatown—formed the residential area sandwiched between the Hastings Mill (at the foot of Dunlevy) and the False Creek flats, which at high tide afforded some beach-front property along Prior Street.

The waterfront streets, called Crescent Grove and Park Lane, were briefly fashionable in the 1890s, but quickly fell from favour when the City established its main garbage dump at Heatley and Prior. Later, during the First World War, the False Creek tidal flats were filled by the Canadian Northern Railway for yards and industrial property. The rest of the district contained the large homes of Vancouver's founding fathers, cheek by jowl with small factories, stores and the cottages of immigrants and working men. A bit of a backwater even in the 1890s, it avoided redevelopment because the CPR pulled Vancouver's development westward. Ironically, the area got its name from Lord Strathcona (Donald Smith), the former Hudson's Bay Company governor who was one of the founders of the CPR.

Immigrants used Strathcona as their first port of call before their assimilation into Vancouver society and eventual move into outlying areas. During the 1890s, most of the immigrants were working-class British and Irish. Waves of Greeks and Scandinavians and Eastern Europeans came around the turn of the century. During the Great War years, there was a Jewish "ghetto" on the 500 through 700 blocks of Georgia and Keefer. The Jewish community built its Schara Tzedeck synagogue at the corner of Pender and Heatley. Union Street from Gore east to Campbell was the Italian neighbourhood. The Battistoni's Venice Bakery—now one of the largest on the Lower Mainland—was established at 561 Union. The brick oven in the back yard was laid by a neighbour named Vaglio, whose name remains with a fireplace and bricklaying firm on East Hastings. Next door to the Venice Bakery was Minichiello's Grosseria di Prima Qualita. Families who lived on Atlantic Avenue and Prior Street kept cows and grazed them on the False Creek flats. The alley between Prior and Union still has several two-storey hay barns, and was called "Cowshit Alley" by local kids, in acknowledgement of an old man who made his living as a cowherd and shepherd, and returned his charges along the alley. Cows destined for the P. Burns slaughterhouse at the foot of Woodland Drive were driven along Pender Street, through Chinatown and east to the swamp at Campbell Avenue.

During the Twenties and Thirties, the Pender Street area around Hawks became solidly Ukrainian. In the Forties, zoot-suited gangs protected their "turf" around the Princess cafe at Princess and Hastings. Single working men lived in cottages like the set at Heatley and Pender, or in the row-housing at Jackson and Keefer. Families built tall wooden houses along East Pender, Georgia and Keefer, some with turrets, stained glass and floor-to-ceiling bay windows—much like "Victorian" houses in San Francisco. Nearly all of the houses have the scroll-sawn and die-punched bargeboards, turned columns and pantograph fretwork of the nineteenth-century Gothic Revival, when woodworking was the most popular hobby in North America.

In the 1960s, the old Strathcona neighbourhood was threatened with complete destruction by the proposed Chinatown freeway. Two urban renewal projects on the boundaries of the area date from that period: the MacLean Park Housing project at Gore and Pender, and the Raymur Park project further east at Campbell and Hastings. Neither the projects, nor the philosophy which counselled the razing of "slum" neighbourhoods, have survived well. The old houses were renovated in the early 1970s, house by house, through an innovative combination of government grants, loans and private effort.

CITY OF VANCOUVER ARCHIVES

Lord Strathcona, Donald Smith, one of the founders of the CPR

A.G. Ferrera

Ferrera Court

Agostino Ferrera

Ferrera Court, erected in 1912 at the corner of Jackson and Hastings, is the grandest building in that part of town. The carved stone entranceway on Hastings has remained intact, although the overhanging cornice with its brackets and lions' head motif has been removed. Georges' Coffee Shop and James' Grocery are long gone, replaced with a Salvation Army Thrift Shop.

Ferrera Court was built by Cavaliere Agostino Gabriele Ferrera, the Italian consul to Vancouver, a Knight of the Crown of Italy and one of the city's first gourmet restaurateurs. He guessed in 1912 that False Creek (then stretching east to Clark Drive) provided such a natural barrier that the city would be forced to expand east along Hastings Street. Ferrera was born in Piedmont, Italy, in 1857. He was sent to relatives in New York in 1869, arriving there with $15 in his pocket. He came to Vancouver in 1897 and by 1902 owned a restaurant and five blocks of stores, and had acquired the title of Italian Consul. Ferrera's first restaurant was the Savoy, on West Cordova on the site now occupied by the Woodward's parkade. The Savoy opened in 1898 with the trumpeted promise to teach plebeian Vancouverites the joys of European cuisine. It was successful—people flocked to dine on imported oysters and be seen there, and Cordova's cobbles clopped and squeaked to more hooves and carriage wheels than anywhere else in town. One story which Ferrera was fond of telling concerned a turtle which had been purchased as a pet by the captain of a steamer bound "from the South Seas" to Vancouver. The turtle expired before reaching port; the captain mentioned this to Ferrera, who promptly bought the corpse. For years afterwards the shell was a fixture in the restaurant's window and turtle soup was available to discriminating patrons.

In 1901, Ferrera leased the northeast corner of Pender and Granville, the site of a bankrupt Bicycle Riding Academy, and built a sumptuous new restaurant. On February 15, 1902, the Maison de la Ville opened "with much éclat." Dozens of would-be patrons had to be turned away. The fifty-cent dinner included salad, soup, fish, two entrées, roast of beef, pudding, "fried cream topped with brandy" lit by Ferrera himself, and a small bottle of California wine. After five years, Cavaliere Ferrera, overloaded with his consular duties, decided not to exercise his option to purchase the property. The corner was purchased by Jonathan Rogers, who demolished the restaurant and, in 1910, erected the Rogers Building.

In 1913, Ferrera retired from his consular duties, bought a farm near Chilliwack and began to work at perfecting his own "Alpine-flavoured" cream cheese. His advertising slogan during the Twenties said: "A Meal Without Ferrera's Full Cream Cheese Is Like A Kiss Without A Squeeze!" In the last years of his long life, he moved back to the city and lived quietly at 2341 Quebec. He died in September, 1948.

Chief Malcolm MacLellan

The East End's reputation for violent crime was cemented by the March 20, 1917 murder of Vancouver Police Chief Malcolm MacLellan in an apartment above a grocery store at 522 East Georgia. The fact that the murder was perpetrated by a Negro drug addict, who was living with his "white paramour," fueled respectable citizens' fears that lawlessness and drug abuse had reached epidemic proportions.

The apartment above the little grocery store had been rented that January to a "Mr. and Mrs. Russell"—in fact, a 32-year old Detroit native named Robert Tait with a long Vancouver police record, and 28-year-old Frankie Russell, a "known prostitute and opium user" who had been arrested a number of times for offences including vagrancy, theft, drunkenness and inhabiting disorderly houses.

On the evening of March 20, landlord Frank King attempted to collect three months unpaid rent, but was met by a shotgun-toting man who said, "I'll blow your brains out." King retreated but returned shortly thereafter with three policemen, including Detectives Russell and Cameron. Russell knocked on the door and identified himself. Tait retorted: "I know you, Russell. You used to be a decent sort but I've been double-crossed too often. I've been acting stool too long. Before you take me I'll go through with it." Tait fired the shotgun through the frosted glass on the door, hitting Cameron in the face and peppering the others with shattered glass and pellets. They retreated. Tait then turned his attention to the front window, and gunned down and killed nine-year-old George Robb, who was crossing the road from his home at 548 East Georgia to buy candy at the store.

Police quickly cordoned off the area. A large crowd gathered east of the house and near Jackson Avenue, and talked of lynching Tait. Chief MacLellan attempted to talk the "confirmed hophead" into surrendering, but when that proved futile attempted—with the Deputy Chief and a few detectives—to storm the apartment. An axe borrowed from a neighbour was used to chop through the door into the darkened apartment. A tremendous gun battle ensued, with Tait firing a variety of weapons from the barricaded bedroom. The police, having emptied their service revolvers, were forced to retreat again, leaving Chief MacLellan mortally wounded in the kitchen. Reinforcements were sent for, and the Fire Department illuminated the back yard to prevent Tait slipping out the back. Two constables took up positions in the house across the street and riddled Tait's apartment with bullets. There was no returning fire, and the police paused to consider their next step. A decision was made to smoke Tait out. The fire department was in the process of preparing two sulphur pots in commandeered garbage cans, when shots and a crash were heard in the apartment.

Detectives covered the line of fire into the apartment, while Constable Berry crawled in to retrieve the Chief's body. They heard the voice of Frankie Russell calling for help from the bedroom. A

WILLENA STONE

Next page: the siege of the house at 522 East Georgia on March 20, 1917, which resulted in the death of Police Chief Malcolm MacLellan and "confirmed hophead" Robert Tait. Above: some members of the Vancouver police force, photographed two weeks after the death of the Chief. The composite of the Chief is third from the right, in front. At the time, Vancouver had a police force of about 250 men and a population of slightly over 100,000. The police were "well armed with baton and revolver, and of fine physique, the police regulations calling for six feet in height, a chest measurement of 37 inches, and a minimum weight of 165 pounds." In the event of an arrest, the officer was not allowed to march the culprit through the streets–"a disagreeable sight in many cities more advanced than Vancouver"–but had to phone, using one of the hundred electric patrol boxes scattered throughout the town, for a motorized police wagon.

few moments later, she appeared in the doorway with her hands above her head, framing Tait's gory remains. The gunman had blown the top of his head off with a shotgun, using his toe to pull the trigger.

The Sun's headline the next day blared: "Sensational Gunfight With Giant Drug Crazed Negro on Georgia Street, East, Results in Death of Three." The city mourned Malcolm MacLellan, who was only 44 years old and left a wife and two young boys. Ironically, the man who was killed by a drug addict had devoted much of his time to the plight of Vancouver's drug addicts, and had proposed the establishment of a medical asylum to aid in their rehabilitation. The old grocery store was torn down and replaced by a "Vancouver Special" bungalow—the only modern home on that quiet block.

(Above) *The Schara Tzedeck synagogue at Heatley and East Pender in 1926. The synagogue replaced a house at 514 Heatley, on the lane, which had served as the first school and place of worship for the Jewish community clustered in the surrounding blocks of Pender, Georgia and Keefer. When the Jewish community moved out after the Second World War, the building was bought by sportsman Rufus Gibbs and operated as a boys' club. The inscription "Gibbs' Boys Club" is still visible on the front façade of the dilapidated building. Nearly all of the windows were bricked up during the boys' club days; the building is now a boarded-up shell, after two reasonably-successful arson attempts on the interior. The Jewish community there disintegrated in the 1920s, when the Jewish Community Centre was built at 11th and Oak (now "Construction House"); later, a new synagogue was built further up Oak Street and, in the 1950s, the Jewish Community Centre moved to new premises at the corner of 41st and Oak, on the site of the old Vancouver Trapshooting Club. (Left) The East End grocery, on Princess Street at Pender, was one of several little groceries ringing Strathcona School, dispensing 10 for a penny sweets. The store, pictured here in 1909, disappeared when Princess Street was closed off to give the school an expanded play area and parking lot. In addition to candy, fruit and Blue Ribbon Tea, Japanese grocers, in the period before the First World War, brought kegs of cider from the Okanagan. After a month or two of slow sales, the cider fermented in the barrels and intoxicated any local kid with a spare nickel. The police were not amused, and put a stop to the practice. (Next page) A historical pageant on June 14, 1912, in the 400 block East Hastings Street. The Coral Rooms building (now the Orwell Hotel) and the Ferrera Court (extreme background, left side) are the only two substantial buildings left standing.*

135

Shaughnessy Heights

The Canadian Pacific Railway "built" Vancouver. Until the First World War, it pushed and pulled people from one residential area to another as the city grew from the ashes of the Great Fire. During the 1880s and 1890s, Blueblood Alley was the fashionable spot to live; later, the West End was the most desirable. One of the railway's few unsuccessful ventures was an attempt made in the early-1890s to sell Fairview Slopes as the attractive alternative to the West End, but that was quickly scotched by the pre-Klondike depression and the pollution from False Creek's sawmills.

After 1897 Vancouver boomed, spurred on by the Klondike Gold Rush. "In 1910, Vancouver Then, Will Have a Hundred Thousand Men" was the slogan on merchants' and developers' lips. One alliterative banner on Hastings Street in 1909 said: "Many Men Making Money Means Much for Vancouver!" So, in 1907, when the CPR announced that they were going to create another prestigious development, the market was ready. On the morning of the property sale, the line-up extended from the railway's station and headquarters almost to Hastings Street. The subdivision in question was 250 acres, occupying the area between the interurban line and Oak Street on the steep hill above 16th Avenue. It was to be named after Sir Thomas Shaughnessy, the CPR president, and many of the streets were named after CPR officials: Sir Augustus Nanton was a CPR director, as were Richard B. Angus, Sir Edmund Osler and W.D. Matthews; C.R. Hosmer was head of the Telegraph Department; Marguerite was the daughter of Sir Thomas.

Shaughnessy Heights was the first Vancouver subdivision to have its streets laid out following the natural contours of the land. The lots varied in size from one-fifth of an acre to one-and-one-half acres. Land was reserved near 41st and Oak for golfing links, and restrictions were set on the minimum price and size of dwellings. The M.P. Cotton Co. got the contract for much of the road grading and sewering throughout the area. Day after day, wagon loads of stone left the South Vancouver rock pit (now the Quarry Gardens at Little Mountain) to macadamize Shaughnessy's roads. Concrete sidewalks were poured. Angus Drive and Osler were laid out with broad, treed boulevards; two parks—a small one west of Granville on Angus and the splendid Crescent east of Granville—were planted. Soil for gardens was brought by the wagon load from the Marpole Midden. Life in Shaughnessy was to be the most elegant west of Mount Royal!

The first home, for CPR western superintendent Richard Marpole, was built in 1909 on a huge, almost block-sized lot at 1615 Marpole Avenue. Others followed immediately on the slope below and on the Crescent, most notably the huge Hycroft estate for General A.D. McRae, just above the corner of 16th and Granville on McRae Avenue. The pace of building barely slowed for the First World War, and by 1920 the original subdivision had been almost completely filled, all the way to King Edward Avenue. The area's formerly fashionable rival—the West End—was rapidly converted from big family homes into rambling rooming houses. Newcomers stayed at the Glencoe Lodge on Georgia at Burrard while their Shaughnessy homes were being completed.

Pressure to subdivide the estate-sized lots of Old Shaughnessy in the early Twenties forced the CPR to open a second phase, still called Shaughnessy, south of King Edward to 33rd Avenue. The lots were smaller and the houses more modest. A later expansion, announced in February, 1926 extended south to 41st Avenue. It produced an area around 39th and Angus Drive which has much of the grandeur of the original subdivision. Land prices were not excessive: the half-acre lot at 5391 Angus Drive was offered for $2,540. The CPR Land Division offered attractive terms: one-tenth down, one-tenth in six months and the balance in eight equal annual installments at six percent interest. The golf course was within walking distance.

The Twenties—a giddy, spendthrift time even for common people—were the heyday of old Shaughnessy. Packards with rumble seats, sporty Stutzes and Cadillacs, dozens of servants, costume balls, golf and lawn-bowling and tennis (at the Vancouver Lawn Tennis Club, then located at the southeast corner of King Edward and Granville), jazz, contract bridge and imported wines were the order of those carefree days and filled the Society pages of the newspapers. The influence and exclusivity of the area was reflected in the easy passage by the Provincial Government in 1922 of the Shaughnessy Heights Building Restrictions Act, which limited any subdivision or tenancies in the area.

Two dark clouds spoiled the picnic. The sensational murder of Janet Smith at 3851 Osler in 1924 (page 142) focussed a lot of unwelcome attention on the habits of Shaughnessy's partying crowd. As well, the inquest pried the lid off a cauldron of bigotry, political influence and police favoritism. The purchase of W.L. Tait's Glen Brae estate that same year by the Kanadian Knights of the Ku Klux Klan further coloured the public's perception of the area.

These were minor disruptions compared with the Wall Street crash in 1929. Many of the homes were barely supportable when mortgaged to the hilt in good times; in the Dirty Thirties, the area was called "Poverty Heights" or "Mortgage Hill" and many of the homes stood empty and deteriorating. The Shaughnessy Heights Property Owners Association was given the authority by its provincial statute to control zoning and prosecute offenders in the area, and it spent much of its time in litigation. One notable case—to stop businessman James Anthony Pappajohn from building a retail store on the northwest corner of Granville and King Edward—was taken by the government all the way to the Supreme Court in December, 1936. (The lot remained vacant until the late Seventies, when a large house was trucked from a lot elsewhere

Col. Alfred Markham (1841-1935) cleared Shaughnessy Heights for the CPR. During World War I, he started the returned servicemen's club in the Oakley house at the southeast corner of Cambie and Georgia. Later, he moved it to the old Vancouver Club.

Augustus Meredith Nanton, CPR director, the namesake of Shaughnessy's Nanton Avenue.

Richard B. Angus, after a mercurial, 12-year rise from clerk to general manager of the Bank of Montreal, became a director of the CPR.

W. Foster Huntting, born in Iowa in 1879, formed the Huntting-Lea lumber company on False Creek in 1902. It burned on August 21, 1909. In 1914, he established the Huntting-Merritt Shingle Mill at the south foot of Granville on the Fraser. His home, at 3689 Angus Drive, was well-known during the Twenties for the entertaining of Mrs. Marion D. Laing, his widow.

A. Edward Tulk, born in Hamilton in 1877, was a barrister, liquor merchant, Conservative, Anglican, and one of the founders of the Vancouver Athletic Club. He built the $250,000 Rosemary, named after his only daughter, at 3689 Selkirk.

The western edge of Shaughnessy Heights in the summer of 1911, looking north from the corner of Cypress and Matthews. The Shaughnessy area south as far as 41st Avenue had only recently been logged–the stumps and slash were heaped into huge piles by steam donkeys and burned during the summers of 1909 and 1910. By the summer of 1911, there was nothing left north of 41st which cast a shadow. Miles Penner Cotton quarried the stone for the roads at the South Vancouver rock pit, now the Quarry Gardens on Little Mountain.

and put on the site.) Shaughnessy split into two camps—an increasing minority who could manage to keep the area up, and the rest who were quietly taking in boarders and subdividing their large homes.

By 1943, Shaughnessy Heights and its ratepayers were extremely unpopular. The city was gripped by a housing crisis: the papers regularly published pictures of houses (like the one at 2351 The Crescent) which were vacant, crumbling and overgrown with morning glory, alongside pictures of homeless war widows, muni-

tions factory workers and families. Emergency wartime legislation was passed, allowing conversion of some of the old homes into rooming houses.

By 1948, Shaughnessy Heights was classed as "another blighted area" by the Town Planning Commission's F.E. Buck. A few homes, like the one at 1812 West 19th at Pine Crescent, were converted into frat-houses by owners taking advantage of the wartime housing relaxations. In 1949, "frat rats" were said to be "sprawled across the lawns drinking beer." The Hollies, at 1350 The Crescent, operated as a fashionable wedding reception hall until slapped with an injunction by the S.H.P.O.A.

In 1959, Shaughnessy's zoning was rewritten to allow the status quo of rooming houses to continue. New prosperity brought moneyed families back into the area. Fortunately, the grand streetscape has stayed much as it was in Shaughnessy's heyday.

A.D. McRae

Hycroft is the most imposing mansion in Old Shaughnessy. Built for Colonel, later General, later Senator, Alexander Duncan McRae, it is one of the earlier Shaughnessy homes, begun in 1909 and completed in 1911. The house is in the classical style, with huge columns supporting a porte-cochère. The interior plasterwork and carving by Charles Marega, particularly around the den fireplace, is unusually rich, even for Shaughnessy. The downstairs ballroom was the scene of many of the grand masked balls of Shaughnessy's salad days, since the McRaes favoured elaborate entertainments, including an annual fancy dress ball, which received much attention in the newspapers.

Alexander Duncan McRae, according to his obituary, would be chiefly remembered for his "powers of promotion and organization." He was born on November 17, 1874, in the little town of Glencoe, Ontario. He left Canada in 1895 for Minnesota, where he assisted an uncle in operating a chain of local banks. He started an insurance business in his spare time, which made him a $50,000 stake by the time he sold it in 1903. He returned to Canada and organized the Saskatchewan Valley Land Company, cashing in on the Prairie colonization and land boom. McRae and his associates bought 500,000 acres from the Federal Government at $1 an acre and another 50,000 acres from the railroads; they attracted some 250,000 new settlers to the west and made a cool $9 million. Like most wealthy men, he was an officer in the Canadian Expeditionary Force when war broke out, and went overseas with the Second Division of the C.E.F. in 1915. He was made Director of Remounts for Western Canada and Director of Supply and Transport for the Regiment. In December, 1916 he was made Quartermaster-General of all the Canadian Overseas Forces and promoted to the rank of Brigadier-General. At the end of the war, he held the rank of major-general and was the head of the Ministry of Information under Lord Beaverbrook.

In the Twenties, McRae became active in provincial politics. He was the primary fundraiser and president of the Provincial Party, a breakaway group formed of remnants of the Young Conservatives, the Soldiers' Party, and the United Farmers of B.C. Their major ambition, leading up to the 1925 election, was to prove fraud in the PGE railway dealings of the McBride, Bowser, and Oliver governments. They lacked a newspaper as a forum, so published an incendiary pamphlet called "The Searchlight," which featured headlines like "B.C. is Saved! The People Turn on Their Betrayers!" Premier Oliver noted that McRae's own investments in Port Mann during the CNPR boom before 1912 wouldn't stand up to investigation. All three provincial leaders— McRae, Bowser, and Oliver—were defeated in the 1925 election, and the Provincial Party disintegrated soon after. McRae then joined the federal Conservative Party and won the Vancouver North seat in the 1926 election. His organizational ability was

Residential View on Shaughnessy Heights. Vancouver, B.C.

used by Calgary lawyer Richard B. "Bonfire" Bennett (so named because he talked so fast) to make the latter Conservative party leader. In the 1930 election, which brought Bennett's Conservatives to power, McRae lost his seat. He was made a senator the following year.

After McRae's first wife died at Hycroft in 1942, he donated the mansion to the Federal Government as a convalescent home for disabled war veterans. It opened as an annex of Shaughnessy Military Hospital in 1943, and was vacated on June 1, 1960, when a large addition was completed at the main hospital. Two years later, the University Women's Club took it over and has restored it.

McRae married the former Mrs. Allan Rodes of El Paso, Texas in October, 1943 and established Eaglecrest, a lavish home with a 3700 acre model farm, at Qualicum Beach. McRae didn't enjoy it long—he died on June 26, 1946. The home burnt down in March, 1969.

Looking southwest from 16th Avenue at General McRae's Hycroft in Shaughnessy Heights. The building is now the University Women's Club. Huge poplars have since grown up along the concrete wall on 16th.

A.D. MacRae

Eric Hamber

Greencroft, the Eric Hamber house at the northeast corner of Cypress and Matthews. The location and angle of the painting is almost identical to the picture of the road grader on page 137. Greencroft today is almost completely hidden by trees.

Eric Hamber

Greencroft was built in 1913 by the newly-married Mr. and Mrs. Eric Hamber—he a banker (and later-to-be lieutenant-governor during the late Thirties), she the daughter of mill-owner John Hendry.

Eric Werge Hamber was very good at everything he put his hand to. He was born on April 21, 1879, in Winnipeg, where his father was headmaster of St. John's College. Although not remembered as a scholar, he was possibly the best Canadian all-round athlete of his time. At St. John's College, he was captain of the rugby team, which he led to a western Canadian championship in 1901. He became associated with the Toronto Argonauts in their glory years from 1902-06, and was captain of all three of their teams— hockey, football and rowing. He rowed for the Argos at Henley in 1902, and later captained a Winnipeg team in the Stanley Cup when it was an amateur championship. He was described in the sporting press to be "as clean a player as has ever stood on skates." He claimed later that he developed his muscles by carrying pails of water several blocks from the public pump to his Winnipeg home. Later in life, Hamber was known on the west coast for the *Lady Van*, an R class racing sloop, and for the *Vencendor*, a three-masted, iron-hulled former British training ship which was the finest yacht in the RVYC

regattas of the Twenties and Thirties. He developed a passion for thoroughbred racing, and maintained a 1,000-acre stock farm in Coquitlam called the Minnekhada Ranch, now a Regional Park.

As a businessman, he "never lost the aloof look of a banker. He was always distant and withdrawn." Hamber got his first job in 1897 as a bank clerk at $16 a month. By 1906, he had transferred to Calgary as the manager of the Dominion Bank. In 1907, he was moved to Vancouver, and in 1910 to London, where he became the manager of the bank's main office. A year later, he met and courted Aldyen Hendry, who was visiting London with her parents. The couple announced plans to marry and insisted that the ceremony take place in London, thus annoying the elder Hendry, who was reluctant to cancel the berths he had already booked for his family and Hamber on the maiden voyage of the *Titanic*.

The next year, after the marriage, the couple came to Vancouver, and took up residence at Greencroft. Hamber started work with his father-in-law's B.C. Mills, Timber and Trading Company. Directorships followed, as did control of the company after Hendry's death in 1916. Hamber also became a leading figure in public service organizations like the Vancouver General Hospital, the Boy Scouts, the Red Cross and the B.C. Cancer Foundation. He was made an honorary Colonel of the Seaforth Highlanders.

His public-spiritedness made him a popular lieutenant-governor from 1936 to 1941. During that time, the Hambers entertained Franklin Delano Roosevelt (in May 1937), and King George VI and Queen Elizabeth during their Dominion tour in 1939. After his viceregal term expired, he became Chancellor of the University of British Columbia. He continued his business and horse-racing activities through the Fifties, finally selling the stock farm in 1958. He died in 1960. The couple had no children, and Greencroft was subsequently sold.

(Preceding page) The white, Tuscan-style house at 3390 The Crescent contrasts with the Tudor homes which dominate Shaughnessy Heights. Villa Russe (the Russian house) was built in the early Twenties for Misak Yremavitch Aivazoff, who held some of the great parties of the Twenties and Thirties for fellow Russian exiles like pianist Sergei Rachmaninoff, White Russian Generals Merkuloff and Semenoff, the Grand Duke Alexander, and Prince Obelinsky. Aivazoff was a Russian Armenian, born in the village of Tiflis on the Kura River. He organized 22 co-operative groups of peasants and made three separate fortunes on Czarist-era wheat crops. His godfather, the governor of Azerbaijan, warned him to flee the country, as the Russian police considered his attempts to organize the peasants to be seditious political agitation. Aivazoff landed in San Francisco and moved north to Prince Rupert, where he established a construction firm which built the courthouse and owned the town's only theatre. He came to Vancouver in 1919, and, in addition to his entertainments, he was active in the Russian Greek Orthodox Church. Aivazoff sold Villa Russe to Dal Grauer in the late Thirties and moved to 1304 Jervis Street, where he died, aged 78, in June, 1954.

CITY OF VANCOUVER ARCHIVES

Andrew Robert Mann, the president of Northern Construction Ltd. and an executive of Canadian National Railways, moved from Winnipeg in the early Twenties and bought The Hollies at 1350 The Crescent.

Walter Cameron Nichol (left) was a newspaperman who, in 1921, became lieutenant-governor of B.C. Born in Goderich, Ontario in 1866, he came to B.C. in 1897 to pursue his interest in gold mining. He became the editor of the *Province* when it was a Victoria weekly, moved it to Vancouver and turned it into a daily in 1898. Before moving to his new home at 1402 The Crescent (above), Nichol lived in the "Steamboat House" on the Fairview Slopes (page 149).

Janet Smith

The comparatively modest home at 3851 Osler was the scene in 1924 of one of the most controversial and brutal murders in Vancouver's history. On July 26, 23-year-old Janet Smith, a Scottish nanny working for the Frederick Baker family, was ironing clothes in the basement. Workmen next door could hear her singing, and commented to each other that she was "a Scottish nightingale." Suddenly, shots were heard; the houseboy, Wong Foon Sien (or Sing), said that he ran down the stairs and discovered Smith lying in a pool of blood, an army-issue Colt .45 in her hand and a wound over her right eye. Wong phoned his employer to say that "nursey" was hurt. Baker called the Point Grey Municipal Police and rushed to the scene. Constable Green, who arrived with Pt. Grey Medical Officer Dr. Bertie Blackwood, picked up the gun and blurred any fingerprints. Blackwood noted that the iron was still hot and the girl's body still warm. Within a couple of hours, a hearse arrived and removed the body. City Coroner Dr. Brydone-Jack approved a partial embalming of the body, during which the bullet hole was filled with plaster of paris. After a hasty investigation the following day, and although the bullet had still not been found, a verdict of accidental death—implying suicide and despondency in the young, singing girl—was returned and the body was buried in Mountain View Cemetery. During a cursory inspection of the premises the next day, the bullet was found lodged in the basement wall, in a position which made it obvious that Janet Smith had not fired the gun. Provincial Attorney General A.M. Manson stepped in and ordered a second inquest, which opened with sensational publicity on September 4.

The Bakers, well-connected with old Shaughnessy money—the McRaes, Foleys, Stewarts, Rogerses—were alleged to be part of a Packard and jazz set who partied the nights away on bootleg liquor, then raced along Marine Drive in fast convoys to Spanish Banks for delicious, champagne-warmed skinny dips. It was alleged that Smith was having an affair with Baker or one of his friends, and that she had witnessed Baker's involvement in a cocaine deal.

Frederick Baker told the inquest that the family was borrowing the house from his brother, who was vacationing in Europe. The revolver was owned by Baker, who kept it in a haversack by the front door. It was loaded because he had "tried to remove the cartridge [himself], but it was jammed in so [he] just left the safety catch on." A Barrister was hired by the Scottish Society to ensure that the second investigation wasn't a whitewash, and rumblings were heard in the press from the anti-Asiatic leagues, the Ku Klux Klan and old-country-dominated labour unions. Tensions increased between east side and west side representatives, and it was said publicly that it wasn't possible for a servant girl to get justice. The body was exhumed, an autopsy performed, at which it came out that Smith had been pushed down the basement stairs, either before or after the gunshot. The Bakers had had a party at the house the previous night, and some of the guests had not returned from sudden trips out of the country. A new verdict of murder was entered. Meanwhile, Wong the cook was kidnapped by a Chinese private eye, beaten, given the "third degree"—during which a confession was extracted—and finally dumped at the Vancouver Police Station, where he was arrested. Wong was formally charged with murder, but finally acquitted. The murder remains unsolved to this day. The ramifications of the event extended beyond Shaughnessy's little world. The image of the Vancouver "establishment" was tarnished and the cause of inter-municipal cooperation among South Vancouver, Point Grey, and Vancouver received a setback.

(Next page) The Baker house at 3851 Osler, the scene of the brutal Janet Smith murder in July, 1924.

Janet Smith, photographed a few days before her murder.

William Disbrow Brydone-Jack, the physician and city coroner who approved Janet Smith's embalming before performing a complete autopsy. Born in 1860 in Fredericton and educated at McGill, he graduated from the University of Edinburgh in 1884 and arrived in Vancouver five years later. He was connected with the Vancouver General Hospital from 1892-1912, and helped organize the Victorian Order of Nurses and St. John's Ambulance in Vancouver. From 1923 to 1935 he was the official coroner for Vancouver. He died in August, 1938.

J.W. Stewart

J.W. Stewart

The house at 1675 Angus Drive, called Ardvar, was the long-time home of Major-General John W. Stewart, CB, CMG, DSO, one of the great railroad contractors and military heroes of the First World War era. The son of a Sutherlandshire crofter, he was born in 1862 and came to Quebec in the early 1880s with ten shillings in his pocket. He came to Vancouver with the CPR in 1885, and worked on the survey party which cut Granville Street and laid out the Fairview area.

Stewart courted and married one of the seven Moran girls. Patrick Welch and Jim Foley, also married to two of the Moran girls, became Stewart's business partners in the largest independent construction firm of the pre-War years—Foley, Stewart and Welch. They built a large part of the Grand Trunk Railroad, double-tracked the CPR from Fort William to Winnipeg, and built the revolutionary spiral Connaught Tunnel in the Rockies for the CPR. Between 1913 and 1915, Stewart was the first president of the Pacific Great Eastern Railway (now B.C. Rail), and supervised its construction from Squamish to Fort George and Quesnel.

In 1916, Stewart took a battalion of Canadian Railway troops to Belgium and was, in the words of British historian T.O. O'Connor, "one of the men who really helped win the Great War." Stewart was the road and rail genius who pushed miles of light railway through the Flanders mud under heavy shellfire. He was showered with honours at war's end, and, to quote O'Connor: "If I had been Prime Minister, [Stewart] would have found a seat in the British House of Lords." The Prince of Wales, during his visit to Vancouver in 1919, stayed with Stewart in the Angus Drive house. Upon his return to Vancouver after the war, he invested heavily in the *Vancouver Sun*, and was credited with promoting accountant R.J. Cromie to publisher, a move which resulted in the *Sun*'s domination of the Vancouver publishing business. His last major enterprise was a railroad and industrial development program on the Gold Coast of Africa in the Twenties. He died in 1938.

(His brother Angus [1875-1953] was the first white man into Kitimat and explored and surveyed much of the then-remote Kitsault area during the early years of the century.)

Lord Shaughnessy

Lord Thomas Shaughnessy, a Milwaukee Irishman "with an almost bloodless devotion to material ends," was hired in 1882 during the construction period as quartermaster and comptroller for the Canadian Pacific Railway. His efficiency and organizational ability saved the railway's financial bacon, and he became its General Manager in 1885 and President in 1899. During his term, which spanned the Edwardian era, he fought the great battles for control of southeastern B.C. with James Hill's Great Northern Railway, sponsored the building of the Kettle Valley Railway and piloted the CPR to its pre-eminence as a globe-spanning transportation empire. Shaughnessy was knighted in 1901, and made Baron Shaughnessy of Montreal in 1916. He died in 1923. His wife, Elizabeth Bridget Nagle of Milwaukee, died at age 85 in 1937 as Dowager Lady Shaughnessy.

Samuel Maclure

Samuel Maclure (self-portrait, left) and Cecil Crocker Fox were two of Vancouver's most successful architects during the first few decades of the city's history. Maclure, particularly, developed a large practice specializing in picturesque, "English countryside," half-timbered Tudor Revival homes in New Westminster, Vancouver and later Victoria. Born in New Westminster in 1860, he attended the Spring Garden Art School in Philadelphia and worked for the Esquimalt and Northern Railway as a telegraph operator in 1885. He had a passion for painting, which he taught from a cluttered studio in Victoria in his later years. His "best" home in Vancouver is "Gabriola," at 1531 Davie Street in the West End, built in 1901, a decade earlier than his Shaughnessy efforts. With his partner Fox—who was influenced by English architect C.F.A. Voysey, designer William Morris and the Arts and Crafts Movement—Maclure dominated the early development of Shaughnessy Heights, completing a remarkable number of Tudor-style homes in the period immediately prior to the Great War. (The one home which, according to architectural historian Harold Kalman, most reflects Fox's architectural personality is the Foster Huntting house at 3689 Angus Drive.) Among the team's designs are the Walter C. Nichol house at 1402 the Crescent, "Rosemary" at 3689 Selkirk, the John E. Tucker house at 3802 Angus, the aforementioned Huntting home, the Brenchley house at 3351 Granville, the Morrison-Mrs. Ernest Rogers house at 1789 Matthews, the Rear-Victor Spencer house (Aberthau) at Locarno Beach, Brock House at Jericho Beach and the E.P. Davis home (now called Cecil Green Park) at UBC.

Grandview

Grandview, initially called Grand View, is the area between Venables and First Avenue above Commercial. It indeed has a grand view, and was promoted in the years before the 1912 as a middle-class alternative to the West End and Shaughnessy Heights. Lot sizes were very flexible, and the successful businessmen and industrialists who decided to move into the new area bought as many of them as they could, giving the area a hodgepodge of mansions, cottages, odd streets and blocks unlike any other area in Vancouver.

The area south of Hastings along Victoria Drive was logged at the turn of the century. Commercial Drive became a major shopping street, thanks to the interurban, which had passed along it since 1892, and a Grandview-4th Avenue streetcar line which served more local needs. There were few farmers and homesteaders in the area; one of the first was a blacksmith, Obel Gooldrup, who anticipated the building boom by a few years when he established his blacksmith shop at the corner of Victoria and Grant in 1905. Successful families like the Odlums, the Copps and the Millers built huge, walled and turreted mansions along Salisbury and Victoria Drives, which rivalled much of what was being built in Shaughnessy at the time. Most of these homes were impossible to maintain in the depression-war-depression cycle which followed the collapse of the real estate boom in 1912, and, by the 1920s, many had been converted into private hospitals (like the Glen Hospital, formerly the Miller residence, on Salisbury, and the Grandview Hospital at 1090 Victoria, across the street from the old W.H. Copp house). Many were chopped into apartments, while others were demolished and the estates subdivided. Most of the later housing is decidedly more modest. The area east of Victoria Drive is an unusual collection of narrow streets, tall houses and mid-block grocery stores—a neighbourhood without the strict zoning enforced in the Municipality of Point Grey.

Grandview has been called "Little Italy" since after the Second World War, when the Italian community left the Union Street area more or less en masse and settled around Commercial Drive. Bocce —a sort of Italian lawn bowling—is played regularly at Victoria Park at Grant and Victoria, across the street from the site of Gooldrup's blacksmithery. Many theatre and music connoisseurs visit the Vancouver East Cultural Centre, the old Grandview United Church at the corner of Venables and Victoria.

CITY OF VANCOUVER ARCHIVES

The first house in Grandview, at 1617 Graveley Street. At the time of its construction, in 1891, the area was only reached by logging skid roads, and the interurban railway half a block away on Commercial Drive was still under construction. The house was built for Mr. and Mrs. John Mason. It was demolished in the Fifties and replaced by a walk-up apartment building.

J.J. Miller

John J. Miller's fabulous Kurrajong (the name reflecting his Australian birth: it is a tree which is widespread in eastern Australia), at the corner of Napier and Salisbury in Grandview.

CITY OF VANCOUVER ARCHIVES

CVA

J.J. Miller

John J. Miller built the huge home at 1036 Salisbury Drive which, for the past several decades, has operated as the private Glen Hospital. The turreted mansion with its stone wall was one of the finest homes built in the area in the grand, palmy Edwardian years before the Great War. Miller represented the City at the coronation of George V in London in 1911, and sent back glowing reports of the pomp and circumstance for the *World* newspaper. A more bizarre, North American claim to fame was his holding of more Masonic Lodge degrees than any other man in Canada.

Miller was an Australian, born in 1860 in New South Wales. At the age of 30, he became the mayor of the grazier's country town of Cootamundra. Within ten years he had left Australia for good, and landed in Vancouver in 1903 aboard the *Aorangi*. He started an auction business which became fabulously successful: on one record-breaking day, he sold $1,250,000 worth of Prince Rupert town lots. With the proceeds he moved to Grandview and built his mansion.

Miller was a booster and a promoter: in 1908 he got a group of friends together to start the Vancouver Exhibition—now the Pacific National Exhibition. He negotiated the civic lease on Hastings Park and was elected president of the Exhibition Board, a position he continued to hold for thirteen years. Miller Drive in Exhibition Park is named for him.

Miller served as alderman for Ward Four in 1917. He died in December, 1950, leaving six daughters.

Prof. Edward Odlum

Grandview, in its boom years before the First World War, attracted its fair share of promoters and successful real estate agents. Professor Edward Odlum, who built the rambling home at 1774 Grant, was an anomaly—a theologian, scientist and educator with a world-wide reputation.

Edward Odlum spent many of his 84 years travelling the world, lecturing, engaging in scientific and ethnographic research and promoting the British Israelite movement and the Methodist Church. He arrived in Vancouver for the first time in 1889, when he took up real estate and business activities (the forerunner of the Odlum, Brown stockbroker group); the second time, in 1904, he built the large home on Grant Street to which he returned throughout the rest of his life.

Edward Odlum was born in Tullamore, Peel County, Ontario on November 27, 1850. His family—which traced its Irish roots to a group of soldiers who fought for King William in 1690—had long-standing military associations. His grandfather was an officer in Wellington's army; his uncle was actively involved with the Fenians. Young Edward served with the 36th Peel County Regiment during the Fenian Raids of 1866 through 1870 and, in recognition of his efforts, he received 100 free acres of land in Ontario.

In university, he worked with a Dr. Hansel to produce the first electric light used in Canada, and the first telephone used for public purposes. He was always interested in scientific research, but his consuming passion was comparative ethnology. He was a prominent evolutionist: once, during world travels in the Antipodes, he studied Australian bushmen to disprove the then-popular sentiment that they were barely a step above the orangutan. He was appointed president of a 600-student college in Tokio during the Nineties, and was the first North American to study the origins of the Japanese. He wandered continually, studying Laplanders, Finns and Northern Russians in the days of the Czar; he propagated theories on the roots of the British people, and studied in Persia and Babylonia to find further clues. At age 72, he took off on another world tour, which occupied him for years among native Indians in the United States and obscure tribes in the South Pacific.

He also managed to find time to run a mine in the Cariboo, write a report on the value of B.C. trees for the botanical section of the 1893 Chicago World's Columbian Exposition, and lecture widely in Britain and Europe to promote Canadian immigration. He served two sessions as Alderman in Vancouver: once in 1892 and again in

Professor Edward Odlum's house at 1774 Grant, in Grandview, was one of the earliest large houses built in the area. Its yard originally occupied much of the block east of Commercial, but in more recent, modest times, a small, stucco bungalow was built onto its sideyard.

1904. In his latter years, he was a regular voice on the "British Israelite Hour" on syndicated radio. On Sundays, he lay-preached for the Methodist Church. He married twice: the first time to Mary Elvira Powell, with whom he had four sons; the second time to Martha Thomas of Vancouver, with whom he had two sons (Mary Elvira died while they were living in Japan). Of the children, one (Victor) achieved some fame as a newspaperman and military figure; two continued to live in Grandview: Edward F. lived at 1880 Grant, while carpenter Arthur G. Odlum lived at 3056 Commercial Drive. Professor Odlum died in May, 1935.

Professor Edward Odlum

Fairview Slopes

Fairview Slopes today is a Vancouver echo of San Francisco's elegant, steep Russian Hill and North Beach neighbourhoods. Some of the most exciting-looking townhouses and condominiums have been artfully fitted onto the steep slope, to make the most of a beautiful view across False Creek to B.C. Place, with the downtown skyline and mountains beyond.

The headlong rush to redevelop Fairview Slopes since the early 1970s parallels the cleaning up of False Creek, formerly the city's main industrial slum and inner-city sewer. As long as False Creek was lined with smoky sawmills and the tangled, abandoned remnants of 70-year old machinery and railyards, there was little incentive to improve the decrepit housing above it.

The area first attracted settlement in 1891, when it was subdivided and sold by the Canadian Pacific Railway, with the help of enterprising realtors like Thomas Calland. Seventh Avenue was the first street pushed through to connect Mount Pleasant with the new North Arm Road (Granville Street). The opening of the Fairview belt streetcar line the following year made the slope an attractive, accessible place to build, and although the Fairview Slopes subdivision was abandoned during the 1893-4 Depression, it prospered again in the Klondike years. Concurrently, though, Vancouver's sawmilling and log booming industry began to fill the Creek: sawmills like Rat Portage, Hanbury, the Alberta Lumber Co., Huntting-Lea, and the predecessors of B.C. Forest Products took up residence. Combined with the creek-cum-sewer outfall which drained at the foot of Ash Street, these smoke-belchers quickly took the shine off the area.

Many fine houses were built there, nevertheless, including the 1891 home once occupied by *Province* publisher and Lieutenant-Governor Walter C. Nichol. This "Steamboat House," built for Sir John Watt Reid at 1151 West 8th in 1891, is so called because of its Mississippi riverboat style woodturning. Two other houses from the period are the James England house, with its beautiful bell turret, on the steep lot at the corner of 7th and Birch; and the Hodson Manor, built in 1894 for steamboat Capt. J.J. Logan and moved in 1974 a few blocks to its current location at 1254 West 7th.

More characteristic of the Fairview Slopes since the First World War is the Yoda tenement at 1017 West 7th, built in 1913 on the steep slope above 6th. The building presents a very modest front to the street but descends down the hillside in a series of steps, and provided dozens of small apartments for the Japanese workers at the False Creek sawmills and shipyards.

During the Sixties, the Fairview Slopes community organized vociferously, though unsuccessfully, against the coming onslaught of higher-priced accommodation. City Manager Fritz Bowers, then an Alderman, said: "Never have so many fought so hard for so little."

The fire at King Edward High School at 12th and Oak Street in June, 1973. The old school, built as the Vancouver High School and opened in January, 1905, was the first large building in Fairview. Its landmark turret (page 91) is invisible in the smoke. The King Edward gymnasium, built in 1940 at the western end of the block, survived the fire to become the nucleus of the King Edward campus of Vancouver Community College, which has since moved to the site of the old China Creek cycle track on Broadway near Clark Drive. All of the college buildings were demolished in 1983, and the Vancouver General Hospital has expanded onto the block.

Vancouver General Hospital

Vancouver General Hospital is one of the largest medical facilities in Canada. Scarcely a year goes by without some modernization and demolition, the latest being the building erected at the corner of 12th and Oak on the old King Edward High School site. Unlike St. Paul's, which was established by the Catholic Church in 1894 at the end of the Burrard Street trail, and has remained "religious" ever since, Vancouver General is an outgrowth of the 1888 City Hospital at Cambie and Pender in the Victory Square area.

Nursing in Vancouver had begun when Emily Susan Branscombe Peabody Patterson arrived at Hastings Sawmill in 1872 with her stevedore husband. Although John Patterson moved to Moodyville two years later, his wife continued to row across the Inlet to give care. A Mrs. Roberts, who had trained in London, managed the City Hospital after it opened, and kept "...bright fires burning in the stoves, [so that] the beds with their snowy coverlets looked the embodiment of rest." Her successor, Elizabeth Crickmay, received $40 a month, while regular nurses received $25 a month for a 12-hour day. The hours of duty were 7 a.m. to 7 p.m. with one hour off. Once a week there was a free afternoon after 2 p.m. If a good excuse could be presented to the Superintendent, late leave was granted for one evening a month. In the early days of "paying patients" at the hospital, dinner trays had linen and silver service.

The hospital's Women's Auxiliary—The Charitable Women of Vancouver—were a doughty lot. In 1888, they had made a city-wide appeal for 50 yards of cotton required for patients' nightshirts. When organizing in 1902 for the new hospital, "the women stood resolutely on street corners, they invaded Chinatown where the response was generous. Greatly daring, they gathered their sweeping skirts about them and stepped into the saloons, risking ribald remarks of drunken sailors. Their bravery was rewarded with quantities of dirty crumpled bills. The treasurer washed and ironed this precious currency and then hid it under the stair carpet of her home until it could be banked the following Monday." Women like Mrs. W.H. Griffin spearheaded the campaign for a new hospital ambulance, a glorious green-painted, gold-striped carriage with blinds, glass windows, a pneumatic rubber mattress strapped to a stretcher, three silver conductor lanterns, a zinc-lined water tank and a pair of fine horses. Along with almost all vehicles in early Vancouver, the carriage with its skinny coach wheels easily became bogged in the mud on side streets, requiring the horses to be unhitched and the ambulance pushed by young men.

By 1902, City Hospital had grown to accommodate 50 beds, but the city had grown considerably more. Citizens under the banner of the Vancouver Medical Association petitioned for a hospital management free of any profit motive or religious affiliation. A vote was held in January, 1902, which led to the purchase for $5,500 of two square blocks in the Fairview area, east of the future site of King Edward High School. In June, Vancouver General Hospital was incorporated by the provincial legislature.

A year later, plans were developed so that a money plebiscite could go to the city's voters. It was passed, and a hospital "of pressed brick with stone trimmings for all the walls facing north, east and west, and good hard brick with stone trimmings for the rear wall" was constructed. There was "provision for ultimately 300 beds, 100 immediately; building to be three storeys." Electricity was to be generated on the premises. Two elaborate wrought-iron lamp standards were donated, by the Canadian Electric and Canadian Foundry companies, to adorn the entranceway.

In January, 1906 (when the city's population stood at about 50,000) 47 patients were driven in horse-pulled ambulances across the old Cambie skid-bridge and up the trail to the Tenth Avenue hospital buildings. Among the last to move from City Hospital were two infectious cases, who were later housed in cottages in the grounds of the main VGH building. The cottages were surrounded by a high wooden fence, and visiting was done through knotholes and gaps in the slats. By the end of the year, the hospital had 104 patients, and had recorded 25 births.

Over the next decade, three isolation wards and a military annex were built, and a "temporary" annex (which lasted until the Banfield pavilion was opened in 1973) was thrown together to cope with the 1918 Spanish flu epidemic. The Main Building, which became the Heather Pavilion, became a city attraction for its splendid gardens framing the front driveway. Many more buildings were erected in response to the growing population. Centennial Pavilion, the current "main building" on Twelfth Avenue, opened in 1959.

The parking lot across 12th from the Centennial was the site of the Fairview Shacks, the forerunner of the University of B.C. until the latter moved to Point Grey after the First World War. The location of the early University came about in 1913, when the Royal Institution for the Advancement of Learning, McGill University College of B.C., moved into one of the hospital buildings.

G.G. McGeer & City Hall

Vancouver's imposing, modernistic City Hall commands a strategic site on Cambie Street, mid-way between east and west, overlooking downtown with the city's best view of the Lions on the north shore mountains. Its grandeur, rather stark design, and choice site—plus the fact that it was built during the darkest years of the Depression—are fitting tributes to the shrewdness and drive of its flamboyant creator: His Nibs, also known as Hizzoner, Senator Claghorn, and His Worship Senator The Honourable G.G. McGeer, Esq., K.C., Mayor (as his letterhead supposedly said). The key to his success was his "common touch"; everyone in Vancouver felt they could call him "Gerry." When he died suddenly in August 1947, there was an unparalleled outpouring of emotion: the funeral cortège from Christ Church could barely move through the 20,000 people jamming the streets, and over 5,000 lined up to view the body in the rotunda of "his" City Hall. Some pundits, though, claimed that most of the mourners showed up to make sure he was dead.

He was certainly the most dynamic and controversial mayor Vancouver had produced. As well, he stitched together a remarkable career over four decades of representing western interests in Ottawa. His idol was Abraham Lincoln, and he owned one of the best collections of Lincoln memorabilia on the continent. He was quoted as saying: "Whenever I think of Abe Lincoln, I feel very humble." Kindly commentators called him "the foe of inertia."

Like Abe, Gerald Grattan McGeer had humble origins. Born in Winnipeg on January 6, 1888, he was just two when the family moved west to a little dairy operation on the Westminster Road. The farm was across from M.J. Henry's nursery at 15th and Kingsway; its barn stood on the city boundary at 16th and Fraser. He had three brothers and five sisters. His father Jim was "a huge Irishman" —the star attraction at political rallies at the old Temperance Hall on 10th Avenue in the Nineties. Gerry was a tough kid and an organizer, "handy with his fists," the laird of Trout Lake. He used to drive the milk wagon on Fraser Street to Lulu Island, a journey he found so boring that he "started making speeches to himself."

Against the advice of his parents, he quit school at 14 to become an iron moulder. By age 19, he was an executive of the Iron Moulders Union, local 286. He was elected as the representative for the Vancouver Trades and Labour Council, and attended a Quebec City meeting, during which he got into a fiery argument with then-Labour Minister MacKenzie King. He came back convinced that he had to understand law in order to get anywhere, so crammed four years of high school into five months and enrolled in law school. After a time at UBC, during which he was "the highest paid law student in Vancouver," and two brilliant final years at Dalhousie, he emerged in 1915 and formed a partnership with his brother James and Gordon Wismer (Attorney-General of B.C. in the late Forties).

CITY OF VANCOUVER ARCHIVES

Mayor Gerry McGeer commanded the political will to build a City Hall in the middle of the Great Depression. The possible sites had been disputed since 1928 when, in preparation for amalgamation, the City had abandoned the overcrowded Market Hall at Hastings and Main (page 14) and moved into temporary quarters in the Holden Building at 16 East Hastings. Town planners Harland Bartholomew and Associates, who had prepared a Master Plan for Vancouver's amalgamation, foresaw a major civic centre for the crest of land at Davie Street above the new Burrard Bridge. Other interests pushed for the revitalization of the city-owned land around the old Central School and Larwill Park downtown along Hamilton and Cambie. McGeer, who wanted to seal the allegiance of the new municipalities, chose the old Strathcona Park at 12th and Cambie, as central a site as possible, for the new City Hall. The building was formally opened during Vancouver's 50th birthday jubilee.

He became bored with the law practice almost immediately, and the next year ran for election provincially in the Richmond-Point Grey riding. He won in a Liberal landslide, and was re-elected in 1920. He fought for the establishment of grain elevators and other federally-owned shipping facilities in the Port of Vancouver, and began his life-long struggle against the unequal freight rates of the 1897 Crows Nest agreement (finally revised in 1983). Feeling that the future of the west lay with a strong Liberal Party against the entrenched eastern-dominated Tories, McGeer resigned his provincial seat in 1921 and ran unsuccessfully against Tory Cabinet

Minister and western advocate H.H. Stevens. He was defeated again in both 1926 and 1930—the latter the Tory sweep which brought R.B. Bennett to power.

During that period in the political wilderness, he memorized half the New Testament, continued to advocate western (mainly Port of Vancouver) issues federally, and became almost fanatical about currency reform and credit control, culminating in the 1935 publication of his book *The Conquest of Poverty*. He also made an advantageous marriage to Charlotte Emma Spencer, the daughter of department store founder David Spencer, who bore him one son and one daughter.

In 1933, his political career clicked again, when he was elected provincially in the Vancouver-Burrard riding. He had barely taken the seat before he ran for Mayor in Vancouver, making headlines all over the continent with his allegations of corruption and promises of a "police shakeup." He won by a huge majority. One of his first actions was to resolve the ongoing City Hall dispute by deciding, with the prompting of the CPR, that it would be built on the old Strathcona Park at 12th and Cambie (which the railway owned and wanted to trade for city-owned land elsewhere). The city couldn't afford the million dollar construction program, so he floated "baby bonds" to finance it. Concurrently, he decided that—Depression or not—the city needed a grand Diamond Jubilee. As part of the lavish celebrations in 1936, a fountain was placed in the middle of Lost Lagoon and the Lord Mayor of London arrived in Vancouver to help open the City Hall and hand Gerry a glittering ceremonial mace for the Council chambers. McGeer, who loved the finery of office, had already ordered robes and a civic chain to spruce up the mayor's image. He was so busy he managed to keep two chauffeurs on the go; his predecessor, former South Vancouver reeve J.W. Cornctt, had barely kept one awake.

While still Mayor, he resigned as MLA and was elected to the federal Parliament, where he stayed until his old foe MacKenzie King appointed him to the Senate in 1945. There, he reputedly broke all records for number and length of Senate speeches. The Prime Minister called McGeer "a pioneer in untried reforms" and fought with him publicly over Liberal policy; McGeer's publicly-stated intention to succeed King as Prime Minister was greeted with guffaws. McGeer then put out feelers for B.C. Premier John Hart's job, but was rebuffed. So he ran for mayor again in 1946.

Two weeks into the campaign, he was stricken with appendicitis and peritonitis and banished to hospital. Over the next few weeks, to the dismay of his doctors and nurses and the amazement of the country, he ran his election campaign and managed his Senate histrionics from his bed. The hospital corridor became a waiting room for everyone from city police to his political advisors. He was on the phone constantly, barking orders to his lieutenants. He won the election, promising to shake up the police again and expose "ringers" in fixed fights at the Gardens, with a record majority. His tactics attracted scorn, particularly from the *Vancouver Sun*. "When you work for McGeer you keep your mouth shut," said "inside sources."

McGeer continued his breakneck pace, until the night of August 11, 1947, when, having retired with a briefcase full of papers to his den at 4812 Belmont Avenue, he died suddenly of a heart attack, aged 59.

Kitsilano

In 1882 Sam Greer, an Irishman who had fought for the Blues in the Civil War and done some unsuccessful gold digging in the Cariboo, bought 160 acres (bounded by First Avenue, Trafalgar and the beach) west of the Indian village of Snauq. He claimed to have got it from the original pre-emptor, a man named Preston, but later maintained he bought it from "Charlie and Joe," perhaps Jericho Charlie and one of his pals. He installed his wife, daughter, a cow and some chickens in a small cabin at the site of the Kitsilano beach bathhouse. His idyll continued until 1884, when the CPR began proceedings to prove that his claim to the land was worthless, and that the railway had legal title to the land. The CPR announced plans in 1886 to build a deep sea terminal and railyards on Kitsilano Point and opened the Kitsilano trestle across False Creek to reach it. In 1890, after an unsuccessful civil suit against Greer, the CPR gained permission from the New Westminster assize court, presided over by Cariboo-era "hanging judge" Matthew Baillie Begbie, to evict Greer. The latter, however, had prepared to fight by purchasing a ten-foot gun, "a piece of ordnance which he proposes to mount on a fortification on his property on English Bay." While attempting the eviction, Sheriff Thomas Armstrong was winged with buckshot by Greer, who then capitulated after negotiations conducted by newspaper editor and M.L.A. F. L. Carter-Cotton. Greer appeared before Judge Begbie, who called him a "perjurer, liar and forger," and was convicted of common assault in September, 1891.

The CPR did little with Kitsilano Point during the 1890s. The depression of the early part of that decade slowed their rate of expansion; attention was turned to dredging False Creek and building a deep-sea terminal near their new roundhouse on the north shore of the creek. The company extended its tracks along the beach to the foot of Balsam, and erected (since removed, along with the tracks) a small cairn on the bluff above the sea, 2710 miles from Montreal. Vancouverites who found English Bay too crowded took to rowing across it, or walking from the bridge at 3rd and Granville; they camped on Greer's Beach (as it came to be known; tiny Greer Street also commemorates Sam) for the summer. Towards the end of the century a bandstand, primitive dance hall and bathhouse, offering boats for hire, were built on the beach. This first effort was demolished in 1904, but quickly replaced with a larger one. The tent city—in some spots three deep—thrived until 1908 when the city forbade further camping due to the unsanitary conditions (the city had learned its lesson from the typhoid outbreaks of twenty years before). Thomas Calland, J.Z. Hall and other prominent local residents could see the writing on the wall, and purchased the first five acres of Greer's Beach in 1909 for a city park; they were later reimbursed by the City, which purchased the rest of the beach area.

Sam Greer's claim to the Kitsilano Beach area, where he settled in 1882, was never recognized, but he steadfastly refused all access and rights-of-way. Telegraph lines crossing his land were cut, and government coal miners had their hole filled in while prospecting below. After his altercation with the Sheriff (see main text), Greer was convicted in September 1891. He was treated as a political prisoner, and could often be seen taking his lunch on the beach near the prison in Victoria. He died in 1925 at the age of 82.

(Left) The corner of 4th and Yew, looking west in 1909. The building on the right, on the site of Plimley's, is the West Fairview School, built in 1907 to serve the expanding district. The new Kitsilano School at 10th and Trafalgar opened in 1920 (the present building in 1927). From 1943 until its demolition in 1946, West Fairview School was called the Seaview School, and was run as a training centre by the Royal Canadian Air Force. The Vancouver police force dressed like London "bobbies" until the First World War years, and a mounted patrolman was an occasional sight through sparsely populated suburbs like Kitsilano. The businesses on the left include John Huxtable's confectionery, Boyle's drug store, and William Tupper's blacksmith shop. The streetcar tracks were laid in October, 1909, though the only resident west of the Trafalgar city limits was James Quiney, at Dunbar. (Right) The foot of Dunbar, in 1910, was a popular picnicking and camping spot. A barn and summer cottages shared the bank above the beach.

(Above) The Crickmay camp, near the foot of Bayswater Street by the English Bay Cannery, in the early 1890s. For several years following their arrival in the city in August, 1888, the family maintained a summer camp "out in Jericho" (Kitsilano then being unnamed). William and Frances Crickmay arrived in Vancouver from England with nine children and assorted relatives. William built the Imperial Opera House at Pender and Beatty. His daughter Elizabeth, later Mrs. A.R. Sherwood, was the second matron of the City Hospital on Beatty Street, and nursed "a rather rough lot of men, the type that flock into frontier towns." Son Alfred founded Crickmay and Bermingham, one of the earliest customs brokerages in the city, which lasted from 1889 to 1947. Alfred and his descendants homesteaded in North Vancouver in 1895. (Right) Looking down the hill from 4th and Yew in 1915. The steepness (and muddiness) of the hills contributed to the difficulties of settling the area in the pre-automobile days. Second and Third avenues were brick-paved in 1913 (remains of this paving are visible at 3rd and Arbutus).

The CPR did some clearing around the corner of Ogden and Maple for a hotel, which was to be the resort for the deep-sea port on the point. The streetcar track was extended to the foot of Vine Street, and a turntable was built there.

By the time Kitsilano was named in 1905, a small community was flourishing on Fourth Avenue, centred around Yew Street. The major drawbacks to settlement there were the great distance to the nearest streetcar stop (3rd and Granville), and the steep hills, which were muddy and difficult to negotiate with horse and wagon and, later, mechanically-braked, wheezing autos. The northeast corner, around First and Cedar (now Burrard) on the edge of the Indian Reserve, became known as a Sikh area. A Sikh Temple stood for years at 1866 West 2nd Avenue. (During the *Komagata Maru* incident in the Spring of 1914, white children were warned away from the Temple and the Indian Reservation forest. The *Komagata Maru*, chartered by Gurdit Singh, arrived in Vancouver with a boatload of Sikhs. Singh contended that his passengers were Commonwealth citizens. The Canadian authorities maintained that "Hindoos" were banned under Canadian racial exclusion laws. After a bitter and sometimes violent standoff, the ship was forced to leave.) There were tenements and workers' cottages along the lower streets and a few small factories on Cypress and the intersecting avenues.

Some residents worked at the Rat Portage Saw Mill at the foot of Fir Street and some of the other mills along False Creek; they walked east through the Indian reserve, where the Sikhs grazed their cows. Boaters and picnickers used the old Indian wells for their water. The landmark was the Women's Christian Temperance Union orphanage (built in 1891 as a hospital, later Alexandra Neighbourhood House), which occupied the block between 6th and 7th at Pine Street. St. Mark's Church stood at the corner of First and Maple. When it snowed, "the brick street" (3rd Avenue east of Arbutus) was blocked off for tobogganers. The interurban ran from its depot at the south end of the Granville bridge through the area to its first stop at Broadway. Kids jumped on it at Broadway and off at

Talton Place (16th Avenue), where the Kerrisdale fares were collected. The industrial tone of the area south of Broadway was set by the opening of the Reifel's "West Fairview" brewery (now Carling's) at 12th and Vine in 1908.

The steep slope above Kitsilano beach contained many fine homes built before the First World War; the best remaining one, in a greatly modified state, is the Stearman residence at First and Larch. Numerous box-like walk-up apartments from the Fifties now crowd the hillside.

To spur development of Kitsilano Point, the CPR in 1909 built five fine homes amidst the stumps. The first, at 2030 Whyte Avenue, was bought for $5,000 by William Evans, the driver of the first locomotive to reach Port Moody on July 4, 1886. The next year, the house at 1343 Maple was occupied by J.S. Matthews, the future Vancouver City archivist. The swampy condition of the land gave everyone problems during the winter, so in 1913 the Pacific Dredging Co. pumped sand through huge pipes on floating pontoons from as far east as Granville bridge, where False Creek was being dredged for the new deep-sea terminal. The muskrats were driven out of the sloughs by the sand and were caught by school kids (Matthews' sons). The fill beside Matthews' house was 13 feet deep.

The western edge of the CPR land grant was Trafalgar Road. It was at that point that the CPR's surveys ran up against the slightly more erratic ones in D.L. 540 (though not as erratic as the ones on Ontario Street, the eastern end of the land grant, which, between 16th and 25th, dog-legs every block). Developers took advantage of the cheaper land west of Trafalgar to build the first apartment buildings in Kitsilano: a three-storey, bay-windowed building at 5th and Trafalgar, and the large, brick Wellington apartments at York and Trafalgar.

In 1931, jeweller Harvey Haddon bequeathed the land at the end of Kitsilano Point to the city, hence the name Haddon Park. The expanded beach was a major attraction for Vancouver residents, particularly as it was so easily reached by the Kitsilano tram.

During the 1920s, the old bathhouse was demolished and replaced by a gabled, two-storey one with Union Jacks fluttering from the flagpoles. In 1927, over 80,000 people regularly used the beach, and people remarked that Kitsilano was almost always more crowded than English Bay. The year 1931 witnessed the establishment of a tidal-filled swimming pool, which opened for swimming trials with great fanfare and relatively clean water; it lasted until the late 1970s, when the modern pool—with a filtration system equal to Vancouver's harbour water—was built. The Kitsilano Yacht Club opened its clubhouse alongside the old City wharf at the foot of Balsam Street on Coronation Day, May 12, 1937. Bathers who wanted more privacy continued to use the Indian Reservation beach, and children swam from the tram trestle and little rafts in False Creek. During the Depression years, bathers shared the shoreline with the Bennettville squatters around the Burrard Bridge. The old streetcar tracks to the Vine Street turntable were removed during the Fifties, but the right-of-way lay fallow until the Seventies, when a set of townhouses was built along it by the CPR's real-estate division, at addresses like 1405 Maple Street.

On January 8, 1941, John Coughlan & Sons announced that they had negotiated a lease with the Squamish band ($13,000 a year for the 40-acre reserve) and were about to build a shipyard on Kitsilano Point, occupying the entire area between Chestnut Street and the bridge. Residents, who had been trying to keep industry out of the area since the turn of the century, fought back; their efforts were intensified in 1942 after the shelling of the Point Estevan lighthouse by a Japanese mini-submarine. The shipyard plans never got off the ground, but in 1942 the Air Force decided to use the Indian Reserve as an equipment depot. (The Vancouver School of Music, next to the Planetarium, is a greatly-modified World War II warehouse). In May, 1943, a commando raid, with smokescreen, landing craft and anti-aircraft barrage, was staged at the foot of McNicholl Street as part of the Fighting Services Committee war

bond drive.

In 1946, Bert Emery, the unofficial "mayor" of Kitsilano, tried to get the ball rolling for a $1 million tourist hotel along the beach, with a Malkin bowl-style theatre and a Coney Island-style amusement park. In 1952, residents in the eastern part of Kitsilano fought a protracted battle against industrial development interests, seeing the establishment of a Coca-Cola bottling plant (now the Chemetics Building) and the planned Sick brewery (now Molson's) at the south end of the bridge as harbingers of an unwelcome future. In 1953, Gerald Sutton-Brown, the city's planning director, brought in new standards for dwelling conversions on Kitsilano hill which eventually meant the demise of the single family dwelling. It allowed rooming and boarding houses, ostensibly only "where quality and property values of the neighbourhood would not be depreciated." However, although City Council backed Sutton-Brown and committed itself publicly to retaining the character of Kitsilano, it rezoned the lower slope between Vine and Larch in 1954 for apartments. The residential interests beat out the industrial near the south end of the Burrard Bridge when, on November 23, 1956, the area around the south foot of Burrard Bridge was rezoned to allow future mayor Tom "Terrific" Campbell to build his three-cornered, highrise Parkview Towers at the corner of Chestnut and Cornwall.

In 1958, Vancouver-Burrard MP John Taylor proposed a combination park, marina, fisherman's wharf and restaurant on the Indian Reserve, much like the plan which eventually became the renovated Granville Island. It wasn't until the mid-Sixties, though, that the Planetarium and Museum complex were built, finally determining the fate of that part of Kitsilano.

The first white residents west of Sam Greer were probably the Crickmay family, who tented at the foot of Bayswater during summers in the early 1890s. The English Bay cannery was built at the foot of Bayswater around 1900, shortly after the area was logged by

(Left) The first Quiney home, in the forest at what was to become the northeast corner of Fourth Avenue and Dunbar, in 1907. There were no roads, light, telephone or neighbours. Their water came from a well. At the corner of 16th and Collingwood in 1908, Quiney shot a bear, which had been bothering some "Hindoo" loggers, then discovered that it had a cub. He brought the latter home and kept it chained to a stake in the yard, where it became something of a family pet. The Quineys moved in 1909 to the house at 1820 Waterloo; when the streetcar line was completed, Quiney opened up the area and sold real estate until the collapse of the boom in 1912. (Right) The first run of the streetcar on Fourth Avenue, in October, 1909, looking east toward Waterloo. The area was commonly known as District Lot 540. Jonathan Miller was asked by the CPR in 1905 to come up with a name for the area bounded by Cedar (Burrard), Fourth and Trafalgar. After consultations with anthropologist Charles Hill-Tout and other local residents, he settled on the name Kitsilano, which translated means "Man of the Lake," after Chief Khahtsalano, the grandfather of August Jack (page 98).

(Above) Jessie Hall, Sam Greer's daughter and the grande dame of Killarney (right), built in 1908 at the corner of Bayswater and Point Grey Road. (Far right) "Edgewood, The Most Beautiful Home West of Granville Street," was built in 1904 on the bluff above the beach between Trafalgar and Stephens streets. It was the residence of Alderman and real-estate promoter Thomas H. Calland and the first home in that part of Kitsilano. Access to the house before the Kitsilano streetcar line opened in 1906 was by rowboat across English Bay, or by a long walk from the Granville Bridge at 3rd Avenue. At a garden party at the Calland's in 1907, a Mrs. Bulwer of Kerrisdale commented on the confusion caused by the duplication of street names throughout Vancouver at that time, and suggested that streets west of the CPR land grant be named for famous British battles. Thus Alderman Calland, who was an influential member of Council, arranged that Boundary become Trafalgar, Richards become Balaclava, Cornwall Blenheim, Lansdowne Waterloo and Campbell Alma.

the Hastings Sawmill Co. The cannery was bought in October, 1905 by R.D. Rorison. His purchase included the cannery, a wharf, some cottages and surrounding land. The next May, one of the cannery buildings on the south side of Point Grey Road burnt to the ground. Rorison dismantled the cannery and used the structural beams for a home at 3148 Point Grey Road—an imposing, Queen Anne style turreted house which looked even more impressive when it was surrounded by vacant land. The wharf, from which Rorison often launched his canoe, lasted for years, though, and the cannery's location was marked by a pile of metal scraps which had fallen through the floor onto the beach.

James Luke Quiney was a Cockney who had lived in Verdun, Manitoba, since emigrating to Canada after his service in the Boer War. He landed with his family in Vancouver in the spring of 1907, worked to get a stake together (his pocket had been picked on the train) and then moved his family to a tent in the woods at the foot of Balaclava Street. The only road to the area was the old Point Grey Indian trail, which had been expanded to a wagon's width through the salmonberry thickets in order to reach the Admiralty Reserve and Jerry Rogers' logging camp.

Late in 1907, the Quineys bought property from R.D. Rorison and built a small house in the middle of the forest at the northeast corner of 4th and Dunbar. The lumber came from the demolished English Bay cannery. There were no numbered houses—in fact, no other houses at all. They drew their water from a well and bought groceries at Webster Bros. at Drake and Granville, which the kids packed home across the Kitsilano Trestle and along Point Grey Road.

Quiney and the other owners in the area successfully convinced the B.C. Electric Railway Co. to extend its streetcar line along Fourth from Granville to Alma—the boundary of the Admiralty Reserve. In 1909, a crew of Italian labourers cleared the right-of-way, which opened to traffic in October. Quiney then moved his family to the small house at 1820 Waterloo and went into the

real estate business. He did quite well until the real estate boom collapsed in 1912. By the beginning of the War, the area from Blenheim to Alma north of 4th Avenue was mostly built up with stone-foundationed, bay-windowed "Swiss Cottages." The local swamp took longer to drain; early photographs show the residents on Waterloo using plank sidewalks suspended high above the skunk cabbage. Cars were swallowed practically whole by the ruts and puddles on side streets.

Some of the old houses remain on Collingwood, Waterloo and Dunbar around First Avenue. At the foot of Dunbar, the site of an old farm and summer cottages from Quiney's time, is a pathway leading to Cameron Avenue, one of the shortest streets in the city, with a superb view of downtown. The first cottages there on the water side were built at the turn of the century by West End families with a desire for remote summer residences. At the corner of Cameron and Alma is Hastings Mill store, moved on floats from its old site at the foot of Dunlevy Street in 1929 when the Hastings Mill was demolished. Built in 1865 and operated now as a museum by the Native Daughters of B.C., it is the oldest building in Vancouver.

Quiney, always a soldier, went off to war in 1915 and returned an invalid, unable to make payments on his deflated D.L. 540 holdings. His land was repossessed. In April, 1919, he and his family moved west of Blanca on Spanish Banks and squatted in a shack on the beach. Quiney fixed up an old car as a hot water wagon, and made a meagre living supplying campers and picnickers along the beach.

Point Grey Road is Vancouver's Ocean Boulevard. The water side of it has been the preserve of the extremely wealthy since the early years of the century. R.D. Rorison was not the first permanent resident there. Thomas H. Calland, who had made a fortune in Vancouver real estate, decided in 1902 that he liked the idea of living south of False Creek (he was familiar with the area and a great favorite of the livery stables, as he would often rent horses to take his clients on wild and woolly jaunts to examine property in

Fairview). On February 10, 1902, his wife, Kate Alice Gertrude Calland, purchased the property at 2601 Point Grey Road, which was in fact the entire block of waterfrontage between Trafalgar and Stephens Street (just outside the CPR land). The Callands left the West End in 1903 and camped in tents at the foot of Trafalgar during that summer, while their palatial residence "Edgewood" was built.

During the first year, Calland had to ride his bicycle over the Point Grey trail and along an abandoned logging road to reach the streetcar stop at 3rd and Granville. After 1905, the Kitsilano tramline terminated at the foot of Vine Street, only blocks away, a boon in 1906 when the ailing Mrs. Calland had to be carried by stretcher to hospital.

Other Point Grey Road pioneers were the Halls: John Z. had arrived "with the mob" in 1885. He became the manager of the T.R. Pearson stationery store, then the city's first notary public, but preferred to be known as the city's "first volunteer soldier." His wife Jessie was the daughter of Sam Greer and the first white baby born in the Cariboo (in 1872). In 1906 they purchased the land

Sir William Whyte, vice-president of the CPR Western Lines, and namesake of Whyte Avenue on Kitsilano Point. Other streets there were named for General Counsel A.R. Creelman, Senior Vice-President David McNicholl, and V.P. of Finance I.G. Ogden.

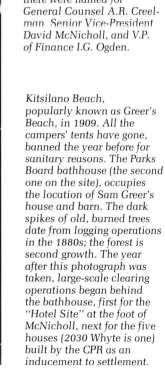

Kitsilano Beach, popularly known as Greer's Beach, in 1909. All the campers' tents have gone, banned the year before for sanitary reasons. The Parks Board bathhouse (the second one on the site), occupies the location of Sam Greer's house and barn. The dark spikes of old, burned trees date from logging operations in the 1880s; the forest is second growth. The year after this photograph was taken, large-scale clearing operations began behind the bathhouse, first for the "Hotel Site" at the foot of McNicholl, next for the five houses (2030 Whyte is one) built by the CPR as an inducement to settlement.

Above: Capt. The Hon. Robert Garnet Tatlow, MLA, in "Vanity Fair," London, in June 1909. Tatlow worked with Henry Ogle Bell-Irving in the shipping business and made a fortune in real estate and insurance as Tatlow & Spinks of Cordova Street. He was a rising Tory–well-connected to old Vancouver money through his marriage to Henry Cambie's elder daughter–and Minister of Finance in Richard McBride's cabinet. He was killed on April 11, 1910, when the horse pulling his carriage through downtown Victoria ran away; he fell from the careening vehicle and died instantly. In a bizarre near-repetition of that accident, his daughter Helen–Mrs. R.G. Wilson–was killed in a fall from a horse in Victoria in December, 1935. Right: Tatlow's name is remembered in Tatlow Park, on Point Grey Road just west of Macdonald, shown here in 1918. In the background distance is Seagate Manor, built in 1912 for Harry L. Jenkins, the president of the Vancouver Lumber Co., Vancouver Trust Co., and the Midway Ranch. Jenkins died in the early Twenties; his effects, including solid mahogany furniture, Persian rugs and a Baby Grand Steinway, were auctioned on June 5, 1926. The house was taken over by American E.A. Woodward, who had established a grain terminal elevator at the foot of Salisbury Drive in 1923. Woodward's daughter Shirley married Dal Grauer. The house was demolished in April, 1977, for a park.

bordered by 4th, Bayswater, 6th and Balaclava, and while clearing it lived on the site of the English Bay cannery. In 1908, they built a stone mansion called Killarney, across the road from the cannery site, which for forty years was the hub of Kitsilano's social wheel. The house was certainly grand: it had oak and mahogany woodwork, elaborate stained glass, bathroom tiles set with gold, a massive fireplace inlaid with carved shamrocks and a fully-outfitted ballroom with a sprung floor in the basement.

Jessie Hall's energy and ambition were expended in such diverse organizations as the Victorian Order of Nurses, the Hart-McHarg Society, the Native Daughters of B.C., the Kitsilano Ratepayers, the Women's Auxiliary of Christ Church and the Conservative Party. Her patriotic activities during the First World War included supporting an entire field hospital in France. Killarney was the site of innumerable garden parties, meetings and formal balls, including the visits of Countess Haig in July, 1925 and Viscountess Willingdon in 1927.

Kitsilano Beach, summer of 1928. Cornwall Street is quiet, with no through traffic, as the Burrard Bridge was not yet built. The recently added tennis courts are at the foot of Yew Street. The "Kitsilano" streetcar is at its terminus, on the turntable, at the foot of Vine Street.

160

Kitsilano Beach, looking north from the foot of Yew Street, during the Twenties. The streetcar directly from downtown, across the Kitsilano trestle, made the park as easy to reach as English Bay. All park flagpoles flew the Union Jack.

When Jessie Hall died in 1949, an era ended for Kitsilano. Seven years later, developers bought the old mansion, threw one last party in the ballroom and demolished the building. In its place was built the palatial Killarney apartments, which retain the mansion's stone wall and much of the grace and charm of an earlier era.

Almost across the street from Killarney is a "view park," developed on the site of Seagate Manor. The house was torn down in the mid-1970s as part of a Parks Board plan to clear the houses from the water side of Point Grey Road. The decision to create a waterfront drive with a view dates from 1927, when the St. Louis firm of Harland Bartholomew and Associates were hired to write the city's first Master Plan and Zoning Bylaws (in preparation for amalgamation with the municipalities of South Vancouver and Point Grey). The plan recommended, among other things, the building of the Burrard Bridge and the upgrading of Cornwall, Cedar Street and Point Grey Road from their quiet backwater status; the purchase of all vacant lots along Point Grey Road; and the expropriation of the 112 lots with beach access.

This was the forerunner of several plans for the Point Grey Road area, mainly reflecting the "Riviera" or "Ocean Boulevard" idea. Engineer Neville Beaton published one in 1956, envisaging a waterfront freeway and park. In 1962, City Council asked the Provincial Government for the 1.3 miles of foreshore between the Kitsilano Pool and Alma Road for a roadway; in 1964, Mayor Bill Rathie threw his support behind the project, suggesting it would be an excellent Centennial Project for 1967. The newspapers headlined the "Waikiki Beach Plan for City" and "Glamour Parkway Scheme." Five months later the project was abandoned when 40 waterfront owners refused to give up their properties.

So Point Grey Road has stayed small and slightly rustic, following the path of the Indian trail from Quiney's days. One early property owner who lost interest in the area was J.S. Matthews. One day in 1908, he went looking for a lot he had purchased near Fourth Avenue and Macdonald. He entered the forest at the foot of the old Macdonald logging trail, became lost in the almost impenetrable salmonberry and salal thickets, floundered around for several hours, and finally emerged at Quiney's homestead at Fourth and Dunbar!

W.C. Stearman

The Stearman house, at the crest of the hill at First and Larch, was the first house built west of Larch Street, in 1908, and commanded an unobstructed vantage point from its logged-off promontory. The house has since been added to on the east (left) side, and converted into expensive apartments.

The finest house on Kitsilano Hill was built in 1908 at 2500 West First, at the corner of Larch. It commanded the crest of land there, on a treeless hillside, cleared over the preceding decade in preparation for settlement. Before 1908, Fourth Avenue, the area's commercial street, had extended only as far west as Balsam, limiting housing development to the eastern part of Kitsilano. The announcement of an impending agreement among the B.C. Electric Railway, the Municipality of Point Grey, and landowners like James Quiney to extend both the streetcar line and 4th Avenue west to Alma Road, acted as an inducement to settlement.

The house was owned by William Charles Stearman (1873-1960), a pioneer Vancouver hardware merchant who came to Van-couver at age fourteen and started his first store at 546 Granville in 1894. Stearman's motto was: "Crazy Copy Creates Customers," and he endeared himself to generations of Vancouverites with advertisements like: "Get 1-2 day 4 Xmas gifts 4-2-morrow may B-2 late!" He moved his store in 1913 to 613 Granville, and installed a sign with a neon steer at one end, a neon number "4" at the other, and "STEARMAN'S" in the middle. Locals knew it meant "Steer for Stearman's." He was "4ced 2 Vacate" in 1939, and opened his last store at 1082 Granville Street. Throughout his life, he wore a common nail as a tie pin, a habit he developed during the Klondike years in Vancouver. When asked why, he said: "anyone can buy a pearl sticker, but show me a man who can find a common nail!"

W.C. Stearman

General Victor Odlum

General Odlum's house on Point Grey Road was the finest estate between Calland's and the public beach. The house still stands, though modern townhouses have been built on its grounds.

General Victor Odlum

The small, elegant estate at 2530 Point Grey Road was owned during the Twenties and Thirties by General Victor Odlum, one of the great soldiers produced by the city and well known as a newspaperman. Odlum was the product of a "Puritanical Sunday School upbringing" at the hands of his extraordinary father—Professor Edward Odlum of Grant Street in Grandview.

Born October 21, 1880 in Cobourg, Ontario, Odlum came to Vancouver with his family when still a boy. He got his first job at age 17 in a Vancouver lumber mill. At 19 he enlisted in the Second Battalion of the Royal Canadian Rifles and went to South Africa to fight the Boers. He was promoted to Lieutenant while there. On his return to Vancouver, he tried his hand as a reporter for Louis Taylor's *World*; by age 25 he was editor-in-chief of the paper. His spare time was spent as William Hart-McHarg's "understudy" in the Duke of Connaught's Own Rifles, headquartered just up the street from his newspaper office in the World Tower. Odlum also found time to make money in the family brokerage business during the prosperous years before 1912.

Odlum was in the first wave of Vancouver volunteers who went to France after mobilization. When Hart-McHarg was killed at Ypres in April, 1915, Odlum took command of the 11th Canadian Brigade. He was, like his father, a bit of a puritan in his personal habits—he neither smoked nor drank, and earned the nickname Pea Soup Odlum for replacing the soldiers' rum ration with soup in the trenches. He was wounded twice and mentioned seven times in dispatches. One dispatch described him as "one of the most fearless fighters on the Western Front."

On his return to Vancouver in the Twenties, he threw himself back into his newspaper career, buying the *Vancouver Daily Star* in 1924. He was a prominent advocate of Prohibition in western Canada, and a major political influence. His motto: "Do Good, or Do Nothing At All" was sometimes said to be at odds with the editorial stance of his newspaper. He entered the newspaper field a final time in 1964 as the publisher of the ill-fated *Vancouver Times*.

Odlum sold the Point Grey Road house and moved to a five-acre estate at Whytecliffe, where he lived until 1959. He then moved into town to a home at 3437 Osler in Shaughnessy. He died in April, 1971, aged 90.

Kerrisdale

The centre of Kerrisdale is the shopping district on 41st Avenue (formerly called Wilson Road) at West Boulevard. The train tracks there date from 1902, when the CPR built a line to the Steveston canneries. The twice-a-day trains were instantly dubbed the "Sockeye Limited" or the "Sockeye Special," and the name stuck to the B.C. Electric's interurban trains after 1905, when the latter took the line over from the CPR. The other legacy from CPR days is Kerrisdale Field, between 41st and 37th avenues from East Boulevard to Maple Street. The area was cleared and planted with vegetables for the railway's passenger and hotel operations. Called the CPR Gardens, it had a watertower and stables at about the corner of 39th and Maple. The gardens were later taken over by Woodward's; the eastern end in 1928 became the site of Point Grey School. So much manure had been dug into the cedar-acidic soil that, in the rainy season, rugby-playing schoolboys reeked of it after games.

The first interurban ran on Tuesday, July 4, 1905, through a wilderness of stumps and berry bushes south of the 9th Avenue car stop. Wilson Road and the CPR Gardens were the only signs of habitation between Kitsilano and Eburne Station. The few settlers lived over the hill to the west. "Kerrisdale" was painted on an inverted coal oil can, hung over a post at the corner. After Syd Bell established his store and post office at the northwest corner of Wilson Road and the tracks, the interurban waited at the stop while passengers from as far away as the Southlands farms dashed in for their mail.

One of the first property owners north of the Southlands farms was the Baroness C.J. de Vos Van Steenwyck (1868-1960), who bought 20 acres at the foot of MacKenzie in 1906. Other new settlers included Frank Bowser, the brother of Conservative Attorney-General William J. Bowser, who in 1907 built a large home at 6000 Macdonald Street, on the edge of his 20-acre stump farm. The next year, William Morrisette built at 38th and Blenheim, and Michael Robson at 39th and Balaclava (later the first Athlone School). There was no school within miles, and as twelve children were required in the area before one could be established, Bowser persuaded General Duff-Stuart, who ran a sort of "summer camp" on Magee Road, to lend him two—"Frankie and Robbie"—to make up the numbers. Miss Marjorie Watson, Mrs. Bowser's niece in Victoria, was also brought to Kerrisdale as another potential student, and by these means Kerrisdale School was able to open at 41st and Carnarvon in 1908. Miss Ethel Parks was hired as teacher, with duties which included drawing water from the school's deep well. Several more families of substance moved into the area before 1910: Dr. Archibald Smith, who built a home with twelve fireplaces at the northeast corner of 37th and Trafalgar; R.S. Ford, who built Huron Lodge at 45th and East Boulevard, now the site of the Dickie Substation; Mrs. J.A. Mackin, the city's first librarian, who built

the large home just west of Macdonald on 41st; Chris Spencer, president of Spencer's department stores, who built at 49th Avenue and West Boulevard.

Residents like these on the west side of the city objected to the Municipality of South Vancouver's penny-pinching policy on civic improvements, and led the secessionist movement which culminated in the incorporation of Point Grey municipality in 1908. Kerrisdale became the municipal centre, and a rambling, multi-gabled, half-timbered Municipal Hall was erected at 42nd and West Boulevard. The Municipal Hall was also the headquarters for the motorcycle-equipped Point Grey police force. The building became a community centre after Point Grey's amalgamation with the City of Vancouver in 1929.

The first substantial commercial building was erected across from Bell's store by Frank Bowser for the Bank of North America (it now houses the Bank of Montreal). A.C. Bruce, a realtor in an adjoining building to the south, announced that "Kerrisdale—Sunny Southern Slope" was "The Place For Your Permanent Home." A few doors west along 41st Avenue was the Masonic Hall, also called the "Jolly Bachelors' Hall." A single-track streetcar was established along 41st Avenue, and ran as far west as Dunbar Street.

The Lulu Island interurban, Kerrisdale's lifeline in the early years, continued in service until February 28, 1958. B.C. Hydro

Miss Ethel Parks, first teacher at Kerrisdale School.

The Kerrisdale Lumber Co., on 45th near West Boulevard, delivered throughout the area by horse and wagon during the First World War years. It moved to its present site at 46th and West Boulevard in 1923.

Wilson Road (41st Avenue) and West Boulevard in 1914. The dark shape on the right is the freight and passenger platform and shed for the Lulu Island Electric Interurban Railway, more commonly known as the Sockeye Limited. The streetcar is travelling towards Dunbar, on the left-hand side of the road. The bank building on the corner was erected by area resident Frank Bowser in 1911 for the Bank of British North America, and is now occupied by the Bank of Montreal. On the left in the distance is the Municipal Hall, built in 1908 as the administrative centre for the recently-seceded Point Grey Municipality. It was torn down in 1953 after a decade-long controversy and replaced with the library, gymnasium, pool and Health Unit which are now the Kerrisdale Community Centre.

General J. Duff Stuart, born in 1866, came to Vancouver in 1889, was active in Cariboo gold mining, and founded Clark & Stuart Co. stationers at 550 Seymour (his partner was one of the backers of the Vancouver "Beavers" baseball team). As an officer in the militia, he commanded the Vernon internment camp during World War I. He died in a motorcar accident on Sumas Prairie in 1936.

CITY OF VANCOUVER ARCHIVES

freight trains still chug along the line a few times a day, and there are plans to use the right-of-way in the future for the second phase of Vancouver's rapid transit system. The old interurban was certainly rapid, especially on open stretches through Lulu Island and along the east side of Quilchena Golf Course between 33rd and 25th, where it would sway and buck along at about 50 mph. Evidently, the trick was not to be caught in the bathroom cubicle when the train hit a sharp bump; occasionally, a lady with all her stays down would hurtle through the thin bathroom door and onto the floor in full view of the passengers.

Progress in the early 1950s brought the rubber-tired bus, which, unlike the streetcars, could pull over to the curb to pick up passengers—never a problem in the early days before automobiles became so numerous. The Kerrisdale community held a pageant in 1952—with street parades, a marching band with cheerleaders, and speeches in the Arena—to mark the passing of the streetcar and inauguration of the Arbutus trolley line.

Left: the Kerrisdale Theatre, just west of the Boulevard on 41st Avenue, in 1930. It was a typical theatre for its time–built for showing movies, as opposed to the Orpheum or Strand, which started as vaudeville houses. Showing at the Kerrisdale on the day of the photograph was The Trespasser, a "Deluxe Drama of Domestic Troubles" starring Gloria Swanson. The showcard on the sidewalk announces that this Edmund Boulding production is the "New First All Talking Picture" (Mother Knows Best, shown at the Capitol in June, 1928, was the first talkie in Vancouver). The Friday and Saturday feature that week starred Mary Pickford and Douglas Fairbanks. The theatre, crippled by television during the Fifties, retreated to 15 cent kiddie matinees (with a couple of cartoons and the Pathé newsreel) before going bankrupt. The building was then converted into a post office, and has since been further modified into shops.

Right: the north side of the 2100-block West 41st, just west of the interurban tracks in Kerrisdale. The street was decked out with Union Jacks, ensigns and bunting for the 1939 visit of King George VI and Queen Elizabeth–the tour of the Dominion aboard the "Royal Hudson" to boost morale for war. The two major chain foodstores in Vancouver were separated on 41st only by Henry's barber shop. Piggly Wiggly had a huge warehouse in the 1000-block Hamilton Street and stores all over town. Safeway began to expand in earnest after the completion of its distribution centre on Homer Street in 1937.

Helen MacKinnon

The MacKinnon house, at 2941 West 42nd, was the second house built in Kerrisdale, in 1903, the year after the estate was built which later became Crofton House school (page 51). The land was logged off and the dirt streets were muddy for much of the year.

Helen Flora MacKinnon

Kerrisdale was named by Helen Flora (Ross) MacKinnon (1881-1933), the great grand-daughter of Kenneth MacKenzie of Gairloch, on the coast of Scotland opposite the northern tip of the Isle of Skye. MacKenzie—a descendant of one Hector Roy, who had fought for King James IV against the MacLeods in 1494—returned to his ancestral parish in 1790 after ten years in the army and built Kerrysdale House on the Kerry River near the Kerrysdale Forest. The name is a corruption of the Gaelic *A Chathair Bheag*— " The Little Throne."

Helen Ross married William Bundock MacKinnon of Elford-leigh, Devonshire, and came to Vancouver in 1897. In the summer of 1903, they built the second Kerrysdale House on the newly-cleared road between Macdonald and Carnarvon Streets, just west of the CPR boundary, at 2941 West 42nd. The home was the second one in the district—the preceding year the von Alvensleben-Cromie estate had been built at Wilson Road and Blenheim.

It was Rochfort Henry Sperling, general manager of the B.C. Electric Railway Co., who asked Mrs. MacKinnon to name the Wilson Road interurban stop (Wilson Road became the stop because of the CPR Gardens; it was the first stop south of 9th Avenue, though Talton Place at 16th was added later). The "Kerrisdale" sign was erected soon after at 41st and the Boulevard. The MacKinnon's Kerrysdale House was demolished in the Sixties and its lot subdivided—two "Vancouver Special" houses occupy the site today.

Royal

Royal was typical of the many farms, nurseries and businesses which thrived in remote parts of Vancouver during the early years. When they vanished, even the names were almost forgotten; occasionally, when they were swallowed by urban expansion the names were attached to the suburban community (like the little community of Lochdale at Hastings and Sperling in Burnaby).

R.D. Rorison, the founder of Royal, was "a great lover of flowers," and created the largest botanical garden in B.C., with the intention of stimulating a wider interest in horticulture in the area. He and his son, Lt. Col. W.D.S. Rorison, began to do business in 1908, with a sales office downtown on Granville Street. From the Royal Station at 51st Avenue, which was simply a freight platform, a spur line led to their greenhouses along the interurban track. Cottages for the workers flanked the eastern boundary of the property at about Laburnum Street. North to south, the property ran from Magee Road (49th) to 51st, a total of 40 acres.

Another owner in the area was Capt. J. Reynolds Tite, who bought five acres on Magee Road about a half mile west of the Magee Road station. Chris Spencer's house at Magee Road and West Boulevard became Athlone School in the early Fifties. Cougar were a regular sight in the forest which bordered the area's narrow roads.

The last time Royal made the news was the evening of August 4, 1914. A group of Vancouver Rotarians had accepted the invitation of member Lt.Col. Rorison, to inspect the surroundings and have dinner there.

After the dinner, which was laid on tables stretching the length of one of the greenhouses, the cigars came out, port was served and throats were cleared for speeches. The first up was the parish priest, the Rev. Leslie Pidgeon, who announced—in case anyone hadn't heard—that Great Britain and all her Dominions had just declared war on Germany. Many of the "jolly clubmen" obviously hadn't, and abruptly excused themselves. The advent of war wrecked more than Rorison's soirée; Royal went bankrupt and disappeared, leaving little trace, sometime before 1918.

The elder Rorison, who had earlier owned the English Bay Cannery and built the large, turreted home at 3148 Point Grey Road, was not one to be discouraged by setbacks like the bankruptcy of Royal. He later made a fortune selling industrial land in Bridgeport, the area of Richmond near the end of the Oak Street bridge.

Above: a Rotary Club luncheon in one of the greenhouses at the Royal Nursery, on August 12, 1913. To stimulate a wider interest in horticulture, R.D. Rorison built what was probably the best nursery in Vancouver, on the east side of the interurban tracks, between Magee Road (49th Avenue) and 51st. The painting on the next page shows the Magee Road interurban stop, just north of Magee Road, looking south toward the nursery. The "Royal Nursery" sign was visible from the tracks, as were the greenhouses and gardeners' huts, which stretched along Laburnum Street. All around was vacant bushland. There were few houses in the area until the Twenties.

Robert Douglas Rorison (1848-1934)

Southlands

The first permanent residents in the Vancouver area were farmers who established themselves near the mouth of the Fraser River in the years immediately following the 1858 Cariboo Gold Rush. Hugh McRoberts arrived from Ireland in 1858, and farmed 1400 acres, which he called Richmond, on Sea Island. McRoberts' nephews, 23-year old Fitzgerald McCleery and his older brother Samuel, left Killeagh, near Belfast, and, after a leisurely journey, arrived in Esquimalt on April 27, 1862. Intent on the Cariboo Gold Fields, they set off for New Westminster, arriving there May 1, and thence headed for Barkerville. After a brief stay there, during which they found every hump and hollow staked, they returned to New Westminster and worked for the Colonial government at $30 a month each, building the River Road to the Musqueam village at Mahly, at the foot of Camosun. (It was from this village in 1808 that an Indian party had blocked Simon Fraser within sight of tidewater.) Deciding to try their hand at farming, they pre-empted District Lot 315 for Fitzgerald (the land bounded by Marine Crescent, 49th, the Marine Drive golf course, Carnarvon and the river, including 40 acres north of Marine Drive for which he paid $120) and District Lot 316 for Sam (the Marine Drive Golf Course; his provincial tax bill in 1881 was $0.79). In addition, Fitzgerald bought 000 acres of Sea Island, which he sold in 1880 for $20 an acre. The brothers built a cabin on the riverbank which—due to the religious services they held there—became known as St. Patrick's Cathedral.

Other farmers followed. In 1863, Henry Mole pre-empted the land between Blenheim and the Indian village, now Point Grey Golf Course. On April 6, 1867, Hugh Magee paid $191 for the 191 acres of District Lot 194—the land bordered by Carrington, 49th, Carnarvon and the river between the McCleerys and the Moles. Further east, George Garypie had pre-empted the land around Marpole. In 1892, freighter William Shannon bought land between the south end of the CPR's land grant (at 53rd Avenue) and Garypie's and established the Shannon dairy farm.

The McCleery's farm was both the first and the last operating farm within the City of Vancouver. The brothers developed their "Garden of Eden" as an oasis of civilization and piety in the wilderness. When their cabin on the riverbank got flooded out in 1873, they built the first permanent home in Vancouver, on the hillside above the farm near the site of the 10th green of the McCleery golf course. Nine years later, in preparation for Fitzgerald's marriage to Mary Wood of St. Williams, Ontario—"the loveliest bride in the city"—they built an addition at the back of the house. That year (1882), Samuel suddenly died.

The McCleery's farmhouse became the first "hospital" in the Vancouver area, and the scene of dozens of births and deaths. A deeply religious family, they helped build the Methodist Church at the Marpole end of the North Arm bridge in 1871. In July, 1886, they founded the Sea Island Presbyterian Church (now the Mar-

pole United) on Sea Island, to which they rowed (and occasionally skated) every Sunday.

Fitzgerald McCleery was an industrious farmer. He floated 300 pounds of seed potatoes down the river from New Westminster and, from them, harvested a three-ton crop. He went with George Black to Oregon and drove ten heifers back to the Lower Mainland, bringing them by barge into Steveston and finally swimming them across the river to the farm. The cows produced the first butter in Vancouver.

A second farmhouse was built in 1892 (demolished 1977) at 2610 Marine Drive, for the arrival of Fitzgerald's older brother John, his son Sam and three daughters. Sam (1884-1970) married neighbour Annie Mole (1882-1959) in 1907. Fitzgerald's daughter Evelyn Elizabeth married H.B. Barton and the couple built the house at 2104 South West Marine in 1913. Fitzgerald's younger daughter married Thomas Mackie (1878-1955), who retired to a 150-acre farm on Sea Island in 1914, and finally sold the property to the city for the Municipal Airport in 1929. The Mackies lived at 8698 South West Marine. Another daughter, Marion (1878-1959) married Harry Logan and continued to farm the property until 1955. Fitzgerald died in 1921, aged 83.

By the Twenties, the pressures of the encroaching city had already begun to make the farm difficult to manage. Taxes which were $413 in 1908 had risen to $5533 in 1923. They were triple what competing farms were paying, and the City insisted on collecting what it felt to be its due. The family sold off 56 acres of the original homestead for residential purposes, and ploughed the proceeds back into tax arrears. In the final years, the Logans hung on grimly and continued to farm 72 acres. Quilchena Golf Club held an option to purchase the property, but demurred. Finally, in June, 1954, the family capitulated and sold the last 72 acres to the city for $135,000. Construction of McCleery Golf Course commenced immediately. The farmhouse—the oldest permanent residence in Vancouver—was destroyed to accommodate the golf course layout.

Hugh Magee started farming the property just to the west of the McCleerys' five years after the latter had gained a toehold on civilization. After applying for his 191 acres, he purchased a home in New Westminster, floated it downstream by barge, and landed it in a grove of spruce trees at about the foot of Blenheim Street. It remained there for 10 years, until high water forced him to move it across the flood plain and up the hill to 3250 West 48th.

In that home, called Spruce Grove even after it was moved, was born Charles Wesley Magee (1871-1957), Kerrisdale's first baby. His older sister, later Mrs. Carolyn Dester (1868-1960), was born in an Indian canoe on the Fraser River in the vicinity of the Oak Street bridge. When Mrs. Magee's labour pains began on July 20, she was placed on a mattress in the borrowed canoe by her two eldest sons,

Fitzgerald McCleery

Mary (Wood) McCleery

Hugh Magee

The Fitzgerald McCleery farmhouse, at 6750 Macdonald Street just below Marine Drive, in 1947. It was the first house built in Vancouver, the front part in 1873, the back in 1883. Hugh McRoberts (1814-1883), who had a career in the Cariboo and Australia before deciding to settle on Sea Island, homesteaded the original 160 acres on April 24, 1862. His nephews, Fitzgerald and Samuel, took it over on September 26. The home was known as "The Garden of Eden," and was renowned for its hospitality. In the wilderness that was to become Vancouver, the farm was the centre of every communal activity. The house was demolished during the Fifties due to the construction of a golf course on the old farm.

William Shannon

who were paddling upstream for New Westminster when nature intervened. The rowboat and canoe trips to New Westminster were not that unusual; Hugh Magee made them regularly to market his produce.

Hugh Magee was hauled into court in September, 1907, and fined $10 for breaking the peace after hitting a horse with a club. The unfortunate equine was pulling a dairy cart on a disputed right-of-way through his property. The feisty old man was forced to relinquish his control over the farm in November, 1908, when his family asked the courts to appoint merchant James Webster as manager. Magee died a year later, leaving an estate valued at $100,000 and a rather complicated will.

He had provided in the will that his wife receive half the income for life from his acreage; the children were to receive the other half, in a proportion depending on their current circumstances. There were seven boys and six girls, eleven of whom survived him, and the fighting started after the mother's death in 1927. By November 19, 1934, when the estate was appealed to the High Court in London, England (at the time the final authority for the Dominion), it was worth $142,000. When the dispute was finally settled by court order in November, 1962, 53 years after Hugh Magee's death, all of his children had died.

The farm property was broken up and sold during the years when the estate was in dispute. During the Fifties, a man named Hyland Barnes operated a nursery at the old farmhouse; he sold the house to a Keith Dewar, who tore it down in January, 1959 and divided the two-acre parcel of land into six lots. Small houses now occupy the site. A great grandson, G.B. Timleck, operates the Magee Pharmacy at the corner of 49th and West Boulevard.

Another farmer was William Shannon, whose career was typical of men who came to British Columbia during the Cariboo Gold Rush days. Born in Ireland in 1841, he came to Ontario at age six. The restrictions on his prospects in that established part of the world prompted him to go to California when he was twenty. He wandered north after finding that California's opportunities had already been seized by others, and arrived in the Vancouver area in 1863. He worked for years in the Interior as a trader, miner, lumberman and cattle rancher, and established a reputation as one of the best freighters in the Cariboo. Shannon settled in Vancouver in 1887 and bought his south slope property. He also had considerable interests in Cloverdale. The Shannon farm was swallowed up by urban expansion during the Twenties and Thirties, but the dairy—headquartered in later years at 8584 Granville— did not cease its regular deliveries until 1951, at which time it had 5,000 customers. Shannon built a home on Haro Street in the West End in 1890, and lived out his final years in a house at 1872 Nelson Street. He died in July 1928, aged 87.

Henry Mole

Henry Mole's farmhouse, on the farm which became, in 1922, Point Grey Golf Course, on Marine Drive at Blenheim.

In 1863, a year after Samuel and Fitzgerald McCleery settled on the bank of the Fraser, Henry Mole quit the Cariboo gold rush and drifted back to the coast. He pre-empted District Lot 314, between Blenheim Street and the Musqueam Indian village of Mahly and began to farm it. After being flooded out of his small cabin near the riverbank, Mole built a large, square farmhouse on the slope just below the River Road (Marine Drive). To provide power for his threshing machine, he installed a red-painted waterwheel in the creek which flowed past his front door. The creek was full of spawning salmon, which Mole took out of the stream with a pitchfork.

In 1922, Mole's son John sold the farm to the Point Grey Golf and Country Club, and retired to Langley. The old farmhouse became the clubhouse, and was finally demolished in 1959 when the current structure was built. Although the waterwheel is long gone, the creek-bed is still visible in front of the 12th tee.

Austin Taylor

The Shannon Estate on Granville at 57th. Financier Austin Taylor bought it in the mid-Thirties, and occupied it until his death in 1965. The estate grounds are now a luxury condominium development, but the mansion and coach-house have been preserved.

Austin Taylor

The Shannon Estate on South Granville, though built by B.T. Rogers, was the long-time residence of Austin Taylor, one of the best examples of a generation of Vancouverites who became wealthy in the mature city of the Twenties and Thirties. He was neither a pioneer nor the scion of established wealth, and made little money in real estate—the favorite game of the preceding generations of Vancouverites.

Taylor was born in 1889 in Toronto. He first attracted the attention of Joseph Flavelle, the chairman of the Imperial Munitions Board, when he converted the Montreal Locomotive Works to wartime production in 1915. Flavelle put him, along with a young forestry operator named H.R. MacMillan, in charge of the procurement of "airplane spruce" on the Queen Charlottes.

Taylor's career took off in 1929, when Messrs. Stobie, Forlong and Co. had a stock debacle over gold mining shares on the Bridge River. Taylor and his associates, under the name Bralco, took over the company and started the Bralorne Mining Co., one of the most prosperous gold mines of the century, and one of the few things that made any money in B.C. during the Thirties.

Almost overnight, Taylor was in the social columns as often as in the business ones. He was a big, square-shouldered, quiet man with a brusque exterior, "not an after-dinner speaker." He was best-known internationally for his A.C.T. stock farm, built on part of the Hudson's Bay Company's old Fort Langley farm, where he raised jerseys and racehorses, amongst them "Indian Broom," which recorded wins at Santa Anita in 1938 after a third in the 1937 Kentucky Derby.

In early 1936, the Taylors held an "at home" in the Hotel Vancouver for several hundred acquaintances. That June, they bought Shannon. Prominent among the Taylors' friends was Joe E. Brown, the then-celebrated Hollywood comedian. The debut of their elder daughter Kathleen in 1938 was heralded with front page pictures in the *Province*. The Taylors' younger daughter, Patricia Aldyen Austin married an up-and-coming American political figure named William Francis Buckley Jr. in 1950.

Austin Taylor returned to public service during the Second World War as a "dollar-a-year-man" working for War Minister C.D. Howe. He was B.C. Provincial Chairman of the 1941 Victory Loan, lent the country (through War Bonds) a million dollars on March 17, 1941 and in 1942 chaired the B.C. Security Commission (the "Jap Removal Commission," an unpleasant job which he insisted "should be done in the British manner"). After the war, he chaired the B.C. Emergency Flood Committee to help ruined farmers in the Fraser Valley, and "personally raised over $1 million on the phone," according to a newspaper editorial.

Taylor was a staunch conservative on political and fiscal matters. One of the few times he spoke out politically was in March, 1957 against Premier W.A.C. Bennett's mining legislation, accusing the government of "killing the goose...now they're busy eating the egg."

By 1958, the 10-acre Shannon estate was costing $9,500 a year in taxes, and Taylor suggested a rezoning with the intention of razing the mansion and redeveloping the estate with apartments. Nothing was resolved until after Taylor's death; arts organizations entered the 1967 controversy over the fate of the property, with an idea of using Shannon as an arts centre. In 1972, after a bitter battle among neighbours, Wall and Redekop Realty, the arts groups and the Taylor family, the property was developed with luxury townhouses. However, the mansion, coach house and perimeter wall were saved.

Austin Taylor died November 1, 1965; his wife, Kathleen Ruth Taylor, died September 28, 1972. The estate was valued at $10.2 million.

The Reifels

Casa Mia, on Southwest Marine Drive above the Fraser River

The two spectacular Spanish mansions on the bluff above the Fraser flats—Casa Mia at 1920 and Rio Vista at 2170 Southwest Marine Drive, were built by sons of pioneer brewer Henry Reifel. The name Reifel is today best-known for the Reifel waterfowl refuge on Westham Island in the South Arm of the Fraser River delta. The 860-acre island and tidal flats were dedicated in 1965 by George H. Reifel in memory of his father, George C., who died in 1958.

In 1888, Henry Reifel (1869-1945), with the help of his brother Conrad, started the family fortune by opening the Union Brewery in Nanaimo. Under the name of Vancouver Breweries, he amalgamated with Charles Doering and absorbed the old Mount Pleasant brewery at 7th and Scotia. The next year, he formed the Canadian Brewing and Malting Co., which built the large brewery in "West Fairview" at 12th and Vine now owned by Carling's. In 1924, he purchased the B.C. Distillery in New Westminster. The distilling activities gained him an interest in the Frank McMahon-controlled Alberta Distilleries Ltd., still a giant in the Canadian liquor business.

Henry's son Harry Reifel built Rio Vista, the earlier and more expensive of the two Reifel homes. Renowned for their conservatories and Pompeiian pools, they were highlights of the 1940s "Garden Beautiful" tours in aid of charity and the war effort. Harry also owned the Bellavista Farm at Milner in the Fraser Valley, where he gained recognition as an expert Jersey breeder. His quiet life had one bizarre twist, in 1955, when there was an attempt to extort $50,000 from him and $150,000 from W. Vincent Astor of New York. The instigator was an Austrian immigrant named Heinz Adam, living at 640 Lakewood. Adam, who was unemployed and had a sick wife, sent a letter to Reifel stating: "There is a certain gentleman who needs your help, and you will extend that help to the extent of $50,000 which you will cable to [account] at [a bank on Granville Street downtown] within five days. If that is not carried out there is a black spot in your life and I will spread it through the newspapers of the land and you will never again occupy a place in the social register. [Signed] Ku Klux Klan." The case was broken by "sleuth RCMP Constable B.C. Johnson" who traced the bank account and the typewriter used to Adam, a former employee of Reifel's at Bellavista.

The second son, George C., was prominent in the family business as a brewmaster, and later as the vice-president and general manager of Alberta Distillers. He built and operated a brewery in Japan, which he sold to Japanese interests in 1919.

CVA

George C. Reifel

CITY OF VANCOUVER ARCHIVES

Harry Reifel

Point Grey

Looking down the hill from 4th and Trimble during the 1920s. The large home in the middle distance is Aberthau, now the West Point Grey Cultural Centre. Sand traps and fairways of the Jericho Golf Course are visible on the right, as is the Jericho seaplane base, later (1976) the site of the United Nations Habitat Forum Conference.

The western end of the Vancouver "mainland" abounds in Spanish names, in honour of the crew of Commander Narvaez, who first sighted the wooded cliffs in 1791. In June, 1792, Captain George Vancouver explored the area, naming the peninsula Point Grey after his friend, Captain George Grey. The Spanish presence (at that time exploring north from their California base) is noted in many of the names in the area: Locarno Beach, Spanish Banks (after Vancouver's meeting there with Galiano and Valdez, who are remembered by two of the Gulf Islands), Langara Street (after the Spanish name for the Vancouver area), Blanca Street (after a Spanish commander) and so on.

Before the 4th Avenue tram line opened in 1909, the area was considered quite remote, and suitable only for farming and a school for "bad boys"—the Industrial School on Fourth Avenue, now the site of the Jericho School for the Deaf and Blind. Logger Jerry Rogers' 15 waterfront acres were sold in 1905 to the Jericho Golf Club, which had a nine-hole course laid out on the sand flats of the Admiralty Reserve there. The remains of the E-yalmu Indian village were still in evidence at the foot of Discovery. In 1905, a feed and grain store, with bay-windowed lodgings above, was built at

the corner of Belmont and Sasamat. Five years later, the building was converted into a general store and became the post office for the Langara district. It survives as a coffee house and store. A dairy farm was established by John L. Stewart on the logged-off "Plains of Abraham," the bluff above Marine Drive between the first and second ravines west of Blanca. Stewart's cows grazed throughout the stumps and alder on what was to become the University Endowment Lands. The concrete foundation of his dairy barn is still visible in the forest, but the funicular railway, which brought the milk down the steep hill to Marine Drive, had disappeared by the late Twenties. The first substantial house in the area was built at 4397 West 2nd in 1909 for James S. Rear. Called Aberthau, it was the long-time residence of Colonel Victor Spencer, and is now the West Point Grey Cultural Centre. By the First World War, many houses had been built near Locarno Beach, including Brock House at Jericho Beach. The Jericho seaplane base was established on a portion of the Admiralty Reserve immediately after the War. After the outbreak of the Second World War, the golf course was abandoned and the area occupied by Pacific Command of the Royal Canadian Air Force. Some of the military buildings still exist, though the golf course land is now largely public park.

The area on the hill above was made accessible to housing by a single-track streetcar line which ran from 10th and Alma up the hill to Sasamat, down Sasamat to 4th (the reason why Sasamat is wider than the other streets in the area), and west along 4th to Drummond Drive, where there was a turntable. The Sasamat line was one where the motormen "passed the baton" at sidings—the streetcar which had the baton had the right-of-way on the single-track. The entire Endowment Lands area west of Blanca was surveyed and prepared for subdivision. Two areas were developed in the mid-Twenties—one adjoining Blanca Street, and other near the present University Hill School. The patches of young forest, mainly alder, which are visible along Chancellor Boulevard date from the early Fifties, when the forest was cleared for an unsuccessful subdivision. The area is now parkland.

Spanish Banks figured largely in Jonathan Rogers' Park Board plans during the Twenties. In 1929, the foreshore was deeded to the city for park purposes; in 1932, Spanish Banks beach was consolidated and developed and the first problems with erosion (which has reduced the sand cliffs at Wreck Beach ever since) were noticed. The beach almost became an airport, after a 1955 study by the Vancouver Board of Trade recommended it for light aircraft and seaplanes. The study mentioned the "dangerous congestion" at Sea Island, but in the end the Department of Transport wouldn't support the proposal, fearing that it would be too close to the existing International Airport.

Col. Victor Spencer, long-time resident of Aberthau, and the most socially-active member of the Spencer department store family (page 52).

Jerry Rogers

Jeremiah Rogers was the most respected and best-known lumberman on Burrard Inlet in the 1860s and 1870s. He was a business partner of Captain Edward Stamp, the founder of the Hastings Mill, and came to British Columbia in 1858 to do contract logging. He started working for Stamp, building a mill on the Alberni Canal on Vancouver Island, and was engaged in the lumber and spar business in the Puget Sound and Port Neville areas. Later, he cut naval warship spars for the French, Russian and Dutch governments.

When Stamp abandoned his mill after he went bankrupt in January, 1868, Rogers sued him for $6,000 in back wages. Under the new San Francisco owners, Rogers continued to log the Point Grey peninsula and was one of the mill's largest suppliers of raw logs.

Jerry Rogers was born about 1820 in New Brunswick. Very little is known of his early life, but he attracted people by his straightforwardness and honesty—qualities that made him a Justice of the Peace in his last years on the inlet. He built a house near his main logging camp by the Admiralty Reserve at what became known as Jericho—either a corruption of "Jerry's Cove" or of "Jerry & Co."

The name "Jericho" first appeared in a newspaper article on the "Battle of Jericho" in 1871, when Police Chief Tomkins Brew and a posse cornered two murderers near the site.

Rogers complained, to anyone who would listen, about the standard English broadaxe, which was woefully ill-suited for the huge trees on Point Grey. He designed his own axes and was able to demonstrate them to Lord Dufferin when the latter made his tour of the new Colony in 1876. Rogers also experimented with steam traction engines, which had arrived too late for the traffic boom on the Cariboo Road, but turned out to be valuable for skidding logs through the forest.

Rogers died on October 24, 1879. His operations on Point Grey were taken over by his sidekick Angus Fraser. During the ensuing twenty years, the rest of the prime timber on the peninsula was removed by small-scale logging operators, some of whom diverted creeks and built log chutes down the steep cliffs to get the logs out of the forest. Most of the trails in the University Endowment Lands got their start as skid roads.

Jeremiah Rogers, the namesake of Jericho, and one of the most successful contract loggers for the Hastings Mill.

The Jericho Boys' Industrial School was built "way out in Point Grey" to keep the bad boys away from temptation; its particular site, at 4100 West 4th, was apparently chosen as it was high and dry: to the east was a hollow and a swamp. When the school opened, about 1908, it could be reached only from the nearest streetcar at Kitsilano Beach, a long walk along Point Grey Road (then a wagon trail through the forest), and continuing over a narrow corduroy road crossing the swamp (now the low part of 4th Avenue by the old Quiney place at Dunbar Street). There were deer, bear and cougar in the forest, which undoubtedly made the boys stay put. In October, 1920, the school moved to Bisco, Coquitlam. The building later became the School for the Deaf and Blind, later known as the Jericho Hill School. The Justice Institute of B.C. now occupies part of the grounds; the Department of National Defense another.

Jericho Air Station

Jericho Park is one of the newest and most attractive parks in Vancouver, with duck ponds, bridges, paths and hundreds of yards of beach. The wharf and ruined foundations at the west end are the only remnants of the park's predecessor—the Jericho Air Station, a seaplane and flying boat base for the Royal Canadian Air Force. (The eastern part of the park was, from 1892 to 1939, the Jericho Golf Links, page 232.) The air station dates from the time of open cockpits, rumrunning and carrier pigeons, when golfers would time their backswings to avoid distraction from a blatting Curtis HS-2L struggling off English Bay.

After the First World War, there was a long and bitter debate in the Canadian Parliament on the value of a permanent Air Force, resulting in the Air Board Act of June, 1919 to control all aspects of Canadian aeronautics. The Board established a framework for a series of training bases across the country: in that year, Joe Hobbs of the Air Board and Seaforths' veteran Earl MacLeod selected Jericho as a suitable spot for a west coast air station, and, on November 1, 1920, the Air Board moved from the Metropolitan Building to Jericho. By the summer of 1921, a slipway had been built and two canvas-covered Bessoneau hangars erected for the four Curtis HS-2L flying boats which were operational there. Drift logs and debris—the bane of early golfers—had been heaped and burned in preparation for building a small community of offices and huts. The next summer, the canvas hangars were replaced with permanent structures.

The pilots spent most of their time doing aerial mapping, exploration, and forestry and fisheries patrols. Jericho had the best pigeon loft in the country: carrier pigeons were often used instead of radios to save weight, and when a flying boat was forced down with engine failure a pigeon was dispatched, bearing an SOS. The flying boats did the first aerial mosaic of Vancouver with photographer Clarence Duncan, and piloted customs officers around the islands looking for drug and liquor smugglers.

Once MacLeod piloted customs officers Harry and Norman de Graves after the ex-submarine chaser S.S. *Trucilla* near Jumbo Island. The flying boat glided in and the officers were able to board the rumrunner before the crew had a chance to come on deck. De Graves met the crew "dramatically, with drawn pistol when they appeared on deck." Another time, a flying boat crew located a bootleg still on Texada Island.

The Air Board was disbanded and replaced by the Royal Canadian Air Force when the latter was formed on April 1, 1924. Number One Operations Squadron was formed exactly a year later, based at Jericho Beach. It was employed on civil government air operations until transferred to the non-military Directorate of Civil Government Air Operations in July, 1927. Commanders A.E. Godfrey and, later, J.H. Tudhope retained the four Curtis flying boats. The operation was reorganized in 1927, but had its wings clipped by the Depression. In April, 1932, the strength of the RCAF was cut by one-fifth. Civilian responsibilities were largely eliminated, and service units were formed, like the No. 4 (Flying Boat) Squadron at Jericho on February 17, 1933. Three years later, the Jericho Base became Western Air Command, with control over all operations in B.C. and Alberta. The Canadian government had finally recognized the need for air defence.

Nevertheless, Number Four Squadron spent its first five years involved in civil government operations—particularly in stepped-up activities against illegal immigration. In January, 1938, it was redesignated for General Reconnaissance work and began service training, mobilizing on September 10, 1939. A month later, it started anti-submarine duty and bombing reconnaissance, which were continued until it disbanded on August 7, 1945.

A feature of life at Jericho in the early war years was "Maw's"—a coffee house and dancing spot in the old Park Board pavilion at Locarno Beach. Run by a Mrs. Susan Williams, Maw's was the unofficial hangout for the Jericho airmen. For a nickel, slot 15 on the jukebox played The Inkspots' "I Don't Want To Set The World On Fire."

In 1945, when the base officially closed and peace was at hand, controversy started on the fate of the waterfrontage and old golf course. The confused ownership of the land, and the vagaries of wartime expropriation, made a decision on its future even more difficult to achieve. Initially, the provincial government had owned 140 acres at Jericho and the golf club only 9, including the clubhouse. In 1941, the Department of National Defense negotiated a rather open-ended lease for the province's land and bought the clubhouse and 9 acres for $55,000. In 1947, the D.N.D. bought the province's land for $2,500 an acre. The Spencer house was then in use as an officers' mess, and the clubhouse, surrounded by a barbed wire fence, became a recreational area for the base's officers. Pacific Command for the R.C.A.F. was established there officially in the late Forties, with supply depots, provost corps, the Search and Rescue Centre, a hoard of other departments, and a round-the-clock manned warning centre against enemy attack.

In March, 1948 the golf clubhouse burned. It was completely destroyed, mainly because firemen had to chop through the barbed wire fence before they could reach the blaze. That year, the city made its first moves to acquire the site for a park. Over the next decade, they were only able to get 16 acres. After another fifteen years of "gifts," threats and counter charges among the various levels of government, the final 54 acres was turned over to the city in March, 1973. The property included the remaining old flying boat hangars and the heating plant. The hangars were renovated imaginatively for the 1976 United Nations-sponsored Habitat Forum conference. Over the ensuing five years, all of the hangars either burned or were torn down, amid great public protest. The site today contains some private sailboat storage and moorage.

A Curtis HS-2L flying boat, moving off the slipway at the Jericho Air Station during the early Twenties. All of the hangars are now demolished, and the land behind them, formerly the Jericho golf course, is park. The Curtis HS-2L, with a 400 h.p. Liberty engine, was designed in 1918 for the U.S. Navy.

R.W. Brock

Brock House, at Jericho Beach, was built in 1913 for Philip Gilman, but got its name from a later owner, Dean Reginald Brock, who lived there until 1935. The house is now used as a senior citizens' centre.

Dean Reginald Walter Brock

Brock House commands a sweeping view of Jericho Beach, Burrard Inlet and Howe Sound. Built in 1913 by architects Maclure and Fox for Philip Gilman, it earned its name from a later occupant—Dean Reginald Walter Brock. One of the best geologists in Canada, the Dean of Applied Science at the University, chairman of the Vancouver Harbours Board, President of the Royal Society and Commander of the First Battalion of the Seaforth Highlanders, Brock was an explorer and adventurer, as well as one of the best-known academics in the country.

Brock and his wife were killed on July 30, 1935 during an aerial excursion to Alta Lake aboard a Boeing flying boat. The airplane crashed after failing to clear a line of trees at the end of the lake. Picnickers managed to get Brock, his wife and the pilot out and onto a passing PGE train to Squamish. Mrs. Brock was the only one still alive when the three were loaded onto Col. Victor Spencer's yacht, which happened to be at Squamish. She expired before the yacht reached the Horseshoe Bay road to Vancouver. Brock was 61.

A military funeral, which jammed the streets around Christ Church, was held on August 4, 1935. The students at UBC erected a memorial to him—the old Student Union building called Brock Hall, which was opened in December, 1939. Brock House at Jericho Beach is now a seniors' centre.

Hastings Townsite

"Fighting Joe" Martin, one of the largest landowners in the Hastings Townsite area, was one of the most controversial politicians in British Columbia at the turn of the century. He was born in Ontario, and came to Vancouver in 1897, after a career which included a term as an M.P., and one as Attorney General of Manitoba. He was elected to the B.C. Legislature in 1898. That August, he recommended to Lieut. Gov. Thomas McInnes, since Robert Beaven had been unable to form a government, that Cariboo rancher Charles August Semlin be appointed Premier. There were no political parties. Semlin selected Francis Carter-Cotton, a Conservative, as his Minister of Finance, and Martin, a Liberal, as his Attorney General. Both men had substantial followings, but no one commanded a majority in the house. Martin fought Carter-Cotton with such enmity that the government's activities were brought almost to a standstill. On March 1, 1900, the lieutenant-governor fired Semlin, and asked Martin to become Premier. The MLAs promptly voted no confidence in him, and walked out of the house, led by James Dunsmuir. The gallery cheered, hissed, laughed and hurled abuse at Martin and McInnes. An MLA named Price Ellison led "a football rush" back into the chamber, shouted "We are the people!" and threw his hat repeatedly into the air. After four months of fancy legal footwork, during which Martin ran the province with only six supporters, he was forced to go to the people, and was soundly trounced on June 14 by Dunsmuir. McInnes was eventually fired by Prime Minister Laurier. Martin made a fortune on his "Hastings Manor," then left the city and got elected as the M.P. for East St. Pancras in London. He made two later attempts to re-enter B.C. politics, and ran unsuccessfully for Mayor of Vancouver in 1915. He died in Vancouver, at age 72, in 1923.

Sarah Bell Cook and her sister Lillian Lucy on the front porch of their new house at 2376 Wall Street, about 1902. The Cooks were among the first to settle permanently along the old trail and boardwalk connecting Granville Townsite with the New Brighton Resort.

Victoria Drive north of Hastings marks the eastern limit of industrial Vancouver, although the grain terminals and docks occupy the foreshore all the way east along the CPR mainline to Port Moody. The residential area south of the grain terminals and sugar refinery is an enclave of tidy, gingerbread-trimmed cottages, interspersed with row housing for the single dockyard workers. Frances Street east of Clark Drive still has the "granite sets" and brick on the streets from the tram days.

Wall Street, which runs along the bluff above the CPR mainline, commanding a view of Burrard Inlet, was cleared in the 1870s by one of Vancouver's early chain gangs, under the supervision of Constable Jonathan Miller and his one-armed jailer, John Clough. The path followed the bluff above the waterfront from the Granville Townsite to New Brighton resort.

The residential area to the east of the industrial area became known as Hastings Townsite, extending from Nanaimo to Boundary Road and from the waterfront to 29th Avenue. Its main street was named for Admiral George Fowler Hastings of the British Pacific Fleet, who charted the inlet and supervised surveying in 1869. Hastings Townsite was a separate municipality within Greater Vancouver until a referendum on December 12, 1910, when the residents voted overwhelmingly to join the City.

The big homesteaders in the early years included "Fighting Joe" Martin, who owned Hastings Manor—an area bounded by 5th Avenue, Charles, Clinton and Boundary; and Max and Frances Sinner, who homesteaded "Hyde Park," the land from Nootka to Rupert, 13th to 20th avenues. A family named Fitzpatrick operated a small sawmill at Renfrew and Charles during the logging of the Martin estate. Hastings Townsite was rapidly settled in the years after 1910, when the McGill Street tram line opened to reach the Vancouver Exhibition on the Hastings Park Grounds.

One landmark of the 1920s was the Yale Street Juvenile Detention Home. The complex started as a Children's Aid Foster Home on the site of the Burrardview Park, where the old home's foundation is still visible. In 1931, the present Family Court complex was built adjoining it. Although it was built for only 46 children, it became the only juvenile detention facility on the Lower Mainland. After twenty years of scandals and headlines like the Sun's 1950 "Children Caged Like Animals," new facilities were built elsewhere and the old detention building demolished.

Second Narrows Bridge

Archie Cowan, an alderman for the City of Vancouver, was one of many who were enraged when the Second Narrows bridge was knocked out of commission in 1930. He collected 1,782 toll tickets from disgruntled commuters, and attempted to force the Second Narrows Bridge Co. to redeem them. When he got nowhere with the company, he fumed: "Citizens are being fleeced out of thousands of dollars." The newspapers quoted him, and the company promptly sued him for slander. After much debate and with the prodding of Mayor Louis Taylor, City Council decided to back his defence (the matter was finally dropped by both sides, when the bridge reopened in June, 1934). A.C. Cowan arrived in Vancouver in 1907, and opened the Cowan Dodson Bakery at 275 East 8th in Mount Pleasant, a building now occupied by Royal City Antiques. He was the president of the Master Bakers' Association and became an alderman, representing the Mount Pleasant ward during the Thirties. Having made his fortune in Vancouver, he went to England to take a War Post in the British government. Shortly after his return, on October 11, 1941, he was rounding up sheep on a farm he kept on the Island of Aill, off Argyll, Scotland, when he dropped dead, apparently from a heart attack.

The Second Narrows bridge linking the city with North Vancouver and forming part of the Trans-Canada highway system is the third to span Second Narrows. All three bridges have been jinxed, a phenomenon attributed to the removal, in 1923, of a small islet in the middle of the channel, which was subsequently used for ballast for Ballantyne Pier. The islet, called Hwa-Hwoi-Hwoi, was the dwelling place of numerous evil spirits, according to local Indians, who considered it taboo after a medicine mask from another tribe was found there.

The first bridge opened in 1925. It had a series of small spans and trestle-piers to cross the inlet; a lifting section was provided, using a bascule (heavy concrete counterweight) arrangement. The bridge, which had a railway track down its centre lane, contributed to the growth of North Vancouver until September 19, 1930, when the freighter *Pacific Gatherer* took out the main span. Cars by the hundreds were stranded on the northern side. When the Second Narrows Bridge Co. announced that, due to the Depression, they were unable to make the necessary repairs, citizens were outraged.

The bridge finally reopened in June, 1934. It was a "navigational steeplechase" for boats, logbooms, cars and locomotives, and was replaced by a modern, high-level arched bridge in the late Fifties. The new bridge collapsed during construction on June 17, 1958, throwing painters and ironworkers hundreds of feet into the churning narrows below. Of the seventy-nine men working on the bridge that afternoon, eighteen died, including the two engineers whose mathematical oversight had overloaded the falsework. One ironworker, wearing 40 pounds of tools, fell the equivalent of 14 storeys; the plunge ruptured his eardrums and broke every rib in his body. The impact shattered all his top teeth and cracked his neck. He survived. Many others, less lucky, rode girders down into ten fathoms of water and never came up.

The evil spirits were not yet assuaged. The old bridge, which had been used since 1960 for trains only, was replaced by a railroad bridge nine years later. On October 12, 1979, *it* was knocked out by the freighter *Japan Erica* and put out of commission for a year.

Marpole & Eburne

Richard Marpole, the CPR western superintendent after whom the district was named in 1916. Born in 1850 in Wales, he started railroading at age 18, and assumed the general superintendent's office after the retirement of Henry Abbott. He resigned that post in 1907, and died in 1920 in Vancouver.

Jacob Grauer (1861-1936), pioneer farmer and storekeeper in Eburne, and the father of the last president of the B.C. Electric Railway Co.

Marpole, the area along the Fraser River at the southern end of Granville Street, is a residential community that for years has been dominated by heavy industry and commuter traffic. Eburne, the bucolic little farming community on Sea Island, has completely ceased to exist due to the expansion of the Vancouver International Airport.

About 2,000 years before white immigration began, the bluff above the Fraser River had been abandoned by the Squamish Indians, who had used it for generations as a garbage dump or midden. The Marpole Midden, as it came to be called, covered about four-and-one-half acres, from the modern site of the Fraser Arms Hotel east to the corner of Hudson and Marine and north to about 75th Avenue. In some spots the midden was about five metres deep, full of clam shells, bones, bits of crockery and other remnants of the culture—everything but wood, which had rotted away. The midden was discovered and thoroughly excavated beginning in 1892 by a group led by Charles Hill-Tout—a prominent local anthropologist who was the Principal of Buckland College on Burrard Street. A section of the midden was removed during the excavation for the Fraser Arms Hotel and now is preserved in the B.C. Provincial Museum in Victoria; a National Historic Site cairn at the small park at 75th and Cartier commemorates it.

The Marpole area was homesteaded by George Garypie on October 18, 1865. Harry Eburne, a lad from Coventry, bought the land in 1875 and began to farm it. In 1885, surveyor Lauchlan Hamilton's North Arm Road, later called Granville Street, was cut through the forest to connect Vancouver with the North Arm farms. In 1889, a connection was forged between it and Sea Island. The San Francisco Bridge Co. built a narrow, two-lane structure from the foot of the bluff (below the Fraser Arms Hotel) to the point where the Arthur Laing bridge now reaches Sea Island. A sign on the bridge read: "Parties driving faster than a walk over this bridge will be prosecuted according to law."

Sea Island was settled by Hugh McRoberts, who started farming there around 1862 on what became known as the Richmond View farm. After the bridge was built, Eburne expanded quickly—it had a post office and general store under the proprietorship of Syd Bell, later taken over by Jacob Grauer, who farmed the area immediately adjoining the Eburne townsite. There was a fine hotel there serving travellers. Lulu Island was occupied by the small community around Steveston, the London farm at the foot of Number Two Road, the Brighouse farm near the Dinsmore bridge, the Bicknell farm to the south of that, and a few others.

Aviation at the time of the First World War was limited to a few daredevils at the Minoru and Lansdowne Racetracks on Lulu Island—now Minoru Park near Number Three Road and West-minster Highway, and Lansdowne shopping centre, respectively. (The Earl of Lansdowne was a Governor General; Minoru won the English derby in 1908, the same year the racetrack opened.) The Sea Island aerodrome didn't open until 1931 and shared the island with the remaining farms until the 1970s, when the latter were expropriated and bulldozed by the Federal government for airport expansion.

The Vancouver side of the Fraser River was comparatively unimportant in 1910. The interurban stopped at "Eburne Station" at the foot of Hudson Street, then swung south across a rickety little bridge (still in use) onto Lulu Island, wound through open farming country and passed the Minoru and Lansdowne racetracks and the rifle range of the Vancouver Trapshooting Club, before arriving at Steveston. Residents of Eburne walked or drove their carriages across the little bridge.

The Vancouver side developed quickly after 1901, when a swingspan was built between the foot of Hudson Street and Eburne. This bridge became the most hated structure in Vancouver during the Forties and Fifties—it was so low that it had to be opened for anything taller than a rowboat, and it frequently jammed, causing long traffic lineups. The congestion on Hudson Street was, however, good for business, and a thriving shopping centre grew up around the corner of Hudson and Marine. In 1912, the future was considered to be so promising that the Grand Central Hotel was built on the northeast corner of Hudson and Marine. The proprietors went bankrupt—the hotel being neither grand nor central. In 1916 the area was named Marpole, in honour of Richard Marpole, the Welshman who had been the Canadian Pacific Railway's Western Regional Superintendent.

In 1917 the Grand Central Hotel was refurbished and reopened as the Provincial Home for Incurables, mainly elderly tuberculosis patients. This Marpole Infirmary, as it was generally called, remained as a gloomy landmark until it was finally torn down in the Sixties. It had been the subject of controversy since the late 1940s, when Premier John Hart announced that it would be torn down immediately. A few years later, Health Minister Eric Martin, who knew shoddy accommodation when he saw it (he was the ex-soldier who organized the post-war occupation of the old Hotel Vancouver as temporary accommodation for returned servicemen, and then rode to prominence under the Social Credit banner), called it a "shameful blot on the Province's health care system." The infirmary—a slum for 145, with a flooding basement when heavy rains backed up the Hudson Street sewer—was finally closed on May 7, 1965. The infirmary's staff house was converted into a minimum security jail, which it remains today.

The infirmary wasn't the only "slum." In June, 1957, the new Oak Street bridge opened, diverting commuter traffic five blocks

The North Arm Road bridge, at the foot of Granville Street, was completed in the autumn of 1889. The photo looks north from Sea Island to what was to become Marpole. The building on the extreme right is the original Methodist church. Harry Eburne's warehouse, for kerosene and fodder, is the building in the centre. Travellers could also go to Lulu Island via the Twigg Island Bridge from the foot of Fraser Street –the "other" North Arm Road. Built in 1893, it was regularly wrecked by river barges (in 1925, 1955, 1966 and 1970), and in its later years, before its demolition in 1974, was as much an obstacle to motorists as to river traffic. It had the last hand-cranked swingspan on the Lower Mainland, and was opened an average of three times a day by the attendant, who blocked the traffic at the Fraser Street end with gates, walked 650 feet to the other end and closed the gates there, inserted a ten-foot bar onto a socket in the centre of the roadway, and, pushing the bar, walked in a circle 25 times to open the bridge. Traffic jams were massive, especially when the Marpole bridge got stuck open, as was regularly the case. The opening of the Oak Street bridge in 1957 streamlined traffic, but on its first day, motorists taking the Twigg Island Bridge to dodge the 25 cent toll caused a traffic jam north on Fraser as far as 30th.

Marpole Midden

The excavation of the four-and-one-half acre Marpole Midden brought to light many facts about the "Marpole" period of pre-history, as it came to be called to distinguish it from the earlier "Locarno Beach period." The Marpole midden revealed that the Indians had hunted elk, deer, seals, ducks and geese and fished for salmon and sturgeon around the mouth of the Fraser River, much as their ancestors at Locarno had. However, the excavations also turned up remains of herring nets, which were a new development for the culture. Many human skeletons survived, including the skulls of "mental patients" who had been trepanned—a hole was drilled into the patient's skull to allow evil spirits to escape, a common operation around the world a few thousand years ago. Much of the midden was taken by the wagon load to provide soil for the gardens in Shaughnessy Heights in the years before the First World War. The midden is one of the few National Historic Sites in Vancouver, a fact recorded by a small cairn and descriptive plaque in the triangular park at 75th and Cartier.

The Marpole end of the first Eburne bridge, looking north at the turn of the century. Marpole was not so-named until 1916; before that it was known as Eburne Station, an adjunct to the more established community of Eburne on Sea Island. The interurban stopped near the foot of Hudson, so many Eburne residents walked across the bridge.

east. The Hudson Street business area went into a swift decline—of the 50 thriving stores in 1956, only 20 were open for business in 1961. Many buildings were boarded up. The Marpole Chamber of Commerce attempted to rescue the situation by suggesting that Marpole become a Kingsway-style motel area. The second blow to the Marine and Hudson part of Marpole was the Arthur Laing Bridge, built specifically to serve the airport. The entrance and exit ramps at the foot of Hudson give the area the look and feel of the many American inner-city neighbourhoods which have been over-run with expressways. The old Marpole business centre is now a tiny enclave, serving the large number of senior citizens living in the apartment area which has occupied much of Marpole south of 70th Avenue.

The modern Marpole business district is the strip of Granville south of 63rd Avenue—a much more convenient location for commuters and car-oriented residents than the old. In the Twenties, the south end of Granville was the location of the White Spot, a fancy new-fangled drive-in restaurant owned by a young entrepreneur named Nat Bailey. Other than the White Spot, with its car hops and 10-cent hamburgers, there were a few blueberry farms and orchards, the Shannon farm, an occasional house, a few billboards at the foot of Granville Street, a plume of smoke from Eburne Sawmills' beehive burner, and the Point Grey Garage, dispensing "Violet Ray" gasoline to the motorists on the long trek from central Vancouver.

A direct route from Vancouver to the American border had been discussed since before World War I. Before 1937, all American traffic came north through White Rock and Crescent Beach, then swung east past Ladner to New Westminster, where it struggled across the Great Northern's railway bridge there. The Pattullo Bridge was only constructed in the late 1930s, and was considered adequate for the few residents of rural Ladner. It took the flamboyance and ambition of Highways Minister "Flying" Phil Gaglardi and the persistent lobbying of Ladner blacksmith George Massey to get the Oak Street bridge built and the revolutionary Deas Island (now George Massey) tunnel laid across the South Arm. Before that, there was no way across the south arm of the Fraser River, other than the Woodward's Landing ferry (see map, page 11).

City Airport

During the Twenties, Vancouver's civic administration had little faith in the future of aviation as other than an amusement for crazy people. Charles K. Hamilton made the first local flight in late 1910, when he piloted a Curtiss pusher biplane from the infield of Minoru racetrack on Lulu Island. Others, like William Templeton (who later managed the Vancouver Airport for its first 19 years of operation), followed over the next few years, piloting flimsy biplanes and autogyros from cow pastures and race tracks on the Richmond flats.

"Respectable" aviation started after the Great War, when the Canadian Air Board established the Jericho flying boat station, and enterprising bush pilots operated primitive charter services from Coal Harbour. The public was captivated by the exploits of E.C. Hoy, who in August, 1919, became the first man to fly across the Rockies in a war-relic Jenny biplane, and the Air Board's Halifax-to-Vancouver air relay over an eleven day period in the Fall of 1920.

It was Charles Lindbergh who indirectly provided the impetus for the creation of Vancouver's Civic Airport. His 1927 New York-to-Paris flight caused a world-wide sensation, and his subsequent well-wishing tour was eagerly awaited all over North America. Lindbergh spurned Vancouver, though, "because there's no airport there fit to land on." Thus goaded, the City administration selected the Sea Island site as the best of nine alternatives, allocated a princely $600,000 to it, and set about clearing the land for an airport. Manager William Templeton's staff consisted of three men and a horse. If a pilot arrived after dark, the staff put out storm lanterns along the edges of the runway. In emergencies, the public responded to calls for help over the radio, and lighted the landing strip with car headlamps. Pilot Joe Bertalino recounted a typical early weather report: "If you can see Mount Baker, it's going to rain; if you can't see it, it's raining." Vancouverites thronged to the airport for its official opening on July 21, 1931, and thereafter to watch the "crazy flying" and to embark on sightseeing flights. During the easy-going days of the Thirties, pilots with no passengers took shotguns and hunted ducks along the slough behind the old administration buildings near the South terminal.

Scheduled air transportation had begun in 1928 from a Lulu Island pasture near the Lansdowne track. A twelve-seat Ford tri-motor operated a Vancouver-Victoria service under the B.C. Airways banner. International flights began on July 1, 1934, when United Air Lines started a regular service to Seattle from the Sea Island airport. Competing air services sprang up, including Trans-Canada Air Lines (now Air Canada) and Yukon Southern Air Transport (now CP Air), both in 1937. The airport remained the city's property until 1961, when it was sold to the Federal Government. Its expansion paralleled the decline of the railways and steamship companies, which had made Vancouver a world transportation centre in the 1890s.

The "Vancouver Air Port" during the early Thirties, when the main activity for pilots was taking sightseers for a look at the city. Scheduled commercial flights from the airport didn't begin until 1934, when United started a regular service to Seattle.

The White Spot

WHITE SPOT LTD

A typical busy Sunday at the White Spot on Granville at 67th, on a winter day during the early Forties. The billboard scene on the right shows a wartime convoy in the North Atlantic.

The White Spot at 67th and Granville has been a favorite of Vancouverites since the Thirties, when the automobile first became very common. Three generations of Vancouver families have courted and spooned in cars at the familiar parking lot on South Granville at 67th. The name White Spot was synonymous with sportsman and philanthropist Nat Bailey, who got his start after the First World War bagging peanuts at the Denman Arena in the winter and the Athletic Park in the summer. On a sunny spring day in 1924, Bailey decided to try selling food to the adventurous motorists who were touring the newly-opened Marine Drive loop around the university. He set up on the back of a Ford truck at Lookout Point on Marine Drive (the spot just west of Shaughnessy Golf Course which commemorates Simon Fraser's arrival at the coast in 1808) and started selling ice cream cones (5 cents), sandwiches (10 cents), ice-cold drinks (10 cents) and hot dogs (10 cents). He later built a kiosk and hired some local kids to deliver the cones and dogs to the cars parked at the point. They would "hop to it," and thus were born Car Hops.

In June, 1928, Bailey opened a small log hut at the corner of 67th and Granville in Marpole, calling it the "White Spot Barbecue" and advertising "barbecued sandwiches." It was particularly popular for Vancouverites on the newly-invented Sunday Drive, but was considered too far from the heart of the city to be a success. Bailey picked the spot as the only piece of commercial property he could afford. Besides, it had the added advantage of being close to the corner of 70th and Granville, where the Marine Drive traffic returned to civilization.

The new White Spot featured the paintings—mainly coastal and farming landscapes—of Jim Osborne. (The job was later taken over by Pete Hopkinson, who still paints them.) Osborne's painting became quite an attraction—families stopped regularly to kibitz with him on the progress of his work.

The big seller in the early years was chicken, and Bailey inaugurated "Chicken in the Straw" after American Beverley Osborne's "Chicken in the Rough."

Bailey was successful enough to open a second location at Hastings and Slocan in 1930, but concurrently, the Second Narrows bridge was knocked out by the *Pacific Gatherer* and commuter traffic at that end of town virtually ceased. Not surprisingly, the second location failed, but people kept coming to the South Granville White Spot. A new building called "Granville House," featuring a dining room, was erected in 1937. Expansion followed rapidly after the Second World War, and Bailey eventually sold the chain to General Foods in 1968. (It has since returned to local ownership.)

The University of British Columbia

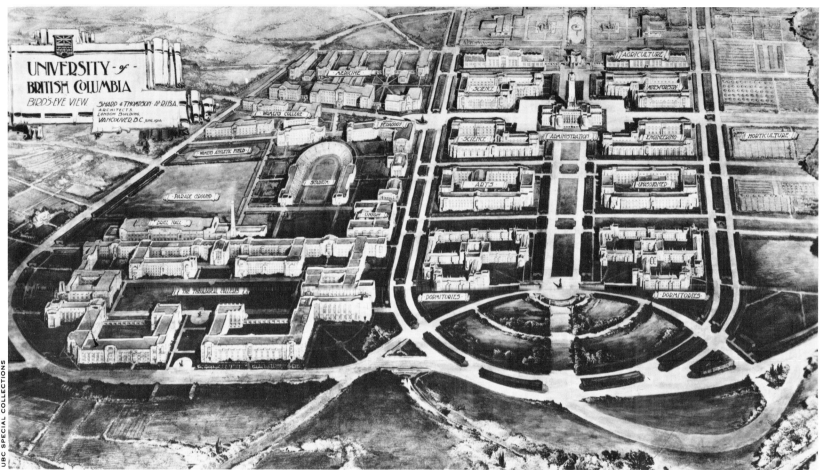

UNIVERSITY -of-
BRITISH COLUMBIA
BIRDS-EYE VIEW. SHARP & THOMPSON M: RIBA.
ARCHITECTS
London Building
VANCOUVER B.C. June 1914.

The Sharp and Thompson
master plan for the
University of B.C., approved
in June, 1914. This view
looks south from a point just
east of Point Grey. The
basic layout of the campus,
with East, Main, and
West Malls, has survived, but
the rest was a victim of
changing governments, the
war, and financial res-
traints. Only the Science
building was built on the
location indicated on the
master plan.

Frank Fairchild Wesbrook,
a pathologist and bacteriolo-
gist, was offered the presidency of the new University
of B.C. on February 10,
1913. Born in Brant, Ontario,
in July, 1868, he was
educated in Manitoba and
England, and had been the
dean of the University of
Minnesota Medical College
before his appointment to
UBC. He died in July, 1918
after a year-long illness, "a
broken and disappointed
man" because the War
caused all his plans to
collapse. His name is
remembered in Wesbrook
Mall at UBC.

In 1908, in the midst of Vancouver's *Belle Époque*, interest in higher learning crystallized into a coherent plan to create a university. The provincial government passed legislation that year creating the University of British Columbia, and suggested that the tip of the Point Grey peninsula was a suitable location (the forested land west of Blanca and Camosun was given to the university as an endowment, to provide a source of funds for the university's development and operation, in 1923). An international architectural competition was held to determine a suitable design for the campus. It was won by the local firm of Sharp and Thompson, which submitted Gothic-inspired plans for a campus community laid out along three malls, the central one ending at a viewpoint overlooking Howe Sound. A campus near Point Grey was cleared in 1912. The following year, Dr. Frank Wesbrook, the university's president, went east to find a staff, "the very best that Canada, the

U.S., Great Britain and possibly Germany have to offer." The next April, Premier Richard McBride declared that the University, to be "the best in the world," would open at Point Grey in the fall of 1915. On June 8, 1914, the architect's plans for the library and Science buildings were approved and a master plan accepted. Construction began immediately on these two central structures, but no sooner had the steel and concrete frames been erected when the Great War began. Construction ceased.

Meanwhile, the McGill University College of B.C., which had been installed in the old City Hospital buildings on Pender, was providing the first two years of university instruction. Vancouver General Hospital entered into negotiations with McGill for the development of a formal medical teaching program. A new building at the hospital site in Fairview was "temporarily" occupied by McGill, and the next year, on September 30, 1915, classes in sci-

Looking northwest from the Science building across the Main Mall, in August, 1929. The buildings in the background, occupied later by Administration, Mathematics, and the "old auditorium," were intended as temporary buildings, to be replaced during the Thirties. They are still in use. The cairn in the left foreground commemorates the Great Trek of 1922, when students successfully lobbied the Provincial Government to move the campus from its Fairview Shacks to the Point Grey campus.

ences and the arts began in the "Fairview Shacks," across 12th Avenue from the main hospital buildings. The students wore academic gowns piped with khaki in honour of the war.

By 1919, the numbers of students at the new university had been swollen by returned servicemen, who agitated repeatedly for the completion of the Point Grey campus. The science building skeleton, four storeys high, continued to rust in the rain. Nearly 1,200 students were enrolled at the Fairview campus, and attended classes in wooden buildings, shacks, tents, basements and attics.

In the summer of 1922, with no action forthcoming from the province, a student campaign committee was formed and gathered over 50,000 signatures on a petition addressed to the Provincial Government, demanding the immediate completion of the Point Grey campus. On October 28, the committee held a huge downtown parade and rally, after which the students boarded streetcars

and transferred their way up to 10th and Sasamat, on the edge of the forest, where they reassembled for the "Great Trek" to the campus. The students climbed the girders of the unfinished science building for photographs, and filled a small cairn (on the Main Mall) with stones carried to the site. Two weeks later, Premier John Oliver announced an immediate grant of $1,500,000 to restart construction. Classes finally commenced at Point Grey in 1925.

The campus remained quite small and "village-like" until the mid-Sixties, when the sudden boom in higher education caused it to expand with parking lots and buildings in every direction. The Endowment Lands remained largely a second-growth wilderness (with the exception of the University Golf Course, some cordwood cutting around 16th and Imperial, and an abandoned subdivision east of University Hill School) and, after a fierce controversy in the early Seventies, were dedicated as parkland.

E.P. Davis

Cecil Green Park, one of the finest homes in the University area, got its name from its last occupant, an Applied Science Dean and university benefactor. Cecil Green donated the home to the UBC Alumni Association, which keeps the entertaining rooms available for wedding receptions and other functions.

The home was built for, and originally occupied by, Edward Pease Davis, the most important barrister and solicitor in early Vancouver. Davis declined the offer of the province's chief justiceship in July, 1898, as it would have meant his removal to Victoria. From 1910 to 1914, he represented former Lieutenant-Governor James Dunsmuir in the celebrated lawsuit by railroaders MacKenzie and Mann. (The latter had bought Dunsmuir's Nanaimo coal mines, in 1910, for $11 million. Dunsmuir claimed that the sale didn't include the company's various steamers and bank balances. He lost in the Privy Council and had to pay $1,500,000 damages.) In 1917, Davis defended Foley, Stewart & Welch in the breach of contract lawsuit with the Provincial Government over the P.G.E—the "Province's Greatest Expense." He regularly journeyed to London to appear before the Judicial Committee of the Privy Council, then the final authority on all Dominion legal matters. As the head of the law firm Davis, Pugh, Davis, Hosie and Lett, he had in 1905 built the Davis Chambers (demolished 1977), a fine small office building at 615 West Hastings.

Davis was born in Waterdown, King's County, Ontario in 1860, and educated at Upper Canada College and the University of Toronto. He was called to the bar of the Northwest Territories (then Alberta, Saskatchewan and everything north) in 1882, and resided in Calgary for four years before coming to Vancouver. He was made a Queen's Counsel in 1894, and continued to practice until 1931, when a stroke forced his retirement. Davis, although at one time the president of the B.C. Liberal Association, was comparatively inactive in politics. He supported the Borden Union Government during the war years, and briefly endorsed General A.D. McRae's quixotic Provincial Party in 1924.

He originally lived on Seaton Street, but moved to 6251 Northwest Marine Drive before the Great War. His first wife, Adelle

Louise (b. 1876), was the daughter of Royal North-West Mounted Police Commissioner T.W. Herchmer. She died in 1936, and the following year Davis married the widow of one Algernon Strang. Davis died in 1939. One of his sons was killed in the Great War; the other, Ghent (d. 1959), was a prominent lawyer. "Birdie" (Strang) Davis died in July, 1970, outliving her second husband by slightly over 30 years.

The view from the dining room of the E.P. Davis house, built just before the First World War, takes in a panorama from Howe Sound practically to downtown Vancouver.

Edward Pease Davis

Road Building

East Hastings in 1914. Although the sidewalk was still a boardwalk, the street has been paved, perhaps in anticipation of a rush of traffic! The area between the streetcar tracks is poured concrete, although it has been marked to simulate brick (note the expansion joints every 20 feet). Most of the streetcar track paving of the time was done with grey paving stones called "granite sets," blocks about 5" x 10" x 4" deep, which were laid on both sides of the streetcar rails but not cemented into place, the theory being that a rail could be replaced at any point without tearing up the street. Hastings Street was a good example of the very common wood-block paving method. Cedar blocks, cut locally and pressure-treated with creosote, were laid on a half-inch sand bed which was put on top of a thin concrete base. The fir or cedar blocks were then sealed with asphalt and sprinkled with a light coating of sand.

Before the turn of the century, all of the sidewalks in Vancouver were boardwalks. There was an excess of cheap lumber coming out of Vancouver-area sawmills, and boardwalks had the advantage of being set up on rot-resistant cedar posts above the quagmire; without proper drainage, concrete walks would crack and break up. After 1900, the City of Vancouver had its own sidewalk crews, like the one at right with George Ledingham as general foreman—sixth from the left in white overalls. At that time sidewalk-building was a hand operation; the cement sacks were mixed with sand and "navvy jack" (the pea gravel in the middle), delivered to the site on drays pulled by horses. In 1905, George Ledingham started his own contracting firm, which built many of the sidewalks on the west side of the city. His "G.W. Ledingham" imprint is visible on many of them.

191

Sidewalk paving crew on Columbia Street just above Broadway about 1910 (the blur in the background is the Fairview Belt-Line streetcar). The hills above Broadway on the Mount Pleasant streets were paved with red brick (which came as ballast on lumber-carrying windjammers, mainly from Scotland) to give the horses a bit more traction. The "granite sets" used for paving between the streetcar tracks were usually quarried at Deep Cove and on Nelson Island. Evans, Coleman & Evans Ltd. was one of the big cement suppliers; cement boats from Bamburton landed at the company's wharf at the foot of Columbia in Gastown. The men on the right with the big knee-pads were concrete finishers.

BRUCE LEDINGHAM

Paving on 21st Avenue near Dunbar in 1925. In the background, sacks of cement have been piled on the street awaiting the paving machine. Note the vacant lot on the left, a common feature on Vancouver streets until after the Second World War. The roads were poured in sixteen or twenty foot sections, a lane at a time, within the forms held up by wooden pegs; a thin board between the sections was removed once the concrete set, leaving space for the asphalt expansion joint which, on hot summer days, tended to melt between small boys' toes (and thus find its way indoors).

Highway construction in 1921. The Ford one-ton batch truck is dumping into the hopper of a 27E Koehring paver. The hopper dumped into the mixer which fed the bucket on the long boom at the back. This boom was hinged at the machine end, so the paving crew could angle it from side to side in order to pour a six inch slab from the bucket, which ran back and forth on little wheels.

Batch truck of Ledingham and Cooper, contractors, loading about six sacks of cement with sand and gravel for Pacific Highway construction in Washington during 1921. The truck is a modified Model T.

Gas Stations

The petroleum industry arrived in Vancouver in 1888, when the Standard Oil Co. opened an agency of its San Francisco branch on Cambie Street at Smythe. An oil warehouse was built there in 1895. The operation incorporated itself as the British Columbia Oil Co. in January, 1898, and amalgamated a year later with the Imperial Oil Co. of Petrolea, Ontario.

The first service station in Canada and, allegedly, in the world, was opened in 1908 at the southwest corner of Cambie and Smythe, with future archivist J.S. Matthews manning the station. A large, red-brick tank held the gasoline, and a ten-foot length of garden hose with no nozzle did the filling. Gasoline was 20 cents a gallon. Lubricating oil was also sold. There was no air, water, or wiping of windshields, and all transactions were strictly for cash.

Until 1918, Imperial Oil had the only gas stations in Vancouver. The second station was established at Broadway and Granville, the third at Cordova and Columbia, and the fourth at Seventh and Main. The Broadway and Granville one was the finest-looking, with a red-tile roof and, during the latter years of the Great War, young lady attendants in short khaki frock-coats with belts, breeches, leather leggings, bobbed hair and no hats, "all from well-to-do families." After 1919, when the soldiers returned, there were no more lady gas attendants.

The first car repair garage in Vancouver was the Vancouver Auto & Cycle Company, at 108 East Hastings, which opened in 1904. The building was originally a livery barn, and had large front doors which permitted the entry of carriages, and horses in need of shoeing. About 1900, the owners cleaned it up, wallpapered it, and re-opened it as a bicycle sales shop, hoping to cash in on the cycling boom. However, on March 5, 1902, James Stark accepted delivery of a gas-powered motorcar. When it needed fixing, he, being also an avid cyclist, took it to the bicycle shop, as there was nowhere else. The little garage got its gasoline from Imperial Oil, buying a case containing two four-gallon cans. The garage expanded and eventually became the Begg Motor Co., which operated for many years on Georgia between Burrard and Thurlow. By 1911, it was owned by W.H. Morrison and called the East End Cyclery, specializing in Indian-brand motorcycles. Later, it was converted into the Universal News store, and finally demolished in the Seventies.

Below: the Ever-Ready Garage and Service Co., at 4th and Macdonald in Kitsilano, opened in the Twenties as a Studebaker agency, and has been known since 1934 as Tremblay's Motors. Below right: a typical Shell station during the Twenties, across from Ferrera Court on Hastings at Jackson.

The Strathcona Garage, at 39th Avenue and West Boulevard in Kerrisdale, in 1945, did everything a garage possibly could, including neighbourhood towing with its converted Model A.

(Next page) Motoring outside the city limits was an adventure. This group on West Vancouver's Marine Drive in the late Twenties would have crossed Burrard Inlet on the new road and rail bridge at Second Narrows. The road stopped at Horseshoe Bay. "Tyres" needed as much as 90 lbs. of air, and often lasted as little as 300 miles on the primitive roads. With the exception of the paved Pacific Highway to the U.S., Vancouver motorists were cut off from the outside world. Few took their cars to Vancouver Island, as all gasoline had to be drained from them to meet shipping regulations. Passable roads continued as far east as Hope, so anyone wishing to take a vehicle to the Interior was forced to ship it by train, until 1924, when the rugged Fraser Canyon Road opened (the Hope-Princeton wasn't completed until 1951). Until January 1, 1922, residents of Vancouver Island and the Lower Mainland abided by a "keep to the left" rule-of-the-road, while people elsewhere in the Province and in the United States drove on the right. The transition was successfully completed at 6 a.m. New Year's Day, 1922, with little effect on motorists, there being few cars. Greater confusion was experienced by streetcar conductors, whose doors opened on the wrong side; horses, who were used to walking on the left; and pedestrians, who didn't know which way to look when stepping off the curbs.

196

Recreation

Stanley Park

Stanley Park is an entire peninsula, with seascapes, harbour views, formal gardens, a zoo, a bird sanctuary, a world-class aquarium, tangled rain forest, open picnic areas and playgrounds.

The first decision of the first Vancouver City Council was that Mayor Malcolm MacLean petition the Dominion Government for the use of its West End Military Reserve as a park. The Dominion agreed, though it retained title to the land. The park was opened on September 27, 1888, by MacLean's successor, David Oppenheimer, and officially dedicated by Governor General Lord Stanley in October 1889.

The prescience of that decision, from the perspective of a century later, was remarkable. In 1886, the park was dense forest, but so was everything else—the Cambie Street Grounds (now the Vancouver Bus Depot) was the major city park, and was on the outskirts of the built-up part of town. There were a few logging trails through Stanley Park, cleared by Jerry Rogers and Jonathan Miller during the 1860s in preparation for Stamp's Mill at Lumbermen's Arch. A logger named Oben set up camp by a stream near Nicola and Georgia in the 1880s, and, in 1885, a small logging firm named McMahon, Carr and Wright had a thirty-man crew camped at the foot of Bidwell. One could ride a horse from Gastown to Stanley Park without difficulty, but the new bicycles were useless in the mud and tangled roots.

The Vancouver Board of Trade, in its first meetings in 1886, had considered possibilities for developing a proper water system for the city. Supply at that time came from shallow wells, which often shared backyards with outdoor privies, contributing to intermittent outbreaks of typhoid. Private interests undertook the first surveys in 1887 in the Capilano watershed. The Vancouver Water Works Co. commenced the Capilano project that year, after winning the franchise away from the Coquitlam Water Works Company. The latter attempted to supply Vancouver from Coquitlam Lake, but was defeated by a vote of ratepayers, 86 to 58, in June, 1887. The first water main was laid across First Narrows, through Stanley Park (down Pipeline Road), across Lost Lagoon on a trestle in August, 1888 and along Georgia Street— which had only recently been cleared by the CPR for settlement. Vancouverites used Capilano water for the first time on March 26, 1889. The Vancouver Waterworks Co. opened negotiations in 1890 with the city, hoping they would purchase the system; two years later, ratepayers voted by 189 to 11 to buy the water supply system at the arbitrated price of $440,000.

The pipeline trestle across Lost Lagoon was joined by a bridge from the foot of Georgia Street into the park. City Council had voted

106.705. Band Concert, Stanley Park, Vancouver, B.C.

$20,000 for park improvements in 1887 and was prepared to spend more, with the support of the 5,000 residents of the town. Henry Avison, who lived in a little cottage on the park side of the bridge, was named Park Ranger. He diligently cleared trails and picnic sites around his cottage and supervised roadbuilding. In 1898, Mrs. Avison started the Stanley Park zoo—they had a bear cub which Avison had caught in the forest and kept on a long chain at the cottage. One day, so the story goes, "the rector's wife" was visiting and took offence when the fully-grown bear was snuffling around her. She poked it in the ribs with her umbrella; the bear wheeled around and took her dress off with one swipe of his paw. The men politely turned away, while the women ran for blankets. The upshot was that Avison dug a bear pit and built a small aviary, which was the beginning of the proper zoo. The bear took to climbing the small, dead maple tree in the middle of the pit, and staring balefully at the panama-hatted tourists with their box cameras.

In the 1880s, the Indian village of Whoi Whoi still existed at the approximate site of Lumbermen's Arch. A smallpox epidemic in 1888 alarmed authorities, who resettled the survivors and burned the village to the ground. The city then decided to pave the park

A concert in the old bandstand in Stanley Park, about 1910. The bandstand stood on the present site of the Malkin Bowl, a few hundred yards inside the park entrance.

Marion Malkin, wife of Mayor W.H. Malkin, whose death in 1934 prompted the building of the Malkin Bowl.

Looking north on Chilco toward the Stanley Park entrance in 1919. The arch is decorated for the visit of the Prince of Wales, later King Edward VIII. The old Coal Harbour bridge is visible on the extreme left, as is the Vancouver Rowing Club on Coal Harbour in the left distance. The Stuart Building, erected in 1909 on the corner, was demolished in 1982 following an extended controversy over its heritage value.

drive with calcined shells from the village midden, a prehistoric garbage and shell dump, which was about three acres in extent and averaged six feet in depth. This work was completed in 1890 and gave the city one of its first properly-graded roads, and thus one of the first decent places to ride a bicycle. The safety bicycle (low wheeled, as opposed to the dangerous penny-farthing high-wheelers of the previous decades, which were still used for races at Brockton Oval) swept the world in the 1890s; groups like the Terminal City Cycle Club, with over a hundred riders, regularly held rallies in the park. Many families kept horses, but a non-owner could rent a decent one downtown at the Stanley Park Stables at Seymour and Dunsmuir and canter around the park. The women, with their full skirts, rode side saddle.

Just outside the park's entrance, on Georgia Street, was the huge Horse Show building, erected at the corner of Gilford in 1898, and destroyed in an enormous fire in 1960. It was the second largest building of its type in North America, after Madison Square Garden. Vancouver's elite rented private boxes for the annual horse shows, which were considered to be the height of the social season. Laurier once spoke to a packed hall during an election campaign. After 1914, it was called the Stanley Park Armouries and used by the Irish Fusiliers. On the shore of Coal Harbour was the Denman

Arena, erected in 1911 by Frank Patrick for the Vancouver hockey team (which won the Stanley Cup in 1915), and the first artificial ice rink in Canada. The land adjoining was occupied after 1929 by a small Boeing seaplane and flying boat plant.

The bridge across Lost Lagoon was decorated in October 1889 for the visit of Lord Stanley. At the Georgia Street end, behind the huge Douglas Fir which stood in the middle of the street (it was felled after the Great War), a clapboard wooden arch was erected, with "STANLEY PARK" lettered in dowelling and a painted sign stating: "Walk Your Horses; No Carriages 2-5 p.m. Saturdays and Sundays. Keep To The Left." (At the other end of the bridge, a little later, the signs were changed to read: "No autos 2-5 p.m. Saturdays & Sundays. To Right, Buffaloes; To Left, Big Trees.") Stanley's carriage proceeded across the bridge and around the newly "calcined" road. He passed along Coal Harbour to the next peninsula, called Anderson's Point after the dairy farmer who had a cottage there. (After the turn of the century, buffalo grazed there—hence the sign on the bridge.) Further on was Deadman's Island, then the clearing for the Athletic Club's Recreation Grounds, later developed as Brockton Oval. At Hallelujah Point, near Brockton Oval, was the little cottage of retired Chief Constable Tomkins Brew. Stanley's carriage then arrived at the modern site of Lumbermen's Arch. It is here (not back at the entrance of the park) that Lord Stanley made the speech dedicating the park "To The Use and Enjoyment of People of All Colours, Creeds and Customs For All Time." He spoke from a small, hastily erected platform at the side of the road; at the end of his speech, he set into the earth a small cairn containing samples of B.C. mineral ores. In 1933, when archivist J.S. Matthews went in search of it, he found it had disappeared, along with the platform and a small gazebo that had decorated the shore across the road.

Henry Avison retired in 1906 and a new park ranger's house was built at the English Bay side of the park, where the Vancouver Parks Board offices are now located. The Lost Lagoon bridge was removed in the Twenties and the "mouth" of Lost Lagoon filled, providing land for the motor-route and causeway.

Lost Lagoon became a permanent lake and waterfowl sanctuary. The streetcar still stopped at Chilco, where there was a little candy stall and a Boats-for-Hire sign; Vancouverites punted around with their parasoled and crinolined ladies, looking like Oxford undergraduates. Boaters used either Coal Harbour or Lost Lagoon; if they were energetic, they dragged their boats along the little stream through the weeping willows between Lost Lagoon and Ceperley Park, and boated in English Bay.

The Vancouver Rowing Club, founded in 1888 and amalgamated eleven years later with the Burrard Inlet Rowing Club, moved from the foot of Bute Street to Coal Harbour before the Great War and built a Tudor-style clubhouse there, having found sheltered Coal Harbour an ideal spot for training. Just across the park drive above the clubhouse is a monument to "Queen Victoria The Good,"

erected by the schoolchildren of Vancouver on May 24, 1906 (her birthday; she died in January, 1901). The stately bronze and stone monument was made by McIntosh and Sons Sculptors, who worked at Westminster and Dufferin, a stone's throw from Mountain View Cemetery. On the hill above is a monument to poet Robbie Burns, commissioned locally and unveiled on August 25, 1928 by Ramsay MacDonald, Britain's first socialist Prime Minister.

The hillside and grove around these monuments is a delightful one at any time of the year. Huge maples and oaks shade the grass and the beautiful flowerbeds, and provide homes for the legions of large, well-fed squirrels. A sidewalk from the entrance to the park at Georgia and Chilco crosses an ivy-covered bridge over the park drive and continues up a tree-lined alley to Lord Stanley's statue, set dramatically in a grove of cedars. The statue, bearing an inscription of the key passages of the park's dedication, is a recent arrival. It was sculpted by Sydney March of Kent, England in the Fifties, following a private subscription drive among some prominent Vancouver citizens. The impressive bronze statue with upraised arms was unveiled by Governor General Vanier on a rainy day in 1960. It was instantly lampooned by *Vancouver Sun* cartoonist Len Norris, who suggested that Lord Stanley was raising his arms only to determine whether it was raining!

Past the Stanley monument is the old Zoological Garden, which was cleared in 1887 as a picnic ground. It was one of the few places where strollers could promenade without tripping over roots, sliding in mud or searching for patches of sunshine among the tall trees. A bandstand, the model for the one at Alexandra Park, was erected there on what is now the site of the Malkin Bowl. Crowds of Vancouverites, in Strathcona double collar with four-in-hand tie, snap-on linen cuffs and bowler (the women in petticoats over whalebone corset), walked down muddy Georgia Street in Cuban-heeled Blucher-cut boots into the park to hear the bands play. Smart families spent a nickel on the tram to the Chilco loop. Vancouverites also came to the bandstand to hear speeches. On September 22, 1919, it was the Prince of Wales, who entered the park under a huge, cedar-bough "Welcome" sign on the site of the old Stanley Park arch. On July 26, 1923, U.S. President Warren Harding made a whirlwind visit. He was in Vancouver only ten hours, but managed to fit in nine holes of golf at Shaughnessy, a ticker-tape parade on Granville Street, an unscheduled visit to the Press Club and a walk into Stanley Park, escorted by a U.S. Marine Honour Guard. At the bandstand, he made a speech to thousands of well-wishers, in which he likened Canadians to good neighbours "from whom one could borrow an egg." Harding died a week later from shellfish poisoning, contracted on a just-concluded visit to Alaska. He was a Kiwanian, and two years later the local Kiwanis erected a splendid monument to him, guarded by two eagles and two rather Roman-looking figures holding shields and grasping an olive branch, "in memory of a great occasion in the life of two sister

The Lumbermen's Arch picnic area, just east of First Narrows, in 1913. It was a popular picnic and camping spot. The arch, erected for the visit of the Duke of Connaught the previous year, was re-erected in the park on the spot which Captain Stamp first chose for a lumber mill on Burrard Inlet, at the northern end of the present-day Stanley Park zoo and aquarium complex. It was the site of the Whoi Whoi Indian village, whose largest lodge stood exactly where the arch was erected. The Whoi Whoi midden, which provided the shells for the Stanley Park drive, extended over the surrounding three acres, and was in some spots as deep as eight feet. The last potlatch was held there in 1875, with about 2,000 Indians attending, and hundreds of dug-out canoes drawn up on the beach. A smallpox epidemic in the village a decade later prompted authorities to put it to the torch. Lumbermen's Arch was demolished in the early Fifties, and a new, simpler one was erected slightly to the west (right) in 1952.

nations."

The Stanley Park bandstand was torn down and replaced in 1934 by the Marion Malkin Memorial Bowl, erected by the former Mayor. Within sight of the Malkin Bowl is the Air Services Memorial—a tiny garden and small stream near the Stanley Park Pavilion. It was erected by the Women's Auxiliary to Air Services in 1948. Two symbolic additions in honour of Canada's allies are there: in front, beside the bronze plaque, is a piece of Australian sandstone; the white stone in the foreground is from the church of St. Stephen in Nijmegen, Holland.

The Stanley Park Pavilion, designed by Otto Moberg and built in 1911, is designed along the lines of a Swiss Chalet. It has the picturesque rustic look of most of the park's buildings, including the old Ferguson Point Teahouse (since renovated into a posh restaurant) and the Beach House near English Bay. For years, the Pavilion had a stuffed cougar—the last one shot in Stanley Park—in its dining room. This particular beast attracted the park warden's attention in October, 1911, when some deer went missing over the high fence around their zoo pen. A hunt was organized with bloodhounds; the cougar was treed and came to grief on October 26.

The Stanley Park zoo is set amongst towering cedars in which one can often see herons' nests and even the occasional eagle high in the trees. The zoo occupants, a horde of bears, snakes and monkeys, and a rabble of seals and otters, are interesting but are overshadowed by the attractions of the Vancouver Aquarium. The latter has come a long way since its tiny beginnings in the old English Bay bathhouse; it now lures the visitor with killer whale shows and the Graham Amazon gallery, opened by Queen Elizabeth in 1983. The outskirts of the zoo are populated by flocks of flamingoes, peacocks, swans and ducks, descendants of the residents of the first duck pond, dug there before the Great War.

A path lined with flowering Japanese cherries leads from the Harding Memorial to the Japanese War Memorial, erected in 1920 for Canadians of Japanese descent who died in the Canadian Expeditionary Force during World War I. The monument is in the shape of a lotus with a fluted obelisk rising from the centre to a small pagoda; the "petals" of the lotus around the base list the names and dates of the great battles of the war—Mons, Ypres, Passchendaele (spelled without the final "e" due to lack of space), the Somme and so on. Japan was the British Empire's ally during the First War and there were many military visits to Vancouver in the years after the

Everyone who visited Stanley Park had to visit the Hollow Tree in Stanley Park. Top left: a family at the turn of the century. Bottom left: butcher James Inglis Reid rented a horse and carriage to show the park to a visiting relative about 1910; the photograph, taken by a man with a booth set up near the Hollow Tree, was printed onto a postcard-backed card. Top right: the gay young set ("the University Crowd") in a Cadillac during the Twenties. Bottom right: a motor-driven sightseeing car, probably the first in Vancouver, in 1911. Its tour extended through the city, to see Fairview and Mount Pleasant via Broadway, the fine homes in Shaughnessy, Kitsilano and the West End, and a tour around the park, returning to the Hotel Vancouver. The car had solid tires and a bulb horn.

CADILLAC EIGHT IN BIG TREE,
STANLEY PARK, CIRCUMFERENCE
65 FT. VANCOUVER, B. C.

Russo-Japanese war of 1905. That friendly relationship, and Vancouver's Japantown, were terminated abruptly in 1941.

Lumbermen's Arch, on the approximate site of Whoi Whoi and the midden, is a simplified version of the first arch. The British Columbia Lumber and Shingle Manufacturers' Association had erected a large, Parthenon-like arch on Pender near Hamilton for the 1912 visit of the Duke of Connaught. It was re-erected in Stanley Park to commemorate Captain Stamp's first chosen site for the Hastings Mill, and became a place to drive the car through when showing off the park to out-of-town relatives. The arch was dedicated to its designer, Capt. G.P. Bowie, who was killed at Ypres in July, 1915. The beach there was a very popular spot to picnic, camp and swim. In the Thirties, when the city became a bit more organized, a tide-filled pool was built and B.C. Electric ran buses there for the *Vancouver Sun's* Free Swimming School.

The picturesque shoreline west of the Brockton Point lighthouse contains two memorials to Vancouver's maritime heritage. The dragon figurehead from the *Empress of Japan* commemorates the CPR White Empresses (the *India, China* and *Japan*) which, beginning in 1891, made Vancouver a world port for the Orient's silks and teas. The second memorial is somewhat less romantic. On July 21, 1906, the small steam tug *Chehalus*, with a group of sunbathers aboard, was bobbing about just west of Brockton Point, enjoying a sunny Saturday afternoon. The new *Princess Victoria*, a "honeymoon steamer" on the CPR's high-speed triangle service connecting Vancouver, Seattle and Victoria, had just left the CPR wharf at the foot of Granville, and was making fifteen knots rounding Brockton Point. Capt. Thomas Griffin of the *Princess* noted the *Chehalus'* aimless movements and steered starboard to ensure a wide clearance. Suddenly, inexplicably, the *Chehalus* veered and turned right across the *Princess Victoria's* bows. Engines reversed and sirens blew but to no avail—the *Chehalus* was struck amidships and sank quickly. Nine people were killed. Griffin was arrested and charged with manslaughter. The litigation ran for years and, although the captain was eventually acquitted, the affair ruined his career. As a result of the sinking, the monument just west of Brockton Point was erected and—more significantly—the speed limit in the harbour was set at ten knots.

The Brockton Point lighthouse continues to blink a warning to small ships in the harbour, but its storm warning function was eliminated in 1951 with the universal adaptation of radio. After 1898, when the lighthouse was built, the lighthouse keeper was busy: he had to fire the Nine O'Clock Gun, run the foghorn and keep lanterns lit, plus hoist signals onto the storm warning mast 200 yards off the Brockton Light. When a westerly gale was forecast, a three-foot high wicker cone was hoisted up the mast, point up; when a heavy gale was predicted, a three foot wicker "pot" or drum was hoisted underneath.

Brockton Oval—the old Athletic Club grounds—was the scene of high-wheeled cycle racing, lacrosse, cricket and more recently

Meralomas' football. The first cricket match was held there on August 8, 1891: Vancouver beat California, 228 runs to 122. The first athletic meet—featuring high and broad jumps, hurdle races and shot putting—was held that September 26. The old clapboard grandstand burned in the Sixties. There is a good colection of totem poles, including the historic Wakius pole, on the site known as Johnny Baker's Clearing, adjoining Brockton Oval, as well as a dugout whaling boat dating from the Whoi Whoi days.

The water around Deadman's Island is crowded with the boatsheds and wharves of the Royal Vancouver Yacht Club (RVYC's other "squadron" is at Jericho Beach, next to Brock House). The name of the island, Deadman's, hails from the 1860s when whites first settled around the Inlet. At that time, Indian corpses were put to rest in the branches high in trees on the island; there were still burial boxes in the trees in the 1880s. An 1875 survey by John Jane recommended moving the cemetery from Deadman's Island to Brockton Point, but nothing was done. The burial of Sam Brierly in 1886 caused an outrage, as the island was already crowded with 25 white graves, so the Provincial Government promised land for a cemetery in Cedar Cottage. In the meantime, some burials took place in Johnny Baker's Clearing. In the 1890s, Deadman's Island was used as a smallpox isolation hospital, and a footbridge was built connecting the island with Stanley Park Drive. The Squamish tribe became positively apoplectic at the turn of the century, when it appeared that the island might be logged. Theodore Ludgate's Vancouver Lumber Co., based at the foot of Cardero on the Bayshore Inn site, claimed in 1908 that it had that right, and occupied the island with sawmill employees. The city got an injunction which, because of the complications of the Stanley Park lease, was ignored by the company. The city was then forced to occupy the island with a small police force, until Ludgate finally capitulated.

In 1901, the footbridge to the island was removed and the smallpox hospital fell into disuse. This was encouraging to the small community of Deadman's Island squatters who had established themselves along the south and east sides of the island during the preceding ten years. Among the characters there were Dutch Pete and one Portuguese Joe, possibly Joseph Silvia Simmons, a Delta cattle drover, who married one of the Musqueam chief's daughters in 1867 and opened a grocery store and saloon in 1868 at Water and Abbott in Gastown. Joe was evidently an unsavoury character in at least one sense of the word—he made dogfish oil, which he sold for 25 cents a gallon. Most of the others on the island were part-time fishermen who had small boats—some sail-assisted rowboats but a few with putt-putt gasoline engines—and worked to the tune of the Nine O'Clock Gun. The remaining squatters were finally kicked off the island in the early Forties; a permanent causeway was built to Deadman's Island to HMCS Discovery, the naval cadet's training school which opened in 1944. On Trafalgar Day each October the island plays host to scrubbed and gloved debutantes with their barbered escorts, attending a social event eons distant from elevated burial boxes and fishoil salesmen.

Fishermen operating in the Coal Harbour area at the turn of the century had to contend with too many fish. The waters literally teemed with salmon, to the point where one dip of a gill net often caught more fish than the boat could sell to the Burrard Inlet canneries. Often, fishermen with filled nets would have to toss some of their catch overboard. Some of these belly-up, odorous salmon were carried by the tide around onto Greer's and English Bay beaches. The canneries decided they needed a start-stop signal, so in 1898 a cannon was purchased and installed, on the last point before Brockton, in a wooden fort-like structure. It was fired at 6:00 every evening during the season as a start-fishing signal, and then again, usually a half hour later. As catches declined and demand increased, the use of the gun as a fishing signal ceased, and the city took it over as a sort of explosive timepiece. It has been fired ever since at nine o'clock in the evening, and became known to Vancouverites, not surprisingly, as the 9 O'Clock Gun.

The grassy field along the beach by the gun, which was originally called Brew's Point, has been recognized officially since 1948 as Hallelujah Point—a name in use informally for years—in honour of the Salvation Army prayer meetings and picnics held there since the 1880s. On those long-ago quiet evenings, Vancouverites swore they could hear the hallelujahs drifting over Coal Harbour from the picnic site. The Salvation Army had its barracks in the Alhambra Hotel at Carrall and Water in Gastown and would troop down to the Union Steamship dock at the foot of Carrall, whence a small ferry chugged quickly across the harbour to the Brockton Point wharf to disgorge its pious flock. (More hedonistic Vancouverites also used the Union Steamship service to Hallelujah Point.)

Long before the Brockton Wharf was built, a little sidewheeler steamer called the S.S. Beaver was plying the coastal waters, connecting New Westminster and Burrard Inlet with the established Hudson's Bay trading post on Vancouver Island. The Beaver was launched in Blackwall, England in 1835, fought her way around the Horn and played a major role developing the west coast of British Columbia, Washington and Oregon, until she was wrecked on the rocks below Prospect Point on July 26, 1888. A cairn at Prospect Point, directly above the Beaver's grave, marks the spot. The walking beam from the ship is set onto a couple of concrete posts along the sidewalk by the Prospect Point observation area (a walking beam connects the paddlewheel to the piston of the steam engine).

Prospect Point provides the most panoramic view of the Lions Gate Bridge, West Vancouver and the outer harbour. This vista has been admired since the park first opened, by visitors like "The Divine Miss Sarah" Bernhardt (the chanteuse who was the toast of Paris during the Gay Nineties), Governor General Earl Grey, and countless relatives from out of town. On the site of the totem pole at the observation point was a small, cedar-bough-roofed (later shingled) gazebo, much beloved by cyclists who were exhausted by the long climb up the hill from Pipeline Road. A sign nailed to the tree at the spot of the S.S. Beaver cairn warned people not to throw

Lions Gate

BASED ON AN IDEA BY MAC MATHESON

THE VANCOUVER PROVINCE

Al Beaton (1923-1967) drew cartoons for the Province from 1953 to 1961, before moving to Toronto. A graduate of the Vancouver School of Art, he travelled extensively and served overseas with the RCAF during the Second World War.

The automobile's domination of Vancouver was confirmed in the late Thirties by the opening of the Lions Gate bridge, a daring, modern structure spanning the First Narrows. Its erection, by British investors led by the Guinness family, came at a time when Europeans were attempting to find safe havens in North America for their money, and it represented, more than anything else, the end of the Depression and the hopes for a prosperous future. Vancouver, still suffering from record unemployment, benefited greatly from the "two years of labour at fair wages" that the bridge provided.

Plans for crossing the First Narrows had been first entertained by Stuart Campbell, of Campbell and Dodson Contractors, and Liberal lawyer Jim Campbell in the early years of the century. They, however, had conceived of a tunnel to the north shore. Their studies were rediscovered in the Twenties by engineer A.J.T. Taylor, who envisioned a bridge connecting Vancouver with an exclusive residential suburb, high on the North Shore Mountains. From the earlier studies, Taylor discovered that approvals to build his bridge would have to be obtained from the Provincial and Federal Gov-

ernments, City Council and the Parks Board, as well as the municipalities of West Vancouver and North Vancouver. Undaunted, he formed the British Pacific Properties Ltd. and, by 1931, had interested Guinness in financing the scheme. Along the way, BPP bought the bankrupt Marine Building at Burrard and Hastings, and, in 1932, acquired about 4,000 acres of Hollyburn Ridge.

BPP made its first approach to the City in early 1933 with the proposal for a road through Stanley Park. On May 9, "the door was slammed in their face." A storm of condemnation from the public, the newspapers, and organized labour led the city administration, prodded by Mayor Louis Taylor, to reconsider. On May 15, the Parks Board announced that their "refusal was too hasty"; three months later, they approved the road through the park. Debate centred on whether the bridge would be high enough and the remaining channel wide enough to allow the world's ocean-going traffic into the harbour. The newspapers published tables showing heights of bridges in various cities in the world, and heights of ships' masts. On November 10, Council agreed to the BPP proposal, subject to the results of a civic plebiscite. On December 13, Vancouver's citizens voted to approve the agreement. The Guinness franchise was to last until 1988, with fixed bridge tolls. An added advantage was the suggestion of a scenic toll road to Garibaldi, which would make Vancouver "even more attractive to visitors." In short order, BPP worked out agreements with every other government body, except the Federal Government.

R.B. Bennett's Conservatives examined the question for three years, at first refusing because First Narrows needed widening, then because it would make the repairs to Second Narrows bridge uneconomic. It was no secret that the Canadian Pacific Railway, which had massive investments (much of it in recent foreclosures) in Shaughnessy Heights, did not want the competition from the British Properties. The CPR had been, since John A. MacDonald's day, closely allied with the Tories. MacKenzie King's Liberals, who were returned to power in late 1935, approved the bridge in April, 1936.

Mayor Gerry McGeer and City Jubilee manager J.K. Matheson formally requested that BPP call it the Jubilee Bridge, an idea that met with distinct lack of enthusiasm from BPP's investors. The bridge opened to traffic on November 17, 1938, and was officially named the Lions Gate Bridge and declared open by the King and Queen on May 26, 1939. The Provincial government purchased it in March 1955, installed the cloverleaf at the north end, and erected its own toll booths. The bridge's three lanes have been a source of annoyance to commuters ever since the motoring and commuting boom of the post-war period. Taylor had wanted four lanes, but Guinness was only willing to invest $5,500,000, which meant a three-lane bridge. Taylor had attempted unsuccessfully to interest Eastern Canadian financiers in a fourth lane.

rocks over the edge because of the sightseers and souvenir hunters on the wreck below.

At Third Beach, just before the road reaches Ferguson Point, is the Pauline Johnson Memorial. Many legends and rumours surrounded Tekahionwake (her Indian name), the poetess who named Lost Lagoon, where she loved to paddle her canoe. She died in 1913 at the height of her fame; for her funeral on March 10 thousands lined Georgia Street near Granville. Crowds followed the hearse to Mountain View Cemetery, where she was cremated. The ashes were placed in a tin box by Mrs. Elisabeth Rogers—strangely enough, proper burial urns were not available in Vancouver at that time. A public subscription drive was started for a memorial in Stanley Park. The original proposal for a $30,000 monument by sculptor Charles Marega was rejected in favour of a simple carved stone memorial with a small reflecting pool by James Hurry of 4586 Sophia Street. It was unveiled in 1922 by the Women's Canadian Club of Vancouver. A bronze plaque included with the scupture was spirited away later by vandals. At the ceremony, Mrs. Rogers placed the tin box and copies of Johnson's two books, *Flint and Feather* and *Legends of Vancouver*, between white silk cushions in a concrete box below the left side of the memorial.

On a grassy field in front of the Ferguson Point teahouse a gun emplacement was maintained during both world wars by the Royal Canadian artillery. The guns were placed there in 1914 following a report that the cruisers *Leipzig* and *Nuremberg* of Admiral von Spee's Pacific Fleet were planning a gold reserve raid; the gold was shipped to neutral Seattle and inland to Winnipeg. Premier Richard McBride was anxious about "the coast defences or lack of it," and bought two used submarines in Seattle for $1 million. On the lawn to the east of the Teahouse, a gun tower—the same as the surviving two at Wreck Beach—was erected. A small, bunker-like concrete command centre was hidden in the trees across the park drive.

The creek which drains Lost Lagoon, and was the skid path for the Coal Harbour rowboaters, winds through a willow glade to Ceperley Park before draining into English Bay. The park drive skirts the pitch and putt golf course, the lawn bowling greens and tennis courts and passes the rambling, half-timbered Beach House. The names for Ferguson Point and Ceperley Park honour two supporters of that first City Council resolution in 1886. Lauchlan Hamilton, the CPR surveyor and alderman, moved the resolution requesting the creation of Stanley Park on the Admiralty Reserve.

CITY OF VANCOUVER ARCHIVES

Mr. Ross, the brother-in-law of Mayor MacLean, and the Member of Parliament for Lisgar, Manitoba (who was called the "CPR member" due to his unstinting support for all things railway) steered the request through the Federal parliament. Ross had gone to Manitoba and a safe Tory seat in order to get elected; in his other life he was a partner in Ross & Ceperley, prominent insurance agents in early Vancouver. Ceperley was brother-in-law to Mr. A.G. Ferguson, who was elected the first chairman of the Parks Board in 1888. Ferguson invariably paid the bills for Stanley Park out of his

Above: the historic sternwheeler S.S. Beaver, wrecked on the rocks below Prospect Point in 1889. Above right: the Brockton Point lighthouse, with the lightkeepers' cottage, commanded the entrance to Vancouver's inner harbour. The light's automation and modern ship navigation ended the need for a keeper, so the house was demolished during the Fifties.

Brockton Point Lighthouse, Stanley Park, Vancouver, B.C. Canada.

own pocket after the city funds had gone. In his will, he left money to Mrs. Ceperley, with the suggestion that she leave it to the Park if there was any left.

MacLean's successor as mayor, David Oppenheimer, is honoured by a statue, set on a marble plinth by a large bed of daffodils, at the Beach Avenue entrance to the park. Oppenheimer was mayor from 1888 to 1891, yet when the statue was unveiled in 1911 by Premier Richard McBride it was noted that the lettering said: "Mayor of Vancouver 1889 1890 1891 1892." The numbers were changed.

John Grove (1864-1935), the lighthouse keeper at Brockton Point from 1895 to 1930.

207

English Bay

English Bay has a long shoreline, extending from Kitsilano all the way around to Stanley Park's Siwash Rock. But "English Bay," the locality, is a small strip of beach from Alexandra Park to the Stanley Park entrance. Even in winter, when the gales blow from the northwest and the sea turns into a pepper and salt froth, English Bay retains its *à la récherche du temps perdu* atmosphere.

It was to this sylvan watering place that Vancouverites of the 1890s, hemmed in by the forest and isolated in their town of 5,000, came for summer solace. The popular enthusiasm for seaside vacations, good health and physical exercise was indulged. Women bathing at English Bay wore boater hats and yards of blinding white cotton; on the hottest days, the more daring might roll down their stockings. Mature, respectable men wore brown serge and homburgs, their collars starched and held with a four-in-hand tie, and sat fully shod on the sand in the shimmering heat. Young athletic men wore the characteristic one-piece cotton suit with long sleeves and shorts, sometimes striped. Young chaperoned women waded in voluminous black satin skirts and long black stockings, with a protective parasol always covering the face. A suntan was very unfashionable: it indicated either that the woman had to work outdoors at coolie labour, or that she had been sick and had taken a sun cure at a sanatorium.

Before the turn of the century, many small cottages were built along the beach near the foot of Davie. Boardwalks and small piers extended from their doors to the water line—a rather unstable and dangerous place due to the logs and debris tossed there by waves and the tide. The opening of the Davie streetcar in 1898 increased English Bay's popularity and accessibility to the public, and caused the city to look at it as more than a private resort. Between 1902 and 1911 much of the property along the beach was bought up, to provide a public area around the $6,000 wooden bathing pavilion at the foot of Denman. The pavilion had changing rooms on its ground floor and a breezy, shaded verandah at the top, allowing a good view over the bay. On sunny days, gawkers stood shoulder to shoulder along the railing, and the sand below was packed like a Coney Island.

The lifeguard at English Bay was Seraphim ("Old Black Joe") Fortes, a native of Barbados who had arrived in Vancouver in 1885, moved to English Bay in the mid 1890s and lived in a cottage on the beach at the foot of Gilford. He supervised the beach diligently every day. Protective West End mothers were more concerned with the dangers of the forest than of the sea, and thought nothing of releasing their children with the parting admonition: "And you stay close to Joe!" After he died in 1922, a memorial to him was sculpted by Charles Marega, with the inscription "The Children Loved Him," and erected on the Beach Avenue side of Alexandra Park.

Alexandra Park, named for the consort of Edward VII, was one of

The Beach, English Bay, Vancouver, B.C.

English Bay, showing Englesea Lodge and Sylvia Court, Vancouver, B. C.

English Bay, Vancouver, B.C.

Top left: English Bay beach looking northwest in 1912, after the pier was built and the old cabins cleared off the water side. All of the fine homes on Beach Avenue were demolished during the Fifties and Sixties, and replaced by luxurious apartments. Bottom left: the view, also northwest, in 1914, after the Englesea Lodge was built on the water side at the park entrance. The Alexandra Park bandstand was a popular spot during the summer months, as was "The Prom" dancehall on the end of the pier. The four-cornered tower of the Imperial Roller Rink is visible on the right, framed against the side of the tall Sylvia Court Hotel. Above: English Bay beach in 1910, with both new and old bathhouses visible. The old bathhouse on the right had breezy verandahs for gawkers intent on staying out of the sun. The two-storey building behind that bathhouse, with the Tetley Tea sign on the roof, is now the English Bay Cafe. Other billboards advertise fish and chips and the Pantages Theatre on East Hastings.

several pre-World War I improvements which so added to the elegance of English Bay: a new, bigger concrete bathhouse was erected, and a bathing pier was built in 1909, extending one hundred yards into the water, from which people launched boats and swam. At the end of the pier was the Prom, a glassed-in dance hall, featuring bands like Len Chamberlain and His Twinkletoes. Summer evenings were enhanced for the promenaders and hand-holders by music from the Alexandra Park bandstand, a copy of the one in Stanley Park, erected on the eve of the Great War. The pier was a fixture of the beach until its demolition in July, 1938.

An attraction for the rambunctious and modern was the Imperial Roller Rink, built on the triangle (now a park) bounded by Denman, Morton and Beach. Roller skating was a craze of the times comparable with card-playing and the safety bicycle. Vancouverites flocked to the rink in the pre-war years to learn to skate, or to watch polo played on roller skates. Until it burned down in the early Twenties, its campanile-style four-cornered tower was a landmark for mariners approaching Vancouver. The "triangle" on which it stood—the last portion of John Morton's original estate—

was given to the City for "the perpetual beautification of Vancouver" during Canada's 1927 Diamond Jubilee of Confederation.

The second generation of buildings along the waterfront reflected the fashionableness of the neighbourhood. The Simpson Apartments at the corner of Davie and Denman had patterned brick sides, ornate entrance arches, leaded glass and lightwells ("Quebec Manor" at 7th and Quebec in Mount Pleasant, and the "Manhattan" at Thurlow and Robson, are similar). The last building on the beach, until its demolition after a fire in 1981, was the Englesea Lodge at the entrance to Stanley Park. The only survivor from that period is the 1912 Sylvia Court, a hotel since the Thirties. Its top-floor, "Dine in the Sky" restaurant was *the* place for a business lunch or fancy dinner during the Forties and Fifties.

Other attractions included the salt-water Crystal Pool at the foot of Jervis which opened in 1928. A new Vancouver aquarium, to replace one at Hastings Park (with crossed whale jawbones forming a doorway), opened in the English Bay bathhouse buildings in 1939, featuring Oscar The Octopus. The aquarium quickly ran out of space, and relocated to Stanley Park in 1956.

Joe Fortes

Seraphim Fortes came from Barbados to Vancouver in 1885. For nearly ten years, he worked as a porter and second bartender at the Sunnyside Hotel in Gastown, where he earned a reputation as a nice, responsible character and the nickname "Ol' Black Joe." Joe's flower-and-vine-choked cottage at the foot of Gilford was one of the last dwellings on the beach side. Before the First World War, when the city was clearing the cottages off the beach, citizens prevailed upon Mayor Buscombe to allow Joe to stay. A compromise was reached and Joe's cottage was moved into Alexandra Park, beside the bandstand, where he lived for the rest of his days. Practically every kid in the West End learned to swim with Joe telling him to "kick yo feet!" He had been given the authority of a special constable, was listed in the City Directory as a swimming instructor, and patrolled the beach constantly—except for Sunday morning, when he attended Mass. In January 1922, Joe fell ill with a severe case of pneumonia, and died in Vancouver General Hospital.

Joe Fortes, the beloved lifeguard of English Bay, in front of his little cottage, about 1920. The cottage stood originally at the foot of Gilford Street, in front of the site of the Sylvia Court Hotel, but was moved to the bank above the beach, at 1708 Beach Avenue, in 1905. Fortes, whose occupation was described in the City Directory as "swimming instructor," died in 1922.

Trythall's Cabin

*William Trewartha Trythall
(1867-1932)*

Energetic hikers in early Vancouver frequently ascended the North Shore mountains, usually on the Grouse Mountain trail. The B.C. Mountaineering Club was formed in 1909, and had a membership of 125 by the outbreak of the war. It owned five acres on Grouse Mountain and built a commodious club cabin there. The Grouse Mountain Chalet, the first commercial exploiter of winter in Vancouver, opened in September, 1926. The painting depicts the Trythall cabin, near Mosquito Creek close to the base of the Grouse Mountain Chairlift. Built well before the First World War, it was the first recreational cabin on the North Shore, and was a welcome resting spot for hikers attempting an ascent to the peak. A return journey to the Grouse summit took three days: one from the ferry landing at the foot of Lonsdale to Trythall's, a second to the summit, and a third to descend to the ferry. The cabin's door was always open, and hikers and skiers used it for thawing feet and brewing tea. William Trewartha Trythall, a printer by trade, owned 160 acres around the cabin, and used it for holidays. He sold 12 acres of his pre-emption to the district of North Vancouver for a municipal waterworks and dam. The cabin was ultimately abandoned, its usefulness negated by the Lonsdale tram, and eventually the chairlift.

White Rock

Entertainment

After the day's work was done, people in small, isolated Vancouver looked in vain for entertainment. For a long time, there were only the many stand-up, brawling saloons, dating from the day in September, 1867 when John Deighton floated his whisky barrel ashore and started Gastown. Later, as Vancouver developed a downtown populated with businessmen, prestigious bars flourished, like the Strand at 624 West Hastings, opulent with leaded glass and carved wood.

At the turn of the century, saloons were open all night, four-year-old rye whisky cost $4 a gallon, and alarmed temperance advocates were pushing for reduced hours, from 6 a.m. to 11 p.m. The freewheeling days continued, however, until 1914, when the First World War practically eliminated the saloon business. Many bars were forced to close due to a lack of customers, and the advent of Prohibition on December 20, 1916 closed those that remained. Although many speakeasies operated quite openly in violation of the Liquor Act during the Twenties and Thirties, cocktail lounges were not licensed to operate until July, 1954. Then, following the liberalizing moves of the new W.A.C. Bennett government, a lounge opened in the Sylvia Hotel. Prior to that, hotel beer parlours were the only place where a man, or a "lady with escort" (to discourage prostitutes) could get served any drink.

Vancouver's first legitimate theatre was Frank W. Hart's Opera House, on Carrall south of Dupont (Pender) on the edge of False Creek, which operated from 1887 to 1889. Hart bought a roller-skating rink, which dated from the CPR construction days, in Port Moody, dismantled it and reassembled it on piles on Carrall Street. The interior was lined with white cheesecloth, and seats were provided for nearly 700 patrons. The town's first indoor Salvation Army meeting was held there on December 10, 1887. The next year, a boxing match was held, with visitors Lord Lonsdale and the Marquis of Queensbury as, respectively, referee and timekeeper.

In May, 1889, Hart's was superseded by the Imperial Opera House on Pender Street at Beatty, built by A.E. Crickmay. In 1892, it was converted into a drill hall, and when the Beatty Street armoury opened nine years later, it was re-converted into a roller-skating rink (later replaced by one at English Bay).

The Imperial's two years of pre-eminence ended in 1891 when the CPR's new Opera House opened on Granville at Robson. The Emma Juch Grand Opera Company was brought to Vancouver at a cost of $10,000 to open it. Sarah Bernhardt, the toast of Europe, appeared there in "Fedora" that September. The CPR had, in 1886, promised the Opera House and a big hotel to purchasers of West End building lots, but delayed building the former for five years. Legal action had been mooted by some disgruntled owners. Its opening attracted Vancouverites in furs, jewels and evening dress, and streetcars waited outside for the end of performances, disrupting schedules throughout the system. When St. Andrew's

(Preceding page) White Rock, in 1917. South of Vancouver almost on the American border, it was a sleepy little summer resort, served regularly by the Great Northern Railway. The station was built in 1913, the same year as the pier was built. White Rock was less established than the Union Steamships' Bowen Island resort, and became popular in the early years of the century as the "Bay of Naples of the Pacific." Cottages were built along the shore, and a settlement grew up around the corner of Oxford Street and Marine Drive by the station. The first hotel opened there in 1912. The white rock, just south of the station along the shore, is an ice age deposit.

THAT WAS THE END OF MY DREAM (2).

I never knew what parting meant until you went away,
I never thought the rose was sent only to fade some day,
I never dreamt that love could die, once it had reigned supreme,
I only knew when you whispered " Good-bye," that was the end of my dream.

Above: a postcard, with song lyrics reflecting the sentiment of the First World War years.

Presbyterian Church was renovated, services were held in the Opera House, scandalizing some members of the congregation. More robust attractions included Pollard's Lilliputian Opera Company from Australia, Ethel Barrymore, Ellen Terry performing a one-woman show of Shakespearean heroines, and pugilist-turned-actor John L. Sullivan, who accidentally knocked out another actor on stage. The CPR sold the Opera House before the First World War. Renamed the New Orpheum, it featured vaudeville until the Twenties, when it was converted into a cinema and renamed, successively, the Vancouver, the Lyric and the International Cinema. It was demolished in the late Sixties for the Eaton's-Pacific Centre development.

In 1898, the Savoy Music Hall, also known as the Grand Theatre, opened on Cordova near Abbott, sharing the block with Kemp and Simpson's Undertakers and Jack Abray's saloon. The ground floor of the narrow building was occupied by the Savoy saloon and A.G. Ferrera's fashionable Savoy restaurant. A side door led upstairs to the music hall, which was reputedly a hangout for fighters and promoters. In March, 1899, there was an appearance by the notorious "Klondike Nugget," Miss Gussie Lamore, whose passion for eggs had caused Swiftwater Bill to buy every "cackleberry" in Dawson City. In 1906, when box seats cost 25 cents, a young Al Jolson played there. The building was demolished in 1940 for the expansion of Woodward's parkade.

The Alhambra, mid-way in size and reputation between the Opera House and the Savoy, opened on March 13, 1899, "with great éclat" and a performance of "The Pearl of Pekin." Located at the northwest corner of Pender and Howe Street, the theatre had 800 chairs for seats and a balcony at the back, from which patrons shouted insults like "Supe, Supe" and "23 Skidoo" at performers and, on occasion, threw orange peels, peanuts and crackerjacks at the stage. Its gaudy curtain was blocked into squares containing advertisements. The theatre was a welcome addition to the city, however, as it was large enough to accommodate stock companies. It hosted a variety of entertainments, including Charlie Chaplin, the city-sponsored Queen's birthday party in 1900, and major political meetings, like the raging debates on the Grand Trunk railway. It was renamed the Royal in 1901, the People's in 1902 (under Pearl R. "Dad" Allen and his Vaudeville Players), then the Orpheum in 1906. It was demolished after the First World War.

Rather than indulge in evenings at the theatre, families in the early days bought sheet music from Woodward's or Spencer's and contented themselves with quiet evenings around the piano. Popular songs during the pre-War years, which were played by bands in the city parks as well, included "Alexander's Ragtime Band" by Irving Berlin (spelled Berling in the Woodward's catalogue); "Oh, You Beautiful Doll"; "There's A Mother Old and Grey Who Needs Me Now"; "Baboon Baby Dance" ("very popular"); "School Days"; "Mammy's Shufflin' Dance" (performed by "coon-singer" Ruth Nolta when she played the Savoy in 1899); and "My Hula Hula Love" (with a cover on the sheet music showing a woman in ancient Egyptian headdress). For those of a more serious bent, a lot of classical music had been transcribed for solo piano during the preceding fifty years, including the ever popular "Beethoven's Fifth," which had been adapted by virtuoso Franz Liszt.

The first decade of the century saw four large theatres open. Alexander Pantages, a Klondike bar-sweep who separated the gold-dust from the sawdust off the floor and came home with a fortune, opened the Pantages Theatre at 142 East Hastings on

Alex Pantages' second theatre, at 20 West Hastings, was a true vaudeville palace. As an independent, the theatre had difficulty bucking the theatre chains' monopoly over first-run movies. The theatre–and the surrounding area– declined during the Thirties and Forties, and was eventually abandoned and demolished for a parking lot.

Frank W. Hart (1857-1935), born in Illinois, came to Vancouver in 1877. He owned Vancouver's first theatre, Frank W. Hart's Opera House, on Carrall near Pender, which operated from 1887 to 1889. As an associate of Mayor MacLean, he helped convince reluctant Granville merchants to adopt the new name "Vancouver." He owned the city's first undertaking establishment, hearse and silk top hat, and made the first burial in Mountain View Cemetery. Later, he speculated wildly in the town of Dyea, hoping that it would become the terminus for the White Pass and Yukon Railway. When Skagway was chosen in 1898, he was wiped out. He settled in Prince Rupert after 1912, and had a successful career there as a furniture merchant.

Labour Day, 1906. (Pantages hated the written word, and so disliked signing his name that he had his signature embossed onto a rubber stamp.) He featured vaudeville there (and at a chain of theatres in Canada and the U.S.) until 1917, when he built the Beacon at 20 West Hastings (see below). The East Hastings theatre was sold to showman Charles E. Royal (who gave Georgia Street girlie-show promoter Isy Walters his start), and operated as the Royal through the Thirties. He sold it after renting it to the Workers' Unity League in March, 1933, when a bomb exploded and shattered the theatre's front. The building reopened as, successively, the State, Queen's, State and Avon. In 1953, the Everyman Theatre Co. mounted a performance of Erskine Caldwell's *Tobacco Road*, which was dubbed an "indecent, immoral and obscene performance" by the Vice Squad. Seven members of the company were convicted and fined $20 each. The Avon became the "hippie" City Nights Theatre in the Seventies, and survives today showing Chinese cinema.

Another popular theatre was the Empress, at Cordova and Gore, opened in 1908 by a gala performance of *Dorothy Vernon of Haddon Hall*, featuring Miss Jane Kelton. Helen Hayes played Victoria the Queen, and Anna Pavlova danced, before the theatre was demolished in 1940.

Main Street near Union had two fine theatres: the Avenue at 711 Main, and the Imperial at 724 (built in 1912, it survives today as a soft-core pornography cinema). The Avenue dazzled Vancouverites in December 1915 with D.W. Griffith's *Birth of a Nation*, billed as "the greatest art conquest since the birth of civilization." In April, 1922, Ethel Barrymore appeared there in *Déclassé*. It was demolished for an expansion of the B.C. Electric gas plant at the east end of the Georgia Viaduct.

The Great War took a lot of the "pizzazz" out of Vancouver's social life. Vaudeville entertainment by the end of the War was expected to be family-oriented, with no more lewd or suggestive jokes. Erotic dancers in the style of Lola Montez, Lotta Crabtree or the vivacious Klondike Kate (who appeared in Vancouver on the same bill as Ruth Nolta and contortionist Zeda the Great) were shown the door. In their place came the antics of Capt. M.W. Plunkett and the Dumbbells, a theatrical review started in Flanders in 1917 which had taken the world by storm. The music of the war years, including "Pack Up Your Troubles in that Old Kit Bag"; "How Ya Gonna Keep 'Em Down On The Farm, After They've Seen Paree" ("...and who the deuce can parlez-vous a cow"); "Mademoiselle from Armentières, Parlez-Vous!" ("You might forget the gas & shells, but you'll never forget the mesdesmoiselles"); and "Tipperary," reflected the changing times, the "loss of innocence," and predicted the difficulty returned servicemen would have re-adjusting to life in Canada.

Alec Pantages expanded his empire on June 18, 1917, when the $350,000 Beacon Theatre opened on Hastings west of Carrall. Stars like Sally Rand, Roy Rogers and Duke Ellington played there dur-

ing the Twenties, but the theatre's business collapsed in 1929 when, as an independent, it couldn't get the major talking pictures. It continued with vaudeville and repertory theatre during the Thirties, re-opened in November, 1946 as the Odeon Hastings, and was demolished for a parking lot in the early Seventies. In 1919, the Allen Theatre chain built the Strand Theatre at Georgia and Seymour (now the Scotia Tower site), which featured vaudeville acts in the tradition of the Ziegfield Follies. Eight years later, the opulent Orpheum Theatre opened on Granville Street, with name acts from the States, especially comedians like Jack Benny, Bob Hope, Eddie Cantor, Bill "Bojangles" Robinson, and Burns & Allen. At Charlie Doctor's Capitol Theatre on Granville, opened in 1921, cinema was the main attraction; before the film rolled, Calvin Winter and the Capitolians played a concert from the orchestra pit. The Capitol got the city's first "talkie," *Mother Knows Best*, in 1928, and the city's first Cinemascope in the Fifties. After 1919, classical music came into its own with the formation of the Vancouver Symphony Society.

By the early Thirties, the dance-band craze had gripped Vancouver. People went to the Alexandra on Robson, the Palomar on Hornby near the all-night liquor store, the Peter Pan on West Broadway, the Georgia Hotel, the Alma Academy Ballroom at Broadway and Alma, or the Crystal Ballroom in the Hotel Vancouver. At the latter's Spanish Grill, Len Chamberlain and His Twinkletoes entertained a refined clientele until 1928, when Lafe Cassidy's orchestra moved in (Chamberlain played then for years at the Prom on the English Bay pier). In the dance halls, mirrored balls spun and flashed, much as they did forty years later during the disco craze. Floors were oak, and sprung with seaweed or horsehair. A memorable evening meant bringing a mickey and sharing a club sandwich. There was not much of a seating area. "It was a ballroom, period," said Mart Kenney, the leader of the Western Gentlemen, describing a typical night spot. "People came to dance." A lighted roller sign beside the band told patrons which dance was next—Waltz Quadrille, Fox Trot, Military Two Step, Moonlight or Home Waltz—so partners could be engaged.

Musicians hung around Dick Perks' Vancouver Music Company until it went broke in 1928. They spent time at Ward's on Hastings, talking and examining sheet music. The time after concerts, until two in the morning, was spent eating "spaghetti-con-chili" at Sid Beech's Vancouver Tamale Parlour in the Orillia. Ivan Ackery, who managed the Orpheum for over 40 years, remembered that some would go to the bootleggers' and Hogan's Alley clubs—"you had to behave yourself there"—but that after the symphony or ballet everyone ended up at Beech's—"the attorney general, you name it." The jukebox there played Rudy Vallee's "I'm Just A Vagabond Lover" and Sophie Tucker's "My Gal Sal."

The established local bands in the late Twenties and Thirties included the Calvin Winter Home Gas Orchestra, which played in the Crystal Ballroom; Lafe Cassidy, whose orchestra played at the Spanish Grill and during the summers at the CPR's Banff Springs Hotel; the Earle Hill Hotel Vancouver Orchestra, which was later the first band to play in the Cave nightclub on Hornby; the Harry Pryce Orchestra, which opened the Hotel Georgia in 1927; the Bob Lyon Orchestra, which opened the Commodore in 1937; the Sandy de Santos Dance Band; Mart Kenney and His Western Gentlemen, with their famous 1934 theme song "The West, A Nest and You Dear," who played across Canada and highlighted the summer season at Chateau Lake Louise in the Rockies; and Charlie Pawlett's 10-piece Commodore orchestra.

Dining out meant going to Scott's at 722 Granville, the Chanticleer Cafe at 776 Granville with the jaunty red neon rooster, or Love's Grill across the street. Couples with cars went to Love's Seaside Gardens on Marine Drive at Spanish Banks, which was a cabaret-style dance pavilion and bottle club. Later, they trekked to the Second Narrows Supper Club on the North Vancouver side of the bridge, for Sunday afternoon dinner dances, or drove to The Dolphins English Restaurant near what is now Totem Park along Marine Drive. The menu standards were pork chops, clubhouse and "turkey nip" sandwiches, fried chicken, and hot beef sandwiches swimming with gravy. Every restaurant was a brown bag bottle club. Normally, the brown bagged bottles stood on the table, but when the heat was on, slim mickeys were fitted into slotted shelves built into the restaurant tables.

By the early Thirties, music and entertainment in Vancouver had begun to reflect the Depression. From June 12 to August 1, 1931, there was a marathon walk and entertainment spectacle in the Denman Arena. The hit of 1932 was "Brother, Can You Spare A Dime." Taxi dancers, at 10 cents a dance, were called jitney dancers in Vancouver (after the jitneys which competed for customers during the Great War years). The musical ballads of 1933 were "Smoke Gets In Your Eyes" and Hoagy Carmichael's "Stardust." The new breed of bandleader was solid and respectable like Mart Kenney, with none of the boozy excess of Twenties' jazzmen like Bix Biederbecke. The CPR—which paid the enormous sum of $17.50 a week to musicians at the Tea Dances—was the organization that everyone wanted to play for. Orchestras like Mart Kenney's found that they weren't hired into the Hotel directly from a private ballroom, so they had to tour. In September, 1935, Kenney

(Above) Boys' bands were the usual starting point for Vancouver musicians, who graduated quickly to the pit orchestras in vaudeville houses during the Twenties. (Below) Len Chamberlain and His Twinkletoes, a popular orchestra at the Alma Academy and the Prom, relaxing on Bowen Island.

MARGARET PAWLETT

WILLENA STONE

216

was finally hired for the Spanish Grill, after a spring tour and a summer engagement at Chateau Lake Louise.

The new popular entertainment of the Thirties and Forties was radio, and Vancouver orchestras were quick to exploit the possibilities. The first radio station in Vancouver, CJCE, broadcast from the World building in 1920 with a 50-watt transmitter. Radio station CJOR broadcast from the Alexandra Ballroom beginning in 1932. The Home Gas Hour of Music played on CJOR on Sunday night. When the radio station wasn't doing "remotes" from the ballrooms, it had orchestras playing from its basement studios in the Grosvenor Hotel (demolished 1983) on Howe. The master of the new medium was Kenney, who had a network program called "Sweet and Low" on the Canadian Radio Broadcasting Commission, forerunner of the CBC (the CRBC got started in the CNR station on Main Street but moved into a little studio on the Hornby Street side of the unfinished Hotel Vancouver in 1936). Dance programs, some of which were picked up by NBC in the States, were broadcast Wednesdays and Saturdays. The "Purity Flour Show" had vocalist Judy Richards and Bobby (Ca-Na-Da!) Gimby playing the trumpet.

When the Panorama Roof opened in 1939, the Len Hopkins band came from the Chateau Laurier in Ottawa to play. New bands and leaders like Dal Richards began to play the influential sounds of Benny Goodman, Arty Shaw, Harry Jones and Glen Miller. "Tuxodo Junction" was a big hit. Many of the old guard of Vancouver musicians left for new fields: Bob Lyon headed for Australia in August, 1939, and became a Colonel playing for MacArthur's troops. After the war, he returned to town and became manager of the Grosvenor. Charlie Pawlett joined the Air Force. At demobilization, the Air Force offered to train him to become a barber. He declined and joined the Ministry of Transport. Charlie See, who played sax and clarinet originally with Jackie Souter's band in the Strand before the advent of the talkies, moved to Los Angeles and played a circuit of clubs around Las Vegas, Reno and Dallas. After the war, he got a good day job, as he had "had it up to here" with music and being on the road. Of the pre-war musicians, Mart Kenney held on the longest—until 1970, when he became a real estate agent. Some orchestras continued, but the Fifties was the era of the small jazz combo. Dancing went out of fashion as television came in.

(Above) A small tea-dance orchestra in the late Twenties, photographed on the roof of the old Hotel Vancouver. The two large buildings in the background are the Credit Foncier tower at Hastings and Howe (visible between band members) and the distinctive Post Office Clock Tower at Granville and Hastings. (Below) The Home Gas Optimists during the 1934-35 season, a smaller version of the huge Home Gas Concert Orchestra which, under the direction of Calvin Winter, played in the Crystal Ballroom in the Hotel Vancouver. The Optimists were featured on the Home Gas Hour of Music, Sunday evenings on CJOR.

Charlie Pawlett

One of the most popular and best-known dance bands in Vancouver during the late 1930s was Charlie Pawlett and the Commodores. Like most musicians of the time, Pawlett moved around from band to orchestra scratching out a living. Along with most of his contemporaries, he more or less ended his professional musical career after the Second World War, when financial security and raising a family became important.

Charlie Pawlett was born in 1902 in Nanaimo. His father was a music teacher who was very actively involved in the Anglican Church in Nanaimo, and spent much of his spare time organizing church boys' bands and playing in regimental bands. After he died, the family moved to Vancouver.

During the Twenties, Charlie played in the pit orchestras in theatres like the Orpheum. He was adept with the violin, although it was an instrument he never enjoyed because of the harsh discipline of his father's teaching. In addition, he played the trumpet and the banjo, so found ready employment in dance orchestras. In late 1927, he was playing banjo with the Harry Pryce Orchestra at the Hotel Georgia, when it was officially opened by the Prince of Wales (later King Edward VIII and, after abdication, the Duke of Windsor), who that summer and fall did a grand tour of Canada with his brother Albert. In the late Twenties and early Thirties Pawlett played the summer season at the Banff Springs Hotel, first with Pryce, later with Lafe Cassidy from 1932-4, then with Earle Hill in 1935. In the off-season, he played for tea dances at the Hotel Vancouver, did stints at the various ballrooms, and played regularly at the big Shaughnessy parties of families like the McRaes, Taylors and Foleys—"the University Crowd." With the variety of the engagements, Pawlett became sufficiently well known to rate an entry in *Who's Who in Western Canada* in 1937. At the time, he, with wife and baby, was living in a basement suite, with a cold-water sleeve on the side of the woodstove, on Denman near English Bay. Rent was $30 a month, and the phone cost another $4.

When he came back from the Banff Springs in 1936, Pawlett was out of work for two weeks and things were really tough. He got on with the Bob Lyon Orchestra. Lyon had an old Packard tourer and another member of the group had a Chevy, so they headed for the Interior and tried their luck playing at the lakeside pavilions and country halls for the harvest season. They went to Christina Lake in the Kootenays, Nelson, Kelowna and finally to Lillooet. It wasn't successful: after deducting expenses from the first two weeks' pay, he was able to send back $4 to his wife and two children. A better deal was playing with the Home Gas Optimists for CJOR's Home Gas Hour of Music, though wages were so low that they rehearsed on Sunday from two o'clock until supper time, then played the concert for $4 each.

(Above) A young Charlie Pawlett, standing with violin, with a small orchestra somewhere in Vancouver in the early Twenties. (Next page) The Bob Lyon Orchestra, on tour through the Interior, outside the Victoria Hotel in Lillooet. (Right) A self-portrait.

In 1937, by which time the Commodore had opened, Bob Lyon's orchestra broke up; Bonnie Shannon, Jack Milne and Jack Heath decided to go with Lyon to an engagement at Chateau Lake Louise, while the rest of the band stayed in Vancouver with Pawlett as band leader. Pawlett was then making the fabulous sum of $30 a week, so the family moved into Stanley Park Manor on Chilco. Charlie Pawlett and the Commodores became one of the best-known of the city's dance bands, and played charity events like the Snowball Frolic in aid of the *Daily Province* Santa Claus Fund. Their vocalist was Betty Ann Petch, and the theme song was "For You."

Pawlett played for the Earle Hill Orchestra when they opened the Cave in 1938, then joined the Air Force when the war broke out. On his return, he kept small bands together, playing first at the old Howden Ballroom at Pacific and Granville. When that reduced to two nights a week, then finally closed, Pawlett moved his band to the Arcadian Ballroom at 6th and Main and finally to the Peter Pan. In 1946, the family had bought three acres and a house in Lynn Valley in North Vancouver for $6,000. Pawlett played briefly at the Second Narrows Supper Club, heading off down Mountain Highway on a bicycle with his trumpet and peddling back afterwards. In the late Forties, seeing the writing on the wall, he took a job with the Department of Transport. He died in 1981, aged 79.

Liquor Control

The Roaring Twenties was the decade of the infamous Volstead Act in the United States, when bootleggers fought gangsters, hatchet-faced men in pinstripes carried violin cases with sinister contents, Dodges had solid running boards and Bix Biederbecke's cornet wailed above the clink of glasses in speakeasies. All of urban America wanted a drink, and Canadians set out to provide it.

Canada had had its own experiment with Prohibition, partly brought on by the need for austerity and self-sacrifice in the War years. The western provinces had pushed the Laurier government to hold a national plebiscite on Prohibition in September, 1898. All of the provinces except Quebec voted for it—B.C. voted 5731 to 4756 in favour of total prohibition—but Quebeckers were so against the idea that the Liberal government felt entitled to declare the plebiscite a failure.

Regional plebiscites followed. British Columbia went dry on December 20, 1916. The ensuing four years saw a remarkable charade of increasing lawlessness hidden behind a façade of public probity. "Temperance beer," which was sold with only two percent alcohol on the dry Prairies, could have four percent in British Columbia. Prohibition Commissioner Walter Findlay went to jail for contempt of court after being arrested for stealing 74 cases of whisky. Smuggling began between the provinces, and down the coastline into the United States. Sikhs on streetcorners in the downtown area kept bottles concealed in their turbans and sold drinks to passersby. Sympathetic physicians prescribed alcohol "for medicinal purposes" to anyone with a bit of money, especially during the Spanish flu epidemic of the winter of 1918-19, when booze was considered an effective preventative. In one month, the dry squad raided 108 bootleggers and 18 disorderly houses and collected $9,750 in fines. In August, 1920, the police offered "$1 an hour and free smells at the broken bottles" to people willing to help move 5,700 cases and 130 barrels of seized liquor to the police station from the Canadian Pacific Wine Co. warehouse.

On October 20, 1920, the government held a plebiscite to consider an end to Prohibition. There was still a strong desire among the populace to prevent a return to the freewheeling abuses of the bars, "treating" and free lunches of earlier years. Unlike the Prairie plebiscites of that year, the B.C. government (resisted by the federal government) presented an alternative to the voters: they could opt for a government-controlled monopoly over the liquor business with all sales from government stores in sealed packages. By a 25,000 majority, they chose that. Thus was born the organization dubbed in later years "Bennett's Dairy." The government-monopoly option had been strongly promoted by a Moderation League headed by Sir Charles Tupper and ex-Mayor Fred Buscombe, who were in favour of liquor sales but keeping the bars banned. Unwittingly, perhaps, they hit upon a gold mine for the government—in the first years, the liquor stores made a million

and a half dollars profit (in 1922, Vancouver's share was $75,000). The new Liquor Act was introduced by Attorney General J.W. deB. Farris in February, 1921. A warehouse and liquor-bottling facility was established at 871 Beatty near the Cambie bridge.

After British Columbia went wet, locals turned their attention more and more to the dry states to the south. Some liquor was shipped to dry Alberta and Saskatchewan, most notably a convoy in 1922 which was chased at high speed through Crow's Nest Pass by the RCMP, one of whom was gunned down by notorious bootlegger Emilio Picariello. But most of the liquor went south, and rumrunning became a household word.

"Rum Row" consisted of about 40 large vessels—the mother ships in a loosely organized smuggling fleet operating from Victoria and Vancouver. A small amount of the liquor came directly from England and Holland, but most of it was loaded from bonded warehouses on the Vancouver harbour—at a 50 cent a case fee to a Vancouver export company which "took care of" the American customs, according to testimony at a Royal commission in January, 1926. Some of the ships involved were converted schooners and sloops—like Archie McGillis' five-masted schooner *Malahat*, 245 feet long and capable of carrying 70,000 cases of liquor, which was launched in 1917 for the Australian lumber trade. Sloops like Capt. Magher's *The Lady Mine* and Capt. Lilley's *City of San Diego* carried smaller amounts. The 573-ton *Quadra*, which had started life as a lighthouse tender and fisheries patrol ship, ended up rusting in San Francisco harbour after arrest by the U.S. Coast Guard. The *Stadacona* started life as the personal yacht of the head of the Singer Sewing Machine Company, became flagship of the New York Yacht Club and served as a U.S. admiral's personal ship during the Spanish-American War. In the rum trade she was renamed the *Kuyakuzmt*, after Kuyakus Mountain, but was later reconverted into a motion picture studio's cruise boat and renamed the *Moonlight Maid*.

These mother ships, which cleared with their bonded cargo from Vancouver and Victoria, were generally bound for Ensenada, Mexico, just a few miles south of San Diego. Forged manifests declared that the cargoes had been discharged there. The Canadian authorities were never able to prove (nor did they want to) that the cargoes had actually arrived. The mother ships travelled south, well off shore, and were met by smaller, faster boats of every conceivable type, including fishboats and 40-knot speedboats that could outrun any Coast Guard cutter sent to arrest them. The *Malahat* had a covey of small "750's," which were purpose-built for the rum trade. The 750's were 35-knot speedboats built along the same lines as motor-torpedo cruisers, and they carried 750 cases of liquor—hence the name. In January, 1933, Capt. A.G. Lilly's speedboat *Kagome* was shelled and captured by the Coast Guard, then towed into San Francisco. She was released two months later,

Captain Stuart S. Stone (1888-1933), was the master of the S.S. Federalship in 1927, carrying over $1 million in liquor, when it was seized by U.S. Customs off San Francisco. After a lengthy court battle there, the ship was released. The next year, it (and Capt. Stone) was shelled and nearly sunk by a U.S. coast guard cutter off Ensenada. Stone quit, and became master of the Malahat, maintaining a liquor "station" between 100 and 200 miles off the Mexican coast for three years.

Norman J. deGraves was born in Melbourne, Australia in 1891. He came to Vancouver in 1913, and worked for Canadian customs, before dropping dead during an after-dinner speech in 1937. He broke up a number of international smuggling rings.

Generations of Vancouverites have laughed at their city through the cartoons of Leonard Matheson Norris, who has drawn for the Vancouver Sun since 1950. Norris, who was born in England in 1913, worked briefly before the Second War in advertising, and received an M.B.E. (Military) for his wartime editing and illustration of Canadian Army technical magazines. He has received every possible award from newspaper and art directors' organizations, and an Honorary Doctor of Laws from Windsor University. He and his wife live in their beloved West Vancouver, a community which, in his cartoons, is a better-than-real-life collection of rural English eccentrics.

"But look at it this way ma'am . . . you're complying precisely with government policy . . . buy it, but don't drink it."

minus her $15,000 worth of liquor, and returned to Vancouver. Rumrunning in small boats was considered by the Workmen's Compensation Board to be the third most hazardous occupation, following aviation and structural steel raising.

By the end of 1933 (when the Volstead Act was repealed), the U.S. government had arbitrarily extended the three-mile limit to twelve miles. The rum ship *Pescawha* was outside the 12-mile

limit on a rough day when Capt. Robert Pamphlett sighted a ship in distress between ship and shore—the schooner *Coaba*, which had lost its masts and was in danger of breaking up on the rocks. Pamphlett and his crew managed to rescue every man aboard the American vessel, then headed for the open sea. While still within the American limit, he spotted a revenue cutter and, instead of running, hove to, hoping to transfer the wreck's crew to the cutter. The cutter, however, arrested Pamphlett and the *Pescawha*, threw captain and crew into jail and confiscated the ship in Portland. The people of Portland, who openly admired Pamphlett's bravery and seamanship and secretly admired the rum he brought, protested to authorities about his imprisonment. Eventually, Pamphlett was presented with an engraved gold watch from the citizens of Portland.

Only one episode of grand larceny marred the cooperation of the happy Canadians and Americans making a living at rumrunning. The schooner *Beryl G.* was hijacked for its cargo in a cove on Vancouver Island, and the boat's owner and his son were murdered. The perpetrators hung for the crime.

In Vancouver, during the Twenties and Thirties, bootlegging occupied much attention. The breweries complained about "the mounting tide of homebrew" affecting their business, while the Dry Squad obtained padlock orders against "blind pigs" in 1932. To discourage bootleggers, an all-night liquor store was opened at 826 Hornby. (It became the downtown "day store" in 1941, and the all-night store then operated from the warehouse at 871 Beatty. It closed due to blackout regulations after December 7, 1941, re-opened five days later, then closed for good in March, 1942 due to wartime liquor rationing.)

Gerry McGeer's election as Mayor in 1936 precipitated a crackdown on vice and bootleggers. The Palms Hotel, at 800 Granville, requested a beer parlour license but was rebuffed, prompting a fight on the number of beer parlours and their conduct. More than 200 bootleggers were said to be operating in the city, but only those on the east side of the city were regularly raided. The situation became ludicrous in June, 1937, when alleged bootlegger Domenic Caruso was padlocked in his house at 272 Union Street (he refused to leave, and thus was locked out, even when he ran out of spaghetti, dubbed "the Italians' favourite dish" in the newspaper), and held out for three weeks until July 13. The following March, 755 bottles of liquor and 200 dozen beer were seized, all of which were returned to the government liquor store and re-sold.

War-time restrictions led to liquor and beer rationing. The latter provoked a storm of protest, most notably the "No Beer, No Bonds" campaign of 1943. After the war, pressure mounted for more liberal laws. A cabaret plebiscite in the late Forties led, finally, to the approval of cabaret licenses in 1954. The Moderates had modestly triumphed.

Crime

By the end of the First World War, peaceful Vancouver began to come apart at the seams. A number of events made people aware of the night-time violence, betting, prostitution and illicit liquor beneath the respectability. The March 20, 1917 murder of Chief of Police Malcolm MacLennan on East Georgia Street (page 132) had profoundly shocked the City. During 1919, Vancouver was plagued by the new menace of automobile bandits—a gang of youths doing stick-ups and outrunning the car-less, radio-less police. Comments in the newspapers linked bootlegging and rumrunning with drugs, white slavery and the smuggling of Chinese and Hindoos. An armed holdup in September, 1922, netted a $76,000 civic payroll.

On the evening of April 12, 1921, the city was shocked by a bloody murder: "Bill" Salsbury, the son of retired CPR treasurer W.F. Salsbury, was gunned down in the street during a robbery attempt. Salsbury had left his home at 719 Jervis Street, and was walking downtown to his office to catch up on some work. Meanwhile, 20-year-old Allen Robinson and 27-year-old Alex Paulson, both carrying guns, on relief but out of money, left a Powell Street rendezvous with the intention of holding up a likely passer-by. They took up a position under the large shade trees in front of Glencoe Lodge at Burrard and Georgia, and, after a brief wait, accosted one man, who refused them money. The pair were about to pursue him when Salsbury walked up. "Stick 'em up!" ordered Robinson. Salsbury, seeing the gun but taking advantage of his position in the shadow of the tree, struck Robinson with his umbrella. Robinson pulled the trigger, mortally wounding him. Paulson ran west to Thurlow, then headed north across some vacant property, pursued by Robinson, who had paused only long enough to rifle Salsbury's pockets. A police dragnet of the area within the next few hours picked up Robinson, who was not identified by two eye-witnesses, but was nevertheless charged with vagrancy. He was later released and went to Moose Jaw, but returned to Vancouver and was arrested a couple of days after Paulson. Both men were picked out of a line-up and formally charged with murder. The two were tried separately, and Paulson turned on Robinson and gave King's evidence. The defence demanded a retrial, and two reprieves were granted before the duo went to the gallows on July 28, 1922. As Robinson stepped over the drop, he said: "Tell the boys to go straight. This game doesn't pay."

The murder of Constable Richard Gordon McBeath, a 1917 Victoria Cross winner, was equally random. On the night of October 10, 1922, McBeath and a fellow officer jumped on the running board of a car being driven erratically along Granville in front of the Austin Hotel. The driver was Fred Deal, whose passenger, prostitute Marjorie Earl, was passed out on the front seat. Deal struggled with McBeath and shot him in the chest, killing him. He then engaged in a wild gunfight with the other constable, and, after wounding him in the hand, managed to escape, but was arrested later that night at Nelson and Howe Street. After sixteen years in prison he was deported to his former home in Jacksonville, Florida. The fact that Deal was "a Negro," owned a gun and lived with the prostitute Earl in an old hotel at 1249 Granville, encouraged the flow of money into the Ku Klux Klan's coffers. Two years later, the latter was able to buy Glen Brae at 1690 Matthews, one of Shaughnessy's grandest mansions, as a headquarters.

Hogan's Alley

An easy dividing line between "classes" of Vancouverites who went night-clubbing in the Twenties and Thirties was whether or not they ever went to Hogan's Alley, where the criminal element was rumoured to congregate. At the Police Court, "scarcely a day passed without some evidence given on the happenings at that busy thoroughfare." People with any degree of respectability stayed on Hastings near the Pantages, or uptown on Granville street around the Orpheum, the Spanish Grill, the Alexandra Ballroom and Scott's Cafe.

The location of Hogan's Alley was often debated. Some put it as the alley behind Puccini's in the 700 block Main—Puccini's jazz bar is still called Hogan's Alley. In the Thirties, it was the alley running from Station to Gore between Union and Pryor, just east of Main Street—a block now completely demolished by the approach and exit ramps of the Georgia Viaduct. This block-long dirt lane was called "a street of mystery to Vancouver's gentlebred" and "a breeding place for crime." Gerry McGeer's 1935 anti-vice mayoralty campaign was directed against the area and the rumours which said protection money was paid to police, who promptly gambled it away in the speakeasies along the lane. Mystery and distrust were added by the allegation that it was home to so many of the city's blacks, who had been involved in highly-publicized murders and bootlegging escapades since the First War years. A newspaper report in the mid-Thirties described Hogan's Alley as "tumble-down shacks, squalid tenements, a stable and the odd trim cottage." Carl Marchi, the self-styled mayor of Hogan's Alley, had a trim cottage at 251½, beside the stable, and an income allegedly based on bootlegging and loan-sharking. Kathleen Moore, the Queen of Hogan's Alley who was regularly arrested for intoxication, claimed that there was a man named Hogan who "was the shining light of the social side of the alley." According to Moore, he had a shack on the alley, more money than his neighbours, and a habit of hosting boozy parties.

On the night of November 26, 1925, a 28-year-old woman named Pearl Traversey was stabbed to death in the cottage at 256½ Hogan's Alley. She died in Vancouver General, after naming one Alex de Bertoli as the murderer. He hanged in Oakalla on July 14, 1926. On May 25, 1930, Mrs. Allan Groat—also known as Bobby Kelly—was shot in the chest at 440 East Pender. "I'm no rat. I won't squeal," she said, and died in hospital two days later. On July 20, 1935, Armando Mori was hit over the head and killed by a pipe-wrench while attempting to break up a dogfight in the alley. No one was ever charged with that murder. Every once in a while, university students ("westsiders" and "frat rats," said the locals contemptuously) would go "slumming" in the alley, harass a few bums and prostitutes and get into mass brawls.

It seemed outrageous to quiet Vancouver in the mid-Thirties. In 1939, City Council debated at length whether to demolish the lane. Residents of the area said it wouldn't make any difference unless the whole area was changed. Citizens felt that the old East End was desperately in need of urban renewal. The war intervened. During the Fifties, plans were made to raze the area, culminating in the construction of MacLean Park and Raymur Park housing projects in the early Sixties. Hogan's Alley finally fell to the wrecker's ball, long after it had lost its notoriety.

MARGARET PAWLETT

The Harry Pryce orchestra in the Hotel Georgia in 1928. Left to right: George Anderson, bass; Harry Hamilton, drums; Bill Arstad, trombone; Wes Mortimer, trumpet; Charlie Pawlett, banjo; Harry Pryce, piano and leader; Fernie Quinn, sax; Harry Carr, sax. The orchestra was the first to play when the hotel was opened in 1927 by the Prince of Wales, later King Edward VIII.

"LAFE CASSIDY'S"
BANFF SPRINGS HOTEL. DANCE ORCHESTRA

(Left) Lafe Cassidy's orchestra was one of many that played during the summer season at the Canadian Pacific Railway's beautiful Rocky Mountain resorts. Both the Banff Springs Hotel and the Chateau Lake Louise offered first-class accommodation, recreation and entertainment for the well-heeled during the Thirties.

(Right) The Bob Lyon Orchestra in the Commodore, shortly after it opened in 1937. Not long after this photo was taken, Lyon and three of the band members went to Chateau Lake Louise; the balance of the members stayed in Vancouver and became Charlie Pawlett and the Commodores.

225

(Left) The Earle Hill orchestra at the opening of the Cave in 1938. The distinctive grotto decor and the club's long-time policy of importing big-name entertainers from the United States made the Cave Supper Club a Vancouver favorite until it was demolished in 1981 as part of the massive Bank of B.C. project. During the Fifties, when all of the old vaudeville palaces had long since been demolished or converted to cinemas, Vancouverites booked months ahead for the Mills Brothers, the Inkspots, Harry Belafonte, Nat King Cole, and Mitzi Gaynor.

(Right) Charlie Pawlett's dance band in the Howden Ballroom in the late Forties. Mabel Howden's little club was not particularly fashionable or successful. It closed and the building was destroyed to make way for the north approaches to the modern Granville bridge. The sign on the right announced the upcoming dances. Other ballrooms, like the Arlington Cabaret and the Peter Pan on West Broadway, operated until the late Seventies for a quiet, respectable (and increasingly aged) clientele.

226

New Brighton

New Brighton resort, looking northeast, near the foot of Windermere Street north of Hastings Park, in 1886. The resort had been established for nearly twenty years as a watering hole and summer place for the people from the Moodyville mill, Hastings sawmill and New Westminster. The trail to Gastown led off to the left. The bar is the low building on the left, the dining room the one in the middle, and the New Brighton hotel the balconied building on the right. Maxie Michaud's hotel was off to the right. The CPR's track-clearing operation can be seen in the distance, at about the modern site of the Alberta Wheat Pool. George Black, "the Laird of Hastings," is standing in the road in front of the boy on the horse.

New Brighton Resort, "The Most Fashionable Watering Place in B.C.," pre-dates the founding of the City of Vancouver by 17 years. As a "remote" summer resort at the north foot of today's Windermere Street near the PNE, it served the earliest settlements of Burrard Inlet—Hastings Mill, Gastown, and North Vancouver's Moodyville—as well as the established residents of New Westminster.

New Brighton owed its existence to the Douglas Road, cut by Royal Engineers based in New Westminster to connect the established city with tidewater and John Thomas' row-boat ferry service to Moodyville. In August, 1865, soon after the road was finished, Oliver Hocking and Fred Houston opened the Brighton Hotel. The next October, a regular daily carriage service by teamster W.R. Lewis connected the hotel with New Westminster. Two years later, following the Admiralty surveys of the area, the townsite was officially named Hastings, although it continued to be called variously "Hocking's," "New Brighton," "1869," "Maxie's" and "Black's" for years to come. The last two names stuck because of two hotel operators: Maxie Michaud, who bought Hocking's hotel in March, 1869; and abattoir owner George Black, who built the Brighton Hotel near the ferry wharf shortly after. Both hotels were a great attraction, particularly with residents of Moodyville, which was dry until 1874 (as "Sue"—Sewell Prescott Moody—was a

teetotaller), and oglers of Maxie Michaud's beautiful consort, to whom he "wasn't exactly married." The pleasant seaside air attracted families, as did swimming and boating in the clean inlet. The thirst-slaking in Black's and conversation with "The Laird of Hastings," as he came to be called, attracted socializers, and the fresh, non-alcoholic entertainment of the regular cricket matches attracted sporting types from as far away as Gastown.

In July, 1869, the first sale of lots was held. Forty-four were sold at $50 each. Oliver Hocking, who continued to live there, was appointed postmaster. When the railroad came through, the CPR established its operations base in Maxie's hotel. The food evidently was better across the road, as on Christmas Day 1885 the CPR's local officials ate at Black's following the successful completion of surveys. Guests at the dinner included the notorious Major "Hell's Bells" Rogers of Rogers Pass, surveyor Jack Stewart, Sam Brighouse, and CPR Western Superintendent Henry Cambie.

During the Eighties and Nineties, the railway ran a regular service to New Brighton, but the town fell from fashion in favour of Larsen's North Vancouver hotel on the Esplanade at the foot of Lonsdale, and later the Union Steamship resort at Bowen Island.

The New Brighton area today bears no resemblance to the tight, hilly, forested little community of a century ago. The foreshore has been flattened, filled and cleared back to the railway tracks; the city and the Pacific National Exhibition have encroached on all sides. The immense Alberta Wheat Pool and Second Narrows bridge dominate the view to the east. New Brighton Park, with a bronze plaque commemorating the old resort, occupies the townsite today. It has a chlorinated swimming pool (replacing a tidal-filled one which became too dirty) and a lot of lawn for picnickers. There is a splendid view of the Inlet and the North Shore mountains.

Pacific National Exhibition

Hastings Park was surveyed in 1863 and was always intended to remain as open space as part of the Admiralty Reserve. It has been the site of a major fall fair and exhibition since August 15, 1910, when Sir Wilfrid Laurier, Prime Minister of Canada and the man on the five dollar bill, came to Vancouver to open it.

Hastings Park occupies a vast, 167-acre chunk of northeastern Vancouver, from Renfrew east to Cassiar and Hastings north to McGill (the southern boundary of old New Brighton). During the 20 years after 1890, it was the scene of casual summer agricultural exhibitions, picnics and the "carny" hucksterism of country fairs. There were few solid buildings—events and people came and went like gypsies. Since then, the fairgrounds have been practically all things to all people. One of the uses has been as a parade ground, for all forms of the military, including "those urchins you see going around with poles, shirts and cowboy hats," as Lieut. General R.S. Baden-Powell, hero of the siege of Mafeking and the founder of the Scouting movement, described his charges at a review of local Scouts at Hastings Park on August 15, 1910. (During his visit to Vancouver, he stayed with R.D. Rorison at the house at 3146 Point Grey Road.) Many of the regiments preparing to leave Vancouver for the battlefields of Europe after August, 1914, were mustered there.

The Vancouver Exhibition—now the PNE—finally got the green light at the beginning of the summer of 1910. B.C. Electric was prevailed upon by Exhibition president John Miller to extend its Powell Street tram line to Hastings Park, so that the population could visit other than on foot. The company responded quickly, and the McGill streetcar line through the forest was opened just in time. Passengers disembarked at Renfrew and Oxford within sight of the strange new pavilions and electrical displays.

At this time, expositions around the world were intoxicating the population with the promise of technological progress. The Universal Exposition in Paris in 1900 had dazzled Europe with electricity, automobiles and sinuous Art Nouveau. The Seattle-Yukon-Pacific Exhibition of 1909 introduced the northwest coast to the pseudo-classicism and boosterism of that prosperous decade. For the Vancouver Exhibition, a number of pavilions were erected—the Industrial Building, the Women's Building, the YMCA and the Manufacturer's Building—which all looked like the "Crystal Palace," with decorative wrought-iron arches and vaults with lots of glass. There was an agricultural area and there are many forestry and logging displays. The exhibition also had a grandstand, from which patrons could watch horse races on the Jockey Club's trotter-track, or the far more exciting dirt-track Blitzen Benz auto races. A roller coaster was erected during the First War, and, within the next decade, Happyland—now Playland— with its collection of rides, amusements and the Midway, began to develop. Visitors during the Twenties could stay at the Hastings Park Auto Camp at Windermere and Hastings Street. Their children played in the forest and along the ravine which occupied the Hastings Street side and the eastern part of the grounds.

Vancouver attracted world attention when it staged the British Empire and Commonwealth Games in 1954, and built Empire Stadium on the PNE grounds. There, on August 8 in brilliant weather, Roger Bannister and John Landy ran the legendary "Miracle Mile"— the first race where two men broke the four-minute mile. The stadium was home through the Fifties, Sixties and Seventies to drenched, generally luckless B.C. Lions football teams, and in the latter years for the soccer-playing Whitecaps, until both teams moved in 1983 to the new B.C. Place Stadium on False Creek.

Little Mountain

Little Mountain is an extinct volcano, a bump on Vancouver's otherwise smooth complexion, at 33rd and Cambie. Princess Elizabeth planted a tree there on October 20, 1951, to begin the development of the world-famous arboretum and rock gardens. Although the bump was officially christened Queen Elizabeth Park in 1940, in honour of the 1939 visit of the King and Queen, old-timers still call it Little Mountain.

Little Mountain's quarry gardens, with their backdrop of city and mountains, are one of the most popular spots in Vancouver for wedding photographs. The quarry part of the gardens is the old South Vancouver rock pit, source of the stone for many of the roads in South Vancouver and all of the roads in Shaughnessy Heights. Tons of basalt were hauled out in drays before the Twenties, when the quarry began to fall into disuse. It was bought by the city as a park in 1929. Small boys chased rabbits and picked berries on the hillsides and climbed the steep sides of the rock pits.

Long before the small boys, Indian legend tells of Chip-kay-am, brother of Chief Khahtsalano and founder of Snauq, hunting bear on the hillside with an old muzzle loader given him by a Hudson's Bay Company trader. He shot once at a bear but failed to drop it. While he scrambled to reload it, the bear mauled him, but Chip-kay-am survived.

By 1908, development had extended far enough into South Vancouver that lack of water pressure during the summer was a problem. To boost the pressure, the city decided to dig two reservoirs at the top of Little Mountain, which remained as uncovered lakes for over fifty years. Finally, in April, 1965, when air pollution and security had become a problem, the city installed a cover. The cover is now a major part of the Little Mountain observation deck and the platform which supports the Bloedel Conservatory and Henry Moore's "Knife Edge" sculpture.

The "triodetic" glass dome of the Bloedel Conservatory, glowing in the night like a flying saucer, was a 1968 bequest from lumber baron Prentice Bloedel—co-founder with H.R. MacMillan of western Canada's largest forest products company. It was one of a number of proposals for a public edifice on top of Little Mountain (the "Van Horne Bowl" proposal of the Thirties would have put a large amphitheatre into the hillside in the quarry area).

The Cambie and Oakridge areas around Little Mountain were bush and farmland during the Thirties. In 1939, Master-Craft Homes Ltd. developed a 42-home subdivision on uniform 60-foot lots, west of Cambie at King Edward. The CPR announced similar intentions, but the war intervened. In June, 1940, work began on a vast training camp, dubbed "Little Aldershot," for at least 10,000 army conscripts. Located in the bushland between Little Mountain and the Oak Street carline, it became the headquarters of Military District Depot 11, which had been operating from the old Hotel Vancouver. The move to the completed buildings at 37th and Heather finally took place in June, 1942. After the war, the 34 abandoned army huts were occupied by squatters—homeless veterans and their families. Eventually, the land was subdivided by the CPR and sold for private housing development.

Beer & Baseball

During the freewheeling days of the late nineteenth century, brewers operated in Vancouver without benefit of or hindrance from the myriad laws which now control the British Columbia beer business. Although "One Hundred Years of Brewing," the mammoth and definitive 1903 study of North American brewing by *Western Brewer* magazine, found few breweries in the province big enough to mention, the output in the Vancouver area amounted to about eight hundred and ninety thousand gallons per year. The largest production of a single brewery was 150,000 gallons, or about 4,800 barrels. Ninety-six percent of the output was lager beer, with the remainder ale and porter. All but a few small ale breweries had installed refrigeration plants by the turn of the century. Over eighty percent of the malt used was imported from the United States.

The small breweries in the Lower Mainland were established at places like Cedar Cottage and Brewery Creek in Mount Pleasant by people like John Benson and Charles Doering. Joseph Kappler and Emil Kerhauser's Columbia Brewery at Powell and Wall Street was typical: it solicited its own customers and provided home delivery by horse-drawn wagon through the muddy streets. Bottled beer typically cost 75 cents for a dozen pints.

By the time Prohibition ended in British Columbia in 1920, the Provincial Government was developing a taste for regulating the beer business, as well as running all liquor outlets in the province. A policy was drafted by Attorney General A.M.Manson in 1924 to sell all beer through the Pacific Brewers' Agency, The provincial government insisted that, to prevent bootlegging, a few breweries which operated in a friendly association should maintain a monopoly on the beer business in B.C. The major intent was to keep any newcomers from getting a chunk of the B.C. market, thus benefiting the Reifel family, which dominated the brewery business and had "a picturesque association with [the Brewers' Agency] and the practical politics of the province," according to a contemporary newspaper article.

Into this tight little group came the Sick interests of Alberta, led by family patriarch Fritz Sick. Born on the Rhine near Freiburg, Germany in 1859, Sick had landed in New York in 1883 with $5 in his pocket, a train ticket to Cincinnati, and a letter of introduction to one of that city's German brewers. After a couple of years' apprenticeship, he moved to California, then north to Tacoma (where he married in 1889), then to Spokane, and finally to Trail in 1896. Spokane at the time was the centre of commerce for the booming mining properties in Washington and B.C. In Trail, Fritz Sick founded the Fernie-Fort Steele breweries in 1896, then moved to Lethbridge, Alberta at the turn of the century and established prosperous operations there. In 1930 he moved to Vancouver, ostensibly to retire, but decided instead to start a new brewery. In 1932, he purchased the Vancouver Malt and Saké Company, which

in 1927 had agreed with Reifel's Vancouver Breweries Ltd. not to brew beer for 15 years, in exchange for a free hand in the saké market. Sick announced to Premier Tolmie that he intended to brew beer, so Vancouver Breweries Ltd. sued for breach of their agreement. Local courts upheld the agreement, but Sick appealed all the way to the Privy Council, which, after two years of litigation, decided in his favour. In February, 1934, the "beer war" ended. Sick's new Capilano brewery was quickly established and opened with much fanfare at 1445 Powell, between the old P.Burns slaughterhouse and B.C. Sugar.

Fritz Sick retired to his home at 6576 Marguerite, celebrated his golden wedding anniversary with Laura (1860-1941), and died in 1945, aged 85 years. His son Emil took over the Capilano brewery, and, in 1939, purchased a baseball franchise from the Western International League and started the Vancouver Capilanos team, headquartered at the Athletic Park at 5th and Hemlock.

Baseball had been well established in Vancouver for the forty years before the Capilanos were formed. It was said that Vancouver was the only Canadian city where a good game of American baseball could be seen. Typically, Vancouverites were divided on the matter. "Baseball has never been highly regarded in Vancouver," wrote J.S. Matthews in 1920. "The men who are associated with it are of questionable integrity." Nevertheless, there were five amateur leagues of "this strenuous variety of the English game of rounders" in the city by the first decade of the century. In 1902, ball was played at the Powell Street Grounds, the Recreation (Cambie Street) Grounds, and the newly-cleared Monastery Grounds—a playing field at 16th and Heather in Fairview. When "Ruby" Robert Paul Brown, nicknamed "sorrel top," started organizing games there, "if you stuck your head out of the bush you had to pay." In 1907, a group of businessmen met in the Hotel Vancouver, and agreed to finance Brown to purchase a franchise in the Northwestern League. The team they formed was the Vancouver Beavers. Property was purchased near 5th and Hemlock, on the south side of False Creek, and the Athletic Park—with 6,000 little squares of turf from the Fraser Valley— opened in April, 1913. A crowd of 6,000 attended on opening day.

Brown managed the team until the league folded up during the Great War. He was a respected manager, making much of his money selling talent to the major leagues, and served on the arbitration group following the notorious Black Sox scandal of 1919 (when the World Series was "thrown" for a gambling racket). He returned to Vancouver later, and managed the Capilanos to a pennant victory in 1942.

The Twenties were the years of semi-pro ball in the Vancouver City League. Teams like the Firemen, Arnold & Quigley, Vancouver Athletic Club, the Arrows, United Distillers, and Home Gas played at the Athletic Park. The Park's grandstand burned in 1926, and

Above: the Capilano Brewery's "Old Style" label, vintage 1946. Right: the Brewery's namesake baseball team, seen in a composite photograph at the Athletic Park at 5th and Hemlock, on the south shore of False Creek.

Fritz Sick

was rebuilt with the first night-lights of any stadium in Canada. Athletic Park was christened Capilano Stadium in 1942; the grandstand burned to the ground in April, 1944, but was rebuilt.

In 1946, the Town Planning Commission announced that Vancouver would have to acquire the Athletic Park for a cloverleaf for a new Granville bridge; the brewery, which had paid $35,000 to the CPR for the park in 1944, agreed to sell it to the City for $25,000 in return for considerations when it came time to build a new stadium.

The new Capilano stadium, which the brewery announced it would erect at Riley Park just east of the new Queen Elizabeth Park, was modelled after pillar-free Hollywood baseball park. The price tag was $300,000. Construction was stalled due to vociferous protests from Riley Park residents in May, 1946. The fire marshal also objected to the proposed plan, citing the difficulty of fireproofing a timber stadium. Memories were still fresh of the enormous Denman Arena fire in 1936. The debate continued until March, 1947, when Alderman Charles Jones suggested that the brewery move the stadium across the street from the cramped 5-acre Riley Park to the 15-acre triangle of land bounded by Midlothian, Melrose and Ontario. This appeared to satisfy all parties, and on April 9, 1947 approval was granted by City Council to build the new stadium. Then, in October, 1948, the brewery announced it was backing out due to unresolved problems with the City, which had agreed to provide drainage and sewerage to the swampy site. A new deal was negotiated in October, 1949, and construction was finally approved on January 24, 1950. The resulting 5,000 seat grandstand was built by the city and leased to the brewery for a 20-year term. During games, it was a common sight to see the parking lot full of kids wearing baseball uniforms and carrying gloves, attempting to catch the foul balls which dented hoods and smashed windshields. The Capilanos played at the stadium until 1955, when the brewery abandoned the team. The stadium was used for amateur sport during the years 1955 and 1956. From 1957-62 and again from 1965-9, it was home to the Vancouver Mounties of the AAA Pacific Coast League, who gave the town its best baseball and received the most loyalty in return. During the late Fifties, there was such a crush of fans that the area inside the outfield fence was roped off to accommodate them. Attendance was aided by the legalization of professional sports on Sundays in April, 1958. In the twenty years since that time, the trees have grown up on "Scotchman's Hill" on Little Mountain, obscuring the view for the aficionados with blankets and transistor radios who listened to Jim Robson's play-by-play on CKWX while watching the Mounties play. The White Spot was a major sponsor during those years—drive-in patrons were given little folding schedules for all the team's games, and the stadium now bears the name of White Spot founder Nat Bailey. After the Mounties folded, the stadium sat vacant and vandalized until the early Seventies, when the Vancouver Art Gallery appropriated it for art exhibits and rowdy rock concerts. In the late Seventies, Harry Ornest got a Pacific Coast League team started again under the name of the Vancouver Canadians, with typography and bankrolling—and the right to sell beer in the stadium—from the Molson's brewery who make "Canadian" beer.

The Capilano brewery had changed its name in 1944 to Sicks' Capilano Brewery Ltd. and adopted a logo of a large "6" for Sicks'. In April, 1949, Sicks' announced plans to build a $2,000,000 brewery next to the Seaforth Armoury at the south end of the Burrard Bridge, on the site of a few abandoned army huts which were then occupied by squatters. The brewery opened in the early Fifties to much fanfare as "The Home of Old Style Beer." (The same typography is still used on Old Style labels.) A feature of the new brewery was a huge "6" on a tower on top of the brewery (now occupied by the Molson's Clock), which changed colour according to the weather forecast—flashing red for approaching rain, green for good weather, and so on.

In 1958, Molson's acquired Sicks', thus bringing to an end the era of the big independent breweries in southwestern B.C. The merger of several companies in the Fifties had consolidated the hold of the "Big Three" eastern breweries over the hearts and tastebuds of Lower Mainlanders. Canadian Breweries bought Western Canada Breweries and the old Reifel plant at 12th and Vine, which eventually became Carling's. Labatt's bought the Lucky Lager brewery in New Westminster and started making "Blue" there.

Golf Courses

Three golf courses in Vancouver have completely vanished. The Jericho Club ceased to exist when the Department of National Defence expanded the Jericho Air Station at the beginning of the Second World War. Shaughnessy and Quilchena lost their leases when the CPR chose to develop the land for housing, though both clubs have been re-established in less central areas of the Lower Mainland.

The first links on the Lower Mainland were established in November, 1892, by the Vancouver Golf Club at Jericho. An organizational meeting, chaired by Dr. Duncan Bell-Irving, got an agreement from J.M. Dalgleish (who in 1886 had purchased 15 waterfront acres from the late Jerry Rogers' former logging and business partner, Angus Fraser) and the Admiralty, for use of the Jericho sand flats as a golf course. For a clubhouse, they purchased a fisherman's shack, which stood at the high water mark on the sand. It cost the princely sum of $35, $25 of which was contributed by visiting golfer Robert Austin. Inside was an open fireplace, at which the lady members made tea, while the men stashed their grog in the sand floor or in private "cellars" under drift logs. The fairways were sandy and marked by drift-log boundaries. Access to the course was by rowboat (or commandeered steam tug) or from the old telegraph trail which became Point Grey Road. During the winter of 1894, heavy gales and high tides flooded the course and moved all the logs around. The members, disillusioned, abandoned it, and re-established themselves the next year at Brockton Point, where nine holes were laid out on the Athletic Grounds. A. St. George Hamersley was elected Honorary President. The golfers found play difficult, owing to the presence of cricket-playing white-suited gentlemen and other sportsmen, so moved the club to the Moodyville rifle range area between Lynn and Seymour creeks on the north shore, where "a sporting nine-hole course was conducted, not the least of its advantages being that golf can be played on all seven days of the week without interference or danger to the public." Another $35 was invested in this club, of which $10 was the cost of making a footbridge across Lynn Creek and cutting some footways. Headquarters were established in the Moodyville Hotel. Play continued there until June, 1899.

After a three-year hiatus, the club attempted to revive golf in Vancouver, when the CPR in 1902 cleared the land west of Granville Street from 33rd to 37th. Richard Marpole assisted with laying out a nine-hole course, but it clashed with F. Todd's subdivision plans for Shaughnessy Heights, so was abandoned. Three years later, a man named McKiver Campbell re-formed the Jericho Golf Club and arranged the purchase of the Dalgleish lands (the Jerry Rogers homestead), and a proper lease of 40 acres of the naval reserve, making possible a new nine-hole course there. On October 6, 1907, Rudyard Kipling played there as a guest of the club.

Although the clubhouse burned down twice, the club prospered, and in 1923 arranged a lease with the Provincial Government for additional land across Marine Drive (now 4th Avenue). A back nine opened on September 1, 1924. The club was abandoned when the Second World War started, and the course and clubhouse were obtained by the Defence Department in 1941. The grand old clubhouse, at which celebrities like the Prince of Wales, Viscountess Willingdon and Mrs. Herbert Hoover had been entertained, burned down in March, 1948. The front nine of the golf course is now Jericho Park, and the back nine is occupied by the Justice Institute of B.C., the Jericho School for the Deaf and Blind, and various Defence Department Pacific Command buildings.

A second attempt was made in March, 1912, to establish a Shaughnessy Golf Club, following the successful development of the CPR's Shaughnessy Heights district. A meeting was held in Richard Marpole's office, at which Sir Thomas Shaughnessy was astutely appointed Honorary President in absentia. A rough layout was agreed to, with the clubhouse on 37th between Granville and Oak, and the links occupying most of the area between Granville and Willow Streets, 33rd and 37th. Wasting no time, the members dispatched W.E. Burns in May, to the meeting of the Pacific Northwest Golf Association, to promote Shaughnessy as the venue for its 1915 championship tournament. He was successful. Construction on the clubhouse began in June, and in November $4,000 was voted for furnishings. On January 1, 1913, the links were officially taken over by the club from the CPR. (The first tournament was held on Christmas Day, 1912, and although 18 holes were completed, the two famous "orphan holes," numbers six and seven, which ran along Oak Street between 37th and 41st avenues, were not included.) The clubhouse was destroyed by fire in August, 1916, but was rebuilt in even grander style, with imported English panelling and cut stone.

After the First World War, the Shaughnessy Club attracted some distinguished golfers, including Walter Hagen, Harry Vardon (who shot a 68, though he had never seen the course before) and Ted Ray. Celebrities like U.S. President Warren Harding and Clark Gable played there during the Twenties and Thirties. Shaughnessy hosted its first major tournament, the Canadian Amateur, in 1933, and the Canadian Open in 1948. Ken Black, a Shaughnessy member who was Canadian amateur champion and the Jubilee Open winner in 1936, held the course record of 63.

The CPR announced, in the early Fifties, that they would not renew the golf club's lease when it came due in 1962. The club looked for alternatives, and considered leasing the University public golf course in 1954. Then, in October, 1957, they signed a lease for 160 acres of the Musqueam Reserve, west of Camosun on Marine Drive, for $29,000 a year (an amount which was to become

The back nine of the Jericho Golf Club, seen from near the corner of 7th and Discovery in the late Thirties. The buildings in the distance on the right are the old Boys' Industrial School, then the Deaf and Blind School. Fourth Avenue crosses in front of the school, and the old front nine and clubhouse are on the flat land below, now a park.

controversial fifteen years later). The new course opened in November, 1960. *Its* clubhouse was destroyed by fire in the late Seventies. The old course and clubhouse were finally demolished in March, 1965, and the area east of Oak Street sold to the Provincial Government for the Eric Hamber School. The balance of the course went to seed until the Seventies, when the Van Dusen Botanical Gardens were established.

Quilchena Golf Course at 33rd and Arbutus was the shortest-lived of the three, lasting for only thirty years from 1925. It occupied a dip of land variously called Asthma Flats or Consumption Hollow, due to the autumn fogs which packed in against the Quilchena hillside. (The name Quilchena means "Sweet Waters.")

The land west of the interurban track, between King Edward Avenue and 33rd, was one of the last large undeveloped bushlands from the CPR's land grant. The northwest part of the property, now the site of the Arbutus Village shopping centre and townhouse community, was left as bushland, but the railway entered into a lease in 1925 with the Quilchena Golf Club for the balance of the property. Two engineers, Ginnis Johnston and Harold Rindal, laid out a nine-hole course along the interurban tracks and built a clubhouse at 29th Avenue and East Boulevard (now Maple Crescent). Within a few years, the course was expanded to a full eighteen, and was rearranged in 1936 to eliminate some of the hilliness of the original layout. Golfers crossed Arbutus at 33rd between the first and second holes, and again between the eighth and ninth. The thirteenth green was the farthest north, practically at the fence of the B.C. Electric substation at King Edward and Maple Crescent. The course was a par 71, 6310 yards long.

Quilchena was given notice in 1953 that the lease would not be renewed when it came due in 1960. The club, after dickering with the McCleery family, voted in October, 1953, to move to the flat-as-a-desk-top Sherwood Farm on Lulu Island. At the same time, citizens in the area began to "raise a row" to save Quilchena as a park. In February, 1956, the city agreed to pay the railway $657,000 for school and park sites on the old golf course. The clubhouse, with its glass-enclosed "snake pit," was thrown in too, but the city chose to demolish it. The new Prince of Wales school opened in 1960. The CPR began property development on the old front nine west of Arbutus, and provoked a storm of controversy in 1964 by proposing the Arbutus Gardens garden-apartment complex at the northeast corner of 33rd and Arbutus (clustered garden apartments were considered the wave of the future in the United States during the Fifties). Other development began on the old course, including the private Arbutus Club and a new Greek Orthodox Church. The CPR's plans to build an Oakridge-sized shopping centre, on the west side of Arbutus Street, roused the ire of local residents, who retained future Mayor Jack Volrich to represent them in a successful battle to reduce the size of the complex.

In the CPR's Quilchena subdivision, the streets were diplomatically named after both railway and civic officials: C.W. McBain was a CPR land agent, J.E. McMullen a member of the company's legal department, J. Edgar was for 27 years with the city's Zoning Appeals Board, Andy Haggart was a former City building inspector, Charles Brakenridge was a City Engineer, and Thomas O. Townley was Mayor in 1901.

The view across Consumption Hollow, looking northeast, to the Quilchena Golf Club "snake pit" at 29th and East Boulevard, in the late Twenties. The twin towers of Glen Brae are visible in the right distance, as is Shaughnessy school, then called Prince of Wales school, at King Edward and Marguerite. The golf course was abandoned during the Fifties, though portions of the fairway layout are visible as Quilchena Park.

Index

Italics indicate picture

Addenda

11. There were a few farms between Marpole and the southern edge of the city, but most of the open land was undeveloped scrub, held for speculation and occasionally grazed over by cattle.

12. House construction continued through the 1920s, especially on the west side of the city in areas such as Second Shaughnessy, Kerrisdale, and Dunbar. Of the few landmarks added to the skyline after the First World War, the most notable was the Marine Building.

18. The Regina Hotel was at the southwest corner of Cambie and Water streets.

22. The original city boundaries were Burrard Inlet, Nanaimo Street, Trafalgar Street, and 16th Avenue. The fire was June 13, 1886.

27. Frank Douglas was Robert Kelly's original partner, and drowned during the sinking of the *Islander.* His brother, Edward, then moved to Vancouver from Minnesota, joined the firm, and provided for Frank's widow.

34. Nanaimo Street was the city's eastern boundary.

48. The "temporary" bus depot on Dunsmuir Street was finally demolished in 1993, after Greyhound moved to the refurbished Canadian National Railways station at Main and Terminal.

52. Chris Spencer commissioned architect Thomas Hooper in 1911 to build the house at 49th and West Boulevard.

53. Sears found retailing at Harbour Centre to be unprofitable; the old Spencer's/Eaton's department store is now the downtown campus of Simon Fraser University.

54. Following years of financial trouble, Woodward's was bought out by the Hudson's Bay Company in 1993, and former Woodward's stores were converted into Bay and Zeller's outlets.

56. The old post office at Granville and Hastings, along with the adjoining Winch Building and Customs buildings, were restored and refurbished in the 1980s as Sinclair Centre, a retail and office complex.

65. The chateau-style CPR station at the foot of Granville Street appeared solid, but the ballast bricks used in its construction were beginning to crumble fifteen years after it was erected.

67. The James Inglis Reid shop closed late in 1986, and was demolished the following year.

71. In actual fact, Mrs. B.T. Rogers terminated Miss Mollison's lease in November, 1931, in a fruitless attempt to find a tenant who could generate more revenue from the building.

76. "Glen Brae" is now owned by the city, and is leased as a children's hospice.

79. The CPR actually had little enthusiasm for the First Narrows and for a time wanted to build its railway and shipping terminus on Kitsilano Point.

81. The B.C. Sugar Refinery was established in 1890, and the first sugar melt took place on January 16, 1891.

83. The ferry wharves for North Vancouver and West Vancouver were at the foot of Columbia Street; there was no turntable for streetcars at the foot of Lonsdale, as the streetcars were "double-enders."

84. Contemporaries who were not as involved in politics as Stevens felt that Charles Gardner Johnson, the Lloyd's agent for B.C. and a shipping broker, was truly "the father of the Port of Vancouver."

89. The former CPR railyards—the Expo '86 site—are gradually being transformed into a high-density residential neighbourhood. The old Roundhouse survives as a community centre.

93. The Canadian National station on Main Street is now a "multi-modal transportation facility" for CN, VIA Rail, Greyhound, and some other bus charter lines; the building itself has been restored, and is officially known as Pacific Central Station.

103. The University Club at 1021 West Hastings closed in the late 1980s.

105. After the retirement of J.H. Turner, Wade was appointed agent general for B.C. in London. He died in England in 1924.

113. The Dunsmuir Street bus terminal was demolished in 1993. Grauer's comment about socialism was probably cribbed from U.S. presidential candidate (1940) Wendell Willkie.

118. The B.C. Sugar Refinery opened late in 1890.

123. The old Federal Agriculture building at 15th and Main was restored in the 1980s and is now known as Heritage Hall.

124. The route of Brewery Creek has been marked with interpretive plaques and cairns. The surviving brewery building at 6th and Scotia was restored in 1992 as artists' studios.

126. The photograph at the bottom right of the page shows the original 1894 Mount Pleasant Presbyterian Church at the northwest corner of 10th and Quebec, being realigned to allow for construction of the 1909 church on the site. The old portion was demolished in 1992 to allow for the renovation of the 1909 church into condominiums. The Davis family has restored a number of houses in the Mount Pleasant area since their rescue of 166 West 10th Avenue.

128. The Ledingham house was built by a contractor named P.B. Fenton in 1894; it was converted into a seniors' residence in the late 1980s in a renovation that left little more than the corner tower standing. The house next door to the west burned down.

130. The city's eastern boundary was Nanaimo Street.

134. The synagogue at Pender and Heatley was refurbished and renovated in the late 1980s into condominiums. The East End grocery stood at the northeast corner of Princess and Keefer.

136. The area between King Edward and 37th Avenue was usually known as Second Shaughnessy, and the 1926 subdivision south of it as far as 41st Avenue was known as Third Shaughnessy.

144. J.W. Stewart supervised Pacific Great Eastern railway construction only as far as Quesnel.

167. The house occupied by Alvo von Alvensleben—now Crofton House school's administration building—was built in 1902 by Richard Byron Johnson.

170 and 172. Elijah Betts was the original pre-emptor, in 1862, of the land that is now Point Grey Golf Course—he sold it to Henry Mole.

174. The old Vancouver Breweries operation at 12th and Vine closed in the 1980s; the site, part of what has become known as the Arbutus Industrial Lands, will be redeveloped with housing.

176. The old feed and grain store at Belmont and Sasamat was demolished in the 1980s.

182. The collision between the *Pacific Gatherer* and the bridge in 1930 was the most serious of a number of accidents that had taken place in the five years following the bridge's opening.

186. The photograph is from 1930 and shows the original Lulu Island airstrip, which occupied about 40 acres of pasture land west of Garden City Road and south of Alexandra Road. It was superseded by the Sea Island (now Vancouver International) airport in 1931.

187. The White Spot at Granville and 67th burned down in the mid-1980s.

209. The aquarium at English Bay was the second one in the city; the first, with crossed whalebones framing the door, was at Hastings Park.

225. Bob Lyon was born Bob Rutherford but his name was too long to fit on a marquee, so he used his middle name. He was the long-time manager of the Grosvenor Hotel, following his return from Australia, where he had been entertainment liaison officer for General Douglas McArthur. Born in 1910, he died on his 77th birthday.

228. The fate of Hastings Park as home to the Pacific National Exhibition was hotly debated through the 1980s and early 1990s. Empire Stadium was demolished in the early 1990s.

230. The Cambie Street Grounds were the block bounded by Cambie, Beatty, Georgia and Dunsmuir (the bus-depot site, also known as Larwill Park). The Recreation Grounds occupied a five-acre site to the southeast of the corner of Homer and Smithe streets, and had a timber grandstand in the years from about 1906 to 1913 for the crowds who came to watch Bob Brown's Aberdeen Baseball Club, later known as the Vancouver Beavers.

234. The fate of the Langara golf course, opened in the 1920s by the CPR and the oldest public course in the province, became a contentious political issue in 1992 due to the Parks Board's plans to upgrade it, charge higher fees, and demolish the clubhouse.